Contemporary Perspectives on Ethnic Studies

FIRST EDITION

Contemporary Perspectives on Ethnic Studies

A READER

EDITED BY Kebba Darboe and Wayne E. Allen

Minnesota State University, Mankato

Bassim Hamadeh, CEO and Publisher
Mieka Portier, Field Acquisitions Editor
Tony Paese, Project Editor
Casey Hands, Associate Production Editor
Jess Estrella, Senior Graphic Designer
Alexa Lucido, Licensing Manager
Natalie Piccotti, Director of Marketing
Kassie Graves, Vice President of Editorial
Jamie Giganti, Director of Academic Publishing

Printed in the United States of America.

To: My widow Sandra, my son Kelefa, and my daughter Sia

I proudly dedicate this book to the loving memory of my first cousin Professor Lamin Sanneh for his lifetime of teaching, research, and scholarship. He had the privilege of teaching at both Harvard (1981–1989) and Yale (1989–2019) Universities, two of the world's bastions of intellect and rationality. He was loved by his aunts, especially my mother, who told us to consider him as our good role model. Dr. Sanneh was an intellectual giant, a great writer, and Gambia's ambassador to the world. He had a good sense of humor, and I enjoyed every second of our long discussions on multiple topics. His life exemplified the classic lines of a scholar in Samuel Johnson's *History of Rasselas: Prince of Abyssinia* (1887): "To talk in public, to read and to hear, to inquire and answer inquiries is the business of a scholar. He wanders about the world without pomp or terror ..." We miss you, Mala. He died on January 6, 2019, and may he rest in peace!

Dr. Kebba Darboe
Professor, Minnesota State University—Mankato

For Justine Mambo Allen, a loyal and loving daughter and sister, a true wife and friend, a great mother, aunty, and grandmother, and a dedicated daughter of God; and to everyone in our Mankon family in Bamenda, Cameroon, this book is in honor of you.

Dr. Wayne E. Allen
Professor, Minnesota State University—Mankato

CONTENTS

FOREWORD

Cultural Diversity Becomes More Important

By Yueh-Ting Lee
Southern Illinois University, Carbondale

I am so honored and privileged to be invited to write this preface for this very important anthology by Drs. Kebba Darboe and Wayne Allen that I cannot help sharing a compelling story with all readers. That is, in 2000, I was hired as a chair of the Department of Ethnic Studies at Minnesota State University, Mankato. I had worked there for five years. Those were among the best days in my academic and administrative career. I was so proud of the colleagues, friends (including Dr. Allen and Dr. Darboe and many others), and students in the department that this initiative brings me back to what we worked on almost 18 years ago. For example, together we discussed and finalized the Department Mission Statement in fall 2000 as follows: The Department of Ethnic Studies, an interdisciplinary program, is academically committed to promoting multicultural and ethnic knowledge and values both within and outside the United States and to preparing our students for effective functioning across the culturally diverse and global community.

During those years, we updated undergraduate curricula and developed two graduate programs collaboratively—an MS in multicultural and ethnic studies program and an online cultural diversity certificate program. These two programs are still very successful. I am even more proud of the department that has been flourishing since I moved to Minot State University in North Dakota in 2005, to the University of Toledo in Ohio in 2007, and then to Southern Illinois University Carbondale in 2015 as a professor and an administrator. Cultural diversity and inclusive excellence (e.g., ethnic studies) are near and dear to my heart as a teacher, researcher and an administrator.

Today we face more opportunities and challenges when we teach or talk about cultural and ethnic diversity. In the United States, we will be either stronger together or may be weaker and more traumatized due to the current political environment. America's culturally diverse groups or underserved groups are like endangered species due to the politically close-minded mentality in the nation. Violence, hatred, and hostility have increased every day since the 2016 election.

Ethnic studies programs also face both challenges and opportunities. Undoubtedly, ethnic studies, like America itself, is at a crossroads. Thus Dr. Kebba and Dr. Allen's book is very important and timely.

This anthology covers a wide range of topics which provides an extraordinary range of knowledge, theories, and research findings for our students, scholars, and researchers, and other readers in and outside the academic area. It includes diverse issues related to Native Americans (or American Indians), African Americans, Latino/a and Hispanic Americans, Asian Americans, Muslim/Arabic Americans, immigrants and other people of multicultural and diverse groups. This volume offers both historical perspectives and current or contemporary topics that are central and critical to all readers. I really enjoy reading it and highly recommend it to all students, colleagues, and friends.

Time flies. Human nature remains hardly changed. Cultural diversity and inclusive excellence will play a much more important role both on campus and in our daily life. To survive and thrive domestically and globally, human beings as a species must not only be in harmony with other beings but also with other species on Earth.

Finally, we salute, and also appreciate, all our colleagues and friends in the Department of Ethnic Studies at Minnesota State University, Mankato who shoulder this important ethnic diversity mission for the region, state, nation, and the world. This anthology absolutely helps all of us to learn, to think and act more critically and more diversely. Reading it is a must!

INTRODUCTION

Introductory Overview of Ethnic Studies

By Wayne E. Allen and Kebba Darboe
Minnesota State University, Mankato

Ethnic studies, like America itself, is standing at a crossroads. In fact, it might not be too presumptuous to say the whole world is standing at a crossroads as we move into the 21st century. Modern technology, globalization, the mass migration of large populations of diverse peoples, and an interconnected world of commerce and culture are redefining who we are as a species. As one human race made up of many diverse populations, we have many challenges before us.

Human beings are extremely diverse in very many ways. People differ in opinions, race, nationality, gender, age, sexuality, ethnicity, socioeconomic class, religion, differing abilities, lifestyle choices, and so much more. Yet, at the very basic level, we are all a single human species—one human race. All people share common traits such as hopes and aspirations, feelings, desires, and needs, and these are all universal to our species. Today, the changes in technology and mass movement that have resulted from globalization have made it pretty much impossible for any population of people to live without interacting with others outside their "in-group." Often people of different cultural and geographical backgrounds meet in differing settings through tourism, international conferences, education exchange programs, sports, etc.

Sadly, the history of differing populations of humankind discriminating against each other based on cultural differences has been with us from the beginning. So many people have died or have been denied their rights because of ethnic conflict, conquest, and oppression. Whole populations and their cultures have been destroyed, as well as peoples enslaved, due to ethnocentrism, a lack of understanding, and xenophobia. Unfortunately, the vestiges of some of these occurrences are visible even today, perpetuated by people who little understand the importance of the uniqueness of our diversity. Little do they know that:

Diversity Creates Richness in Opinion

The complexity of challenges facing the world today requires the input of people from different cultural backgrounds if we are to succeed. A diverse set of opinions and approaches will offer fresh ideas to solve some of our impending problems. Diverse peoples have often been found to be creative and thus produce alternative solutions to problems. Human history is rife with examples of the inventiveness of members of oppressed populations making significant contributions to human advancement.

Diversity Makes us Empathetic and Understanding About Others

When we interact with people not like us and try to understand them, we are actually enriched, both personally and professionally. This helps us empathize with others, understand our differences in a broader context, and learn from one another. We are then able to live in harmony, help one another, and grow together as a community, a nation, and a planet. Cross-cultural awareness and understanding allows us to first listen to others and give the other a fair hearing, and then hopefully to grow and empathize with them in solidarity. Doing so helps us realize that all human beings share the same needs and hopes and dreams. Hatred between people of differing identity backgrounds only diminishes us by denying us the opportunity to live life to the fullest in a vibrant multicultural world.

Diversity is a Growing Trend

Today, no country in the world has only native peoples living there. Each and every day, millions of people are moving from one part of the world to another. Most people are in search of better opportunities, education, and a chance to experience something new and different. In the process, people of different cultural, ethnic, and religious backgrounds often find themselves going to the same schools, working in the same offices, shopping in the same stores, attending the same events, and so on. As citizens of this world, we are, therefore, left with no choice other than to embrace our diversity and learn as much as we can from it. Children really need to be raised in settings that celebrate diversity, as well as taught to live with and respect people who are different from them in some way. In this way, the world will be a more peaceful and prosperous place in which to live.

Diversity Opens Up New Market Opportunities

By embracing and learning about diversity, entrepreneurs have been able to reach new markets in the global economy. Today we have multinationals setting up offices in different parts of the world, and this is not possible without embracing diversity. This further creates employment and travel opportunities for people in all parts of the world.

How to do Ethnic Studies

Ethnic studies is not, and should not simply be, about minorities for minorities. It needs to be relevant to all people as a social and behavioral science discipline. A tendency to emphasize identity politics and make ethic studies about minorities for minorities actually ghettoizes and delegitimizes the discipline. Certainly, the discipline should celebrate diversity along with contributions made by all peoples, and it needs members of underrepresented populations in its ranks. And it should teach about the history of oppression—how and why it is leveled at disadvantaged populations of people, and how real redress really works. But it should not become a broken record refrain of the sad victimology lament listened to while on the treadmill of blame and self pity. And ethnic studies should not try to find its legs by standing on reverse discrimination and quotas. The discipline needs to balance merit with inclusion, and that is not an easy job. But the editors contend that is precisely the challenge, and any ethnic studies program worth its funding will rise to the challenge.

Identity Politics: Strengths and Weaknesses

The strength of identity politics is that people take pride and strength from multiple identities, and everyone has more than one aspect to his or her identity. We live in a world where identity—ethnic, racial, religious, gender, differing abilities, sexual orientation, age, social status, economic class, education level—is as definitive to who you are as your name and your address. We all have to balance and juggle these identities every day of our lives, whether overtly stated or not.

A weakness of identity politics is that it disunites people on the basis of certain physical/social identity characteristics rather than uniting them under the culture and values broadly grouped under democracy, which is meant to be a unifying force in social and political life in a free society. This is seen as a weakening force for nation-states. It is contended that people should be coming together under a shared identity instead of fragmenting off into ever-diversifying interest groups.

The classic push and pull between country unity and country division based on identity categories is at the heart of the national identity dilemma for the West in the 21st century. The American political scene has become more and more partisan these days because factions are no longer reaching out to one another across party lines to get the business of governing done. Ethnic studies, when done properly, can actually help to inform a balance between these seemingly divergent aspects of identity in education, commerce, social and political life, and governance by teaching understanding, cultural sensitivity, and cross-communication skills, as well as the practical value of these things in business, education, politics, and governance.

A Practical Career-Oriented Approach to Ethnic Studies

At Minnesota State University (MSU), Mankato, the home campus of the editors of this anthology, we approach the teaching of ethnic studies in a multifold manner. First, we teach our students about the differing socially constructed categories people use to identify themselves and others: race, religion, ethnicity, gender, sexual orientation, differing abilities, age, and socioeconomic class differences. Then, we teach them about the history of social, economic, and political relations between members of differing identity categories. Next, we teach them about the value and relevance of diverse identities, languages, and traditional practices and customs in the United States and the world at large, as well as how to engage one another in meaningful ways across these identity categories. Lastly, we require our students to gain knowledge and skills in areas of professional concentration: business, government, local and/or international service, education, health care, law enforcement/corrections, and counseling. We teach them to apply what they have learned about diversity within a professional career track and in this way better-serve their community, their home country, and the world.

Ethnic studies as a discipline has fallen out of favor in certain parts of the United States due to its over-emphasis on identity politics, accompanied by the view that it is simply "politically correct studies" and an exercise in reverse discrimination. It is viewed as that portion of the college curriculum that is a "diversity requirement"; the "real" scholars and scientists on campus believe it to be politically correct "fluff" that radicalizes both students and faculty, thereby dividing rather than uniting us as Americans and global citizens. It is for those "other" people, not real scholars and scientists. Such critiques of ethnic studies, however, while valid on some levels, in no way negate the facts concerning the history of racism, sexism, discrimination, and oppression that must be addressed in an attempt to redress the wrongs faced by members of formerly subjugated populations within a modern (post-modern) enlightened society. There simply must be equal treatment under the law and equal opportunity for all if America is to move forward into the 21st century as a viable society. And this is not political correctness, it is common sense—and it is good business. The economy does a lot better if there is peace and harmony, equal opportunity for education, employment, and entrepreneurship, and equal treatment under the law. Conflict is costly. With declining enrollments, impending budget cuts, and an offsetting increase in students from underrepresented populations, challenging these critiques by refining the ethnic studies mission becomes critical.

The Impact on Academic Diversity and Inclusion

Historically, most interdisciplinary programs like ethnic studies owe their intellectual heritage to traditional disciplines like anthropology, education, history, psychology and sociology. It is, therefore, axiomatic that the theories on ethnicity, such as primordialist, constructionist, and instrumentalist perspectives, be derived from social science theories. The purpose of ethnic studies is to provide a compliment to the Euro-American curricula. Ethnic studies programs started in the early 1968 at

San Francisco State University, then spread to other campuses in California and across the country. However, ethnic studies has a much longer history because it is built on the pioneering writings of Carter G. Woodson and W.E. Du Bois; as well as freedom schools of the 1960s, black independent schools, tribal schools, and language immersion schools. Black History Month was created in 1926 in the United States when historian Carter G. Woodson and the Association for the Study of Negro Life and History announced the second week of February to be "Negro History Week." This week was chosen because it coincided with the birthdays of President Abraham Lincoln on February 12 and of Frederick Douglass, a freed slave and African American leader on February 14, both of which black communities had been celebrating together since the late 19th century.

Du Bois stated that the problem of the 20th century is the color line—social relations will be based on racial identity. European imperialism and colonization ended in the 19th century. Subsequently began the decolonization and self-determination struggles of Africa, Asia, and Latin America in the 20th century. In this historical context philosopher Frantz Fanon pointed out that the goals of self-determination and anti-racism of the third-world project are similar to the students of the Third World Liberation Front at San Francisco State College when they proposed ethnic studies "to aid in further developing politically, economically, and culturally the revolutionary third-world consciousness of oppressed peoples both on and off campus" (Okihiro, 2010, p.3).

In addition, the resistance to European imperialism was the impetus of the liberating ideas of Negritude and Pan Africanism. Negritude is a literary movement of the 1930s, '40s, and '50s that began among French-speaking African and Caribbean writers living in Paris as a protest against French colonial rule and the policy of assimilation. The francophone intellectuals, writers, and politicians included Martinican poet Aimé Césaire, Léopold Sédar Senghor (the first president of Senegal from 1960-80), and Léon Damas of French Guiana. They argued for the importance of a Pan-African racial identity among people of African descent worldwide, (Markovitz, 1969).

In this context, Kwame Nkrumah, the first president of the Independent Nation of Ghana in 1957, was a Pan-Africanist. He played an important role in developing the Organization of African Unity (OAU) in 1963, the same year he was awarded the Lenin Peace Prize (Timothy, 1963).

Nelson Mandela is a South African leader who spent years in prison for opposing apartheid, the policy by which the races were separated and whites were given power over blacks in South Africa. Upon his release from prison, Mandela, from 1994 to 1999, became the first president of a black-majority-ruled South Africa in which apartheid officially ended. A symbol of hope for many South Africans, Mandela is also a former winner of the Nobel Peace Prize (Mandela, 2010).

What Ethnic Studies is Not

First, ethnic studies does not teach the separation of America into racial/ethnic groups, neither does it advocate an overthrow of the United States government. For example, on May 11, 2010, Arizona's

Governor Jan Brewer signed HB 2281 into law. The law bans schools from teaching classes that are designed for students of a particular ethnic group or that promote resentment or ethnic solidarity. While the Arizona law deals with primary and secondary schools, the issue is very much alive in higher education as well. What ethnic studies really does is to include all racial/ethnic groups, especially marginalized communities, in a multicultural American curriculum. Consistent with this observation, many sectors of American society, including prominently the military, businesses, and members of the entertainment, sports, and educational spheres know that diversity is not only important, it is good for business. That is why a record number of institutions filed friend-of-the-court briefs arguing that diversity is a compelling interest in the affirmative-action case decided in 2003 by the U.S. Supreme Court in Grutter v. Bollinger. The Supreme Court in a 5-4 decision upheld the University of Michigan Law School's policy that race can be one of many factors considered by colleges when selecting their students.

Another misperception is that ethnic studies can be perceived as lowering academic standards. In reality, ethnic studies curricula are academically based and actually improve disadvantaged students' academic performance and university preparation. Ethnic studies is often falsely characterized as cheating students of color by substituting ethnic pride for knowledge and skills necessary to succeed in the mainstream society. But when ethnic studies is done properly, its interdisciplinary approach offers an academic curriculum that supports diverse student success, as revealed in the research findings at San Francisco State University.

The Benefits of Ethnic Studies Courses

Research at San Francisco State University revealed that colleges should add ethnic studies courses to their curricula in order to address the history of racial division and discrimination in the U.S. Additionally, students who pass an ethnic studies course improved their overall performance in other courses. Further, the data compiled by the college's Division of Institutional Analytics found that ethnic studies majors in general graduate at a rate about 20 percentage points higher than non-ethnic studies majors. Ken Monteiro, the acting director of the César Chávez Institute at the university and former dean of the ethnic studies college, said the data point in one direction, and that is that there should be more ethnic studies courses. According to Monteiro, there are several reasons why ethnic studies affects improved student learning outcomes as compared to other majors. First, ethnic studies faculty members spend more time on advising and supplemental education than faculty in other areas. Second, ethnic studies faculty teach students information that directly relates to them. And third, ethnic studies faculty teach critical thinking skills, as well as interdisciplinary approaches, to show students that they can look at things from a range of different perspectives.

The Future of Ethnic Studies

For a new generation of ethnic studies scholars, the focus is not just—or even foremost—on the relations between white and nonwhite people, but on relations among peoples of all backgrounds that make up the United States of America. If ethnic studies scholars and students fail to articulate a compelling practical social, political, and economic value of the field to any educated person in the 21st century, the discipline will fade into irrelevancy no matter how loud or compelling its narrative. As a result, the threat to ethnic studies comes not from the liberals, who make it into self-interested factionalism, nor from the conservatives, who deride it as a celebration of cultural diversity and multiculturalism that is just a front for politically correct studies. The challenge comes from whether or not ethnic studies can be shown to have practical merit as an academic discipline that is hierarchically integrated with other practical professional disciplines. Therefore, ethnic studies must have some practical criteria for accreditation through application in real-world professional settings, thereby demonstrating its practical merit in a 21st century economy with shrinking budgets. While ethnic studies is about the history of identity politics in America, and its emphasis on multiculturalism and promoting affirmative action as redress for institutional discrimination and disparities in education and the workplace, as well as society at large, is at its core, its relevance in the 21st century is as an interdisciplinary field that offers an academic curriculum that provides cross-cultural diversity training that supports successful professional practice in other practical disciplines in the academy and in business for the betterment of American society and the American economy.

This anthology represents a cross-section of relevant articles in the field that are intended to introduce the student to the substance, relevance, and practice of the discipline of ethnic studies as we move forward into the 21st century. Truly, the discipline is at a crossroads, but that is actually a good thing because a crossroads allows one to look in all directions at once. After all, looking at and celebrating all diverse perspectives has always been the forte of ethnic studies, and it is and ever will be a professional discipline ready to rise to the many outlooks and challenges ahead.

CHAPTER I

Historical Perspectives on Race and Ethnicity

READING 1

Historical Perspectives on Race and Ethnicity

By Kebba Darboe and Karamo Barrow

Introduction

State agencies through administrative fiat have identified four racial minorities: American Indians, African Americans, Hispanic Americans, and Asian American-Pacific Islanders (Lowry, 1982). These groups have suffered discrimination in the process of American nation building; for instance, American Indians were victims of genocide in the Trail of Tears in 1838 and at Wounded Knee in 1973. African Americans are victims of slavery. The Hispanics were conquered and segregated after the Mexican-American War, and the signing of the 1848 Treaty of Guadalupe Hidalgo, which ceded the southwest region from Mexico to the United States. Asian immigrants are victims of racial exclusion, including the Chinese Exclusion Act of 1882 and the internment of Japanese during World War II in 1942 (Schaefer, 2015).

Native Americans

The ancestors of modern Native Americans were the first people in what is now the United States, and they are properly referred to as "First Nations" peoples. A vast variety of peoples, societies, and cultures developed in the Americas before European contact. Native Americans were greatly affected by the European colonization of the Americas, which began in 1492 with Christopher Columbus, an Italian explorer and colonist. After the founding of the United States, many Native American peoples suffered from discriminatory government policies, such as slavery, diseases, warfare, removals, and one-sided treaties. Native Americans became conquered peoples who were placed under the political and economic control of the dominant populations of white Americans through internal colonialism processes. Arguably, the Americanization or assimilation process was done through warfare, reservations, missionaries, boarding schools and mission schools, and land allotment programs.

However, since the 1960s, Native American self-determination (sovereignty) movements have resulted in changes to the lives of Native Americans, though there are still many contemporary issues faced by Native Americans (Schaefer, 2015). The challenges include self-governance, education, economic development, housing, healthcare, land claims and the environment, designation of sacred lands, federal policies, and more. According to the 2010 Census, 5.2 million people in the United States are identified as American Indian and Alaska natives (U.S. Census, 2010).

African Americans

The institution of slavery is as old as civilization. Many nations and empires were built by the muscles of slaves. Slavery was based on the demand and supply of labor. The first Africans were brought to what is now the United States in 1619. In colonial America most Africans and some white Europeans were indentured servants (Takaki, 1993). During the period 1650–1700, tobacco plantations in Virginia needed a steady supply of labor, and slavery was the solution. As a result, African Americans came involuntarily, unlike European immigrants. Today, African Americans are the second-largest racial minority group in the United States of America.

Alexis de Tocqueville (1831), a young French magistrate, who wrote the classic book *Democracy in America*, asked President John Quincy Adams, "Do you look on slavery as a great plague for the United States?"

"Yes, certainly," Adams answered. "That is the root of almost all the troubles of the present and the fears for the future" (Rodriguez, 2007, p.41).

Adams's observations were prophetic. Since the 17th century, through American slavery, emancipation, segregation, and modern civil rights movements, the issue of race and ethnic relations has been salient, as illustrated by the exploitation and violence toward African Americans through slavery as well as the marginalization, violence, and exploitation of the Jim Crow laws of de jure segregation. Arguably, one root cause of racism against African Americans is slavery, which dehumanized them. Slavery did have a devastating effect on the lives of the slaves because of the denial of cultural self-identification, economic and political opportunities (Fogell & Engerman, 1974).

Hispanics/Latinos

Hispanics/Latinos are the largest, youngest, and fastest-growing racial/ethnic minority group in the United States. The Latino population will account for most of the nation's population growth from 2005 through 2050. Hispanics will make up 29% of the U.S. population in 2050, compared with 14% in 2005 (Passel and Cohn, 2008). Latinos are heterogeneous from cultural, socioeconomic, and genetic perspectives. Therefore, they represent a wide variety of national origins, ethnic and cultural groups, and social classes. From a genetic perspective, Latinos are descended from indigenous American,

European, and African populations. The Spaniards tolerated intermarriage between Spanish Christians and Native Americans, the progeny of which were called Mestizos (Morner, 1967).

The term "Hispanic" or "Latino" describes a population with a common cultural heritage and a common language, but it does not refer to race or a common ancestry. The term Hispanic is a mainstream concept, and Latino is a political one. The largest groups are the Mexicans, Puerto Ricans, and Cubans. There are two basic characteristics of Hispanic groups: (1) They are heterogeneous, and (2) they are concentrated in specific geographic areas. For example, Mexican Americans settled in the Southwest region: Texas and California. The Southwestern or borderlands region was settled by Spanish-Mexican-Indian ancestors: the Aztec, Maya, and Inca. Puerto Ricans settled in the Northeast region, primarily New York. Cubans occupied the Southeast region in Florida.

Similar to the Native Americans, Mexican Americans entered the society through direct conquest of their homelands. The Mexican-American War was justified on the basis of "Manifest Destiny," the idea of "Jefferson's homogeneous republic" and American expansionism, resulting in the conquest of the southwest region and Mexicans becoming "foreigners in their own land" (Takaki, 1993, p. 176, 178). In this historical context, Mexicans consider themselves today as migrants not immigrants (Alvarez, 1973). The contemporary chant, "We didn't cross the border; the border crossed us," epitomizes the life experiences of a racialized group: Chicanos/as—Americans of Mexican descent, (Fennelly, 2007, p. 2). The Treaty of Guadalupe Hidalgo is the peace treaty, largely dictated by the United States to the interim government of a militarily occupied Mexico that ended the Mexican-American War (1846–1848), (Fennelly, 2007). The early Chicanos, however, were colonized people, but today many have immigrant roots—Mexicans (Blauner, 1994). The colonized and immigrant models are differentiated by "centrifugal and centripetal" social relationships with the dominant group (McLemore, Romo & Baker, 2001, p.457). For instance, the colonized people (Chicanos) have a centrifugal social relationship with the dominant group characterized by struggle and resistance to assimilation. By contrast, the immigrant group (Mexicans) have a centripetal social relationship with the dominant group characterized by some resistance to assimilation, while aspiring through education and employment to achieve the American dream (McLemore, Romo & Baker, 2001).

Asian Americans

The Chinese immigrated to America fleeing from the ravages of the British Opium Wars and peasant rebellions. Additionally, the 1840s "gold rush" drew Chinese workers to mine along the western coast of the United States of America (Kil, 2012). Initially, they wanted to make money and return to China—sojourner laborers. The Chinese and Japanese had been in America before many European immigrant groups. As "strangers" coming from a "different shore," they have been stereotyped as heathen, exotic, and inassimilable, (Takaki, 1993). Also, they suffered from exclusionary immigration policies such as "the yellow peril," out crowding the white race, etc.

In 1882 the United States Congress passed the Chinese Exclusion Act and President Chester A. Arthur signed it into law (Kil, 2012). The 1882 Chinese Exclusion Act was the first law that prohibited the entry of immigrants on the basis of nationality. The Chinese condemned the restriction as racist. In 1943, the Act was repealed, when China and the United States were allies during World War II. However, this precedent later provided a basis for the restriction of European immigrant groups, for example, Italians, Poles, Russians, etc. During World War II, President Franklin D. Roosevelt signed an Executive Order 1942 to put Japanese Americans in military internment camps because Japan was an ally of Germany (McMillion, 2016). Arguably, what happened to the Chinese and Japanese influenced the reception of the Koreans, Filipinos, Asian Indians, and Southeast Asian refugees (Vietnamese and the Hmong). The Asian population in the U.S. was about 5% in 2005, but Asians are projected to be 9% of United States population in 2050 (Passel and Cohn, 2008). Today, Asian Americans are the model minority for blacks, Hispanics, and whites.

In summary, the nuanced life experiences of the aforementioned racial minority groups have become institutionalized, resulting in institutional discrimination, racism, bigotry, ethnocentrism and racial microaggressions. The scholarly articles in this Anthology highlight some of the challenges and opportunities.

Racial Microaggressions

Racial microaggression is the new face of racism. The term racial microaggression was coined by Chester Pierce (1978) after the Civil Rights period to bring attention to the shift in race relations to subtle and nonverbal behaviors that are 'put downs' of Blacks by offenders, (Ross-Sheriff, 2012). The definition was further refined by Derald Wing Sue and colleagues (2007) to include "commonplace verbal or behavioral indignities" that are hostile, derogatory or racial insults in everyday life. Table 1.1 below shows some examples of microaggressions.

Many Americans believe that the election of the first black president—Barack H. Obama, we live in a "postracial" society, "where one's life chances were no longer significantly determined by race and neither were the basic contours of politics and society," (Dawson, p. 670, 2012). Yet the daily news is replete with all forms of police brutality in black communities, residential segregation, and social inequities between different populations. As a result, there is the rise in activist groups such as Black Lives Matter, public debates on affirmative action, and reparations for slavery, (Zevnik, 2017). While race may be a "social construct," it still has very real effects on society as well as national and global politics.

The table below, taken from Capodilupo, Nadal, Hamit, Lyons, & Weinberg (2010), shows racial microaggressions in everyday life:

Table 1.1 Microaggressions Table

Themes	Microaggression Examples	Implicit Message
Alien in own land: When Asian Americans and Latinos are assumed to be "foreigners"	"Where are you from? Where were you born? You speak good English. You don't even speak with an accent. How long have you been in the States?"	You are not American.
Ascription of intelligence: Assigning intelligence to a person based on their race, gender or (perceived) abilities.	Assuming that Asians are naturally more intelligent in the sciences and math.	Asians are naturally gifted in the sciences and math; they do not work hard for it.
	Assuming that it is unusual for an African American or Latino to be in an academically rigorous program or prestigious university.	People of color are not as intelligent as whites. It is unusual for them to be intelligent or articulate.
	"Oh, you are a bio major? Are you studying to be a nurse?" (when said to a woman)	Women are not smart enough to be doctors; men would rarely, if ever, be asked this question
	"You get a note taker for every class? Why can't you take your own notes?" (when said to a student with a learning disability)	Students with learning or other invisible disabilities are not smart enough.
"Intrinsic Skills" and "Personality Types": Using stereotypes of race, gender, and sexual orientation to assume an individual's interests and talents.	"You're gay? You have to give me some decorating tips!"	All gay men are interested and talented in interior design and decorating
	"Women in power lead by emotion and are too sensitive!"	Women are "genetically" emotional and sensitive; they are not intelligent, rational, and impartial.
	"Are you here on a basketball scholarship?" (asked of African American students)	African Americans are good at basketball, and that is the only way they would be able to attend our college.

Derald Wing Sue, "Racial Microagressions in Everyday Life: Implications for Clinical Practice," *American Psychologist*.

(Continued)

Table 1.1 Microaggressions Table

Themes	Microaggression Examples	Implicit Message
"Color Blindness": Statements that indicate that a white person does not want to acknowledge race (or a heterosexual person does not want to acknowledge sexual orientation). Please note that use of the term "blindness" itself is very problematic here.	"When I look at you, I don't see color."	Denying a person of color's racial or ethnic experiences.
	"America is a melting pot."	Assimilate to the dominant culture.
	"She's so independent, you wouldn't even know she's in a wheelchair!"	Wheelchair users are unable to be independent.
	"There is only one race, the human race."	Denying the individual as a racially or culturally different being.
	"I don't support gay rights because they are 'special rights,' and everyone is equal!"	Denying that queer people are treated differently in our society.
Criminality: A person is presumed to be dangerous, criminal, or deviant based on their race, nationality, and/or sexual orientation.	If something comes up missing or a fight ensues, a black or Latino person is assumed to be the culprit.	You are a criminal.
	If a group of black male students are walking down a street with dark hoodies, they are assumed to be dangerous.	You are dangerous and poor. You do not belong in the university.
	If a group of black or Asian students are sitting together in a public place, they are "self-segregating" or must be talking badly about whites.	You are not to be trusted in a group; you are out to harm the majority.
	"Beware of people wearing a head scarf!" "Why are you dressed like Osama?"	You are part of the enemy. I don't trust you. Your clothing identifies you as a terrorist. I don't need to know anything else about you. I need to be wary of people like you.
	"I wouldn't want my children to be taught by gay/lesbian teachers."	LGBT people are sexually deviant and would try to recruit young people in to the "gay lifestyle" or even sexually abuse them.

Adapted from Patricia A. Burak, Ph.D., Tae-Sun Kim, Ph.D., Amit Taneja, Doctoral Candidate. Syracuse University 2009

References

Alvarez, Rodolfo. 1973. "The Psychohistorical and Socioeconomic Development of the Chicano Community in the United States," *Social Science Quarterly* 53: 920–42.

Blauner, Robert. 1994 [1972]. "Colonized and Immigrant Minorities." In *From Different Shores: Perspectives on Race and Ethnicity in America*, edited by Ronald Takaki, 149–160. New York: Oxford University Press.

Capodilupo, Christina, Kevin Nadal, Sahran Hamit, Oliver Lyons, and Alexa Weinberg. 2010. "The Manifestation of Gender Microaggressions." In *Microaggressions and Marginality: Manifestation, Dynamics, and Impact*, edited by D.W. Sue. Hoboken, N.J.: John Wiley & Sons, Inc.

Dawson, Michael. C. (2012). Racial Tragedies, Political Hope, and the Tasks of American Political Science. *Perspectives on Politics, 10*(3), 669–673. https://doi.org/10.1017/S1537592712001685

Fennelly, Katherine. 2007. "U.S. Immigration: A Historical Perspective." *National Voter*, January, 2007. www.hhh.umn.edu/.../immigration_historical_perspective.pdf.

Fogel, Robert and Stanley Engerman. 1974. *Time on the Cross.* Boston: Little, Brown & Co.

Lowry, Ira S., 1982. "The Science and Politics of Ethnic Enumeration." In *Ethnicity and Public Policy*, edited by Winston A. Van Horne, vol. 1, pp. 42–61. Wisconsin: University of Wisconsin System.

Kil, Sang, 2012. "Fearing Yellow, Imagining White: Media Analysis of the Chinese Exclusion Act of 1882." *Social Identities*, 18(6), 663–677. https://doi.org/10.1080/13504630.2012.708995

McLemore, S. Dale, Harriett D. Romo, and Susan Gonzalez Baker. 2001. *Racial and Ethnic Relations in America* (6th ed.). Boston: Allyn & Bacon

McMillion, Rhonda, 2016. "Internment of Japanese-Americans During World War II Offers Cautionary Message." *ABA Journal*, 1. Retrieved from https://search.ebscohost.com/login.aspx?direct=true&db=aph&AN=117806416&site=ehost-live

Morner, Magnus. 1967. *Race Mixture in the History of Latin America.* Boston, Mass.: Little, Brown and Co.

Passel, Jeffrey S. and D'Vera Cohn. 2008. *U.S. Population Projections: 2005-2050.* Pew Research Center, Washington, DC. (www.pewresearch.org) http://www.pewsocialtrends.org/2008/02/11/us-population-projections-2005-2050/

Pierce, Chester. M. 1978. *Television and Education.* Beverly Hills: Sage Publications.

Pritzker, Barry. 2000. *A Native American Encyclopedia: History, Culture, and Peoples.* New York: Oxford University Press.

Rodriguez, Junius. 2007. *Slavery in the United States: A Social, Political, and Historical Encyclopedia* (Vol. 1). Santa Barbara, California: ABC-CLIO.

Ross-Sheriff, Fariyal. 2012. Microaggression, Women, and Social Work. *Affilia, 27*(3), 233–236. https://doi.org/10.1177/0886109912454366

Schaefer, Richard T. 2015. *Racial and Ethnic Groups*, 14th ed. Upper Saddle River, New Jersey: Pearson Education, Inc.

Sue, Derald Wing, Christina M. Capodilupo, Gina C. Torino, Jennifer M. Bucceri, Aisha Holder, Kevin L. Nadal, & Marta Esquilin. 2007. Racial microaggressions in everyday life: implications for clinical practice. *American Psychologist, 62*(4), 271.

Takaki, Ronald. 1993. *A Different Mirror: A History of Multicultural America.* Boston: Little, Brown and Co.

U.S. Census 2010: https://www.census.gov/library/publications/2012/dec/c2010br-10.html

Watkins, Nicole, David Rivera, and Kevin Nadal. 2012. "Microaggressions: The New Face of Discrimination." Microtraining Associates.

Zevnik, Andreja (2017). Postracial Society as Social Fantasy: Black Communities Trapped Between Racism and a Struggle for Political Recognition. *Political Psychology*, *38*(4), 621–635. https://doi.org/10.1111/pops.12430

READING 2

The Evolution and Consequences of *Kelo v. City of New London*

By Jeffrey D. Eicher, J.D., Jerry D. Belloit, and C. Frank Shepard, Jr., J.D.

Introduction

The first ten amendments to the United States Constitution, the Bill of Rights, were created to save us from what John Stuart Mill called tyranny by the majority. The purpose of the Bill of Rights is to protect the individual from the power of government, and in theory, from the will of the majority by protecting individual liberty. For example, the First Amendment protects the dissemination of unpopular ideas, protects the press, provides for religious freedom, and gives people the right to collectively assemble and complain to and about the government. Each one of these protections has been given specific legal meaning.

At least since *Marbury v. Madison,* 5 U.S. (1 Cranch) 137 (1803), courts have been charged with determining the constitutionality of governmental action. By this process courts have protected the individual from the government, and therefore from tyranny by the majority. Never has a court said that the phrase "Congress shall make no law ... abridging the freedom of speech ..." was not subject to judicial interpretation. Obviously, if liberty of free speech, as provided by the First Amendment to the Constitution, extends only as far as Congress says it extends, then we have no free speech. Since the Bill of Rights was established to protect the individual from the majority, it would defeat its purpose to have the majority determine what freedom of speech meant. Therefore, time and again, courts have given specific meaning to the phrase "freedom of speech" and have continually risen to the occasion by defeating the legislative will and protecting the individual.[1]

The Fifth Amendment to the Constitution states, in part, "... nor shall private property be taken for public use, without just compensation." That clause originally applied only to the federal government, but was made applicable to the states by the Fourteenth Amendment.[2] It is hard to imagine that the drafters of the Bill of Rights envisioned that some of the language they were debating would simply have no meaning. However, the United States Supreme Court made exactly that determination in the case of *Kelo v. City of New London,* 125 S. Ct. 2655; 162 L. Ed. 2d 439 (2005) (*Kelo*).

Kelo vs. New London

The issue presented to the Supreme Court in *Kelo* was the specific meaning of the phrase "public use" as it is used in the Fifth Amendment. In *Kelo* the Court was presented with exactly the situation that the Bill of Rights was meant to prevent. A few families were seeking the protection of law from the power of the majority. The families involved lived in the Fort Trumbull neighborhood in New London, Connecticut. The economic base of New London had weakened considerably in preceding years. The Naval Undersea Warfare Center had closed down in 1996 and many of New London's jobs left with it. The population in and around New London dropped to its lowest level since the 1920s. The most blighted area of New London was its Fort Trumbull area. This area is located on a peninsula in the Thames River.

In the New London area there existed a private, nonprofit entity called the New London Development Corporation (NLDC). This organization was reactivated in January 1998 with the idea of assisting the city with economic development. At about the same time as the group's reactivation, the city of New London received news that Pfizer Pharmaceuticals was planning to build a $3 million research center in the Fort Trumbull area which would, presumably, rejuvenate the area and bring in needed employment.

The NLDC crafted a redevelopment plan which it hoped would complement the new Pfizer facility and revitalize this area of New London. In January of 2000 the New London City Council approved the plan and designated the NLDC as being in charge of implementation. The council further delegated to this private corporation its power to purchase property pursuant to the plan, and to exercise eminent domain in the name of the city of New London if necessary.

The Fort Trumbull area was composed of approximately 115 privately owned properties and 32 acres of a former naval facility. The NLDC's development plan encompassed approximately 90 acres, divided into seven parcels, with a different use contemplated for each parcel. These uses included a waterfront conference hotel, retail shops and restaurants, a pedestrian river walk, a residential neighborhood, marinas and a new U.S. Coast Guard museum.

The majority of landowners in this 90-acre area of interest agreed to sell their property to the NLDC. Nine families, owning 15 properties, could not come to terms and had their properties condemned by the NLDC via the power granted to them by the New London City Council. Eleven of these properties were in Parcel 4A and four were in Parcel 3. As stated in the *Kelo* opinion: "Petitioner Susette Kelo had lived in the Fort Trumbull area since 1997. She had made extensive improvements to her house, which she prized for its water view. Petitioner Wilhelmina Dery was born in her Fort Trumbull house in 1918 and had lived there her entire life. Her husband Charles (also a petitioner) had lived in the house since they married some 60 years ago."

Interestingly, the NLDC had no firm plans for the use of Parcel 4A, a site composed of only 2.4 acres which included eleven of the properties at issue. In fact, the Supreme Court rendered its decision in *Kelo* before any specific plans had been made for the site's use. All the NLDC could tell the Court was that the subject property might be used to support a local marina or as a parking lot for a nearby state park. Parcel 3, which contained the other properties at issue, was to be used as office space for research and development. This area was located immediately north of the newly planned Pfizer facility.

The Supreme Court held that the city's proposed disposition of petitioners' property qualified as a "public use" within the meaning of the Fifth Amendment. In so doing they cited *Fallbrook Irrigation Dist.* v. *Bradley*, 164 U.S. 112, 158–164 as standing for the position that "public use" should be interpreted as "public purpose." They went on to state that the Court has defined the concept of "public purpose" broadly, in deference to legislative judgments as to what public needs justify the use of the takings power of the Fifth Amendment. In other words, the Court was saying that the use of eminent domain is limited only to showings of "public purpose," and local governments are the appropriate parties to determine when "public purpose" is best served by the use of that power. So long as the local governmental body has satisfied its duty of due diligence by "carefully formulating its plan" and "thoroughly deliberating its (the plan's) adoption," the Court will defer to that judgment.

The Court specifically rejected a request that economic development should not qualify as a public use. It also rejected petitioners' argument that for takings of this kind, the Court should require a "reasonable certainty" that the expected public benefits will actually accrue. The Court did recognize that "... the city could not take petitioners' land simply to confer a private benefit on a particular private party. ..." However, it dismissed this important limitation in *Kelo* merely by stating that "... the takings at issue here would be executed pursuant to a carefully considered development plan, which was not adopted 'to benefit a particular class of identifiable individuals.' ..."

In its opinion, the Court cited its decision in *Berman v. Parker*, 348 U.S. 26 (1954) (*Berman*) in which it held that eminent domain could be properly used for the elimination of slums or blight. Interestingly, neither the city of New London nor the NLDC made any allegation that the subject properties in *Kelo* were blighted in any way. Rather, the Court expressly noted that they were condemned only because they happened to be located in the development area. Many of the properties were located on valuable beach front and were being transferred to a private developer by the NLDC. The Court found no problem with this and left the definition of the phrase "public use" completely to the whim of local government—in this case the unelected officials of a development corporation.

How has the interpretation of "public use" evolved into such a broad application that it has supported taking private property to give to another private individual? The Supreme Court in 1798 stated: "[A] law that takes property from A and gives it to B: It is against all reason and justice, for a people to entrust a Legislature with SUCH powers; and, therefore, it cannot be presumed that they have done it. The genius, the nature, and the spirit of our State Governments, amount to a prohibition of such acts of legislation; and the general principles of law and reason forbid them. ..."[3] Today, pursuant to the decision in *Kelo*, "such powers" are an acceptable power of state and local governments. The determination as to what is a public use or a public purpose is now wholly a local government determination, and further, it essentially matters not that the land is taken by the governmental entity and given to another private owner, so long as the government's plan is carefully considered and does not identify a particular individual or group of individuals to be benefited. This dramatic reversal of constitutional determination was arrived at through a slow and incremental process which began in the nineteenth century.

The Evolution of a Decision

In some ways, things have come a long way since the Supreme Court in *Calder* described what was to eventually happen in the *Kelo* case as being "against all reason and justice." In other ways, things are right back where they started. Initially, the Takings Clause, that section in the Fifth Amendment stating the government can take property only for public use and with just compensation, applied to actions of only the federal government. In *Baron v. City of Baltimore*, 32 U.S. 243 (1833), the Supreme Court was confronted with the question of whether the Takings Clause could prevent the destruction of harbor property by the City of Baltimore without just compensation. The Court said it could not, that the states were not subject to the restrictions of the U.S. Constitution. It stated, "The constitution was ordained and established by the people of the United States for themselves, for their own government, and not for the government of the individual states." Therefore, as regarded state action, the definition of public use was left to the states.

History teaches us what happened when the states were given this power. Beginning with the discovery of the Comstock Lode in 1859, mining and mining companies controlled Nevada politics. Thus it was not a surprise when mining interests were able to get the Nevada legislature to declare that any land needed for the mining industry was serving a "public use." Specifically Nevada's statute stated that, "the production and reduction of ores are of vital necessity to the people of this state; are pursuits in which all are interested and from which all derive a benefit; so the mining, milling, smelting, or other reduction of ores are hereby declared to be for the public use, and the right of eminent domain may be exercised therefore."[4] A challenge to this law was brought to the Nevada Supreme Court in the autumn of 1876. A mining corporation decided that it would be easier to transport lumber and other materials to its mining operation if it could take land belonging to James Waddell. Since Waddell had no desire to part with his land, the mining company simply had the local government take his property by eminent domain and deed it to the company. The Nevada Supreme Court found no problem with taking land from a relatively powerless individual and giving it to one of the most powerful interests in Nevada at the time—a mining corporation. The Court obviously did not base its decision on any theory supported by the Bill of Rights, such as protection of individual liberty. As the Court succinctly stated, "... that mining is the paramount interest of the state is not questioned; that anything which tends directly to encourage mineral developments and increase the mineral resources of the state is for the benefit of the public and is calculated to advance the general welfare and prosperity of the people of this state, is a self-evident proposition."[5]

Nevada was not alone in its view of the broad applicability of eminent domain and the broad definition of public use and purpose. As mining interests controlled Nevada, steel companies and railroads controlled Pennsylvania during this era. In 1858, a coal company decided that it wanted to shorten its route to the Monongahela River by building a railroad through the farm of James H. Hays. Since Hays preferred not to lose productive farm land, nor have his peace and solitude destroyed by a noisy and smelly coal fired train, he refused to sell an easement to the corporation. The coal company contacted the local government who took the right-of-way by eminent domain and gave it the company.[6]

Hays brought his argument to the Supreme Court of Pennsylvania. He argued that this taking was not for a public use. The Court rejected this argument, finding that the mining of coal was a financial benefit to the state. James Hays also argued that the company should take a shorter and more direct route to the river that would not damage his land as severely. The Court reasoned that the coal company was best able to determine its own most appropriate route. However the Court did not stop with taking the land of this private citizen to give to a private corporation. It also found it necessary to disparage Hays for his rudeness in thinking that his land should not be made available for taking by a powerful corporation. The Court called him the "unneighbourly owner." It also found that the actions of a private corporation and the actions of the government were one and the same since the government granted the right to take private lands through the *Lateral Railroad Act* 67 P.S. § 781. The Court further chastised Hays for arguing the outlandish idea that private lands should be taken only for a "public purpose." It stated: "The Constitution was not made to prevent or hinder the government from improving the country and promoting the general welfare of the citizens; and when the selfish passions of individuals attempt to set up the instrument for such purposes they misapply it, and cannot expect the courts to help them." At this point in our history, while state and local governments, without the restrictions of the Fifth Amendment, were running roughshod over private landowners at the behest of the powerful, the federal courts, constrained by the Fifth Amendment, were following a different route.

In 1897, a case reached the U.S. Supreme Court involving the Gettysburg Battlefield. Congress had decided to preserve the battlefield and erect tablets and statues at various places on the site. On June 5, 1894, by joint resolution of Congress, and with approval of the President, the federal government was further authorized to take any necessary land by eminent domain. The Court determined that a taking could only occur if its purpose was both a public one and within the powers granted to government by the U.S. Constitution.[7] "It [the government] has authority to do so [take property] whenever it is necessary or appropriate to use the land in the execution of any of the powers granted to it by the Constitution. Is the proposed use, to which this land is to be put, a public use within this limitation?"[8] After an exhaustive analysis of the public benefits of preserving the battlefield, the Court determined that "... when the legislature has declared the use or purpose to be a public one, its judgment will be respected by the courts, unless the use be palpably without reasonable foundation." Thus a two-pronged test emerged for the use of eminent domain by the federal government. First, was the goal within the powers granted by the U.S. Constitution, and second, was there a public use to which the land was going to be put?

Therefore, as we approached the end of the nineteenth century, the United States had two distinct legal approaches regarding eminent domain. One, followed by the states, allowed the taking of private property and subsequent transfer to another private individual so long as the taking indirectly, or even arguably, advanced the economic welfare of the state or its citizens. The other approach required that the federal government, operating under the restraints of the Fifth Amendment's Takings Clause, act only within its constitutional authority and exercise the right of eminent domain only for a truly public use.

It was not until the adoption of the 14th Amendment in 1868 that people began to contemplate the application of the Bill of Rights to state and local actions. Even though Congressman John Bingham, the drafter of the 14th Amendment, argued that he was proposing the amendment specifically to make the first eight amendments to the Constitution applicable to state and local action; the courts did not agree. It was not until 1897 that the first section of the Bill of Rights was incorporated into the 14th Amendment and made applicable to the states.[9]

The decision in *Cincinnati v. Vestor*, 281 U.S. 439 (1930) (*Cincinnati*) is telling on the issue of public use under the new standard of federal liberty guarantees being made applicable to state and local actions. In this case the city of Cincinnati decided to take property via eminent domain for the widening of Fifth Street. No one contested the expansion as being for a public use. However, the city attempted to condemn an area wider than was necessary for the public use. In its decision the U.S. Supreme Court began by laying out what it viewed as current precedent.

> It is well established that in considering the application of the Fourteenth Amendment to cases of expropriation of private property, the question what is a public use is a judicial one. In deciding such a question, the Court has appropriate regard to the diversity of local conditions and considers with great respect legislative declarations and in particular the judgments of state courts as to the uses considered to be public in the light of local exigencies. But the question remains a judicial one which this Court must decide in performing its duty of enforcing the provisions of the Federal Constitution.[10]

This is a statement of the law that gives due regard to the Bill of Rights and the Court's responsibilities to use it to insure our freedoms. In the end, the U.S. Supreme Court did not allow the city of Cincinnati to take the excess property because it could not delineate a public use for it that was specific enough to pass Fifth Amendment or Ohio statutory law scrutiny.

The Court's decision in *Kelo* discounted the earlier case of *Cincinnati v. Vestor* and instead turned to two cases that were decided in the latter half of the twentieth century: *Berman* (above) and *Hawaii v. Midkiff*.[11] Justice Stevens, writing the majority opinion in *Kelo*, relied heavily on these two cases for the proposition that the Court must "... decline to second-guess the city's considered judgments about the efficacy of its development plan." The Court's reliance on these cases is arguably misplaced.

Rather than simply deferring to the opinion of a locally appointed corporation, the U.S. Supreme Court in *Berman* took a hard look at the public purpose involved in the taking. *Berman* concerned a redevelopment project in Washington, D.C. The Court was persuaded to allow the exercise of eminent domain by the fact that the areas being condemned were slums that adversely affected the health and welfare of the inhabitants of Washington, D.C. The Court in *Berman* stated:

> In 1950 the Planning Commission prepared and published a comprehensive plan for the District. Surveys revealed that in Area B, 64.3% of the dwellings were beyond repair, 18.4% needed major repairs, only 17.3% were satisfactory; 57.8% of the dwellings had outside toilets, 60.3% had no baths, 29.3% lacked electricity, 82.2% had no wash basins or laundry tubs, 83.8% lacked central heating. In the judgment of the District's Director of Health it was necessary to redevelop Area B in the interests of public health. The population of Area B amounted to 5,012 persons, of whom 97.5% were Negroes.

It is extremely hard to argue that the eradication of such conditions does not serve a public purpose. Rather than displacing the affected persons. the plan required the construction of low-cost housing that was clean and sanitary. It is extremely easy to see the public use here, and a unanimous Court had no difficulty in finding the eradication of squalor to be a public purpose.

In 1984 the U.S. Supreme Court revisited the issue of public use in deciding an appeal in the case of *Hawaii v. Midkiff.* Hawaii had been settled by Polynesian peoples from the western Pacific. When they arrived they established a feudal system whereby the land was owned by the king. The peasants worked land they did not own, and never could own. By the mid 1960s Hawaii was still owned by only a few people. On Oahu, 72 percent of the land was owned by 22 landowners. Overall, 49 percent of all the Hawaiian Islands was owned by the state and federal government, while 47 percent was owned by 72 private landowners. Hawaii attempted to end the remnants of its feudal system by having the government purchase all land in excess of five acres that was leased to a private individual. It paid the owners just compensation.

Justice O'Connor, who would later dissent in *Kelo*, wrote the Court's opinion in *Midkiff.* She determined that the ages-old Hawaiian land system had "... created artificial deterrents to the normal functioning of the State's residential land market and forced thousands of individual homeowners to lease, rather than buy, the land underneath their homes. Regulating oligopoly and the evils associated with it is a classic exercise of a State's police powers."[12]

In the case of *Kelo*, however, there was no such limitation concerning a public use or a public purpose. In *Berman* and *Midkiff* there was an evil that had been perceived by the state and the state acted to eradicate that evil, e.g., the existence of unsafe, blighted properties and an antiquated feudal system of land ownership. These cases dealt with an easily recognizable public use or purpose in eradicating these recognized evils. Neither problem existed in the *Kelo* case.

In *Kelo,* the City of New London simply made a determination that one private citizen could provide more economic benefit to the community than another private citizen. Perhaps there is some public purpose in attempting to create a better economic climate or to collect more tax revenue. However, as a result of the *Kelo* decision, there is now no distinction between a public purpose and a private purpose. The Court specifically addressed the instance of a "one-to-one transfer, executed outside the confines of an integrated development plan," but found that such a transfer was not present in the instant case, presumably because the beneficiary of the transfer was not specifically identified at the time of the trial. Therefore, the definition of a public purpose is left to the local government so long as its planned use for the property is considered and does not name a specific person or group to be benefited thereby. The logic of this decision would allow a city to condemn a church to build a retail store because it would provide jobs or to condemn modest housing because an expensive high rise would yield higher tax revenue. As Justice O'Connor stated in her dissenting opinion: "The specter of condemnation hangs over all property. Nothing is to prevent the State from replacing any Motel 6 with a Ritz-Carlton, any home with a shopping mall, or any farm with a factory."

Justice Stevens, writing for the majority in *Kelo*, did not provide a standard by which to interpret the phrase "public use;" he simply explained why one standard after another could not work and left the determination to local government. In other words, the Court declined to address the issue. This is more than a little troubling as the question at hand was a fundamental right guaranteed by the Bill of Rights. As stated by the Court in *Cincinnati* (above) "… the question remains a judicial one which this Court must decide in performing its duty of enforcing the provisions of the Federal Constitution." Unfortunately, the Court in *Kelo* abandoned its responsibility to develop standards by which to interpret the Bill of Rights in a way that protects the citizenry from tyranny by the majority. It failed its fundamental task.

The result of the *Kelo* decision has been to return us to the days prior to the Incorporation Doctrine which made the Takings Clause applicable to state action. The protection of individual liberty is essentially now left to the whim of local government.

Post-Kelo

As mentioned above, the petitioners in *Kelo* maintained that for takings of the kind present in the instant case the Court should require a "reasonable certainty" that the expected public benefits would actually accrue. The majority rejected this argument, stating: "Such a rule, however, would represent an even greater departure from our precedent. 'When the legislature's purpose is legitimate and its means are not irrational, our cases make clear that empirical debates over the wisdom of takings—no less than debates over the wisdom of other kinds of socioeconomic legislation—are not to be carried out in the federal courts.'"

Three years after the Supreme Court case was decided, Susette Kelo's house was relocated to another site. The city's redevelopment plan, which figured so prominently in the Supreme Court opinion as justification for the taking, failed. The redeveloper was unable to obtain financing and the redevelopment project was abandoned. The promised new jobs and increased tax revenues did not materialize. In September 2009, four years after the *Kelo* decision, Pfizer completed a merger with Wyeth and in late 2010 chose to close its New London facility prior to the expiration of its tax breaks on the New London site.[13] The land was never deeded back to the original homeowners, most of whom left New London for nearby communities.[14] As of early 2011, the original Kelo property was a vacant lot, generating no tax revenue for the city. The cost to the city and state for the purchase and bulldozing of the formerly privately held property, as of 2009, was $78 million.[15]

Prior to *Kelo* only eight states specifically prohibited the use of eminent domain for economic development (except to eliminate blight). These states were Arkansas, Florida, Illinois, Kentucky, Maine, Montana, South Carolina and Washington. By July 2009, 43 states had enacted some type of reform legislation in response to the *Kelo* decision. Of those 43 states, 22 enacted laws that substantially inhibited the takings allowed by the *Kelo* decision, while 21 states enacted laws that placed some limits on the power of municipalities to invoke eminent domain for economic development.[16]

Conclusion

The Supreme Court Building in Washington, D.C., has a statue of Lady Justice, as do many courthouses in this country. She is a woman, often blindfolded, holding a set of scales and a sword. The sword represents reason and justice, and may be used for or against either party. The blindfold represents her lack of concern for the social status of the individuals before her. The scales hold all of the many items that must be weighed to achieve justice and promise that the evidence will be weighed fairly and objectively. The statue has been prominent since the ancient Greek civilization and adorns courthouses throughout Europe and the Americas. She does not depict law. She depicts justice. The goal of our legal system is not the enforcement of laws, but rather the pursuit of the elusive goal of justice. Justice is made up of many things of which law itself is but one small part. The laws created by our legislature attempt to create justice for the majority. The Bill of Rights in our Constitution protects the minority from the majority, thereby ensuring individual justice.

The U.S. Supreme Court ignored individual justice with its decision in *Kelo*, returning to the days when local government is free to select winners and losers without the constitutional restraint of the Fifth Amendment. Unfortunately, local government is not equipped to balance liberty interests; that can be done only by an independent judiciary.

The *Kelo* decision raises several disturbing issues. First, in light of the lack of standards defining public use, are there any private property rights left in this country? Ownership and future control of property is potentially subject to the whim of local government to favor one owner over another for some possibly nebulous reason such as the desire to collect more tax revenue from the property.

It does not seem difficult for a local governmental entity to satisfy Justice Stevens' requirements of a "carefully considered development plan ... not adopted to benefit a particular class of identifiable individuals." Even more disturbing, as pointed out by Justice Thomas in his dissent, is the possibility that local governments might use eminent domain to rid themselves of housing opportunities for the economically disadvantaged, thus driving the poor from the community.

Ironically, in response to the *Kelo* decision, a proposal was made to take Justice Souter's home in Weare, New Hampshire, through eminent domain and give it to another individual to make a bed-and-breakfast. While the irony of this situation is humorous, it highlights the possibility that local governments might choose to take properties from private citizens for any number of reasons—to create tourist attractions, to advance business interests, to increase tax revenues—merely by arguing that such takings would benefit the local economy.

Following the *Kelo* decision, Riviera Beach, a community in Florida, made plans to condemn much of its waterfront property, potentially displacing thousands of people. On May 4, 2006, the state of Florida passed legislation that prohibited the taking of properties through the use of eminent domain where the properties were to be used for private development. Florida's Governor Jeb Bush signed this legislation on May 11, 2006, but the Riviera Beach City Council voted on the night of May 10, 2006, to authorize signing an agreement with developer Viking Harbor Inlet Properties that the city would use eminent domain to take property for the project. As a result, an 800-acre area full of homes and businesses, including as many as 5,100 residents, was to be replaced with a yachting complex, luxury housing and other private commercial uses.

Riviera Beach's mayor announced that the city believed Florida's new law did not apply to Riviera Beach. Riviera Beach's home and business owners filed suit to stop the use of eminent domain for this private development. Shortly thereafter, the mayor was voted out of office, and new city council members were elected. Responding to public outcry, they made clear that plans to use eminent domain for this project were off the table. An editorial by the *St. Augustine Record*, May 14, 2006, stated:

> That decision [Kelo] paved the way for cities and counties to take private homes or businesses if they 'believed' the development 'might' generate more tax revenue. And according to the Virginia-based Institute for Justice, hundreds used the ruling to prepare or begin condemnation proceedings across the land. And because of the wording of the Supreme Court opinion, governments did not need to demonstrate any need for the property in the foreseeable future. Some simply began to condemn property with the intent of shopping for a developer down the road.
>
> The Justices did, however, say in the ruling that individual states could enact their own laws to provide more protection to owners than did the court.
>
> Thursday, Florida became one of the first. The legislation signed by Bush prohibits transferring property from one owner to another by use of eminent

domain. It forbids the use of eminent domain to eliminate "blight." It does still allow government to take private property, but in the much narrower description written in the state constitution. By contrast, Connecticut's statutes allow eminent domain for developments used for 'any commercial, financial or retail enterprise.'

The Florida law has been heralded by property rights groups as a model for other states, although some commentators argue that it goes too far in forbidding takings to eliminate blight. Unfortunately, in light of the U.S. Supreme Court's ruling in *Kelo,* individual state legislative action may be the only avenue remaining to protect individuals from this particular form of "tyranny by the majority."

Notes

1. Laurence Tribe, *2000 American Constitutional Law,* Foundation Press.
2. *Chicago B. & Q. R. Co. v. Chicago,* 166 U.S. 226, 41 L. Ed. 979, 17 S. Ct. 581 (1897).
3. Calder v. Bull, 3 U.S. 386, 388–89 (1798).
4. Nevada Statute (1875), 111.
5. *Dayton Gold and Silver Mining Co. v. Seawell,* 11 Nev 394 (1876).
6. *Hays v. Risher,* 32 Pa 169 (1858).
7. *United States v. Gettysburg R.R.,* 160 U.S. 668; 16 S. Ct. 427; 40 L. Ed. 576 (1897).
8. Ibid., p. 679.
9. *B. & Q. R. Co. v. Chicago,* 166 U.S. 266 (1897).
10. *Cincinnati v. Vestor,* 281 U.S. 439 (1930), p. 446.
11. *Hawaii v. Midkiff,* 467 U.S. 229; 104 S. Ct. 2321; 81 L. Ed. 2d 186 (1984).
12. Ibid., p. 242.
13. "Pfizer to Close New London Headquarters," *Hartford Courant,* Nov. 9, 2009.
14. "Connecticut Land Taken from Homeowners Still Undeveloped," Associated Press, Sept. 25, 2009.
15. "Pfizer and Kelo v. City of New London," *The Wall Street Journal,* Nov. 11, 2009.16. *www.castlecoalition.org/legislativecenter.*

CHAPTER 2

Native Americans: Brief Historical Perspectives

READING 3

An Exemplary Program for Recruiting American Indian Students

By Mary C. Dowd, Ed.D., Megan R. Heutmaker, M.S. and Kelly S. Meier, Ed.D.

Introduction

> "Educational access and attainment are among the most pressing issues facing Indian Country." (Harrington and Harrington, 2011, p. 1)

The percentage of American Indian students enrolled in college has historically been disproportionately lower than non-Native peer groups. Too often, this disparity is framed as an individual failing rather than the product of a skewed educational system. "What is commonly seen as the 'problem' of Indigenous education is, in fact, a larger problem of an educational system that perpetuates and models the goals and values of Western epistemology" (Maldonado, Rhoads, and Buenavista, 2005).

Because mainstream education is associated with genocide, especially in the minds of elders, there is an understandable aversion to pursuing higher education despite the potential benefits. When American Indians do attempt college, they often find it difficult to live in two cultural worlds with strikingly different worldviews and opposing values. Many otherwise capable students leave school without completing their degree. Abandonment of a dream represents a loss to the student, campus, family, tribal community and society.

Enrollment management strategies rarely take into consideration the unique challenges of recruiting American Indian students. Typically, less attention is given to student populations that do not have a high success rate. Numbers drive decision making, not philosophical discussion. "Native American students are typically defined in the postsecondary literature not by their personal stories but in terms of their retention in or alienation from mainstream institutions" (Khachadoorian cited in Simmons, p. 36, 2011).

Many factors contribute to the underrepresentation of American Indian students in the academy. "It seems rare, given the myriad cultural, worldview and cognitive obstacles that any American Indians— especially those who strive to maintain their cultural identity—can succeed in a higher education system dominated by powerful and persuasive influences of the white majority culture" (Harrington and Hunt, 2010, p. 2). For some individuals, college is not considered an option due to their substandard high school education or their decision to drop out before earning a diploma or GED.

Enrollment of American Indian students has increased somewhat but proportionately less than the percentage of students from other racial or ethnic groups. Aboriginal students in Canada have not had a positive experience in higher education either. Without education, Indigenous people will remain largely walled off from economic prosperity.

The urgent problem of underrepresentation of gifted, intelligent American Indians in college cannot be overstated. Evidence-based solutions are available for institutions of higher learning sincerely committed to disrupting the status quo and wisely tapping this artesian well of overlooked talent.

Paucity of Research

Finding recently published studies on the retention and recruitment of American Indian students is challenging. The limited research available consists of facts and figures on admission, matriculation, retention and graduation. Far less is known about the unique personal stories of students who persisted and those who did not.

Culturally sensitive research is needed to gain insight into the perspective of postsecondary students. Clear understanding of student opinions, attitudes, and expectations would provide valuable data that could inform policy decisions, enrollment management strategies and allocation of resources for effective programming.

Jackson, Smith, and Hill (2003) suggest that racism must be acknowledged as a significant factor in why Native students do not persist at predominantly white colleges and universities. "Though racism has received considerable scholarly attention, we found little research that focused specifically on the personal experience of racism and its relationship to persistence among Native Americans" (p. 557). Jackson, Smith, and Hill further assert that the absence of study in this area is a form of institutionalized racism in itself. They described the frequent disclosures of racism by study participants as "surprising, painful and poignant" (p. 562).

Forced Assimilation

Student Affairs conversations related to recruiting diverse students typically revolve around customer relationship management (CRM) software communications, free admissions applications, and help with the FAFSA. Sentiments are mixed as to how much time and effort should be spent trying to recruit students who are ambivalent about school, at best.

Admissions officers are under pressure to find students who will persist to graduation. "How likely is it that a large, mainstream state-funded college could make fundamental changes for a population of students that probably make up less than 1 percent of the total student body?" (Simmons, 2011, p. 38).

Many American Indian students have limited resources for college. When American Indian students do not respond to communications from mainstream colleges and universities, admissions offices often attribute it to concerns about the cost of college and understandable reluctance to accumulate debt on top of existing poverty.

Nevertheless, even when offered a scholarship from a prestigious institution, high performing American Indian students may hesitate to enroll. Dean Chavers, director of a national scholarship agency, has written extensively on racism and dropout rates. Chavers (2012) states, "My theory is that there is a huge elephant out there started by Captain Richard Henry Pratt at Carlisle in 1878. It's called assimilation, meaning Indians should learn English, how to make beds and plow fields, and not much else. Not much has changed. College is not for them," they feel.

When first founded, prestigious schools such as Dartmouth, Harvard, and Princeton considered it their mission to bring Christianity and Eurocentric values to college-age American Indians. College administrators segregated and treated students differently according to students' socioeconomic background.

The aim of the elite was to educate American Indian youth with the hope that they would take Western European ideas and Christian morals back to their tribe. "Education and conversion [to Christianity] were viewed as mutually supportive practices." The plan failed. Elders complained to school officials that their children were learning ideas and skills that "were good for nothing" (Simmons, 2011).

It was duly noted that young men returning to the reservation after attending college were lazy and too out of shape for running and chasing game. In addition, schools lamented that educated American Indian students were succumbing to the "recidivist influence of their elders" (Simmons, 2011, p. 65) instead of inoculating their tribal members with Western ways of thinking.

From an early age, public education served to oppress and dehumanize Native children by pushing an assimilation agenda. Parents could be arrested and jailed if they did not send their children to public schools or if they attempted to hide them in an isolated area. Rather than deal with resistant parents, government agents rounded children up and placed them in institutionalized boarding schools to accelerate assimilation. Places like the Carlisle school punished children for expression of cultural dress, beliefs, language, and behavior. Treatment was harsh and conditions poor.

Student Development Theory

Conventional enrollment management approaches presume that admissions offices should direct time and money to the recruitment of students who "fit" the current institutional profile—privileged white children. Student development theory in the field of student affairs along with enrollment data corroborate that institutional fit contributes to persistence and timely graduation.

Astin's development theory of involvement and Tinto's assimilationist theory of persistence are among the two theories often referenced in enrollment management models and literature. However, generalizability is limited because the theories are predicated on the study of young, white, middle-class males. Tinto and Austin do not adequately "take into account the unique family, political status, tribal affiliation, language, tribal customs and traditions, and tribal community factors" (p.61).

Tinto presumed that lower retention of underrepresented students is due to lower socioeconomic status and inadequate high school preparation. Tinto does not consider that poor performance may be due to disinterest and difficulty relating to Eurocentric materials and curriculum.

In fact, "Tinto contends that students must reject their attitudes and values from their previous communities to successfully negotiate the separation process and integrate into their new college environment" (Pidgeon, 2008, p. 346). Community college closer to home may be less threatening to first-generation students who may be overwhelmed by the pressures of conformity while attending a distant university far from friends and family support.

Researchers are making strides to fill the gap in the literature with regard to the holistic development of American Indian students. Models are helpful in understanding attrition and identifying corrective action.

HeavyRunner and DeCelles (2002) offer an insightful model of student retention theory known as the Family Education Model (FEM) that helps explain the Indigenous student experience in college. This intervention-based model posits that engendering a sense of belonging is key to retaining Native American students. In this schema, a multicultural staff person serves as a "specialist" who works closely with the student, as well as the family. The specialist wears many hats: mentor, family counselor, academic adviser, and advocate. Similar to a social worker, the specialist also connects the student with campus and community resources, such as transportation, housing, financial aid, tutoring, counseling, child care, cultural ceremonies, and multicultural events.

What is critical to note about FEM, as contrasted to more typical approaches to student retention, is the emphasis placed on college students' perception of need. Eurocentric studies tend to focus more on what institutions must do to reach institutional diversity goals in some strategic plan. FEM maintains that being differently prepared for college does not make students inherently ill prepared for academic success.

Arguably, the underrepresentation of American Indian students in higher education is the proverbial canary in the coalmine suggesting problems on a broader scale. Is it that underrepresented students decide not to attend college in disproportionate numbers, or has higher education chosen not to invite them? Jaquette and Salazar (2018) examined recruitment practices of 150 colleges and universities and discovered that admission offices focus on high schools where students are whiter and richer than the general population.

In an earlier study, Jacquette (2013) found that when schools intensify their efforts to recruit out-of-state students, enrollments of underrepresented, low-income students decline. Admissions visits to out-of-state high schools are disproportionately made to affluent areas. Higher education leaders argue that admissions must focus on families who can pay to offset declining state appropriations.

Opportunity and access should start with a review of the curriculum. Analysis must take into account what material is taught, as well as what content is not taught—by accident or design. The issue is coming to a head as underrepresented students' crash through hegemonic barriers. The U.S. Census Bureau projects that by 2020, more than 50 percent of school-aged children will be a member of a diverse racial or ethnic group. By 2060, only 36 percent of children will be non-Hispanic white.

It is a safe assumption that shifting demographics will prompt revision of the current Eurocentric account of history and shape school culture to reflect the tapestry of diversity that built the United States. The goal is to infuse diversity into core subjects instead of buying into the false dichotomy that teaching ethnic studies takes time away from learning the core skills of reading, writing, and arithmetic. Reading and discussing history develops student's critical thinking skills. Attaining cross-cultural skills complements the back-to-the-basics movement by preparing students to succeed in a global society. Life skills are just as important as knowing how to add numbers or spell without a gadget in hand. The change has profound implications. Studies have shown that test scores increase when students learn more about their identity (Kelly, 2011). Suspension and dropout rates go down. Thus, curriculum reform constitutes a moral imperative.

Students who maintain cultural identity and see how topics connect to their lives are more academically successful. Sensitive educators also look for ways of teaching to different learning styles. They also take into consideration how information is processed and shared across cultures. For instance, Navajo students hesitate to participate in class or talk about themselves because that is perceived as bragging or calling attention to themselves, which goes against a collectivist worldview.

Pidgeon (2008) recommends that college and universities seeking to recruit and retain diverse students should recognize that students of color may view success very differently than other students on a predominantly white campus. Making money is just one desired outcome and marker of a good life. Virtually all students care about finishing college and landing a good job. According to a comprehensive Georgetown University report in 2011, the average wages of college graduates are 84 percent higher than the earnings of workers with a high school diploma.

Thus, it is critically imperative that American Indian students obtain an education. However, the financial benefits of a college degree must outweigh the personal cost and potential risk of assimilation. American Indian students seek to retain and deepen their sense of cultural identity. American Indians are highly motivated to persist and succeed if they are reminded of the special benefits of a degree for indigenous students (Pidgeon, 2008). A well-educated populace has more leverage in self-governance, self-determination, decolonization, and empowerment of self and community.

Retention Factors

Researching all the reasons why American Indian students struggle in college is like asking why a battered woman stays in a violent home instead of examining what keeps her stuck there. Repeatedly dwelling on the low retention rates of American Indians can increase stereotype threat and reinforce racist assumptions about natural ability.

Hunt and Harrington (2010) argue that it is time to stop dwelling on the low retention rates of American Indians in college and focus on those who persist and thrive. The stories of successful American Indians working in all fields and occupations needs to be told. Role models are very important when students imagine possibilities for themselves.

Demmert's (2001) research study found the following:

> Knowledge about characteristics of successful Native students is somewhat limited, but the information that is there tells us that attendance, language competence, motivation, positive life experiences, sense of purpose, early goal setting, the ability to balance conflicts between home and community, and knowledge of basic skills all contribute to a student's ability to successfully navigate the process of schooling. There is much we still need to learn about this area and what is alterable and what is not. (p. 42)

Resiliency Factors

Harrington and Harrington (2011) and Hunt (2010) indicate that American Indian students who do well in higher education are positively impacted by the following factors:

- Cultural ties and strong cultural identity
- Ease of access to financial aid
- Contact with diverse faculty and staff as role models
- Available child care, if needed
- Flexible scheduling that allow students an opportunity to work part-time to pay for school and reduce debt
- Adequate preparation in high school
- Defined career goals
- Availability of needed classes
- Family support
- Faculty and staff mentoring to guide and champion the student's endeavors
- Personal determination and resiliency

Harrington and Harrington (2011) further recommend that additional studies be undertaken to examine how American Indian students' expectations of college influence performance in their first year at college.

Family Encouragement

A study by Jackson, Smith and Hill (2003) produced similar results. Family support was especially pivotal, whether it came from parents, grandparents, aunts, or uncles. "In many cases, the encouragement was almost an imperative to be academically successful" (p. 553). They also noted that participation in multicultural offices and groups was key, even though some students initially hesitated to get involved. A few students who participated in the study commented that membership in a cultural group should be mandatory.

Success Strategies

A study conducted by the National Center for Education Statistics (NCES) examined the graduation rates of underrepresented students at 4,000 colleges. The top five schools were Ripon College, Yale, Scripps, Harvard and Flagler College, all having a graduation rate of 75 percent or more. Commonalities included mentoring, special orientation for first generation students, and attractive financial aid packages.

Similar strategies have been effective at other schools around the country.

Examples include the following:

- Pair American Indian students with alumni who can relate to the student and offer personal support. Alumni connections can feel like extended family.
- Start early. Expand college preparation programs. "As early as elementary and secondary school, American Indian students should be encouraged to consider and plan a college education and participate in college preparatory curriculum" (Harrington and Harrington 2011; Hunt, 2010, p.6).
- Provide tutoring in math, science, reading, and technology. High school guidance counselors and college programs should work together to connect students with summer enrichment, bridge programs, and TRIO.
- Provide academic advising and career counseling in culturally familiar ways. For example, McCormick, Neumann, Amundson & McLean (1999) developed the First Nations Career/Life Planning Model. Student advising sessions incorporate traditional practices, such as the smudge ceremony, talking stick, burning sage and eagle feathers. Familiar cultural metaphors are used to guide students along the career exploration path.
- Integrate awareness of American Indian learning styles into teacher prep curriculums. Stereotypes, microaggressions, and misunderstanding of American Indians can create

unconscious bias that disadvantages diverse student populations. Anyone going into education needs to be culturally competent.

- Wherever possible, colleges should work with local tribal leaders to improve outreach to students and their families. Trust takes time and must be earned.
- Increase admissions fairs and open house events. Although it may cost more, encouraging the student to bring along extended family members can reduce anxiety on the part of the student and relatives. Furnishings and materials should be nice and not second-rate, which would contradict the school's message that these underrepresented students are important and valued.
- Collaborate with two-year colleges to ease the transition to the university. Transferring from a small school close to home to a larger, bureaucratic institution can be stress inducing. Communication between faculty and support staff from both institutions can ease the transition.
- Because American Indian students may hesitate to seek help until it is too late, support staff should take the risk of being seen as intrusive by continually making overtures to connect with students. Obtaining classroom reports can help get students back on track if there is a problem with attendance or homework completion. "Both developmental and prescriptive academic advising sessions should be required to assist American Indian students in the decision-making process of schedule building, academic policies and procedures, and information of campus student services" (Hunt, 2010, p. 10).
- Programming must be frequent and intentional. American Indian students should be encouraged to participate in cultural organizations, planning Pow Wows, family weekend, study groups, etc.
- Connect current students with American Indian mentors in the alumni association.
- Involve undergraduate students in undergraduate research centers directed by Ethnic Studies faculty.

Structural Overhaul

As a microcosm of society, higher education is infected with racism. Courage and honesty are necessary requisites for dismantling barriers. Institutional policies should be reviewed and examined for disparate impacts on certain segments of the student population. It is time to rethink the delivery of education and the many rules that pertain to virtually every facet of college life. American Indians joke about all the "white tape" they encounter just to take a class. Eurocentric notions of time and rigid structure must be examined. Finding ways of promoting life-work balance would benefit all of society.

Commissioned by the Minnesota Department of Education Office of Indian Education, the Midwest Comprehensive Center conducted a meta-analysis of state and national documents pertaining to American Indian education. Using a grounded theory methodology, MCC researchers identified undergirding themes. Researchers found common agreement in how mainstream education must change to better serve American Indian students. Several themes stood out:

1. There exists an urgent need to close the opportunity gap between Native and non-Native populations. Acknowledge and compensate for the different socioeconomic levels that affect educational performance and self-fulfilling expectations.
2. Mandate that all students learn about American Indian culture and history, past and present.
3. Reach out to tribal agencies to build bridges, partnerships, and alliances. Increase capacity to work together in service to students. Honor tribal sovereignty. "An example of such an approach would be for institutions to provide office space on campus for tribal educators and tribal leaders so that they could continue to provide support to Native American students and so that the institution could benefit from their expertise" (Larimore & McClellan, 2005, p. 27).
4. Increase funding for American Indian student opportunity and access at pre-K through secondary levels.
5. Develop a pipeline for developing American Indian teachers and professors. "Provide professional development and capacity-building opportunities for American Indian education" (MWCC Report, 2013).

Larimore and McClellan (2005) suggest that the practice of student affairs and student support services can be enhanced by relying on more culturally diverse models of student development. "Develop a culturally based model of identity development for Native American people" (Larimore and McClellan, 2005, p. 27). Another helpful structural change would be creative use of emerging technologies to expand online education to students on the reservation combined with adequate student service support and easy access to individual assistance with everything from registering for classes to computer glitches.

Colleges and universities can show their sincere commitment to diversifying the student body by offering more attractive financial aid packages and scholarships that appeal to underrepresented students. For example, prestigious Maine colleges—Bates, Bowdoin and Colby—consulted with tribal leaders to establish a full $45,000 per year scholarship for American Indian students. College leaders also agreed to step up recruiting and outreach efforts, starting with students in middle school. Thomason and Thurber (1999) suggested that predominantly white organizations could be more responsive to the professional development of American Indian students by helping them find relevant jobs, practicums, and internships. Working part-time while in school provides valuable work experience, which is advantageous in the job search after college. "Additionally, colleges and universities have come to acknowledge that racial and ethnic diversity within faculty fosters multicultural pedagogy serving to enhance the overall learning experiences of their students" (Hunt 2010, p. 8).

It's All About Family

Bridging the schism between the two worlds of western worldview and Indigenous worldview requires acknowledging differences in core values. "By incorporating family within the educational experience of Native American students, institutions have the opportunity to bridge gaps, heal wounds and build trust" (Guillory and Wolverton, p. 84). Higher institutions of learning must acknowledge that mainstream methods of student recruitment and retention are fatally flawed. Family connections are so strong that students will make great personal sacrifices and tenaciously pursue goals if they believe that getting an education will benefit their families. "It is a reflection of an Indigenous philosophy of putting community before individualism" (Guillory and Wolverton, p. 74).

Mentoring

American Indian programs and services play a critical role in helping students live in both worlds without losing cultural identity. Mentoring and role models empower students and help them feel connected. Mentors mitigate a sense of isolation and help the student find friends and support networks among peers, faculty and other staff at the university. As role models, mentors give hope that it is possible to be true to yourself while succeeding and dismantling racism on a predominantly white campus. Structured, intentional, proactive efforts to establish mentoring relationships for an American Indian student can go a long way in enhancing retention and persistence to graduation at the graduate and undergraduate level.

Three Pillars of Recruitment

Using the framework and recommendations from the literature, institutions of higher education can provide specialized recruitment efforts for American Indian students that will increase the likelihood of persistence and success. The three pillars of recruitment that enhance access for American Indian students include specialized on-campus visits, targeted college fairs, and specialized follow-up in phone calls and virtual contact efforts.

Specialized on-campus visits must include interaction with registered Native students, faculty, and staff. The opportunity for American Indian students to feel a sense of community and a connection with their culture and identity is paramount. A successful campus visit includes a tour of campus (hosted by a Native student leader), a broad understanding of college readiness, specific financial aid information, a panel presentation by Native students about college life, a visit to a college class, preferably taught by an American Indian faculty member, and an opportunity to talk to diverse students and staff. When possible, a campus visit that is paired with an American Indian program and includes an overnight experience is preferable. Hosting specialized campus visits are a critical beginning to the recruitment process. Often, American Indian students feel isolated and in need of advocacy and encouragement.

Another way to engage students in a longer-term campus visit is to implement an American Indian summer camp. Recruitment to the summer camp can be done through campus visits, outreach to American Indian liaisons in the high schools, and word of mouth on American Indian reservations. Using college student staff as the summer camp counselors allows for the natural formation of mentoring for the American Indian high schools students. These summer camp experiences provide students more in-depth information about ACT preparation, financing college, and choosing the right college preparatory classes. An American Indian campus serves as a springboard for deepening the relationship with the institution. Including fun and engaging activities throughout the program breaks down social barriers for the students attending and builds a unique community from this experience. An extended experience like this can help the students feel more comfortable on campus and see that college isn't as scary or impossible as it may seem. Building trust with American Indian communities is a natural, residual effect of this endeavor.

College recruitment offices must be willing to meet American Indian students where they are and where they live. College fairs that are uniquely suited for American Indian students are prevalent. Many are held in schools with a large population of Native students or on reservations. Institutions of higher education must make the commitment to be consistently present at these events. More than the fair itself, the principal of showing investment in the Native communities is equally as important.

Other ways to engage in recruitment efforts include invitations to American Indian community events such as powwows and cultural fairs. Even though there may not be immediate results in terms of enrolled students at your university, a continued, annual commitment is evidence of institutional investment in American Indian students. It takes a long time to build trust with the communities, but once you are faithful in your commitment, a positive reputation ensues.

Building relationships is key. American Indian students and their parents are searching for a college that provides resources and support for Native students. Recruitment efforts that are authentically invested in the success of American Indian students will grow a community that is inclusive and committed. Targeted work and relationship building with American Indian liaisons in the high schools is an effective way to start making connections. American Indian Liaisons are specifically hired to work in high schools to provide additional support for American Indian high school students. Common responsibilities include college prep work, ACT study groups, cultural events, college visits, and advising support in the high school environment.

Colleges and universities must foster a continued relationship with Native students that have expressed an interest in enrolling in college. Intentional follow-up with American Indian students is critical. This can be done with e-mail, phone calls and virtual interaction, which builds a sense of trust and investment in each student who has made a connection with the institution. This follow-up can be as simple as a quick check-in, or it can become more in-depth and include financial aid assistance. Serving as a resource for the student prior to arrival, an engaged and supportive environment is invested in student success. Again, this provides support for American Indian students and their families, creating a connection to the university and the American Indian community.

References

Blue, Elizabeth T., and Priscilla A. Day. 1999. "A Literature Guide: Resources for Holding Institutions of Higher Education Accountable; How Do They Serve American Indian Students?" *Journal of Indian Higher Education, 10*(2). ISSN: 10525505.

Bowman, Nicole R. 2013. "America Indian Education in Minnesota: Analytical Review of Key State and National Documents." *Midwest Comprehensive Center Report*, 1–25.

Chavers, Dean. 2012. "A Handful of Indian Scholarships." *Native American Times*, 5 (June 22). ISSN: 15424928.

Collins, Robert Keith. (2013). "Reducing Barriers to Native American Student Success in Higher Education: Challenges and Best Practices." *American Indian Culture and Research Journal, 37*(3), ix–xvi.

Demmert Jr, William G. 2001. "Improving Academic Performance Among Native American Students." Office of Educational Research and Improvement. Washington, D.C.

Flynn, Ellen E. 2015. "It's All About Saving Face: Working with the Urban College Student. *College Student Journal, 49*(2), 187–194.

Georgetown University Center on Education and the Workforce Report (2011). Retrieved from https://cew.georgetown.edu/cew-reports/the-college-payoff/

Guillory, Raphael M., and Mimi Wolverton. 2008. "It's About Family: Native American Student Persistence in Higher Education." *The Journal of Higher Education, 79*(1), 58–87.

Iris HeavyRunner and Richard DeCelles, 2002. "Family Education Model: Meeting the Student Retention Challenge." *Journal of American Indian Education, Vol. 41(2),* Celebrating 30 years of American Indian Higher Education 1972-2002: SPECIAL ISSUE, pp. 29–37.

Harrington, Charles F., and Billie G. Harrington. 2011. "Fighting a Different Battle: Challenges Facing American Indians in Higher Education." *Journal of Indigenous Research, 1*(1), 1–5.

Hunt, Billie. 2010. "The Impending Educational Crisis for American Indians: Higher Education at the Crossroads." *Indigenous Policy Journal, 21*(3), 1–13.

Jackson, Aaron P., Steven A. Smith, and Curtis L. Hill. 2003. "Academic Persistence Among Native American College Students." *Journal of College Student Development, 44*(4), 548–565.

Jacobs, Michelle R., and Tiffany Taylor. 2012. "Challenges of Multiracial Antiracist Activism: Consciousness and Chief Wahoo." *Critical Sociology, 38*(5), 687–706.

Jaquette, Ozan. (2013). "Why do colleges become universities? Mission drift and the enrollment economy." Research in Higher Education, 54(5): 514–543.

Jaquette, Ozan, and Salazar, Karina. (2018, April 13). Colleges recruit at richer, whiter high schools. The New York Times. Retrieved from https://www.nytimes.com/interactive/2018/04/13/opinion/college_recruitment-rich-white.html

Jaschik, Scott. 2018. "Study Analyzes Where Colleges Recruit and Where They Don't." *Inside Higher Education.* Retrieved from https://www.insidehighered.com/admissions/article/2018/04/16/study-analyzes-where-colleges-recruit-and-where-they-don't.

Larimore, James A., and George S. McClellan. 2005. Native American Student Retention in U.S. Postsecondary Education Report, (109) 17–32.

McCormick, Rod M., Harly Neumann, Norman E. Amundson, and Holly B. McLean. 1999. "First Nations: Career/Life Planning Model: Guidelines for Practitioners." *Journal of Employment Counseling, 36,* 167–176.

Pidgeon, Michelle. 2008. "Pushing Against the Margins: Indigenous Theorizing of 'Success' and Retention in Higher Education. *Journal of College Student Retention, 10*(3), 339–360.

Pidgeon, Michelle, and Cox, Donna G Hardy. 2002. "Researching with Aboriginal Peoples: Practice and Principles." *Canadian Journal of Native Education, (26)2,* 96–201.

Rees, Nina. (2017). "Closing the Gap: College Access to College Success." *HuffPost.* Retrieved from https://www.huffingtonpost.com/nina-rees/closing-the-gap-college-a_b_13657242.html.

Rosales, Joseph. 2012. "U. Aims to Recruit Native American Students, Faculty." *The Brown Daily Herald.* Retrieved from: http://www.browndailyherald.com/2012/02/10/u-aims-to-recruit-native-american-students-faculty/

Simmons, W. S. 2011. Khachadoorian, Angelle A.: Inside the eagle's head: an American Indian college. *CHOICE: Current Reviews for Academic Libraries, 48*(12), 2357. Retrieved from http://link.galegroup.com/apps/doc/A263439413/EAIM?u=mnamsumank&sid=EAIM&xid=d2368a56

Snipp, Matthew C. 2015. "American Indian Education and Poverty." In W. G. Tierney, (ed.), *Rethinking Education and Poverty,* 54–76. Baltimore: John Hopkins University Press.

Thomason, Timothy C., and Hanna J. Thurber. 1999. "Strategies for the Recruitment and Retention of Native American Students." *American Indian Rehabilitation and Training Center,* 1–39. IBSN: 1-888557-84-2

Toensing, Gale Courey. 2007. "Maine Tribes and Colleges Seal Education Partnership." *Indian Country Today.*

United States Census Bureau. Retrieved April 13, 2018, from https://www.census.gov/newsroom/press-releases/2015/cb15-tps16.html

Ward, Lee, Michael J. Siegel, and Zebulun Davenport. 2015. "First-generation College Students: Understanding and Improving the Experience from Recruitment to Commencement." *Journal of College Student Retention: Research, Theory & Practice, 17*(3), 381–385.

Wetschler, Ed. 2011. "After 50 Years, Ethnic Studies Still Controversial." *District Administration,* 46–53. Retrieved from https://www.districtadministration.com/article/after-50-years-ethnic-studies-still-controversial.

READING 4

Native American Sovereignty and U.S. Citizenship

By Robert Keith Collins

What is the relationship between Native American sovereignty and U.S. citizenship? McDonald's *American Indians and The Fight for Equal Rights*, Warren's *The Quest For Citizenship*, and Work's *The Seminole Nation of Oklahoma* offer analyses that examine the nature and origins of this relationship, as discernible from legal, historical, and narrative records. These works encourage the reader to consider potential answers to this question from Native American struggles for civil rights as both citizens of sovereign tribal nations and U.S. citizens. A common assertion made by all authors is that this relationship must be understood as a direct precipitate of the struggles for civil rights, voting equality, educational opportunities, and government-to-government relationships that have shaped Native American lived realities from the late nineteenth through the twentieth centuries.

This perennial question may seem to have been exhausted; however, it is only because American studies of this relationship have historically centered on what the United States did to Native Americans, rather than the agency demonstrated by the people both individually and collectively. Contrary to this approach, McDonald, Warren, and Work focus on what Native Americans did in the face of assimilation, cultural change, discrimination in voting, and legislative efforts to influence tribal sovereignty. Their research illustrates, on the one hand, that to understand this relationship, the experiences and interactions between Native Americans (e.g., Crow, Gros Ventre, Seminole, Sioux, etc.) and the legislators, missionaries, stakeholders, and teachers must be chronicled; however, on the other hand, the active negotiation—not passive reception—Native Americans participated in during these interactions and the formulation of their civil rights and identities as citizens of both sovereign tribal nations and the United States must also be examined. Knowing that Native Americans have experienced discrimination as U.S. citizens is only the beginning. There remains that challenge of examining when, where, and in which contexts this suppression of civil rights has occurred and how Native self-deterministic resistance facilitated their struggles for equality.

Robert Keith Collins, "Native American Sovereignty and U.S. Citizenship," *American Studies*, vol. 52, no. 2, pp. 115-122.

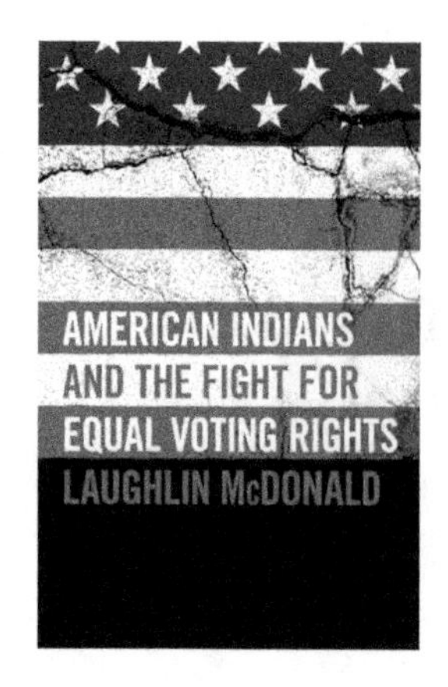

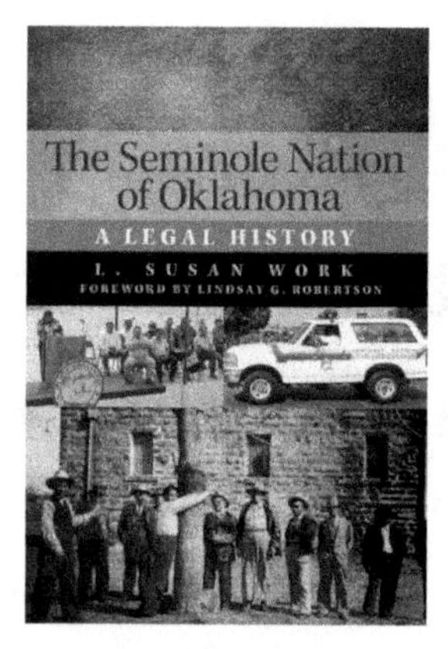

American Indians and the Fight for Equal Voting Rights. By Laughlin McDonald. Norman, OK: University of Oklahoma Press. 2010. *The Quest for Citizenship: African American and Native American Education in Kansas, 1880–1935.* By Kim Cary Warren. Chapel Hill, NC: University of North Carolina Press. 2010. *The Seminole Nation of Oklahoma: A Legal History.* By L. Susan Work. Norman, OK: University of Oklahoma Press. 2010.

This approach taken by the authors is particularly timely, as comparative American studies of Native American civil rights struggles with those of other ethnic minorities (e.g., African Americans) in the U.S. are expanding. No longer is the federal government the sole central focus in analyses of discrimination against Native Americans. Instead, as discussed in all three books, the differences, similarities, and elusive complexities of federal policy towards Native Americans are now being analyzed in tandem with the discrimination that some social and political interactions between Native Americans and non-Natives have produced (e.g., racial polarization in voting, contempt for non-taxation of Native Americans, etc.). Such analyses illuminate the duality of Native American civic existence through an emphasis on the uniqueness of contradictory federal and state policies—as well as social customs—towards Native American sovereignty, while illuminating the struggles for civil rights Native Americans share in common with other U.S. citizens that continue to fight for social equality.

This discourse, premised on the review of primary documentation, offers irrefutable data supporting the notion that federal and state policies were not dictators of the parameters of Native American civic engagement, resistance to discrimination in educational opportunities, and expressions of tribal sovereignty. Collectively, McDonald, Warren, and Work's books remind the reader that federal and state laws on Native American voting, education, and nations building were very specific and followed; however, there were enough communities and individuals who found these laws insufficient, challenged their implementation, and sought reform.

McDonald's *American Indians and the Fight for Equal Voting Rights* engages the significance of these points by examining how citizens of the Crow, Northern Cheyenne, Omaha, Salish—Kootenai, Utes, and other nations have been disentitled from the right to vote in the states of Colorado, Montana, Nebraska, South Dakota, and Wyoming. Through nine highly informative chapters, which focus on litigation filed since the 1980s, the author thoroughly investigates the legal efforts aimed at improving Native American voting rights brought forth by the American Civil Liberties Union (ACLU) Voting Rights Project.

Following a brief introduction that explains the format of the book, the rationale behind the legal historical approach taken, and the implications this approach holds for understanding the lingering impact of historical voting discrimination in the present, the first chapter provides readers with a comprehensive examination of the creation and maintenance of U.S. policies regarding Native Americans from the 1820s through 2008. This discussion centers on the limited and inconsistent salience of the U.S. Constitution and federal policies in Native American civic lives over time. One set of laws—reinforced by subsequent state specific laws and social customs—facilitated the assimilation of Native Americans through the removal of nations from their original homelands, the allotment of tribal lands, the selling of surplus lands to white Americans, the granting of U.S. citizenship to Native Americans, and the suppression of tribal life ways. Another set of laws maintained the reservation system, treaty rights, protects tribal nations as self-governing bodies, and granted religious freedom, while allowing states to assume jurisdiction over tribal lands and—in some cases, as in Wyoming and the *Ward v. Race Horse* case—trump treaty rights with state law (12).

Although the linkage between chapter 1 and chapter 2 is slightly illusive, the second chapter, examines *The Voting Rights Act of 1965*, its function (i.e., prohibiting discrimination on the basis of skin color) for Native American individuals and nations, the similarities and differences in application towards racial groups (e.g., African Americans), and its expansion in 1975 to include "language minorities," which also included Native Americans and Alaskan Natives, Asian Americans, Latinos, and immigrants (35). McDonald makes it clear from Senate reports and testimony that Native Americans have experienced as much discrimination and encroachment upon their voting rights as other minorities in the United States. Despite the granting of U.S. citizenship to Native Americans in 1924, the upholding of Native Americans and Alaskan Natives as entitled to protection under the Fourteenth Amendment—as late as 1948—Native Americans have been systematically refused the right to vote, had their vote suppressed through racial bloc voting by whites, and found themselves the victims of county redistricting to limit their voting power well into the present. All of these phenomena are meticulously explained with context-specific details in chapters three through eight.

Of particular importance in the second chapter, however, is the evolution of this act and its further expansion in 1982, 1992, and 2006 to address persistent discrimination in voting against racial and language minorities, particularly Native Americans, which coincided with their growing political participation. Included in this expansion were provisions requiring plaintiffs to prove racial discrimination in practice. Such proof took the form of court decisions acknowledging discriminatory practices against Native Americans. For example, in the *Oregon v. Mitchell* case, literacy tests were proven to be a weapon—also used against African Americans—to suppress the Native American vote.

Chapter 3, the first of six comprehensive chapters that illuminate the challenges against voting discrimination brought by Native Americans in Montana, South Dakota, Colorado, Nebraska, and Wyoming, examines the first lawsuits (e.g., *Windy Boy v. Country of Big Horn*) in Indian Country brought by the Crow and Northern Cheyenne with the representation of the ACLU. It chronicles the history of discrimination against Native Americans and presents the reader with examples of the dynamics of anti-Native American prejudice, as discernable from individual remembered experiences. Such narratives offer the reader a chance to understand how Crow, Northern Cheyenne, Salish, and Kootenai individuals made sense of white prejudices and their motivations for resistance. Their stories reflect understandings of local race cultures that forbid interracial dating, but also political arenas where white racial bloc voting was championed in order to prevent Native Americans from holding office. Why Native Americans used this same strategy to ensure the election of Native American representation—from majority-Native American districts—onto the Big Horn County Board of Commissioners and school boards of Rosebud and Roosevelt counties, etc. is also discussed.

Although the subsequent chapters examine these discrimination phenomena in other states, it is McDonald's concluding chapters that enlightens and solidifies for the reader the rationale behind the book: the growing importance of the Native American vote. This enlightening chapter reviews how state and federal definitions of citizen voting rights frequently excluded Native Americans, much as they once excluded African Americans, and encourages the reader to question the implications that Native Americans challenging voting discrimination over time hold for the growing importance of the Native American vote in state politics that surround their tribal communities. As tribal nations expand in population and their citizenry begin to exercise collective voting power and actualize their self-determination efforts, their impact can only continue to develop in ways that enrich tribal sovereignty and expand the roles that they continue to play as citizens of the United States.

The larger issue of the relationship between Native American sovereignty and U.S. citizenship is central in Warren's *The Quest for Citizenship: African American and Native American Education in Kansas, 1880–1935*: How have Native Americans thought of themselves as Americans? This question is central because it further illuminates the duality of Native American existence within the United States: being citizens of sovereign tribal governments and belonging to the larger citizen population of the U.S. nation state. While McDonald's work reveals the struggles that Native Americans have endured to find meaning—and cultivate a formidable presence—through civic engagement, Warren's *The Quest for Citizenship: African American and Native American Education in Kansas, 1880–1935* examines similar reactions and struggles by Native Americans in the educational arena and their similarities and differences to those of African Americans. The focal point of this analysis is premised on three questions: "How did blacks and Indians think of themselves as Americans? How did their notions of citizenship get influenced or crafted by white reformers in schools? How did these two groups define American citizenship for themselves despite whites' efforts to dictate those definitions" (5-6).

Warren addresses these questions through a lens of cultural citizenship, which comparatively engages the extent to which education in Kansas was effective in conveying an identity of belonging within the United States to African American and Native American students. Divided into three parts, this book introduces six comprehensive chapters and a brief conclusion aimed at illuminating how government officials, missionaries, and teachers acculturated African American and Native American students into America's racial divide—as well as racially assigned social roles—through segregated education. For Native Americans, this would mean separation from tribal communities, acquisition of the English language and "civilized" manners associated with citizenship, preparation for transitioning into public schools with white students, and possible intermarriage into white society. Similarly, African Americans were to be taught citizenship, however, their contributions were to be through labor and lives kept separate from—but in service of—white society.

Despite these goals that directed the processes of acculturation for both populations, Warren argues, Native Americans and African Americans found the means to resist these prescribed social roles and cultivate their own identities and senses of belonging as Americans through education. Following a thorough introduction, which explains the author's rationale for the book, approach taken, usage of terms, and chapter organization, chapter one presents a straightforward discussion of "Reformer" discourse: questions raised by educators and other stakeholders seeking to solve the "Negro Problem" and "Indian Problem" (13). Warren gives particular attention to the efforts and questions of Elizabeth Comstock and Hervey Peairs, making an important distinction between their intentions and their actions, which often reinforced the racist notions of inferiority and incompetence that Native American and African American students were supposed to transcend. She asserts that reformer pedagogy furthered colonialism within the classroom by not teaching students about their own histories and importance of their origins within the scope of overall human history. Instead, such pedagogy indoctrinated students into rejection of their ancestral life ways and pasts and prepared them to reinforce the social roles white Kansan society expected them to fill. These points, while poignant and thought provoking, require more context-specific examples and explanations of the student-teacher relationships in Kansas classrooms to support them, than is given.

Warren makes up for this, however, in chapter three with an assiduous examination of Native American student navigations and negotiations of the curriculum at Haskell Institute and the limited nature of parental input into pedagogy due to the distance between the schools and tribal communities. This point is juxtaposed with the relatively active parental involvement seen in the education of African Americans in the fourth chapter. She asserts that student strategies for navigation and negotiation included compromise, acts of active resistance (e.g., smoking, stealing food, running away, etc.), and passive resistance (e.g., cultural exchange between students from different tribal nations, doing chores slowly, holding on to traditional values such as sharing with one another, etc.). These discussions are detailed enough that the reader can not only gauge the similarities and differences in experiences according to gender, but also the similarities and differences between their experiences with those of African Americans.

Warren's primary discussion in the following chapter centers on how the collective challenge that Africans American adults (e.g., William Vernon, Booker T. Washington, members of the NAACP, the Conventions of Colored Men, et al.) brought against substandard education enabled greater parental input into school curricula in Kansas than afforded Native American parents. The author does not gloss over the prevalence of segregation in Kansas schools serving African Americans. Yet by not doing so, she illuminates how this marginalization—wedded with active collective resistance—leads to African Americans developing new curricula in segregated schools that moved beyond industrial training and service to preparing students for college, professional jobs, and lives more prosperous than the service roles (e.g., house servant, cook, field hand, etc.) prescribed by white Kansan social custom.

Chapter five illustrates how students, emulating and inspired by such efforts, became teachers themselves and carried on this resistance within the classroom and in the face of school boards and funders that continued to insist on industrial service for African Americans. Both chapters are very deft at describing to the reader how many of the stakeholders who sought to transform African American and Native American students failed to address the underlining barrier to the cultivation of a sense of being American and belonging for both populations: socially constructed and customarily reinforced racial hierarchies.

Warren's book concludes with an intriguing discussion of the American identities cultivated by Native American students. Like the previous chapter the reader is offered a glimpse into the motivational lives of former students turned educators (e.g., Ella Deloria and Henry Roe Cloud) who used their education to analyze, give relevance and importance, and ultimately revitalize the same nations and traditional life ways that their educators sought to degrade and eradicate. Warren wants the reader to grasp how these efforts ignited the flames of the civil rights movements that both groups would later champion, according to their own desired—self-determined—goals and participatory roles as U.S. citizens.

Susan Work's *The Seminole Nation of Oklahoma: A Legal History* offers a unique perspective that contextually highlights the importance of sovereignty in this discussion of its relationship to U.S. citizenship. Drawing on three decades of experience as an Oklahoma attorney, this legal history presents a comprehensive review of twentieth-century legislation, policies, and rulings (i.e., Supreme Court decisions) that have shaped the creation and maintenance of the Seminole Nation of Oklahoma. Preceded by a brief introduction that discusses the author's motivations for the book and understandings of the legislation to be presented in subsequent sections, the first chapter examines the federal laws that governed nineteenth-century Indian Territory. Work asserts that the endurance of the Seminole Nation of Oklahoma in the twentieth century cannot be understood without understanding the direct responses the nation gave to imposed federal laws during the previous century. This section reviews the compacts and rulings (e.g., *Worchester v. Georgia*, the Treaty of 1845 which allowed the

Seminoles to settle away from the Creek, the Curtis Act, etc.) that affected the Seminole, as one of the relocated "Five Civilized Tribes."

Chapter two chronicles the roles that the Seminole Allotment Act played in how the Seminole Nation would experience Oklahoma statehood and the dynamics of their interactions with non-Native American populations. Central in this historical discussion are the provisions associated with Seminole allotment, the tribal divisions it created (e.g., anti-principal chief factions, Citizens by blood, Freedmen, and non-Indian tribal citizens), the functions of citizenship roles in the distribution of lands, the Five Tribes Act, and the Enabling Act in its execution. Work compels the reader to understanding this transfer of land—from collective tribal control to individual title—as the negation of treaty guarantees to tribal ownership of property that occurred as non-Native American immigrants sought to own land in what was becoming the state of Oklahoma.

Focusing on the fortitude that language (Mvskoke), religion, and recreation (e.g., stickball) provided the Seminole people, chapter five discusses how Seminole citizens and government were able to weather this encroachment and persevere in cultural and governmental operations before and after statehood. This strength enabled the Seminole government to remain relatively self-sufficient through statehood; however, actions by Congress in 1916 instigated dependency—which furthered dissent within the nations—when Congress passed a provision that tribal funds could not be spent by the Five Civilized Tribes without congressional appropriations (i.e., except on per capita payments, specific attorney contracts, tribal schools, etc.). Similar acts, in succession, would further facilitate Seminole dependency on the U.S. government and give the federal government increasing influence over Seminole economic and governmental affairs through the late 1960s.

The epilogue that concludes this resource-rich legal history encourages the reader to develop an appreciation for how this past motivated Seminole self-determination efforts. These included—but were not limited to—increased self-reliance and a more integral role within Oklahoma, specifically Seminole County: the establishment of a county-wide road works program, public transit system, Older American Program, and other support services for both tribal citizens and the county at large.

What implications do these texts hold for understanding the relationship between Native American sovereignty and U.S. citizenship? These books illuminate how Native American agency and self-determination has actively shaped this relationship in American civic and educational arenas. The negation of this agency has been both an intended and unintended byproduct of the processes of Native American acculturation into U.S. citizenship. The works of McDonald, Warren, and Work remind the reader that perhaps if the navigation strategies that Native Americans—like African Americans and other minorities—used to negotiate their U.S. citizenship are to be understood, then the effective civic and educational actions the people engaged in to protect their civil rights must be further examined. Students and scholars of American studies of history should find these resource-dense texts an encouraging foundation for future examinations of this relationship and how individual agency and collective sovereignty has shaped the dynamic salience of U.S. citizenship in American Indian lives.

READING 5

American Indian Women in Higher Education

Navigating The Doctorate

By Mary Jo Tippeconnic Fox

In the Twenty-First Century, higher education embraces the principles of diversity and inclusion, but has this equated into students of color having more meaningful experiences in the academy? This essay asserts that American Indian women still face gender bias, racism, stereotypes, discrimination, hostility, and cultural issues which lead to marginality and oppression at the doctoral level in a colonized system of higher education. Additionally, it identifies tactics employed by these women to overcome these challenges and successfully graduate.

As an increasing number of American Indian women aspire to the doctorate, it is important that both they and their universities become aware of the experiences of those who have completed the degree. This helps them understand the encounters of their predecessors, and to identify strategies used to successfully navigate through the educational system. This is especially important for Native women who identify and practice their tribal life ways, as their cultural values often clash with mainstream society on many levels including American higher education. Although, the annual number of doctorates awarded to American Indian women each year is small, each graduate is a valuable human resource for tribes wanting to maintain their sovereignty and self-determine their futures.

Data for this essay is drawn from interviews with thirteen American Indian women who earned doctorates between 2003 and 2008. *Tribal Critical Race Theory* (Tribal Crit) by Bryan McKinley Jones Brayboy (425–446) provides an indigenous framework to understanding the findings and to prove or disprove the thesis. *Tribal Crit* is based upon nine tenets addressing the American Indian experience. The basic tenet of this theory is that colonization is endemic to mainstream American society.

This essay begins with background information about the interviewees, commonalities of experiences at the doctoral level, and concludes with mutual strategies the women employed to graduate. Specific examples and the voices of the women themselves are used to illustrate the findings.

Mary Jo Tippeconnic Fox, "American Indian Women in Higher Education: Navigating the Doctorate," *Studies in the Humanities*, vol. 36, no. 2, pp. 69-76.

Throughout this essay, the identities of the respondents are anonymous due to the overall small number of American Indian women with doctorates.

The sample represents fifteen different tribal groups; three are multi-tribal and only two women come from the same Nation. All but one tribal group resides in the United States; one is in Canada. The majority of the respondents are 40 years or older; three women are 30–40 years of age. Their major fields of study are English (2), German studies, linguistics, American Indian studies (3), educational leadership (2), higher education, social work, and kinesiology. Twelve of the interviewee graduated from higher educational institutions in the United States, and one woman matriculated from a Canadian university. Eight of the women are married, one is divorced, one is separated, two are single, and nine have children. Eight of the women are employed at mainstream universities and colleges as assistant professors, one is a professor at a community college, two are university student affairs administrators, one is a consultant, and one works for the federal government

The data indicates that the American Indian women in this study experienced instances of overt and covert acts of gender bias, racism, discrimination, stereotypes, hostility, and exclusion in their doctoral programs. In addition, the women felt that their cultural traditions and tribal backgrounds were not respected, and the academy wanted them to change.

Six of the thirteen American Indian women experienced gender bias from professors, students, advisors, and chairs. One person commenting on her treatment, "My advisor/chair was a jerk. He would not have treated me this way if I was a man." Another woman recalls only males were called upon in class by her professor, and the female students had to fight to get acknowledged. The men were so aggressive in class which made her feel "simple" and not "smart" especially when she was unable to answer the questions posed by them remarked a Native woman. This was confirmed when she asked a male student about it after class. He said "If I would have asked anyone else, they would have bull-shitted their way through it" making this respondent feel inferior.

Two of the women experienced gender bias related to being a mother. They were deliberately excluded by fellow students from functions and activities because it was assumed that mothers could not attend because they had to care for their children. No one took the time to ask the individuals if they could participate. These same women found it hard to balance their family and academic demands especially when the institutions did not have a support system for students with children. One interviewee had to leave campus once she became a candidate to better deal with child care.

All the respondents acknowledged the existence of gender bias during their doctoral program; however seven women were better prepared to confront it. They attributed this to being from matrilineal societies, raised with the value of equality or were in fields of study where females were the majority. As one interviewee says, "some made comments but I did not feel it, my spirit was strong enough to not see gender as an issue."

All thirteen women experienced racism and discrimination in various forms. One interviewee was invited by her department head to a fundraiser because she was an American Indian student, and the fund was named for a professor whose scholarship involved Natives. Once there, after being introduced by the department head, a professor refused to shake her extended hand. The Native woman was so ashamed thinking something was wrong with her. Then, when she attempted to sit next to her department head at the dinner, she was told by an organizer in front of everyone to sit at a back table facing the wall. Once at the back table, a fellow non-Native graduate student refused to serve her meal. She was completely humiliated by this situation and left early.

The perpetuation of stereotypes and misinformation about American Indians in lectures and discussions was not uncommon. The majority of the interviewees commented about professors using stereotypes about Indians in class; making generalizations or excuses for assimilation policies. When one Native woman challenged the stereotypes, the response of the professor was to use another stereotype. Another interviewee attended a university with an Indian mascot and had to deal with educating fellow students about why it was offensive. In a different incident, a professor called one of the respondents into her office and asked about her accent. The woman did not realize she had an accent. The professor informed her she was speaking "Indian English," and later emailed her information on the topic.

Hostility toward American Indians by students, professors and staff had one woman fighting a voice in her head that said "she shouldn't be here." This statement illustrates how racism can become internalized to the point where one questions their identity and culture including becoming embarrassed by it. One Native respondent encountered an unwelcome climate toward students of color in her department that was created by a head known for not supporting inclusion. Another interviewee using a copy machine in her department office was the recipient of hostile remarks when asked by a staff member "when was she transferring out?" She was shocked and did not know how to respond since it was her first semester.

Interviewees commonly expressed feelings of isolation, exclusion and loneliness. For many of the respondents, they were either the only Native student in their program or one of a small number on campus. Often professors would single them out to speak for all Indians which made them uncomfortable. Another woman recalls being excluded by other students and feeling alone. She was never asked by fellow students to coffee, lunch or dinner during her entire doctoral program, and when she asked white students about assignments, misinformation was given.

All the women dealt with inaccurate and inappropriate comments. They overheard statements by fellow students that in some cases made them doubt their abilities and worthiness to be in a doctoral program. One respondent remembered remarks such as "You will get good grades because professors like minorities" or "you will get jobs because of your gender and race." Another interviewee felt uncomfortable about her skin color when a non-Native peer put his arm next to hers and made condescending assertions about the darkness of her skin.

The respondents were affected by cultural issues in several ways. For example, three American Indian women were told in evaluations or by professors that they needed to speak up, they were too shy. This was a difficult adjustment for these individuals because culturally they were taught to listen and observe before speaking. They felt less capable as they struggled to adjust and find their voices.

Another ordeal for the interviewees was the devaluing of American Indian culture in relation to research. Non-Native mentors and advisors did not understand research topics dealing with indigenous peoples; questioning whether it was good scholarship. For those women in traditional disciplines who wished to focus on Native issues, they found it hard to find faculty to mentor them, serve and chair their committees. One person remarked that during her tenure as a doctoral student, only one American Indian man was available to help her then he left.

The climate of the community where the university was located was not always supportive. Often the institution was located in a town or state without an American Indian population and being Native was trying. For eight of the women, the lack of understanding of indigenous issues and no opportunities for spiritual activities was problematic. Their home communities were not always close enough to visit.

The women's ability to confront and deal with gender bias, racism, discrimination, exclusion, cultural issues, stereotypes, and hostility varied. Six of the individuals in the study felt that they were better equipped to handle the issues they encountered in the academy from the start. They were able to confront the various situations without it affecting them personally. One interviewee said "... by the time I started my doctorate, I had real life experiences, maturity, self-confidence, and I was able to deal with issues of my graduate education." She had developed her voice and used it. Two other respondents echoed the same sentiment with one person stressing it was more of a problem during her Master's degree program.

Four of the thirteen Native women were more positive about their overall doctoral experience. One woman felt her program was rewarding because of the American Indian faculty she had, another interviewee said it was good because it was relatively laid back, and she had good mentors. The third person said her experience was alright or good even when there was a high turnover of faculty in her program, and the fourth individual's program was fulfilling but honestly not as rigorous as she expected.

It is notable that despite their mixed feelings about their doctoral experiences, all thirteen women were generally satisfied with the education they received. As one individual remarked "I earned the degree, but it should not be so hard." In this study, the American Indian women decolonized their experiences in the academy by developing tactics to succeed. Family, support networks, American Indian faculty and staff, strong cultural identity, commitment to community, and keeping a balance are the strategies most often mentioned.

Family was an essential strategy for success for all thirteen respondents. Family—immediate, extended and the larger Native community—provided them with spiritual, emotional, financial, and hand on support. When stressed or discouraged, the Native women would call or visit family members. Their relatives listened and encouraged them even though most of them did not fully understand what their wife, daughter, granddaughter, aunt, or mother was going through as they had not experienced this level of education themselves. They had ceremonies for the interviewees, prayed for them and were free with cultural advice, stories and wisdom that provided motivation to persevere. The extended families recharged the respondents; kept them focused on the larger picture and prevented them from quitting.

Another determinate of success was the establishment of support networks of fellow students, friends, professors, mentors, advisors, and Indian organizations, groups or centers. These associations were comprised primarily of American Indians but also included non-Natives. One woman's husband was part of a drum group whose members became like family. Others got moral support from culture groups and centers on campus. Just being around other indigenous students was empowering.

The women found that the presence of American Indian professors and staff in their programs or at their institutions was a critical asset. Interviewees sought them out as people they could talk to and feel comfortable around; someone that understood tribal communities and their issues. Where Native instructors were not available, some of the women found support from faculty of color and supportive non-Native personnel in and outside their respective programs. Many of these individuals became mentors for the women.

A strong cultural identity provided strength for the thirteen women in the study and helped them deal with the issues confronting them. Empowerment came from knowing who they were and where they came from. One interviewee said her experience in the academy made her appreciate her cultural heritage; others found their Native identity and culture being tested, and they had to work through internal oppression before reconnecting and embracing it.

Commitment to serving American Indians was a strong motivation for the women to complete their programs. All of the interviewees mentioned wanting to achieve their educational goals to serve their people and communities. It was not an individual accomplishment for the women, but a feat for their families, community and all Indian people.

Finding and keeping a balance between the demands of their personal lives and school was essential for the interviewees. They took care of themselves physically, mentally and spirituality by exercising, seeking counseling, eating healthy, and practicing their customs and beliefs. It was important to the women that their families understood the time consuming nature of their doctoral program.

In conclusion, the findings of this study reveal that American Indian women are routinely encountering gender bias, racism, discrimination, cultural issues, stereotypes, exclusion, and hostility in doctoral programs. It also identifies common strategies they used to succeed and graduate. The data confirms the thesis and indicates that colleges and universities, especially at the department level are not always inclusive and supportive environments. The interviewees felt their programs wanted them to change or conform, and European American thought and knowledge dominated the system. "Assimilation" is how one person described her doctoral experience.

The small number of American Indian women pursuing and earning the doctorate makes this population easy to overlook. To fully understand the doctoral experiences of these women, more research is needed besides two excellent studies by Reva Lynn Ballew (1996) and Heather J. Shotton (2008). However, the female voices in this essay make a significant contribution to the larger ongoing conversation about doctoral education and diversity in higher education. Without these indigenous voices, the dialogue is incomplete.

Works Cited

Ballew, Reva Lynn. "The Experiences of Native American Women Obtaining Doctoral Degrees in the Psychology at Traditional American Universities." The University of Tennessee, Knoxville, 1996.

Brayboy, Bryan McKinley Jones. "Toward a Tribal Critical Race Theory in Education." *The Urban Review* 27, 5 (2005): 425–446.

National Center for Educational Statistics, Digest of Educational Statistics. "Doctoral Degrees Conferred by Degree Granting Institutions, by Race/Ethnicity and Sex of Student: Selected Years 1976–77 through 2006-2007." http://nces.ed.gov/programs/digest/d08/tables/dt08_290.asp

Shotton, Heather J. "Pathway to the PH.D.: Experiences of High-Achieving American Indian Females." Diss. University of Oklahoma, 2008.

CHAPTER 3

African Americans: Brief Historical Perspectives

READING 6

Why Do You Call Yourself Black and African?

By Carina Ray

Over the last year, *New African* readers have increasingly enquired about my racial background. I hope that in satisfying their curiosity, their attentions will be directed once again at the content of my columns rather than the colour of my skin.

A little over a year ago, I received an email with the subject line "Ok I wonder why you call yourself 'black' and 'African'" from a self-described longtime *New African* reader. Even if subsequent emails have been less direct in their articulation of the same underlying sentiment, they all point in a similar direction: some people are confused about my racial background and about the way I racially identify myself. Their need to seek clarification suggests that being able to label me is important to the way in which they understand the content of my columns.

I was perplexed at first by this seemingly sudden preoccupation with my race. After all, I had been writing for *New African* for several years and never had anyone raise the subject before. It then occurred to me that these racial enquiries started happening almost immediately after my picture began running with my column. Obviously there was a disconnect in the minds of some readers between my appearance and my writing, especially when I refer to myself as both black and African, and use the collective "we" to talk about the past, present, and future of black people worldwide.

Indeed, the fact that I claim my place in the global African world annoyed one reader so much that he asked: "Why do you keep on writing 'we'?" Just in case he hadn't already made his point clear, he added: "You are not black in my eyes. You look much more Italian or Spanish. I can assure you, if you go to Africa you will be called 'white'." I always find it amusing that people seem to forget the proximity of southern Spain and Italy to Africa. There is a reason after all that Spaniards and Italians from the south look a lot like North Africans—centuries of exchange between the two regions certainly wasn't limited to material goods. And Africans from North Africa actually colonised the countries of the Iberian Peninsula for centuries!

Ironically, however, the reader was partially right. I am a quarter Italian, but I don't look anything like my blond hair and blue-eyed Italian paternal grandmother who came from Turin in the far north of the country. Nor do I look anything like my paternal Irish grandfather. The reader wasn't off the mark either when he guessed I might be Spanish. My mother is part-Spanish. She is also Taíno Indian and African, most likely of Yoruba ancestry, as were many of the enslaved Africans who worked the sugar plantations on the island of Puerto Rico where my mother was born. So there you have it: Taíno, Spanish, Northern Italian, Irish, and yes, African too. Why, you might ask, if I am so thoroughly mixed race do I identify as black and African?

Let me begin by providing the context necessary to understand the particularly unique way in which black is defined in the United States, where I was born and raised. Black, as a legal-cum-racial category, was historically constructed in the broadest possible way In order to expand the number of people who could be enslaved and to limit the legal right of racially mixed people to claim their freedom. Known as the "one drop rule", the idea that a person with even the slightest trace of African ancestry is black has long outlived slavery in America. What was once a legal construction became a socially constructed category that has, and continues, to encompass a broad range of very phenotypically diverse black people.

While the racial landscape of the US is home to black people of all hues, hair textures, body shapes and sizes, and facial features, we do not all experience our blackness in the same way—far from it. Phenotype, class, gender, and geography all play major roles in shaping our individual experiences as black people in America. Hierarchies based on skin tone, alone, have been at the root of painful divisions within the black community, and are often the basis for preferential treatment within the dominant white society. It has not been lost on African-Americans that if Barack Obama was the complexion of his father, he would likely not be our president today.

If blackness in America has been defined broadly enough to claim me as one of its own, that still leaves the question of why I claim my blackness. I could call myself mixed race or even Latino/Hispanic. I certainly recognise that I am multi-racial, but I don't feel a common bond with mixed people simply because we have parents of different racial backgrounds. Equally, I've always been unnerved by the categories Latino and Hispanic to describe people from the Spanish Caribbean and parts of Latin America that are heavily populated by people of African descent precisely because they erase/e-race our ties to Africa.

The categories Black and Latino/Hispanic are often defined as mutually exclusive on Identification forms in the US, such that one is instructed to check "Black" provided one is "not of Hispanic origin" and to check "Hispanic—regardless of race"! Since when has anything in America ever been regardless of race? As history has too often demonstrated, this is a calculated attempt to create divisions between black people based on language and country of origin.

Beyond the historical and political, however, are the biographical details of my life that help to explain why I, a person that could choose to be almost anything, at the age of 13 firmly declared *"I am black and proud of it!"* I was born and raised for the first eight years of my life on a commune called Synanon in California. Synanon was the founding model for the therapeutic community and in its heyday during the 1960s and 1970s was hugely successful in getting drug

Seated next to her aunt, Carina (in pink dress) watches her grandfather play the piano during her first childhood trip to Puerto Rico 27 years ago

addicts clean. My parents met and married there in a 1972 mass wedding of 70 couples, many of whom were interracial.

They were following in the footsteps of Synanon's founder. Chuck Dederich, a white man who married Betty Coleman, a strong, beautiful black woman whose death from cancer in 1977 was the beginning of the end of Synanon, which finally folded in the mid 1990s. My early years were thus spent in an enclosed environment where people from all walks of life lived and worked together.

In 1981, we left Synanon and I quickly became aware of how racially segregated the outside world was. The real turning point, however, was in 1986 when we moved to Orange County, California, a predominantly white and very conservative area. By that time I was already deeply concerned with issues of social justice and racial equality, a fact that marked me as different from my peers, as did my unruly kinky hair and deep olive skin.

One day on the school bus home, an aspiring skinhead turned around in his seat and yelled "NIGGER" at me. I stood up and yelled back "I'm not a nigger. I'm black and proud of it!" When we arrived at my stop with a pounding heart, I made my way to his seat and hit him before making a mad dash off the bus. I was given a demerit. He wasn't punished at all. It wasn't being called a "nigger" that made me realise I was black, but it crystallised in my 13-year-old mind the price one pays for being black and the absolute necessity of embracing, affirming, and declaring one's blackness in the face of both the overt and subtle forms of racism that we regularly encounter.

Yet, to reduce my blackness to an act of antiracism would efface the primary role that the black community has played in my understanding of myself. Home is where we see ourselves reflected in the faces, voices, and experiences of others. Home, for me, has always been in the black community. No embrace has been stronger.

On 15 August 1993, my 20th birthday to be exact, I landed in Accra, Ghana, for the first time and quickly realised that I was "white" in the eyes of the vast majority of Ghanaians I met. While I knew I wouldn't be met with a chorus line of "welcome back our long lost daughter", I hadn't expected it to be nearly impossible to convince people of my blackness. And so I resigned myself to being "white" ... I stopped explaining and started listening and I learned more about race in America during my first year in Ghana through those conversations than I had growing up in the belly of the beast.

What I took away from that experience was the ability to let go of how others see me. For sure, it didn't take going to Ghana to be mistaken for a white person—that happens here in America, but once you assert yourself as black, people more or less recognise you as such. In Ghana I could argue until I was blue in the face and fail completely to alter my putative "whiteness".

Making the journey to Ghana, only to have the very reason I was there denied, might seem like a cruel irony; but it freed me to inhabit my racially ambiguous body in a way that lets others see me through their own eyes. So before I answer the question of why I call myself black and an African, let me say that I have no desire to prove my blackness or to legitimise the views that I express in my columns through recourse to blood quantum disclosures.

Black is the name I call home. Black is the name that called me home. I call myself an African because I am a Pan-Africanist and like the generation that came before me, I recognise Africa as our collective home. I also realise, as did they, that the greatest obstacle in the way of black people worldwide is the divisions between us. Far from advocating a narrow black nationalism, Nkrumah and Nasser envisioned a Pan-Africanism that encompassed all of Africa's children at home and abroad. We still have a lot of work to do.

READING 7

The Case of Affirmative Action Policy

By Michele S. Moses

In this chapter, I delve more deeply into the specifics of the affirmative action case. The legal, political, and legislative contexts of this policy illustrate the moral and political nature of the disagreement about affirmative action and other controversial race-conscious education policies. What is particularly interesting about the case of affirmative action as a moral disagreement, and the numerous court cases and legislative actions that have accompanied it, is all of the flipping back and forth on the issue. Disagreements among the US Supreme Court justices highlight the different interpretations of the ideals of equality, liberty, and diversity [...], and, as such, they parallel the public disagreement as well.

Policy Background

In the last several years, various events and incidents have sparked reexamination of the role of race in American life. Some of these turns were promising, and others were painful reminders of how far we have to go. And they all seemed to take place simultaneously. For example, the governor of Virginia, Bob McDonnell, has declared April to be Confederate History Month in his state. When civil rights leaders criticized the move, Governor McDonnell explained that his proclamation was designed to promote tourism (Kumar and Helderman 2010). The 2008 election brought not only the first black president of the United States but also the first viable female candidate. In another first, in 2009, a Latina was nominated and confirmed as a justice on the Supreme Court. During Sonia Sotomayor's confirmation hearing, Senator Tom Coburn of Oklahoma told the nominee that she would "have lots of 'splainin' to do" for her views, invoking Ricky Ricardo from the television series *I Love Lucy* (Rich 2009, ¶ 4, line 5). Also in 2009, Professor Henry Louis Gates was arrested while trying to enter his own home, triggering a new round of race analyses in so-called postracial America. "'I can't wear my Harvard gown everywhere I go.' Professor Gates said. 'We—all of us in the crossover generation—have multiple identities, and being black trumps all of those other identities'" (Cooper

2009, ¶ 21, lines 1–3). During President Barack Obama's first campaign for the presidency, another campaign was also launched by Ward Connerly and his group, the American Civil Rights Institute, for what Connerly called "Super Tuesday for Equal Rights," to promote five state ballot initiatives that, if passed, would eliminate affirmative action in Arizona, Colorado, Missouri, Nebraska, and Oklahoma. The initiatives made it onto the ballots in Colorado and Nebraska; ultimately, Nebraska followed California, Michigan, and Washington to become the fourth state to abolish affirmative action in public education, employment, and contracting. The same initiative passed in Arizona in 2010 and Oklahoma in 2012, the same year President Obama was reelected. Most recently, the Project on Fair Representation is suing both the University of North Carolina at Chapel Hill and Harvard University on behalf of students who claim they were discriminated against based on race in the admissions process (CBS 2014). The student plaintiffs were recruited actively by affirmative action opponent Edward Blum, who was also behind the *Fisher v. University of Texas* case that I discuss below (McCloskey 2014).[1]

The debate over affirmative action, particularly in higher education admissions, has been a consistent part of the larger analysis of race in the United States. Notably, in 2013, the US Supreme Court made a somewhat unexpected ruling in the *Fisher v. University of Texas* case concerning the use of affirmative action in admissions at the state's flagship campus of the University of Texas at Austin. White plaintiffs who had been rejected for undergraduate admissions sued the university. They lost in US district court, but appealed the decision to the US Supreme Court. In response, the Obama administration filed an amicus brief taking a strong stance in favor of affirmative action in higher education admissions citing the educational and social benefits of a racially and ethnically diverse student body (Jaschik 2010b). Although the brief itself did not invoke egalitarianism specifically, such a position stems from a race-egalitarian philosophy, with the understanding that race and ethnicity continue to play a significant role in American society. Part of the importance of affirmative action is that it is used primarily in the most selective institutions of higher education, the very places that educate many of our nation's leaders, officeholders, and professionals. The state of the US public education system is such that many students of color are underserved and consequently not as competitive in their college applications (Yosso et al. 2004). For example, black and Latino students are underrepresented in Advanced Placement programs (Jaschik 2010a) and in college preparatory courses in general. Such realities lead to the underrepresentation of students of color in selective colleges and universities. This, in turn, produces a dearth of scientists of color, lawyers of color, and doctors of color, to name a few examples (Haycock, Lynch, and Engle 2009; *JBHE* 2010). Research has shown that without affirmative action, selective colleges and universities would suffer significant decreases in enrollment of underrepresented students of color (Hinrichs 2009, 2012; Howell 2010; Long 2007; Long and Tienda 2008). The most selective and prestigious University of California campuses did, in fact, suffer this drop-off after affirmative action policies were banned in that state, even though the number of underrepresented minority students graduating from high school increased

(Moses, Yun, and Marin 2009; Saenz 2010). Similarly, undergraduate enrollment of black students at the University of Michigan decreased to 4.6 percent in 2013 (Vega 2014)—this in a state with a 14.3 percent black population (United States Census Bureau 2013). Still, these realities fail to stem the deep disagreement about affirmative action, which, as I examine in chapter 3, is characterized by the conflicting paradigms of race egalitarianism and color blindness.

Instead of taking the opportunity in *Fisher* to strike down the constitutionality of using race in higher education admissions decisions, the court remanded the case to the lower court to rule on the question of whether the university's admissions program that considers race is narrowly tailored to obtain the benefits of a diverse student body.

The Case of Affirmative Action

In the United States, affirmative action in higher education admissions primarily relates to race, ethnicity, and gender. Quotas are rarely if ever used, based on the *Regents of the University of California v. Bakke* ruling against quotas and set-aside places at universities. *Gratz v. Bollinger* reinforced the impermissibility for numeric set-asides in university admissions, and *Grutter v. Bollinger* upheld the constitutionality of affirmative action (Moses, Yun, and Marin 2009). This conceptualization of affirmative action without quotas evolved over its fifty-year history in the United States (Moses 2002).

Because the Supreme Court has allowed universities to use affirmative action policies, opponents have turned to another strategy to ban such policies, the state-level ballot initiative (Moses and Saenz 2008). Such initiatives to abolish affirmative action in the targeted state have been proposed in nine states, placed on the ballot in seven, passed in six (Arizona, California, Michigan, Nebraska, Oklahoma, and Washington), and defeated in one (Colorado) (Farley, Gaertner, and Moses 2013; Marin 2014). In what follows, I first discuss the key court cases shaping the landscape of affirmative action policy. Then I examine the state ballot initiatives and other state legislation that have eliminated or have intended to eliminate affirmative action in those states. [...] [T]his will provide the legal and political context to inform [...] [a later] analysis of how the turn toward direct democratic ballot initiatives—as well as the campaigns for and against them—relies on ideas and ideals from egalitarian and libertarian political theory.

The controversy over affirmative action has resulted in numerous important court cases and legislative actions that not only have shaped the contours of the policy but also exemplify the public moral disagreement about it. Although I will not examine each case in detail herein, I have chosen to explore key cases and legislation that demonstrate the different interpretations of the ideals of equality and liberty that shape the disagreement. Through a concurrent review of key court rulings and state legislation, I present analyses of some key federal court decisions regarding affirmative action in higher education admissions: *Regents of the University of California v. Bakke* (1978), *Hopwood v. Texas* (1996), *Gratz v. Bollinger* (2003), *Grutter v. Bollinger* (2003), and *Fisher v. University of Texas*

(2013).[2] I also include a relevant K–12 case insofar as it pertains to higher education, *Parents Involved in Community Schools v. Seattle School District No. 1* (2007).[3] In addition, I examine several state political and legal events: California's Proposition 209 (1996), Michigan's Proposal 2 (2006), and the ballot initiative campaign in Colorado.

Key Court Cases: Conflicting Values

Affirmative action causes a "conflicted public mind" (Sandel 2005, 101) due to the simultaneous desire for racial equality and color- blind policies. As I mention in the last chapter, the public mind has become no less conflicted as affirmative action policy has been tested and contested in the courts and at the ballot. These conflicts emerge as the justices of the Supreme Court have deliberated about the constitutionality of using race as a factor in college admissions decisions. I begin with the first case in which US Supreme Court justices ruled on affirmative action in higher education admissions.

Regents of the University of California v. Bakke

Prior to the 1978 US Supreme Court case *Regents of the University of California v. Bakke*, the national mood had been moving in favor of policies and programs designed to support equality of educational opportunity (Moses 2002). Great Society and War on Poverty programs were indicative of this mood. Yet the landmark *Bakke* case marks the beginning of a strong backlash against race-conscious policies. Perhaps the case's most lasting policy effect was to clarify that the use of numeric quotas and set-aside places within admission programs seeking to promote diversity in higher education is forbidden because it violates the Fourteenth Amendment to the US Constitution. Even though the legal legacy of the *Bakke* case is significant, the decision itself was the result of a fractured Supreme Court. The justices held 4–1–4 that "(a) the minority-admissions program of the University of California at Davis Medical School had discriminated illegally against a white male applicant, but (b) that universities could legally consider race as a factor in admissions" (Sobel 1980, 145). Justices Warren Burger, John Paul Stevens, Potter Stewart, and William Rehnquist decided in favor of plaintiff Allan Bakke on both counts; Justices William Brennan, Byron White, Thurgood Marshall, and Harry Blackmun decided in favor of the University of California at Davis Medical School on both counts, and, in the swing vote, Justice Lewis Powell decided *against* the Davis policy, but *in favor of* universities' ability to use race as a plus factor in admissions decisions. Although Powell was the only justice to use the educational benefits of diversity as his rationale in favor of race- conscious admissions policies, his became the court's controlling opinion since he cast the deciding vote for each side. Although its division illustrated the larger disagreement within US society, the Supreme Court indicated to the nation that affirmative action programs were constitutional and could be implemented legally. The four justices who were against both UC–Davis's quotas and the constitutionality of considering race viewed affirmative action as degrading to the ideal of equality. The four justices in favor of affirmative action policy saw it as a legitimate way to further equality.

One especially enduring justification for affirmative action policies, the diversity rationale, came from Justice Powell's *Bakke* opinion. The legacy left by *Bakke* provided the legal guidelines for affirmative action policy, now updated and bolstered by *Grutter*, as discussed below. Although the diversity rationale for the use of affirmative action in higher education admissions remains in place within the legal framework, that fact has not precluded legal challenges to *Bakke*. The dispute over the nature of affirmative action and its consideration of race and ethnicity did not end with the *Bakke* ruling. The next important court case regarding higher education admissions was decided in 1996 with *Hopwood v. Texas*.

Hopwood v. Texas

In deciding *Hopwood*, the Court of Appeals for the Fifth Circuit ruled against race- conscious affirmative action policies in higher education admissions, thus nullifying the US Supreme Court's *Bakke* ruling in the three states in the Fifth Circuit: Texas, Louisiana, and Mississippi.[4] The white female plaintiff in the case, Cheryl Hopwood, relied on a strict interpretation of equality and equal (same) treatment, arguing that she had been discriminated against by the University of Texas Law School's admissions system. *Hopwood*'s three-judge panel agreed with this interpretation and ruled to prohibit the use of race-conscious admissions criteria to achieve diversity at the law school. The panel decided that a state's interest in acquiring a diverse student body was not legally compelling enough to justify an admissions program like the one at the law school. *Hopwood* was the first successful challenge to an affirmative action admissions program since *Bakke*. One year later, Texas Attorney General Dan Morales offered clarification on the *Hopwood* decision for the state, maintaining that its reach extended to programs outside of admissions, including financial aid, recruitment, and scholarships. Subsequent research on the impact of the decision concluded that *Hopwood* had a chilling effect on college access for black and Hispanic high school graduates in Texas (Dickson 2004; Kain and O'Brien 2001).

At the flagship University of Texas at Austin (UT–Austin), officials put a great deal of effort into implementing various policies and programs to mitigate the effect of losing affirmative action. In addition, the Texas legislature passed House Bill 508—the Top Ten Percent Plan—guaranteeing "admission to the top 10 percent of a high school graduating class to any public higher education institution in the state" (Marin and Flores 2008, 226).[5] However, once the US Supreme Court issued its 2003 rulings effectively overturning *Hopwood*, UT President Larry Faulkner indicated that the university would work with the Texas legislature to resume affirmative action policies (University of Texas at Austin 2003a). Having had the experience of operating without affirmative action, President Faulkner was eager to reinstitute the policy. Bruce Walker, vice provost and director of admissions at UT–Austin, said at the time, "We have used race-neutral policies for seven years and still do not have a critical mass of African American or Hispanic students in our classrooms" (University of Texas at

Austin 2003b). Currently UT–Austin uses both race-conscious admissions policies as well as the Top Ten Percent Plan (Chapa and Horn 2007). The *Fisher* case, described later, is the most recent court challenge to UT–Austin's affirmative action policy.

Gratz v. Bollinger and Grutter v. Bollinger

The plaintiffs in *Gratz* and *Grutter* were white applicants who believed that they would have been admitted to the University of Michigan had it not been for the consideration of race/ethnicity in the institution's admissions decisions; Jennifer Gratz sued regarding the undergraduate admissions policy and Barbara Grutter regarding the law school admissions policy. Like Bakke's lawyers in 1978, the plaintiffs' Center for Individual Rights lawyers maintained that the University of Michigan's use of race as a factor in admissions violated the equal protection clause of the Fourteenth Amendment and Title VI of the Civil Rights Act. Again we see anti-affirmative action plaintiffs relying on the idea of equality as sameness, which comes out of a color-blind paradigm. In the final decision in these cases, issued June 23, 2003, the Supreme Court upheld Justice Powell's opinion in *Bakke* that student diversity is a compelling state interest. By upholding the University of Michigan Law School admissions policy as narrowly tailored, the court endorsed policies that follow its guidelines in letter and spirit. It upheld the constitutionality of using race and ethnicity as plus factors in higher education admissions decisions and emphasized the importance of individualized, holistic reviews of applications.

More specifically, in *Gratz*, the justices struck down the University of Michigan's particular race-conscious undergraduate admissions program, emphasizing that any type of quota or numerical point system that automatically awards points to minority applicants does not fall under the permissible standards regarding the use of race and ethnicity in admissions decisions. In its *Grutter* ruling the court affirmed that the educational benefits flowing from a diverse student body served a compelling state interest. The diversity rationale, based on the ideal of diversity in a democratic society, was the central justification in upholding the constitutionality of affirmative action. Writing for the majority in *Grutter*, Justice O'Connor explained: "The Law School's educational judgment that such diversity is essential to its educational mission is one to which we defer. The Law School's assessment that diversity will, in fact, yield educational benefits is substantiated by respondents and their *amici*" (*Grutter* 2003, 328). She also noted that policies could focus on a range of attributes including applicants' varied talents and experiences and possible contributions to the learning environment, as well as academic ability. The key would be to assess each applicant individually. In addition, the *Grutter* decision highlighted Justice O'Connor's idea that affirmative action should no longer be necessary in twenty-five years.[6]

Ultimately, the ruling in *Grutter* invalidated the Fifth Circuit's ruling in *Hopwood*. The *Grutter* decision thus underscored the importance and legal viability of the diversity rationale for affirmative action in college and university admissions. This justification has wider appeal than the remedial justification, as even those who oppose affirmative action sometimes support the idea of diversity (see, e.g., Deardorff and Jones 2007[7]). In fact, even the plaintiffs in *Gratz v. Bollinger* did not contest the importance of diversity to higher education. In addition, the *Grutter* court emphasized that institutions should engage in holistic review of applicants, within which they consider both quantitative (e.g., high school grade point average) and qualitative (e.g., extracurricular activities) assessments of the applicant's qualifications for admission.

After these rulings, opponents of race-conscious education policies seemed to feel a renewed urgency to prohibit the consideration of race and ethnicity in higher education admissions and related programs. Immediately after the rulings in *Gratz* and *Grutter* were announced, Ward Connerly, chair of the American Civil Rights Coalition, announced that he would propose an amendment to Michigan's state constitution opposing affirmative action (see the section below about Proposal 2).

Parents Involved in Community Schools v. Seattle School District No. 1

Extending outside of higher education is a group of court cases involving K–12 race- conscious student assignment plans in public schools. Although these cases are important primarily for the K–12 arena, *Parents Involved in Community Schools v. Seattle School District No. 1* is probably the most relevant to higher education. In 2007 the US Supreme Court took up the issue of voluntary race- conscious student assignment in public schools when it agreed to hear *Parents Involved in Community Schools v. Seattle School District No. 1* and *Meredith v. Jefferson County Board of Education*.[8] The court had changed significantly in its composition since the 2003 University of Michigan cases. Chief Justice William Rehnquist had died and been replaced by similarly conservative Chief Justice John Roberts, whose views on race consciousness stem from libertarian political theory, with a focus on color blindness. In addition, Justice Sandra Day O'Connor had retired, and her spot was filled by Justice Samuel Alito. Justice O'Connor had moderate egalitarian leanings within a divided court and was often the swing vote in contentious cases such as *Grutter*. By contrast, Justice Alito was expected to align with his conservative colleagues on the high court. It was not surprising, then, when the Supreme Court ruled that voluntary racial integration plans in place in school districts in Seattle and Louisville were not narrowly tailored and, thus, unconstitutional (Korrell 2007). However, the decision left the *Grutter* ruling intact and supported the idea of diversity as a compelling interest in both higher education and K–12.

Fisher v. University of Texas at Austin

In another challenge to UT–Austin's affirmative action policy, this time to the undergraduate admissions policy, Abigail Fisher was the plaintiff in a lawsuit that contested her rejection to UT–Austin. She alleged that she was not accepted to UT–Austin because of "racial preferences" (Kever 2008, ¶ 1, line 2). The plaintiff's attorneys from the Project on Fair Representation argued that, per *Grutter*, UT–Austin could use affirmative action only if race-neutral alternatives did not succeed in admitting a diverse student body. At UT–Austin, 75 percent of the available places for freshmen go to Texans who graduated in the top 10 percent of their high school classes. The remaining 25 percent of places are decided through individualized application review, in which race and ethnicity may be considered as qualifying factors. The Fifth Circuit Court of Appeals unanimously ruled in favor of the University of Texas in 2011, saying that the admissions policy was in keeping with what the US Supreme Court allowed in *Grutter*. Fisher then appealed that decision to the US Supreme Court.

The court heard the case in 2012 and on June 24, 2013 ruled, 7–1, that institutions of higher education are permitted to consider race and ethnicity as one factor in the admissions process. Justice Elena Kagan had recused herself from the case due to previous involvement. Importantly, the court also remanded the case back to the Fifth Circuit, instructing the court of appeals to address the issue of strict scrutiny, that is, to examine UT–Austin's policy more closely to determine specifically whether the UT–Austin undergraduate admissions policy was indeed narrowly tailored to its goal, as laid out in *Grutter*. In the majority opinion, Justice Anthony Kennedy wrote, "Strict scrutiny does not permit a court to accept a school's assertion that its admission process uses race in a permissible way without closely examining how the process works in practice, yet that is what the District Court and Fifth Circuit did here" (Supreme Court of the United States 2013, 12). What this means for affirmative action policy is that the court declined to strike down the *Grutter* precedent through *Fisher*. However, at the time of this writing, the Supreme Court has elected to hear the *Fisher* case again during the 2015–2016 session.

Once again, the US Supreme Court reaffirmed the *Grutter* and *Bakke* precedents that highlight the ideal of diversity and allow institutions of higher education to consider race and ethnicity in admissions processes. Nevertheless, efforts at the state level have been undermining and continue to undermine affirmative action, due to discordant understandings of what the ideals of equality and liberty require of education policy.

State Bans of Affirmative Action

> The state shall not discriminate against, or grant preferential treatment to, any individual or group on the basis of race, sex, color, ethnicity, or national origin in the operation of public employment, public education, or public contracting.

The above language formed the primary text of most of the state ballot initiatives seeking to curb the use of affirmative action in public institutions.[9] Anti-affirmative action initiatives have passed in six states: California (1996), Washington (1998), Michigan (2006), Nebraska (2008), Arizona (2010), and Oklahoma (2012).[10] Similar ballot initiatives were proposed in two other states: Colorado and Missouri. In Missouri the initiative did not make it onto the ballot despite three attempts. Perhaps the most interesting development was in Colorado where the initiative was on the ballot but was defeated by a narrow margin. And in two additional states, affirmative action has been eliminated due to a governor's executive order (*viz.*, Florida, 2000) or a law passed in the state legislature (*viz.*, New Hampshire, 2012). In this section I examine the key pieces of state legislation in California, Michigan, and Colorado.

California's Proposition 209

Spurred on by then-University of California (UC) Regent Ward Connerly, who holds libertarian views about equality and who situates himself within the color- blind paradigm (Connerly 2000), in 1995 the UC Regents voted to bar the consideration of race and ethnicity in admissions decisions in the UC system by approving system guideline SP-1.[11] California's Proposition 209 soon followed. Known by proponents as the California Civil Rights Initiative (CCRI), Proposition 209 was a ballot initiative for a constitutional amendment to abolish all "preferences" based on race, ethnicity, and sex.[12] Even though the proposition never mentioned affirmative action by name, its effect was to eliminate affirmative action in higher education admissions (as well as in other state programs). The impact on California's public college student population was felt almost immediately and is visible to this day. In fall 1998, the flagship UC campus, Berkeley, reported a 52 percent decrease in the number of black and Hispanic first-year students for the first class admitted without affirmative action. Because of this, black and Hispanic students made up only 9.9 percent of the first-year class, well below the 20.7 percent of first-year enrollees the previous year (Healy 1998). At Berkeley's law school, there was only one black student in the entering class of 1997–98. In partial response to the negative attention given to the UC system, in 2001 the Regents voted to rescind their ban on affirmative action (Schevitz 2001). Because of Proposition 209, however, the Regents' change of heart was symbolic and did little to stem the rollback of students of color in the UC system, especially the most selective campuses. Frances Contreras (2005) examined the effects of Proposition 209 on college access at three UC campuses: Los Angeles, Davis, and Riverside. Using *parity* as a measure of access (a ratio comparing admissions rates to proportional representation in the K–12 system), Contreras found that although this ratio did not change for Asian American and white students, significant declines were experienced by African American, Chicano, and Latino students. That is, she found significant underrepresentation of these groups at all three campuses studied. Further, consider that UCLA's first- year class in fall 1997 had 221 African American students; by fall 2006, it included fewer than half that amount—100 (Leonhardt 2007, 78). Research consistently has shown that Proposition 209 has not only degraded equality of educational opportunity for underrepresented minority students at the most selective UC campuses but also had negative effects on the campus climate for students in general and students of color in particular (Backes 2012; Hinrichs 2012; Kidder 2012; Moses, Yun, and Marin 2009).

Michigan's Proposal 2

The political campaign for Proposal 2, once again spearheaded by Connerly and his American Civil Rights Institute, was announced the day that the US Supreme Court issued its decisions in the University of Michigan cases. Although it did not garner enough petition signatures to make it onto the ballot in 2004, two years later Proposal 2 passed with 58 percent of the vote. Immediately following the implementation of Proposal 2, both the University of Michigan and Michigan State University reported decreased percentages in freshmen of color for fall 2007 (Baker 2007). By fall 2009, the University of Michigan's enrollment of African American, Latino/a, and Native American first-year undergraduates decreased from 12.6 percent of the class before the state affirmative action ban to 9.1 percent, even as its overall numbers of applications and enrollment increased (Schultz 2008). Higher education officials in Michigan noted their struggle to conduct admissions and still keep diversity in mind under the constraints of Proposal 2. As Wayne State University Law School Dean Frank Wu explained,

> What do we do if we're serious about racial integration, diversity and the competitiveness of this nation in a global economy? What Prop 2 did was eliminate one method of dealing with these issues, but it doesn't take away the urgency of the issue. (quoted in Erb 2007, ¶ 5)

Research on the public discussion during the campaign surrounding Proposal 2 showed that media coverage on the issue was superficial at best and deceptive at worst (Moses and Saenz 2008). Neither relevant moral and political issues nor research evidence were presented to voters, resulting in an important state decision made without sufficient dialogue or attempts at understanding the nature of the dispute. I turn next to the initiative campaign in Colorado, which had a different outcome.

Colorado's Amendment 46

Two states had ultimately unsuccessful state ballot initiative proposals for November 2008—Colorado and Missouri. Some commentators pointed out that the timing of these initiative campaigns was strategic, with the aim of capitalizing on the immigration debates and influencing the outcome of the presidential election (Bello 2007).

In Missouri, the initiative never made it onto the ballot. Colorado's case is particularly interesting. Amendment 46 was defeated by a narrow margin: 50.7 percent against and 49.2 percent in favor (Denverpost.com 2008). During the campaign, sponsors of Amendment 46 collected more than 128,000 petition signatures, well more than the 76,047 valid signatures needed to get the initiative on the ballot (Gandy 2008). As in other targeted states, Colorado has relatively few students of color at its state colleges and universities, with about 72 percent of its 2005 first- time, degree-seeking college enrollment identifying as white (Moses, Yun, and Marin 2009). This is especially true of the flagship institution of the University of Colorado Boulder, where in 2005, only 1.4 percent of first-time, degree-seeking college students were African American, 6.3 percent Latino, and 6.5 percent Asian American (Moses, Yun, and Marin 2009). The defeat of Amendment 46 in Colorado marked the first time such an initiative failed to pass at the state level. Several proposed theories explain why Coloradans voted to defeat Amendment 46, including the governor's public opposition to the measure, President Obama's strong support in Colorado, the state's large Latino population, the confusing language of the ballot initiative, an unprecedented grassroots effort against it, television and radio advertisements, and a state ballot that included thirteen other ballot measures. A study of voter beliefs and attitudes about Amendment 46 and affirmative action in Colorado found that misperceptions and misunderstandings about the intent and consequences of the initiative itself played a part in how citizen voted (Moses et al. 2010). Yet opportunities for dialogue and deliberation about affirmative action prior to the election contributed to greater information and understanding, which I explore in chapter 5. First I explore the moral and political roots of the disagreement about affirmative action and other race-conscious education policies aiming to foster greater opportunities for students of color. The central puzzle here, as I see it, is how it is that people disagree despite agreement on basic moral values. We agree about the importance of equality, yet disagree about whether affirmative action promotes greater equality or inequality. The next chapter delves into this controversy.

Notes

1. These cases are different from previous ones in that the plaintiffs are Asian American, which complicates discussions about race, discrimination, diversity, and social justice.

2. Also at the time of this writing, another affirmative action–related case was heard before the US Supreme Court: *Schuette v. Coalition to Defend Affirmative Action* (2014). And, as mentioned at the beginning of this chapter, two lawsuits involving challenges to affirmative action at Harvard University and University of North Carolina at Chapel Hill were filed in federal court in 2014. This moral disagreement is not going away anytime soon.

3. Although there are other cases related to affirmative action regarding K–12 education, as well as hiring and contracting decisions, an examination of those is beyond the scope of this chapter.

4. Much legal debate ensued after the Fifth Circuit issued this opinion. Some legal scholars argued that the Fifth Circuit did not have the authority to overrule the US Supreme Court (Torres 2003).

5. The Top Ten Percent Plan served as the model for the percent plans later implemented in California and Florida.

6. In O'Connor's words: "We expect that 25 years from now, the use of racial preferences will no longer be necessary to further the interest approved today" (*Grutter* 2003, 343).

7. Deardorff and Jones's (2007) survey of southern and midwestern colleges showed that among the southern schools, although administrators generally did not support or agree with the University of Michigan

decisions, they all agreed that race plays a significant role in our society, and administrators at all schools reported that diversity was important.

8. These cases were combined by the US Supreme Court as *Parents Involved in Community Schools v. Seattle School District No. 1*, 551 U.S. 701 (2007).

9. In Oklahoma, the language of the initiative differed from the other five states.

10. Once passed, such legislation is very difficult to undo. The Supreme Court rulings in *Gratz* and *Grutter* set the parameters for what is constitutionally permissible; they did not overturn California's Proposition 209 or Washington's Initiative 200, which were political actions curbing affirmative action.

11. Because this chapter focuses on college and university admissions, I address SP-1, which eliminated affirmative action in UC admissions policy; SP-2, which eliminated affirmative action in UC hiring and contracting, was passed simultaneously but is not relevant for the discussion here.

12. I place "preferences" in scare quotes because it is a controversial term used predominantly by those opposed to affirmative action. I do not interpret affirmative action as "preferences." In keeping with the ruling in *Grutter* (2003) and egalitarian political theory, I view race as one possible factor among many in the admissions process.

References

Backes, Ben. "Do Affirmative Action Bans Lower Minority College Enrollment and Attainment? Evidence from Statewide Bans." *Journal of Human Resources* 47 (2) (2012): 435–56.

Baker, Julie. "Proposal 2: A Year Later." *State News*, November 15, 2007. http://www.statenews.com/index.php/article/2007/11/proposal_2_one_year_later.

Bello, Marisol. "Affirmative Action May Be on Ballots." *USA Today*, December 27, 2007. http://www.usatoday.com/news/politics/2007-12-27-affirmative-action_N.htm.

CBS. "Affirmative Action Lawsuits Hit Harvard and UNC." November 17, 2014. http://www.cbsnews.com/news/affirmative-action-lawsuits-hit-harvard-and-unc/.

Chapa, Jorge, and Catherine L. Horn. "Is Anything Race Neutral? Comparing 'Race-Neutral' Admissions Policies at the University of Texas and the University of California." In *Charting the Future of College Affirmative Action: Legal Victories, Continuing Attacks, and New Research*, edited by Gary Orfield, Patricia Marin, Stella M. Flores, and Liliana M. Garces, 157–71. Los Angeles: Civil Rights Project at UCLA, 2007.

Contreras, Frances E. "The Reconstruction of Merit Post–Proposition 209." *Educational Policy* 19 (2) (2005): 371–95.

Cooper, Helene. "Obama Criticizes Arrest of Harvard Professor." *New York Times*, July 22, 2009. http://www.nytimes.com/2009/07/23/us/politics/23gates.html.

Deardorff, Michelle D., and Augustus Jones. "Implementing Affirmative Action in Higher Education: University Responses to *Gratz* and *Grutter*." *Social Science Journal* 44 (2007): 525–34.

Denverpost.com. "Amendment 46—Discrimination by Gov Results." *Denver Post*, November 7, 2008. http://data.denverpost.com/election/results/amendment/2008/46-discrimination-by-gov/.

Dickson, Lisa M. "Does Ending Affirmative Action in College Admissions Lower the Percent of Minority Students Applying to College?" *Economics of Education Review* 25 (2004): 109–19.

Erb, Robin. "Colleges Find New Ways to Retain Diversity." *Detroit Free Press*, December 10, 2007. http://www.freep.com/apps/pbcs.dll/article?AID=/20071210/NEWS05/712100377.

Farley, Amy N., Matthew N. Gaertner, and Michele S. Moses. "Democracy under Fire: Voter Confusion and Influences in Colorado's Anti-Affirmative Action Initiative." *Harvard Educational Review* 83 (3) (2013): 432–62.

Fisher v. University of Texas at Austin, 133 S. Ct. 2411 (2013).

Gandy, Sara. "Foes Weigh Next Move Against Anti-Affirmative Action Initiative." *9News.com*, March 28, 2008. http://archive.9news.com/news/local/story.aspx?storyid=88903.

Gratz v. Bollinger, 539 U.S. 244 (2003).

Grutter v. Bollinger, 539 U.S. 306 (2003).

Haycock, Katy, Mary Lynch, and Jennifer Engle. *Opportunity Adrift: Our Flagship Universities Are Straying from their Public Mission*. Washington, DC: Education Trust, 2010.

Healy, Patrick. "Berkeley Struggles to Stay Diverse in Post–Affirmative Action Era." *Chronicle of Higher Education*, May 29 1998, A31–A33.

Hinrichs, Peter. *The Effects of Affirmative Action Bans on College Enrollment, Educational Attainment, and the Demographic Composition of Universities*. Washington, DC: George-town Public Policy Institute, 2009.

______. "The Effects of Affirmative Action Bans on College Enrollment, Educational Attainment, and the Demographic Composition of Universities." *Review of Economics and Statistics* 94 (3) (2012): 712–22.

Hopwood v. Texas, 78 F.3d 932 (5th Cir.), *cert. denied*, 518 U.S. 1033 (1996).

Howell, Jessica S. "Assessing the Impact of Eliminating Affirmative Action." *Journal of Labor Economics* 28 (1) (2010): 113–66.

Jaschik, Scott. "AP: More Pass and More Fail." *Inside Higher Ed*, February 11, 2010a. http://www.insidehighered.com/news/2010/02/11/ap.

______. "Strong Backing for Affirmative Action." *Inside Higher Ed*, April 1, 2010b. http://www.insidehighered.com/news/2010/04/01/affirm.

Kain, John F., and Daniel M. O'Brien. "*Hopwood* and the Top 10 Percent Law: How They Have Affected the College Enrollment Decisions of Texas High School Graduates." Paper presented at the National Bureau of Economic Research Meeting on Higher Education, Boston, MA, November 2001.

Kever, Jeannie. "White Sugarland Teen Sues UT over Admissions Policy." *Houston Chronicle*, April 8, 2008. http://www.chron.com/life/mom-houston/article/White-Sugar-Land-teen-sues-UT-over-admissions-rule-1678257.php.

———. *The Salience of Racial Isolation: African Americans' and Latinos' Perceptions of Climate and Enrollment Choices with and without Proposition 209*. Los Angeles: Civil Rights Project/*Proyecto Derechos Civiles*, 2012.

Korrell, Harry J. F. "No Big Surprise: A Review of the Seattle Schools Case." *Engage* 8 (4) (2007): 11–17.

Kumar, Anita, and Rosalind S. Helderman. "McDonnell's Confederate History Month Proclamation Irks Civil Rights Leaders." *Washington Post*, April 7, 2010. http://www.washingtonpost.com/wp-dyn/content/article/2010/04/06/AR2010040604416.html.

Leonhardt, David. "The New Affirmative Action." *New York Times Magazine*, September 30, 2007.

Long, Mark C. "Affirmative Action and Its Alternatives in Public Universities: What Do We Know?" *Public Administration Review* 67 (1) (2007): 311–25.

Long, Mark C., and Marta Tienda. "Winners and Losers: Changes in Texas University Admissions Post-*Hopwood*." *Educational Evaluation and Policy Analysis* 30 (3) (2008): 255–80.

Marin, Patricia. "The United States: The Changing Context of Access to Higher Education." In *Affirmative Action Matters: Creating Opportunities for Students around the World*, edited by Laura D. Jenkins and Michele S. Moses, 79–98. Routledge International Studies in Higher Education. New York: Routledge/Taylor & Francis, 2014.

Marin, Patricia, and Stella M. Flores. "*Bakke* and State Policy: Exercising Institutional Autonomy to Maintain a Diverse Student Body." In *Realizing* Bakke*'s Legacy: Affirmative Action, Equal Opportunity, and Access to Higher Education*, edited by Patricia Marin and Catherine L. Horn, 219–39. Sterling, VA: Stylus, 2008.

McCloskey, Sharon. "UNC Sued for Use of Race in Admissions." *Progressive Pulse*, November 17, 2014. http://pulse.ncpolicywatch.org/2014/11/17/unc-sued-for-use-of-race-in-admissions/.

Moses, Michele S. *Embracing Race: Why We Need Race-Conscious Education Policy*. New York: Teachers College Press, 2002.

Moses, Michele S., Amy N. Farley, Matthew N. Gaertner, Christina Paguyo, Darrell D. Jackson, and Kenneth R. Howe. *Investigating the Defeat of Amendment 46 in Colorado: An Analysis of the Trends and Principal Factors Influencing Voter Behaviors*. New York: Public Interest Projects, 2010.

Moses, Michele S., and Lauren P. Saenz. "Hijacking Education Policy Decisions: The Case of Affirmative Action." *Harvard Educational Review* 78 (2) (2008): 289–310.

Moses, Michele S., John T. Yun, and Patricia Marin. "Affirmative Action's Fate: Are 20 More Years Enough?" *Education Policy Analysis Archives* 17 (17) (2009). http://epaa.asu.edu/ojs/article/view/22.

Parents Involved in Community Schools v. Seattle School District No. 1, 551 U.S. 701 (2007).

Regents of the University of California v. Bakke, 438 U.S. 265 (1978).

Rich, Frank. "They Got Some 'Splainin' to Do." *New York Times*, July 18, 2009. http://www.nytimes.com/2009/07/19/opinion/19rich.html.

Saenz, Lauren P. "Education Policy by Ballot Box: Examining the Impact of Anti-Affirmative Action Initiatives." PhD diss., University of Colorado–Boulder, 2010.

Sandel, Michael J. *Public Philosophy: Essays on Morality and Politics*. Cambridge, MA: Harvard University Press, 2005.

Schevitz, Tanya. "Critics Say Plan Fails to Counter Image of Bias." *San Francisco Chronicle*, May 16, 2001, A4.

Schultz, Marisa. "U-M Reports Slight Decline in Minority Enrollment." *Detroit News*, October 20, 2008.

Sobel, Lester A., ed. *Quotas and Affirmative Action*. New York: Facts on File, 1980.

Torres, Gerald. "*Grutter v. Bollinger/Gratz v. Bollinger*: View from a Limestone Ledge." *Columbia Law Review* 103 (2003): 1596–1609.

University of Texas at Austin. "Statement on Reinstatement of Affirmative Action in Admission." September 10, 2003a. http://www.utexas.edu/news/2003/09/10/nr_affirmative/.

______. "The University of Texas at Austin Proposes Inclusion of Race as a Factor in Admissions Process." November 24, 2003b. http://www.utexas.edu/news/2003/11/24/nr_admission/.

United States Census Bureau. "Michigan." *State and County Quick Facts*, 2013. http://quickfacts.census.gov/qfd/states/26000.html.

Vega, Tanzina. "Colorblind Notion Aside, Colleges Grapple with Racial Tensions." *New York Times*, February 24, 2014.

Yosso, Tara J., Laurence Parker, Daniel G. Solorzáno, and Marvin Lynn. "From Jim Crow to Affirmative Action and Back Again: A Critical Race Discussion of Racialized Rationales and Access to Higher Education." *Review of Research in Education* 28 (2004): 1–25.

READING 8

The Politics of Gerrymandering

Overview of Supreme Court Precedent

By Congressional Digest, 20(8): 5–8.

The Supreme Court has defined partisan gerrymandering as "the drawing of legislative district lines to subordinate adherents of one political party and entrench a rival party in power."—*Arizona State Legislature v. Arizona Independent Redistricting Commission* (2015). While leaving open the possibility that a claim of unconstitutional partisan gerrymandering could be within the scope of judicial review, the Supreme Court has been unable to decide on a manageable standard for making such a determination.

The *Vieth* Precedent

In its 2004 decision in *Vieth v. Jubelirer*, the Court addressed a claim of partisan gerrymandering, in which the challengers relied on the Fourteenth Amendment Equal Protection Clause as the source of their substantive right and basis for relief.

In *Vieth*, a plurality of four justices determined that such a claim presented a non-justiciable political question. The plurality argued that the standard previously articulated by a plurality of the Court in its 1986 decision of *Davis v. Bandemer* had proved unmanageable.

Under that standard, a political gerrymandering claim could succeed only where the challengers showed both intentional discrimination against an identifiable political group and an actual discriminatory effect on that group. However, another plurality of four justices in *Vieth* concluded that such claims are justiciable, but could not agree upon the standard for courts to use in assessing such claims.

The deciding vote in *Vieth*, Justice Kennedy, concluded that while the claims presented in that case were not justiciable, he "would not foreclose all possibility of judicial relief if some limited and precise rationale were found to correct an established violation of the Constitution in some redistricting cases."

Further, Justice Kennedy observed that while the appellants in this case had relied on the Equal Protection Clause as the source of their substantive right and basis for relief, the complaint also

"The Politics of Gerrymandering: Overview of Supreme Court Precedent," *Supreme Court Debates*, vol. 20, no. 8, pp. 5-8.

alleged a violation of their First Amendment rights. According to Justice Kennedy, the First Amendment may be a more relevant constitutional provision in future cases that claim unconstitutional partisan gerrymandering because such claims "involve the First Amendment interest of not burdening or penalizing citizens because of their participation in the electoral process, their voting history, their association with a political party, or their expression of political views."

In contrast, Justice Kennedy noted, an analysis under the Equal Protection Clause emphasizes the permissibility of a redistricting plan's classifications. When race is involved, Justice Kennedy reasoned, examining such classifications is appropriate because classifying by race "is almost never permissible." However, when the issue before a court is whether a generally permissible classification—political party association—has been used for an impermissible purpose, the question turns on whether the classification imposed an unlawful burden, Justice Kennedy maintained.

Therefore, he concluded that an analysis under the First Amendment "may offer a sounder and more prudential basis for intervention" by concentrating on whether a redistricting plan "burdens the representational rights of the complaining party's voters for reasons of ideology, beliefs, or political association."

LULAC Leaves the Door Open

Subsequently, in its 2006 decision, *League of United Latin American Citizens (LULAC) v. Perry*, the Court was again divided on the question of whether partisan gerrymandering claims are within the scope of judicial review. In *LULAC*, Texas voters challenged a redistricting plan that had been enacted mid-decade, arguing that the plan was motivated by partisan objectives, served no legitimate public purpose, and burdened one group because of its political affiliation, in violation of the First Amendment and the Equal Protection Clause.

However, the Supreme Court disagreed. In *LULAC*, a plurality of four justices opined that claims of unconstitutional partisan gerrymandering are justiciable, but could not agree upon a standard for adjudicating such claims. An additional two justices took the view that such claims are not justiciable.

However, the two justices who had joined the Court since its ruling in *Vieth*, Chief Justice Roberts and Justice Alito, generally agreed with Justice Kennedy's position, leaving open the possibility that the Court might discern a standard for adjudicating unconstitutional partisan gerrymandering claims in a future case. Therefore, in the aftermath of *LULAC*, it seems possible that a claim of unconstitutional partisan gerrymandering could be judicially reviewable, but the critical standard that a court could use to find such a violation and grant relief remain unresolved.

Wisconsin Case Offers Another Look

Recently, in a potentially significant case, the Supreme Court was presented with another opportunity to craft such a standard. In February 2017, under a provision of Federal law providing for direct appeals to the Supreme Court, the State of Wisconsin appealed a three-judge Federal district court ruling involving partisan gerrymandering.

In this case, *Whitford v. Gill*, the district court held, by a vote of two to one, that a Wisconsin State legislative redistricting map constituted an unconstitutional partisan gerrymander. Following the 2010 census, the Wisconsin legislature redrew its State legislative redistricting map, which was signed into law by the governor in 2011.

In the 2012 election, "the Republican Party received 48.6 percent of the two-party statewide vote share for Assembly candidates and won 60 of the 99 seats in the Wisconsin Assembly." In the 2014 election, "the Republican Party received 52 percent of the two-party statewide vote share and won 63 assembly seats."

The Plaintiffs—registered voters in various counties and districts throughout Wisconsin—are "supporters of the Democratic Party and of Democratic candidates, and they almost always vote for Democratic candidates in Wisconsin elections." The Plaintiffs challenged the Wisconsin State legislative redistricting plan as treating voters "unequally, diluting their voting power based on their political beliefs, in violation of the Fourteenth Amendment's guarantee of equal protection," and "unreasonably burden[ing] their First Amendment rights of association and free speech."

The district court agreed, holding that the First Amendment and the Equal Protection Clause prohibit a redistricting map that is drawn with the purpose, and has the effect, of placing a "severe impediment" on the effectiveness of a citizen's vote that is based on political affiliation and cannot be justified on other legitimate legislative grounds.

While acknowledging that the law of political gerrymandering is "still in its incipient stages" and "in a State of considerable flux," the court announced that it is clear that the First Amendment and the Equal Protection Clause protect the weight of a citizen's vote against discrimination based on the political preferences of the voter. Relying on a 1968 Supreme Court ruling that had invalidated a State law that required new political parties to obtain a certain number of signatures in order to appear on the ballot, the court found a "solid basis" for considering the associational aspect of the Plaintiff's claim of partisan gerrymandering.

Examining the evidence presented at trial, the court determined that one purpose of the redistricting plan was "to secure the Republican Party's control of the State legislature for the decennial period." Although the drafters had created several alternative redistricting plans that would have had a less severe partisan impact, the court found that the drafters had opted for the plan that, in comparison with the existing plan, significantly increased the number of districts containing voters who "lean[ed]" toward one political party.

Based on that and other factors, including numerous reports and memoranda considered by the drafters that addressed the partisan outcomes of various maps, the court concluded that even though the redistricting plan complied with traditional redistricting principles, it nonetheless had a purpose of "entrenching" one party in its control of the legislature.

Furthermore, the court determined that the redistricting plan had the effect of ensuring that one political party would maintain control of the State legislature for a 10-year period. This was accomplished, the court found, by allocating votes among the newly created districts in such a manner as to make it likely that the number of seats held by candidates of one political party would not to drop below 50 percent in any election scenario.

The "Efficiency Gap" Test

Notably, in this ruling, the court embraced a new measure of calculating asymmetry among districts, proposed by the Plaintiffs, termed the "efficiency gap" (EG), As described by its creators, EG "represents the difference between the parties' respective wasted votes in an election—where a vote is wasted if it is cast (1) for a losing candidate, or (2) for a winning candidate but in excess of what she needed to prevail."

In other words, as the court observed, EG measures two redistricting methods that are designed to diminish the electoral power of the voters of one party: "cracking" and "packing." As used here, packing refers to the concentration of voters of one party into a limited number of districts so that the party wins those districts by large margins. Cracking refers to the division of voters of one party across a large number of districts so that the party is unable to achieve a majority vote in any district.

EG, the court announced, is "a measure of the degree of both cracking and packing of a particular party's voters that exists in a given district plan, based on an observed electoral result." The EG, the court decided, does not impermissibly require that each party receive a share of seats in the legislature in proportion to its vote share, but instead, measures the degree to which a redistricting plan "deviates from the relationship we would expect to observe between votes and seats."

Relying on the results from 2012 and 2014 elections, academic analyses, and the EG measure, the court held that the Plaintiffs had demonstrated that the State legislative redistricting plan created a burden, "as measured by a reliable standard, on [their] representational rights." In particular, the court found that having "actual election results" confirmed the reliability of the academic analyses so that the court was "not operating only in the realm of hypotheticals," which was a concern that Justice Kennedy voiced in *LULAC*. Therefore, the court concluded that neither the Constitution nor the Supreme Court's rulings in *Vieth* and *LULAC* precluded it from considering the EG in order to ascertain partisan gerrymandering.

Finally, the court held that the discriminatory effect of the plan is not explained by the political geography of Wisconsin, nor is it justified by a legitimate State interest. Acknowledging the absence of explicit guidance on this question from the Supreme Court, the court determined it most appropriate to evaluate whether the partisan effect of a redistricting plan is justifiable, "i.e., whether it can be explained by the legitimate State prerogatives and neutral factors that are implicated in the districting process."

According to the court, although the "natural political geography" of Wisconsin played some role in how the redistricting map was drawn, this political geography was inadequate to explain the significant, disparate partisan effect of the plan as evidenced by the results of the 2012 and 2014 elections.

The most crucial evidence presented, the court said, was that the drafters had produced multiple alternative plans that would have achieved the same "valid" redistricting goals, but with a much smaller partisan advantage to one party, and opted not to use them. After holding that the Wisconsin State legislative plan constituted an unconstitutional partisan gerrymander, the court deferred ruling on an appropriate remedy. However, in January 2017, the court enjoined the State of Wisconsin from using the plan in all future elections and ordered the State to enact a new plan by November 1, 2017, for use in the November 2018 election.

Conclusion

In sum, while the Supreme Court has left open the possibility that a claim of unconstitutional partisan gerrymandering could be within the scope of judicial review, it has been unable to decide on a manageable standard for making such a determination. Currently, the Supreme Court is considering an appeal that presents it with an opportunity to craft such a standard if it so chooses.

READING 9

Michelle Alexander's *The New Jim Crow*

Mass Incarceration in the Age of Colorblindness

By Devereaux Kennedy

The Construction of a Racialized Caste, Part I: Slavery and Jim Crow Segregation

Like Charles Murray, Michelle Alexander has her curiosities, concerns, and passions. The curiosity that sparked her study *The New Jim Crow* was a sign she noticed nailed to a telephone pole in Oakland, California. The sign announced a community meeting sponsored by a local radical group, and said, "The Drug War is the New Jim Crow" (Alexander 2012, 3). She initially dismissed the sign as an example of the hyperbolic tendencies of a lot of radical groups. Still, it made her curious. The more she thought about the sign, the more curious she became.

At the time she saw the sign, Michelle Alexander was a young civil rights lawyer concerned about attacks on affirmative action policies and what she then saw as the lingering effects of segregation on African Americans. "I understood the problems plaguing poor communities of color, including problems associated with crime and rising incarceration rates, to be a function of poverty and lack of access to quality education" (3). She was and is a passionate advocate for the civil, social, and economic rights of African Americans, and of an egalitarian society.

Intellectual and Social Problem Addressed

As we will see below, Alexander's study addresses an intellectual as well as a social problem. The thinking, research, and interviewing that resulted in *The New Jim Crow* led her to conclude that she was wrong about the connection between African American crime, rising incarceration rates, and the legacy of segregation. She no longer thinks that crime and rising incarceration rates in poor African American communities are vestiges of the old Jim Crow. She now thinks they are crucial aspects of the new Jim Crow.

Concepts: Caste, Class, and Race

Charles Murray constructs two new classes to paint his picture of how the contemporary United States looks and works. Alexander constructs a new conception of caste and a new definition of mass incarceration to paint a very different picture. In texts like those we surveyed in Chapter 3, caste is presented as a system of social stratification sometimes found in traditional societies. Traditional India is usually given as the example of a social system once governed by a caste system. (The caste system is officially outlawed in contemporary India, though it still has important effects on social life.) India's caste system is probably thousands of years old and is connected with the Hindu religion. Introductory sociology texts make the point that caste systems like India's are closed systems in which one's status is given for life and is based on one's parents' position in the system. Caste systems are usually contrasted with class-based systems of stratification, which are presented as characteristic of modern developed societies. Class systems are conceived of as open systems in which one's position is determined by achieved characteristics, particularly income and wealth. Class systems are open in the sense that it is possible to change one's position in the system during one's lifetime.

Alexander constructs her own conception of caste and uses it to make sense of the position of African Americans throughout American history. Alexander's uses the concept of caste not to denote a system of stratification, but to characterize a form of social control. "I use the term racial caste ... to denote a stigmatized racial group locked into an inferior position by law and custom" (Alexander 2012, 12).

Historical Narrative

Like Murray's, Alexander's study has a historical dimension. However, she conceptualizes the historical dimension of human social life differently than does Murray. Murray establishes a historical zero point—a point at which the phenomenon he studied, the coming apart of American civic culture, had not yet begun. Alexander uses her concept of caste to construct a narrative that she employs to present a picture of the recurring features characterizing the historical experience of African Americans in the United States. In effect, Alexander uses the historical narrative she constructs to answer a question: is there a way to think of slavery, Jim Crow segregation, and mass incarceration as different instances of the same caste system? To answer her question affirmatively, she "conceives of each as a caste system which takes different forms in different historical periods. ... Jim Crow and slavery were caste systems. So is our current system of mass incarceration" (Alexander 2012, 12).

The Concept of Racial Caste

Race is the ascribed characteristic upon which Alexander builds her concept of caste. She argues that the status of African Americans is determined by the ascribed characteristic of race. She conceives of racialized caste as a closed system that circumscribes the position and status of African Americans in the American social hierarchy. In the caste Alexander has constructed, race is inherited from one's parents and passed on to one's children. African Americans are assigned throughout their lives to the lowest position in American society, one outside and beneath the class system. Alexander pictures African Americans as the United States' untouchables. Like India's untouchables, their caste position is enforced and maintained by law and custom.

Mass Incarceration as a Form of Racialized Caste

Alexander pictures African American slavery and Jim Crow segregation as different forms of racialized caste, one form historically following the other. Her central task in *The New Jim Crow* is to show that mass incarceration is another form of racialized caste, one that historically followed that of Jim Crow segregation. She understands that, on the face of it, this doesn't seem to make sense. At first it didn't make sense to her. "Only after years of working on criminal justice reform did my own focus finally shift, and then the rigid caste system slowly came into view" (Alexander 2012, 12). It was not the social world that changed; it was the way Alexander came to view it that led her to "see" this caste system. It is in this sense that the problem Alexander addresses in *The New Jim Crow* is intellectual as well as social.

This new way of viewing the social world involved conceiving of what she meant by "mass incarceration" differently. "The term mass incarceration refers not only to the criminal justice system but also to the larger web of laws, rules, policies and customs that control those labeled criminals both in and out of prison. Once released, former prisoners enter into a hidden underworld of legalized discrimination and permanent social exclusion. They are members of America's new undercaste" (13). To make her point, she must address the following kinds of objections: (1) surely the status of criminal is achieved, not ascribed; and (2) criminals earn their status the same way middle-class professionals earn theirs. These objections can be refuted if you alter the way you look at the social world in the way Alexander has. She presents her readers with a picture of an American social world in which gaining the status of criminal is a matter of race, not behavior. Central to Alexander's picture is a new conception of the American criminal justice system and how it works.

> The current system of control permanently locks a huge percentage of the African-American community out of the mainstream society and economy. The system operates through our criminal justice institutions, but it functions more like a caste system than a system of control. ... Although this new system of racialized social control purports to be colorblind; it creates and maintains racial hierarchy much as earlier systems of social control did. Like Jim Crow (and slavery) mass incarceration operates as a tightly networked system of

laws, policies, customs and institutions that operate collectively to ensure the subordinate status of a group defined largely by race. (13)

Slavery, Race, and Social Conflict

Alexander uses caste to compare the way mass incarceration came into existence with the way slavery and Jim Crow segregation came into being. To do so, she adopts what sociology texts call a **conflict perspective**. By contrast, Charles Murray takes what those same texts call a **consensus perspective**. Like Durkheim, Murray looks for what ties people together—a civic culture—and then examines how those ties sometimes fall apart. Like Marx and Weber, Alexander looks at the human social world as an arena of conflict within which social groups struggle for power, wealth, and prestige. When she looks at human social life, she tries to identify the groups that are struggling; what they are struggling over; who wins and who loses; and the social consequences of their victories and defeats. Tenuous periods of consensus are reached when one group or coalition of groups is able to successfully work its will over and above the resistance of other groups.

The Lawyer's Brief: Data

Alexander is a lawyer by profession. Her book takes the form of a brief in which she gathers all the evidence she can to make her case. She doesn't bother looking for inconvenient facts that might weaken her case. Accustomed to working within the adversarial American system of justice, she seems to leave that task to her adversaries. Alexander is not a social scientist. With the exception of her citation of court cases, the data she employs consists mainly of secondary sources: books and newspaper and journal articles written by others.

Slavery as a Form of Racialized Caste

Alexander employs the conflict perspective and the concept of racialized caste along with data taken from the works of historians like Edmond Morgan (1975), Charles Vann Woodward (1955), and Gerald Fresia (1998) to construct a picture of slavery as a form of racialized social control emerging out of a conflict between indigenous peoples, indentured servants, free immigrants, and Southern planters during the early colonial period of American history. Southern landowners wanted to build plantations on which to grow commercial crops like tobacco, rice, and, particularly, cotton. They found indigenous peoples and indentured servants unsuitable as a labor force. They turned instead to the importation of African slaves to work their lands.

Figure 9.1 Slavery

Concept: The Racial Bribe

At the time, Alexander argues, indentured servants were not distinguished by race (Alexander 2012, 23). Southern planters employed a "racial bribe" to divide indentured servants by race and then turn them against indigenous peoples. They bribed white indentured servants by encouraging and supporting their efforts to confiscate the lands owned by indigenous peoples. Slavery and taking land from indigenous peoples was justified by the invention of racism and white supremacy. If indigenous peoples were viewed as "wild savages" and "redskins" inferior to civilized white Europeans and their descendants, the confiscation of their lands could be justified. If Africans were seen as an inferior race, their enslavement could be justified. Alexander argues that rich Southern planters won over poor whites by offering them land confiscated from an inferior race of "redskins" and a status superior to that of African slaves (23–25).

In Alexander's historical narrative, the establishment of the United States is pictured as the result of a compromise between conflicting elites in the former Southern and Northern colonies. The US Constitution granted the central government (the federal government) increased power, which elites in the North wanted and those in the South had resisted in exchange for the de facto recognition of a racial caste of African slaves in many of the Southern states.

Abolition, Reconstruction, Class, and Racial Conflict

Alexander has surprisingly little to say about the American Civil War and the contribution of the interracial abolitionist and radical republican social movements to the abolition of slavery. She has more to say about the brief period of Reconstruction that followed the end of the Civil War and the abolition of slavery. In Alexander's historical narrative, the Reconstruction period is seen as a time when racialized caste might have been eliminated but ultimately wasn't.

> The Reconstruction Era ... did appear at least for a time to have the potential to seriously undermine, if not completely eradicate, the racial caste system in the South. With the protection of federal troops, African Americans began to vote in large numbers and seize control, in some areas, of the local political apparatus. Literacy rates climbed, and educated blacks began to populate legislatures, open schools, and initiate successful businesses. In 1867 at the dawn of the Reconstruction Era, no black man held political office in the South, yet fifteen years later, at least 15 percent of all Southern elected officials were black. (Alexander 2012, 29)

Figure 9.2 Black Reconstruction

Populism, Race, and Class Conflict

In Alexander's narrative, the early years of the Populist movement are seen as containing the possibility of an interracial movement of poor people capable of challenging white elites in the South. Alexander selects parts of a speech given by Tom Watson, a Populist leader, to show this early Populist possibility. In it, Watson calls for a union of black and white farmers: "You are apart that you might be separately f leeced of your earnings. You are made to hate each other because upon the hatred is rested the keystone of the arch of financial despotism that enslaves you both. You are deceived and blinded that you may not see how this race antagonism perpetuates a monetary system which beggars you both" (33).

Alexander pictures Populism, in its beginnings, as a budding multiracial social movement. Alexander employs a quote from C. Vann Woodward (1955), the author of *The Strange Career of Jim Crow,* to bolster this view of Populism: "It is altogether probable that during the brief Populist upheaval of the [eighteen] nineties Negroes and native whites achieved a greater comity of mind and harmony of political purpose than ever before or since in the South" (33).

Jim Crow Segregation, Race, and Class Conflict

In Alexander's narrative, Jim Crow segregation is seen as the result of the defeat of the Populist coalition of poor blacks and whites by rich Southern white elites. "Just as the white elite had successfully driven a wedge between poor whites and blacks ... by creating the institution of black slavery, another racial

Figure 9.3 Jim Crow

caste system was emerging two centuries later, in part due to the efforts of white elites to decimate a multiracial alliance of poor people" (35).

At the beginning of the twentieth century all Southern states had laws that effectively denied blacks the right to vote and segregated them in virtually all aspects of life—schools, churches, housing, jobs, restaurants, hotels, even drinking fountains, morgues, and orphanages (35). In Alexander's narrative, the new form of racialized caste, Jim Crow segregation, had replaced slavery as the form of racial caste in the South.

The Civil Rights Movement, Class Conflict, and the Defeat of Jim Crow

The next chapter in Alexander's narrative begins during and directly after World War II. In her picture, this period is defined by the formation of a new interracial coalition of forces that challenge Jim Crow segregation in the South. The mass migration of African Americans out of the rural South; the experience of other African Americans in the Armed Forces; steps toward the integration of the United States Armed Forces; and legal challenges by the National Association for the Advancement of Colored People (NAACP) to segregation all contributed to the formation of this coalition.

Alexander pictures the 1954 Supreme Court decision *Brown v. Board of Education* as signaling to white segregationists a real threat to Jim Crow segregation in the South. "Brown threatened not only to end segregation in public schools, but also, by implication, the entire system of legalized segregation in the South" (Alexander 2012, 36). In response, Southern segregationists mounted a sustained and multi-fronted defense of "their way of life." A Southern Manifesto vowing to maintain segregation by all legal means was signed by 101 out of the 128 members of Congress representing the original Confederate states. White citizens, councils composed primarily of upper- and middle-class white businessmen and clergy were formed in most Southern cities. A revitalized Ku Klux Klan engaged in a campaign of illegal violence against those who supported integration in the South. Southern legislators passed new Jim Crow laws (37).

Figure 9.4 Civil Rights Movement

The segregationist forces were opposed by a growing coalition of white and black activists, who launched a campaign of boycotts, marches, sit-ins, and black voter registration drives challenging Jim Crow laws throughout the South. A bitter, protracted conflict between these two forces ensued, involving nonviolent civil disobedience on the part of the civil rights movement, and arrests and mob violence on the part of their opponents. Much of this struggle was covered in newspaper stories and television reports throughout the world. Alexander, as did Murray, identifies 1963 as a key turning point in American history. "The dramatic high point of the Civil Rights Movement occurred in 1963. The Southern struggle had grown from a modest group of black students demonstrating peacefully at one lunch counter to the largest mass movement for racial reform and civil rights in the twentieth century" (37). On June 12, 1963, President Kennedy announced that he would present a strong Civil Rights Bill before Congress. After Kennedy's assassination, President Johnson announced his commitment to the goal of "full assimilation of more than twenty million Negroes into American life" (38). Under his leadership the Civil Rights Act of 1964 and the Voting Rights Act of 1965 were passed, essentially ending Jim Crow segregation as a form of racial caste.

The Poor Peoples Movement that Wasn't

The same coalition of groups that defeated Jim Crow in the South next attempted to wage a nationwide struggle for the economic rights of poor people. President Johnson responded with the announcement of an "unconditional war on poverty" and led the struggle to pass the Economic Opportunity Act of 1964. "As the Civil Rights Movement began to evolve into a 'Poor Peoples Movement' it promised to address not only black poverty but white poverty as well—thus raising the specter of a poor and working class movement that cut across racial lines" (Alexander 2012, 39).

[...] [I]n Alexander's view, white conservative elites used the rhetoric of law and order and the War on Drugs to create a new form of racialized caste to prevent this from happening.

Study Questions

1. What are Alexander's curiosities, concerns, and passions?
2. If race and crime are the topics of Alexander's study, what is the problem the book addresses? Why is it an intellectual as well as a social problem?
3. What are the major concepts Alexander employs in the construction of the first two parts of her historical narrative?
4. What does Michelle Alexander mean by racialized caste? How does she use this concept to organize her historical narrative?
5. Describe the social forces which, according to Alexander, were responsible for the creation of slavery and Jim Crow segregation as forms of racialized caste.
6. What is the difference between a conflict and a consensus perspective? Which one does Murray employ? Which one does Alexander employ? How does each employ their perspective?

Assignment

1. Determine whether the author(s) of the study you are analyzing employ a conflict or a consensus perspective.
2. Describe the methodical approach to you intend to take in your project. Be sure to include whether you intend to employ a conflict or a consensus perspective (or combination of both) if you think it relevant.

Suggested Further Readings

Alexander, Michelle. 2012. *The New Jim Crow: Mass Incarceration in the Age of Colorblindness*, rev. ed., 20–58 (The Rebirth of Caste). New York: The New Press.

Stamp, Kenneth. 1965. *The Era of Reconstruction: 1865–1877*, 155–217 (Radical Rule in the South and the Triumph of the Conservatives). New York: Random House.

Woodward, C. Vann. 1955. *The Strange Career of Jim Crow*, 31–111 (Forgotten Alternatives and Capitulation to Racism). New York: Oxford University Press.

Image Credits

Fig. 9.1: Henry P. Moore, "Slavery." Copyright in the Public Domain.
Fig. 9.2: Currier and Ives, "Black Reconstruction." Copyright in the Public Domain.
Fig. 9.3: Jack Delano, "Jim Crow," http://www.loc.gov/pictures/item/fsa1998006256/PP. Copyright in the Public Domain.
Fig. 9.4: Carol M. Highsmith, "Civil Rights Movement," http://www.loc.gov/pictures/item/2010636981. Copyright in the Public Domain.

Bibliography

Alexander, Michelle. 2012. *The New Jim Crow: Mass Incarceration in the Age of Colorblindness*, rev. ed. New York: The New Press.

Fresia, Gerald. 1998. *Toward an American Revolution: Exposing the Constitution and Other Illusions*. Boston: South End Press.

Morgan, Edmond. 1975. *American Slavery, American Freedom: The Ordeal of Colonial Virginia*. New York: Norton.

Stamp, Kenneth M. 1965. *The Era of Reconstruction: 1865–1877*. New York: Random House.

Woodward, C. Vann. 1955. *The Strange Career of Jim Crow*. New York: Oxford University Press.

CHAPTER 4

Hispanics/Latinos: Brief Historical Perspectives

READING 10

The Hispanic Category and the Development of a New Identity Politics in America

By G. Cristina Mora

In the late 1960s, activists, government bureaucrats, and media executives each embarked on separate projects to develop the notion of panethnicity. Mexican American activists, eager to recast their movement as a national, Hispanic one, reached out to Puerto Rican and Cuban communities alike. Bureaucrats from the Cabinet Committee on Opportunities for Spanish-Speaking People (CCOSSP) and the Census Bureau began recasting Latin American origin groups panethnically and creating reports on the conditions of Hispanics in the United States. Finally, media executives, eager to grow the market for their Spanish-language programming, expanded nationally, forging a television network that would bring together Mexican American, Puerto Rican, and Cuban audiences across the country.

Throughout the 1970s and 1980s, however, the efforts of these stakeholders would become intertwined. Activists took part in census hearings and supported state officials' work to institutionalize panethnicity. In turn, the Census Bureau sponsored regular workshops to teach activists more sophisticated ways of analyzing Hispanic census data. Media executives also became plugged into these networks by helping the bureau and activists promote panethnicity on their Spanish-language television programming. Indeed, by 1990 a viewer could tune into Spanish-language television, brimming with various panethnic entertainment and public affairs programs, to watch census spokespersons and activists comment on the future of the Hispanic community.

In effect, Hispanic panethnicity became institutionalized over time as activists, bureaucrats, and media executives forged a new field centered around the new category. Within this field, stakeholders developed networks, shared resources, and worked together to advance the notion that Mexican Americans, Puerto Ricans, Cuban Americans, and others constituted a single, national community. As one media executive recalled, "We all came to know each other ... [the] world of Hispanic leaders was small ... we could call one another up easily."[1]

Ambiguity was a critical element of this new Hispanic field. Activists, media executives, and census officials never really defined who Hispanics were, nor did they argue definitively that characteristics like language, place of birth, or surname made Hispanics Hispanic. Instead, they reiterated that, above all, Hispanics were Hispanic because they shared a common set of values and a common culture. The stakeholders used descriptors like *hardworking, religious,* and *family-oriented*—adjectives that could be applied to any group—to describe the unique characteristics uniting Hispanics.

This ambiguity allowed stakeholders to reduce any potential resistance to the idea of panethnicity. By pointing toward a vague cultural definition of panethnicity, stakeholders could position the category as broad and as complementary to, rather than in conflict with, national identity. One did not have to speak Spanish or have a Spanish surname to be Hispanic because panethnicity was predicated on a set of historically based cultural values. More important, stakeholders suggested that one did not have to choose between nationality and panethnicity because one could be both Hispanic *and* Mexican, or Hispanic *and* Puerto Rican. The nationality issue remained open because panethnicity was not about being descended from a specific set of countries, or even about harboring certain feelings (nostalgic or loyal) toward Latin America or Spain. Instead, stakeholders framed panethnicity as a shared if hazily defined set of cultural values and experiences. As a result, an immigrant with close connections to his or her homeland could claim to be as Hispanic as a fourth-generation individual with little or no connection to Latin America.

Equally important, the ambiguous narrative about panethnicity allowed stakeholders to bend the notion in ways that helped them attain their organizational goals. Activists framed Hispanics as an underrepresented minority group that suffered from discrimination, poverty, and other forms of disadvantage. They claimed that Hispanics wanted to contribute to the nation but were held back by an unequal playing field. This framing allowed activists to position Hispanics as a national constituency that merited federal, and not only state, attention. Media executives framed the issue differently. In order to attract advertising revenue from corporations, they described Hispanics as a young national consumer market that was "getting richer" and "growing larger."[2] Their marketing manuals thus combined Hispanic census data with their own claims about Hispanic consumption habits and brand loyalty. For their part, bureaucrats in CCOSSP and the Census Bureau framed Hispanics as a sizable demographic group identifiable through a unique set of economic, family, and cultural patterns.

Over time, as the networks between bureaucrats, activists, and media executives became more extensive, stakeholders learned to appropriate frames from one another. Activists developed Hispanic advocacy organizations and used the "Hispanic market" frame to attract corporate sponsors; contributions to Hispanic causes, they argued, could translate into positive publicity among Hispanic consumers. For their part, media executives employed the activists' frame of an underserved, Hispanic minority to reap special concessions from regulators. For example, the Federal Communications Commission granted special licensing preferences to Spanish-language station owners because it came to consider Hispanics as an underserved population.

Indeed, by 1990 shareholders created a new field undergirded by what sociologist Peter Berger has called a "plausibility structure": a sociocultural web of agreed-upon meanings and accepted roles. In these structures, roles become institutionalized and connected to one another through a broader set of shared meanings.[3] Thus, activists developed His-panic political agendas and reports and soon called themselves experts on Hispanic politics. The Census Bureau created positions for "Hispanic data analysts," and media executives began calling themselves Hispanic marketing consultants. In their new roles, these stakeholders helped to legitimate one another's work. To give one telling example, by 1990 Hispanic data analysts from the Census Bureau were regularly featured speakers at national Hispanic activist conventions, which were covered annually on Spanish-language television.

Ultimately, the history of the Hispanic category invites scholars to revisit understandings of how racial and ethnic classifications are institutionalized. Much of the available research stresses the workings of the state, or the agendas of ethnic political and market leaders, without paying much attention to *how* categories are negotiated and developed through forging networks and relationships. This has obscured the way that processes of co-optation, negotiation, and marketing play a role in determining when new categories emerge and how they will be defined. These processes are interactive; new categories can emerge when conflicts and struggles force stakeholders to cooperate and find areas of mutual interest with their fellow actors.

Again, ambiguity facilitates this cooperation. Categories that are defined narrowly, such as those based on surname or language, make it difficult for stakeholders to develop mutual interests and work together. For example, activists would have had a difficult time supporting a definition of Hispanics as those who spoke Spanish because many second-plus-generation Mexican Americans, including many activist leaders themselves, were monolingual English speakers. By defining the Hispanic category in a cultural manner, however, stakeholders could insinuate that the category was much broader and they could develop their own frames about panethnicity.

Moreover, ambiguity allows for a broad definition that can help to absorb resistance. Ambiguous categories can be combined with others, since their broad definition makes it difficult to discern who lies outside of the group. This allows stakeholders to include those individuals who might have felt shut out of a classification, or to preempt resistance from those who feel that they must give up one identity in order to be part of a new category. The idea that Hispanic panethnicity was complementary to national identity was incredibly important for overcoming resistance.

Ambiguity, however, works in tandem with analogy. Stakeholders recognize that a thoroughly ambiguous category is in danger of becoming irrelevant; as such, they make analogous comparisons between new classifications and existing ones in the hopes of delimiting the category. In effect, analogies allow stakeholders to make a new category seem more familiar by connecting it to an already established category.[4] Thus, when activists claim that Hispanics are like blacks, they want listeners to understand that, like blacks, Hispanics are a distinct, bounded minority group with a long history of disadvantage. And when census officials make comparisons between Hispanic and black communities, they want to convey that, like blacks, Hispanics are a sizable, bounded American demographic community.

At the same time, analogies also allow stakeholders to construct a barrier between categories. When stakeholders use analogies, they are suggesting similarities, but they are also asserting the existence of two distinct categories. The claim that Hispanics are like blacks suggests that while the communities share similarities, the Hispanic category is separate and distinct from the black one. The analogy thus places a boundary around the Hispanic category by suggesting that those who are Hispanic are not black. This distinction of course becomes problematic when we consider the population of individuals who straddle two categories, such as Afro-Latinos.

Nonetheless, as a field forms around a new classification, the origins of a new category become obscured. The web of interconnected positions, resources, and frames makes it difficult to say that one particular interest (political, economic, social) exclusively produced a given category. Stakeholders further obscure their individual interests and actions by drawing on history to persuade people that the new category has deep historical roots. In the Hispanic case, census officials wrote reports contending that Hispanics were united by their "common heritage from Spain," which stretched back to more than five centuries in the Americas.[5] Activists also historicized the notion of panethnicity in the United States by, for example, pointing to the Mexican American soldiers who had fought in the Civil War and contending that "Hispanics," not simply Mexican Americans, had played a key role in shaping American military history.[6]

Over time, the ambiguous category becomes more popular as more actors enter the field and use the new classification to achieve their organizational goals. A sort of collective amnesia[7] sets in as organizations begin to refer to the new category's long history and develop narratives about the rich cultural basis of the classification. By then, the category is completely institutionalized, and the new classification is, like other classifications, assumed to have always existed.

The Organizational Diffusion of the Hispanic Category

This book has mainly focused on outlining the efforts of the pioneering organizations that helped to institutionalize the notion of panethnicity. However, there were certainly other vital processes that emerged later as a result of these pioneering efforts. Beginning in the mid-1970s, for example, NCLR activists, former CCOSSP officials, and congressmen like Edward Roybal placed pressure on the Office of Management and Budget to issue Statistical Policy Directive 15, which it did in 1977. The directive required that all federal data collection agencies institute a Hispanic category, and this was instrumental in further institutionalizing the notion of panethnicity within the federal government.

Yet, while federal agencies could be directed to collect Hispanic data through a federal mandate, state agencies were under no obligation to follow suit. This was challenging for the Census Bureau because officials relied on the states' vital statistics to estimate undercounts. The resistance was particularly acute in places like New Hampshire and Vermont, where vital statistics offices claimed that there were too few Mexican Americans, Puerto Ricans, or Cuban Americans to justify adding the Hispanic category on birth and death certificate forms.

To resolve the issue, officials turned to their activists and ethnic leaders for help. Activists eagerly complied, understanding that more accurate data could aid them in their lobbying and grant-writing efforts. For example, throughout the 1980s, groups like NCLR wrote to vital statistics agencies across the country to argue that Hispanics were a separate community and should not simply be labeled as racially white or black. By 1993, all fifty states had included some kind of Hispanic category on birth and death certificates.[8]

Post-Nixon executive administrations also helped institutionalize pan-ethnicity by creating offices that expanded on work done by CCOSSP. Gerald Ford created the Office of Hispanic Affairs in 1974.[9] Run by Fernando De Baca, the group continued efforts to lobby federal agencies to funnel resources and grants to Hispanic communities. Subsequently, Jimmy Carter established his own Hispanic affairs office, which instituted a series of Hispanic town hall meetings in the late 1970s.[10] The Reagan and Bush administrations also continued the trend by appointing special assistants to advise them on Hispanic affairs.[11]

Throughout the late 1970s and 1980s, activists met with the staffs of these Hispanic affairs offices regularly, seeking opportunities to both garner resources and increase the executive office's awareness of Hispanic issues. NCLR, for example, appealed to these new offices for resources to fund community projects across the country. Moreover, Spanish-language television often interviewed the members of these agencies for news segments about Hispanic political and social affairs.[12]

In addition, by the mid-1970s, the Republican and Democratic Parties had also continued CCOSSP's work by formally instituting plans to secure more Hispanic votes. Both parties created Hispanic advisory groups, whose function it would be to advise their national committees on the needs and political goals of the Hispanic community. Furthermore, both political parties began working closely with marketers to create Spanish-language advertising that would appeal to Hispanic voters. These efforts became more pronounced after a group of Hispanics who had worked with CCOSSP and for the Nixon administration established their own political marketing agencies.[13] Over time, candidates solidified their links to these Hispanic marketing firms and spent an increasingly larger share of their budgets on courting the Hispanic vote.[14]

In addition, important political figures began attending Hispanic activist conventions, bringing even more national attention to the idea of the Hispanic vote. George H.W. Bush attended NCLR's national convention when he was vice president, and he became the first sitting president to attend the convention in 1990.[15] President Bill Clinton also attended the 1994 convention and spoke about issues like immigration and health-care policy.[16]

During the 1980s, the idea of Hispanic panethnicity also spread rapidly through academia, especially in the social sciences. Soon after 1980 census data were released, social scientists used those and other data to write the first compendiums on the United States' Hispanic population. Notable early works include Joan Moore and Harry Pachon's *Hispanics in the United States* (1985) and Frank Bean and Marta Tienda's seminal text, *The Hispanic Population of the United States* (1987).[17]

Additionally, the influx of Hispanic data spurred the creation of new social science journals. The *Hispanic Journal of Behavioral Science* was established in late 1979, and the *Harvard Journal of Hispanic Policy* was founded in 1986.[18] These journals published articles that focused on specific subgroups alongside articles that analyzed the characteristics of the national, Hispanic community. A single volume on Hispanic education might, for example, deal with the specific challenges facing Mexican Americans while also considering how Hispanic education rates compared with those of non-Hispanic blacks and whites. In bringing together these different areas of research, these journals showcased the diversity within the Hispanic community *and* suggested that Latin American subgroups composed a single, national panethnic group.

Indeed, it was only after the idea of Hispanic panethnicity had been institutionalized as a data category that the Hispanic identity became the object of scientific scrutiny. In 1989, Rodolfo de la Garza and his collaborators developed the Latino National Political Survey, which asked individuals to rank identity labels such as "Mexican," "Hispanic," and "Latino."[19] Others soon began to code panethnic identification within their data sets.[20] Important qualitative studies about panethnicity emerged soon after the 1980 census as well. After interviewing Mexican and Puerto Rican community leaders in Chicago, sociologist Felix Padilla argued that a "Latino panethnic consciousness" was a viable element of a personal, albeit situational, identity that was often employed instrumentally.[21] More critical were researchers like Earl Shorris and Shirley Croucher, who pointed to interethnic antagonisms and the importance of national identity as a way to discredit the new category.[22] Still other academics argued that panethnicity fostered a sense of solidarity arising from a common experience of discrimination and marginality in the United States.[23]

Taken together, these Hispanic/Latino studies helped map out new academic domains. Disciplines ranging from sociology to political science created Latino subfields. Research on Hispanic/Latino panethnicity, as well as works on single ethnic groups, became categorized as "Latino studies," a classification that also became institutionalized in academic programs and departments. By 2000, a typical Latino studies program included courses not only on subgroups such as Chicanos or Puerto Ricans but also on panethnic topics such as Latino literature and Latino migration.[24]

Outside of academia, other civic organizations, including several with ties to NCLR and the Forum of National Hispanic Organizations, had also adopted the notion of panethnicity by the mid-1980s. Bodies that had initially focused on representing specific ethnic groups, like the Mexican American–focused League of United Latin American Citizens (LULAC) and the American GI Forum, eventually changed their mission statements to include panethnic language and began recruiting a panethnic constituency.[25] Some organizations even changed their names to reflect their new panethnic status. For example, in 1994, the Mexican American National Association changed its name to MANA—A National Latina Organization,[26] and in 2008, the Puerto Rican Legal Defense and Education Fund changed its

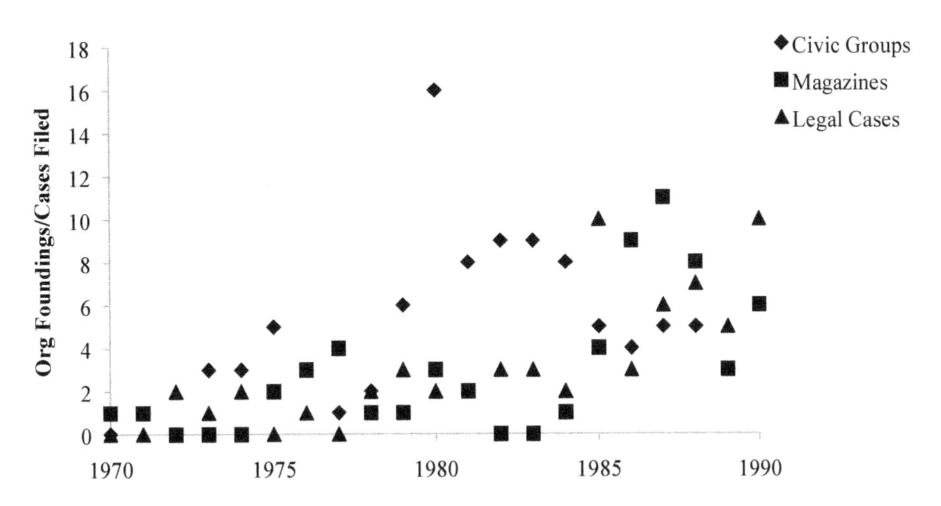

Figure 10.1 Rise of Hispanic civic organizations, magazines, and legal cases, 1970–90 (*Note*: Organizations were coded as panethnic if their names included the terms *Hispanic*, *Latino*, or *Spanish Speaking*, or if they signaled more than one ethnic group in their description. Organizations using the term *Hispanic* to signal persons of Spanish descent [second-plus-generation Spaniards], academic institutes, and government organizations were excluded. All listed, nationally circulating Spanish-language magazines were included in this count, unless the periodical's description or title specifically mentioned a single ethnic group. And finally, all federal and state legal cases that included "Hispanic," "Latino," or "Spanish-speaking" pan-ethnic descriptors were included. Civic organizations data [excluding religious organizations] collected from the *Encyclopedia of Associations, National Organizations* [Detroit: Gale Research Corporation, 1970–90]; magazine data collected from *Standard Periodical Directory* [New York: Oxbridge Communications, 1965–90]; and legal data collected from LexisNexis.)

name to Latino Justice PRLDEF.[27] Many of these activist groups eventually helped institutionalize panethnicity within the legal system as well by filing court cases on behalf of Hispanics/Latinos.

Following the trail blazed by NCLR and state agencies, panethnic professional and nonprofit civic organizations began to emerge during the late 1970s and the 1980s. Examples include the United States Hispanic Chamber of Commerce (established in 1979), the Committee for Hispanic Children and Families (established in 1982), and the National His-panic Bar Association (renamed and reestablished in 1985).

For its part, the media adopted an international strategy to promote panethnicity throughout the 1990s. Univision began exporting its news and entertainment shows to Latin America, where they gained popularity. Univision's *El Show de Cristina* and *Noticiero Univision*, for example, were highly rated in about twenty Latin American countries by 1998.[28] By broadcasting stories about Hispanic families, Hispanic politics, and Hispanic current events, these shows provided Latin Americans with insights into the panethnic world of Latin American immigrants in the United States.[29]

The notion of panethnicity also spread through other forms of mass media. Eduardo Caballero, who had worked for Univision during its initial phase, was an early Spanish-language radio pioneer who brought together stations in the Southwest with those in Miami and New York by shipping songs across the nation. His and other radio stations promoted what the industry eventually labeled the "International" or "Espanol Continental" format, which mixed together music from across Latin America and Spain.[30]

Media entrepreneurs also established magazines with titles like *Hispanic Business* (established in 1979) and *Hispanic Magazine* (established in 1986).[31] The magazines served to further popularize the notion of pan-ethnicity by telling compelling stories about the political, business, and social aspects of the Hispanic community. A typical issue in *Hispanic Magazine*, for example, would include an interview with a Mexican American celebrity, a recipe for a Cuban dish, and an article about Hispanic politics or marketing.[32] Trade magazines like *Hispanic Business* served as synergistic mediums by covering the activities of Spanish-language television and radio as well as the current trends within Hispanic marketing. Such publications thus provided executives with an opportunity to monitor the developments within the broader Hispanic media field.

The accompanying figure examines the founding of Hispanic panethnic civic organizations and the establishment of panethnic magazines. It illustrates how Hispanic magazines and civic organizations grew over time. Moreover, the graph depicts the rise of legal cases filed on behalf of "Hispanic(s)/Latino(s)," demonstrating how the panethnic category expanded to broader discourses. To be sure, there are a considerable number of variables that account for the rise of civic organizations, magazines, and court cases related to Hispanic panethnicity. Nonetheless, the parallel increases in the trends are striking and suggest that the Hispanic panethnic category grew steadily more popular over time.

The rise of panethnicity, however, did not mean that *all* civic organizations and media entities accepted the notion. Some groups, such as the Mexican American Political Association (MAPA) and select Spanish-language radio stations, argued that panethnicity was contrived, an identity imposed on Mexican Americans, Puerto Ricans, Cuban Americans, and others by government bureaucrats and ethnic elites. Some academics supported this argument, noting that individuals overwhelmingly preferred national to panethnic labels. For the most part, though, these were faint voices easily overwhelmed by the growing chorus of organizations that hailed the notion of panethnicity. Indeed, by the 1990s, it was not only the large national political advocacy groups and media organizations that were promoting the idea of a Hispanic culture; an increasing number of small civic and local media organizations were also calling themselves Hispanic. Like the national groups before them, the local civic organizations sought grants and resources to aid the "Hispanic community," and the media organizations developed marketing manuals about Hispanic consumers. Hispanic panethnicity had become a strong narrative that could overpower criticisms precisely because diverse stakeholders bought into its unifying message.

Another category of protesters vigorously disapproved of the "Hispanic" label even though they agreed with the notion of panethnicity more generally. Public commentators and academics argued that the term *Hispanic* was conservative because it seemed to prioritize a cultural attachment to a white, European, specifically Spanish past and thus glossed over the important contributions of indigenous and African peoples within Latin America.[33] Many preferred *Latino* as an alternative way to signify panethnicity.[34] While it was not an ideal term, some argued that *Latino* was the best referent for panethnicity because it less overtly connoted Spain (though I should observe here that the meaning of the *Latino* label itself has remained ambiguous).[35]

Several organizations—including NCLR, the Census Bureau, and Univision—paid attention to the growing debate. The issue of which label and which definition to use had always been a thorny one because narrow categorizations threatened the stability of the relationships among civic and media organizations and federal agencies. Moreover, one label—be it *Spanish-speaking*, *Raza*, *Hispanic*, or *Latino*—never seemed to please everyone. Civic organizations responded to the debate not by taking a firm stance but by referring to a "Hispanic/Latino" panethnicity. Indeed, that *Hispanic* and *Latino* would eventually come to be used interchangeably speaks to the inherent ambiguity of panethnicity itself. The practice of using both terms continues today, although cross-sectional research shows that most persons of Latin American descent have a slight preference for the term *Hispanic*.[36]

Demography and Panethnicity

To be sure, the diffusion of Hispanic panethnicity that occurred in the 1980s was also made possible by Latin American population growth. While national organizations like the Census Bureau, Univision, and NCLR pioneered the effort to define and promote panethnicity in the 1970s, these efforts could have fizzled out were it not for three important demographic processes: the growth of the Hispanic population, the rise of panethnic communities, and the increase in panethnic marriages.

Throughout the 1970s and 1980s, the Hispanic population increased, prompting government, civic, and market organizations to direct more attention to these communities. High fertility rates among Hispanics and an increase in Latin American migration, especially from Mexico, allowed the population to grow substantially during that period. This population increase caught the attention of federal and state agencies, which turned to census reports to make sense of the demographic changes and forge new social policies. Population growth also gave rise to new civic groups, especially professional and political organizations, as well as to commercial media and retail firms that were eager to cater to the burgeoning Hispanic community.

Initially, population growth followed the same historical demographic patterns: Mexicans migrated to the Southwest, while Puerto Ricans and Cubans settled on the East Coast.[37] These two regions became increasingly panethnic as Central and South American migration increased throughout the 1980s.[38] Cities like Miami became home not only to Cuban Americans but also to newly arriving Nicaraguans, Venezuelans, and Argentines.[39] Los Angeles developed vibrant Central American business districts that helped revitalize what were once almost exclusively Mexican American barrios.[40] Also, Puerto Rican mainstays like "Spanish Harlem" became the new home for an increasing number of Dominican immigrants.[41]

The new Latin American migration of the 1980s created panethnic spaces that provided opportunities for subgroups to not only live, shop, and work together,[42] but also to fall in love. Intermarriages between Puerto Ricans and Dominicans in New York and Central Americans and Mexicans in Los Angeles increased significantly, if unevenly, throughout the 1980s.[43] Puerto Ricans and Cuban Americans were much more likely than other Hispanics to marry Latin Americans outside of their subgroup, while Mexican Americans were the least likely. Second-generation immigrants were also more likely to intermarry than were first-generation immigrants.[44]

As panethnic spaces and unions grew, so too did the number of local-level, panethnic civic and market organizations. Community studies on panethnic neighborhoods show that "Latino" and "Hispanic" newspapers, neighborhood groups, religious organizations, and markets emerged in these spaces and catered to the diverse array of Latin American subgroups. Hispanic bodegas in New York, for example, included items from Puerto Rico as well as delicacies from the Dominican Republic and South America.[45] Churches also hosted religious events and services that brought different Latin American subgroups together.[46]

More research is certainly needed to untangle the relationship between demography and the rise of local-level panethnic organizations. Were these organizations significantly more likely to emerge in panethnic spaces? What role did local labor market trends and connections to national panethnic bodies play in facilitating the emergence of these organizations? Were these local-level panethnic organizations more likely to emerge in places where Latin American subgroups experienced occupational segregation?[47] Regardless, what is certain is that the panethnic claims advanced by national market and political organizations provided a Hispanic category that could subsequently be adopted by those in pan-ethnic neighborhoods during the 1980s.

In effect, the developments throughout the 1970s and 1980s created a completely new context for the Latin American diaspora, which continues today. A young Mexican American currently has several panethnic options that were unavailable to her three decades ago. She can join a variety of Hispanic-labeled civic clubs and organizations, tune in and watch Hispanic television programming, listen to bands on Hispanic/Latino radio stations, visit panethnic neighborhoods, and take part in Hispanic marketing and social science surveys. Her birth certificate, school forms, and driver's license will likely identify her as Hispanic. If she chooses to go to college, she can apply for Hispanic scholarships, take courses in Latino studies, and, eventually, she can be hired as a Hispanic marketing specialist, a Hispanic data analyst, or a Hispanic political analyst.[48] Now more than ever, the idea of Hispanic panethnicity has become part of the American cultural fabric.

Hispanic Categorization, Identification, and Politics

As this book went to press, the US Census Bureau announced that it would consider revamping its race question to include Hispanic as an option alongside race categories. The new question would read: "What is your Origin or Race?" Respondents would then be able to choose from options including

Black, Hispanic/Latino, White, Indian, and several Asian nationalities. In a press conference about the proposed new question, the bureau's spokespersons noted that the agency was considering the change because it needed a better way to classify the vast number of Hispanic respondents who had rejected the conventional white, black, and Asian race categories on the last enumeration. These respondents had instead simply checked the "Some Other Race" box and had written in a Latin American country of origin or "Hispanic" or "Latino" on the race question.[49] A final decision will not be made for some time, giving the bureau several years to test different versions of a new racial category.

The decision on whether to change the race question will be consequential for the way that Latino identities are perceived. The two-question format used in the 2010 decennial census asked individuals first to identify if they were of Hispanic/Latino origin and then to choose a race option from categories that included white, black, Asian, and Native American. This formulation implies that persons of Latin American descent can somehow be sorted out among the established race categories. By not providing a Hispanic/Latino racial option, the formulation dismisses the Latino "racialization" thesis, which contends that Latino identities are durable and shape life chances because they signal a nonwhite, racial minority status in the United States.[50] Instead, the census formulation seems to imply that persons of Latin American descent are in fact racially white (or in some cases black or Native American) and that Latino identities, whether they be panethnic or national, are, like European American identities, ephemeral, lasting only a generation or so.[51]

A new combined question would not only help lend credence to the idea that Latinidad/Hispanidad is a durable racial identity that shapes an individual's life chances in meaningful and lasting ways, but it would also better accord with more recent studies on the issue. Indeed, census researchers have found that a significant number of persons of Latin American descent (sometimes more than half) believe that the traditional census categories of white, black, Native American, and Asian do not apply to them,[52] and most recently, in 2006, a national, comprehensive survey on Latino attitudes found that over 50 percent of persons of Latin American descent answered "yes" to a query about whether Hispanics/Latinos composed a distinct racial group.[53] With a combined question, these individuals could simply check the Hispanic/Latino box and move on without having to stumble over a separate race query.

The idea that Hispanics/Latinos might compose a race points as much to the larger issue of racial inequality as to the preference for a particular identity. When we see Hispanics/Latinos as a racial group, we can understand them as a distinct minority yet to reach socioeconomic parity with whites. This perception is not without supporting evidence. Overall, Latinos/Hispanics suffer high poverty rates and low educational attainment rates, they experience high rates of racial profiling, and they are disproportionately represented in the American penal population. Moreover, there is no question that many persons of Latin American descent, whether they are immigrants or not, continue to be stigmatized by a discourse that depicts them as "alien" foreigners in the American landscape.[54]

At the same time, any move toward a racial understanding of His-panic/Latino identity should proceed with caution because it could lead to incorrectly framing Hispanics as a homogenous community with little internal variation. Many, though certainly not all, Cuban Americans consider themselves white, have higher levels of social mobility than other groups, and intermarry with whites more frequently. This contrasts starkly with the experiences of, to take one group, Mexican Americans, who are poorer, less educated, and less likely than other subgroups to marry whites.[55] The issue becomes more complicated when we consider research that finds that Afro-Latinos have a particularly different experience of Latinidad from that of their lighter-skinned counterparts.[56]

The uncertainty and caution surrounding the Hispanic/Latino race issue is ultimately a reflection of how ambiguity upholds the notion of panethnicity in the first place. In attempting to bring such a diverse array of peoples together, the Hispanic category by design resists tight definition. Its broadness gives it strength because it refers to a wide variety of understandings and can thus be molded to conform to different organizational goals and to encompass an assortment of different groups. However, this very flexibility also makes the category's contours difficult to discern at times. Policy makers, census officials, and ethnic leaders would be wise to balance issues of internal diversity with the impulse to cast the category too broadly.

In conclusion, it is important to consider what the history related in this book means for identity politics. That my study reveals the web of interests and organizations that helped to institutionalize the Hispanic category over time does not necessarily mean that panethnicity is somehow untrue or false. All identities are social constructs, and none are completely accepted by every member of a given group. Nation-states had to forge national identities at one point, just as ethnic and racial group leaders have had to do for ethnicity and race, respectively. There are no true or false identities, for each is the product of a sociohistorical process.

In fact, the idea of Hispanic panethnicity is much more popular now than it ever has been. Survey research tells us that Mexican Americans, Puerto Ricans, and Cuban Americans, not to mention Central and South Americans, are more apt to identify with Hispanic and Latino labels today.[57] Whether or not this identity category was widespread in the late 1960s is inconsequential to many who feel that it adequately represents their community now.

Ultimately, Hispanic panethnicity has become a salient form of collective identification in America. This is true despite the fact that organizations frame Hispanic/Latino panethnicity in various ways, and despite the fact that the category still seems ambiguous to many. We should be cautious of any statements that depict Hispanics as a homogenous community with little internal variation. At the same time, however, we should not dismiss the social currents that are attempting to unify subgroups and the potential impact that Latino/Hispanic solidarity can have on American institutions. The challenge for Hispanic/Latino organizations will be to honor their community's differences while emphasizing that community's similarities. The task will be delicate and difficult, but the outcome will certainly affect the American political landscape and change our discussion about race and ethnicity for generations to come.

Notes

1. Emilio Nicolás (SICC vice president, 1962–86), interview by G. Cristina Mora, March 9, 2011.

2. "SIN Pays," *Advertising Age*, April 6, 1981, S17.

3. Peter Berger, *The Sacred Canopy: Elements of a Sociological Theory of Religion* (New York: Anchor Books, 1967).

4. See Mary Douglas, *Purity and Danger: An Analysis of the Concepts of Pollution and Taboo* (New York: Routledge Press, 1966); and Dror Etzion and Fabrizio Ferraro, "The Role of Analogy in the Institutionalization of Sustainability Reporting," *Organization Science* 21, no. 5 (2010): 1092–1110.

5. Armando Rendon, "WE ..." (Suitland, MD: Bureau of the Census, April 1995), 4.

6. "Hispanic Corporate Partnerships: Some Observations and Examples," p. 4, speech delivered by Raul Yzaguirreto the First Corporate/Hispanic Partnership Summit, October 23, 1982, Sheraton Place, San Francisco, NCLR Records, record group 6, series 2, box 11, folder 38.

7. Benedict Anderson, *Imagined Communities: Reflections on the Origins and Spread of Nationalism* (London: Verso, 2006).

8. To be clear, this shift was likely due to a variety of factors, including the desire to mimic other states and pressure from federal agencies such as the National Center for Health Statistics. Activist lobbying efforts, then, were only one part of the shift. See National Center for Health Statistics, "US Vital Statistics System: Major Activities and Developments, 1950–1995," PHS 97-1003 (Hyattsville, MD: Department of Health and Human Services, 1997).

9. See "Briefing Outline," Office of Hispanic Affairs, May 15, 1975, Marrs Files, 1974–76, box 26, "Spanish Speaking People" folder, Ford Library.

10. José de la Isla, *The Rise of Hispanic Political Power* (Santa Maria, CA: Archer Books, 2003).

11. Ibid.

12. Interview with Emilio Nicolás Jr. (SICC/SIN/Univision executive, 1975–89), interview by G. Cristina Mora, March 9, 2011.

13. See chap. 1 in this book.

14. See Arlene Davila, *Latinos Inc.: The Marketing and Making of a People* (Berkeley: University of California Press, 2001); Marissa Abrajano, *Campaigning to the New American Electorate: Advertising to Latino Voters* (Palo Alto, CA: Stanford University Press, 2010); de la Isla, *Rise of Hispanic Political Power.*

15. Michael McQueen, "Republicans Persevere in Their Uphill Campaign to Woo and Win a Bigger Slice of the Hispanic Vote," *Wall Street Journal*, August 10, 1990, A12; and NCLR, "Holding Firm to

Principles," NCLR website, accessed January 13, 2013, http://www.nclr.org/index.php/about_us/history/holding_firm_to_principles/.

16. Paul Richter, "Clinton Pitches His Health Care Plan to Latinos: Reform: President Speaks to La Raza at Miami Meeting," *Los Angeles Times*, July 19, 1994, A14; Michael Wines, "The Health Care Debate: Clinton, on the Stump, Opens a Final Health Care Push," *New York Times*, July 16, 1994, 1.9; and David Rogers, "Conservatives Seek Wider Tax Breaks Tied to Health Care," *Wall Street Journal*, July 19, 1994, A2.

17. See Joan Moore and Harry Pachon, *Hispanics in the United States* (Englewood Cliffs, NJ: Prentice-Hall, 1985); and Frank D. Bean and Marta Tienda, *The Hispanic Population of the United States* (New York: Russell Sage Foundation, 1987).

18. See Henry Ramos, Kennedy School of Government, to Raul Yzaguirre, April 16, 1984, NCLR Records, record group 2, series 2, box 11.3, folder 3, Department of Special Collections, Stanford University Libraries, Stanford University.

19. Michael Jones-Correa and David Leal, "Becoming 'Hispanic': Secondary Panethnic Identification among Latin American Origin Groups," *Hispanic Journal of Behavioral and Social Sciences* 18, no. 2 (1996): 214–54.

20. Alejandro Portes and Dag MacLeod, "What Shall I Call Myself? Hispanic Identity Formation in the Second Generation," *Ethnic and Racial Studies* 19 (1996): 523–47; and John Itzigsohn and Carlos Dore-Cabral, "Competing Identities? Race, Ethnicity and Panethnicity among Dominicans in the United States," *Sociological Forum* 15, no. 2 (2000): 225–47.

21. Felix Padilla, *Latino Ethnic Consciousness: The Case of Mexican Americans and Puerto Ricans in Chicago* (South Bend, IN: University of Notre Dame Press, 1985).

22. Earl Shorris, "Latinos: The Complexity of Identity," *NACLA: Report on the Americas* 26, no. 2 (1992): 19–26; and Sheila L. Croucher, *Imagining Miami: Ethnic Politics in a Postmodern World* (Charlottesville: University of Virginia Press, 1997).

23. Suzanne Oboler, *Ethnic Labels, Latino Lives: Identity and the Politics of (Re)Presentation in the United States* (Minneapolis: University of Minnesota Press, 1995).

24. See Juan Flores, "Latino Studies: New Contexts, New Concepts," *Harvard Educational Review* 67, no. 2 (1993): 208–21.

25. Herman Badillo (cofounder of PRLDEF [Puerto Rican Legal Defense and Education Fund], 1972), interview by G. Cristina Mora, March 25, 2010; Benjamin Marquez, *LULAC: The Evolution of a Mexican American Political Organization* (Austin: University of Texas Press, 1993); and Craig A. Kaplowitz, *LULAC, Mexican Americans, and National Policy* (College Station: Texas A&M University Press, 2005).

26. See MANA—A National Latina Organization website, accessed February 23, 2013, http://www.hermana.org/frequently-asked-questions-faqs.

27. See PRLDEF, Latino Justice website, accessed December 5, 2012, http://latinojustice.org/about/history_2000s/.

28. America Rodriguez, *Making Latino News: Race, Language, Class* (Thousand Oaks, CA: Sage Publications, 1999); see also Cristina Saralegui, *Cristina: Confidencias de Una Rubia* (New York: Warner Books, 1998).

29. The efforts of Univision were ultimately reinforced by transnational migration. Indeed, as US immigrants took trips back to their countries of origins, they explained their Hispanic identity to others. Thus, a Domini-can immigrant to the Untied States could return to his hometown on yearly visits and speak about panethnicity, teaching his family there about a new identity. At the same time, however, the people in the Dominican Republic could tune into Univision programming and watch the Hispanic shows that were imported from the United States. See Wendy Roth, "Latino before the World: The Transnational Extension of Panethnicity," *Ethnic and Racial Studies*, 32, no. 6 (2009): 927–47; and Wendy Roth, *Race Migrations: Latinos and the Cultural Transformation of Race* (Palo Alto, CA: Stanford University Press, 2012).

30. Eduardo Caballero (former SIN executive, 1967–72, founder of Caballero Spanish Media), interview by G. Cristina Mora, November 14, 2007. See also Joel Russell, "Media Deal of the Year," *Hispanic Business*, December 1995, 24–30.

31. Isabel M. Valdes, *Marketing to American Latinos: A Guide to the In-Culture Approach* (Ithaca, NY: Paramount Market Publishing, 2002); and Angharad Valdivia, *Latina/os and the Media* (New York: Polity Press, 2010).

32. John Garcia, *The Success of "Hispanic" Magazine: A Publishing Success Story* (New York: Walker, 1996).

33. For early critics of the notion of panethnicity, see David E. Hayes-Bautista, "Identifying Hispanic Populations: The Influence of Research Methodology on Public Policy," *American Journal of Public Health* 70, no. 4 (1980): 353–56; and Martha E. Gimenez, "Latino/Hispanic—Who Needs a Name? The Case against a Standardized Terminology," *International Journal of Health Services* 19 (1989): 557–71. For the roles of indigenous and African communities, see David Gonzalez, "What's the Problem with Hispanic? Just Ask a Latino," *New York Times*, November 15, 1992, A.6.

34. See Frank De Olmo, "Latino Si, Hispanic No," *Los Angeles Times*, October 24, 1985, C9. See also a retrospective piece on the issue, Darryl Fears, "Latinos or Hispanics? A Debate about Identity," *Washington Post*, August 25, 2003, A01.

35. Edward Murguia, "On Latino/Hispanic Ethnic Identity," *Latino Studies Journal* 2, no. 3 (1991): 8–18.

36. See Paul Taylor, Mark Hugo Lopez, Jessica Hamar Martinez, and Gabriel Valasco, *When Labels Don't Fit: Hispanics and Their Views of Identity* (Washington, DC: Pew Hispanic Research Center, 2012), 10.

37. Bean and Tienda, *Hispanic Population of the United States.*

38. Laird Bergad and Herbert Klein, *Hispanics in the United States: A Demographic, Social, and Economic History, 1980–2005* (Cambridge: Cambridge University Press, 2010).

39. Alejandro Portes and Alex Stepick, *City on the Edge: The Transformation of Miami* (Berkeley: University of California Press, 1994); and Guillermo Grenier and Alex Stepick, introduction to *Miami Now! Immigration, Ethnicity and Social Change*, ed. Guillermo Grenier and Alex Stepick, 1–18 (Gainesville: University Press of Florida, 1992).

40. See Roger Waldinger and Mehdi Bozorgmehr, *Ethnic Los Angeles* (New York: Russell Sage Foundation, 1996).

41. See Roger Waldinger, *Still the Promised City? New Immigrants and African Americans in Post-industrial New York* (Cambridge, MA: Harvard University Press, 1996).

42. There were small areas that had been panethnic since the late 1960s. Padilla, for example, describes sections of west Chicago as home to both Mexican American and Puerto Rican residents. Nonetheless, panethnic spaces became more pronounced with the increase in Central and South American as well as Dominican migration throughout the 1980s. See Padilla, *Latino Ethnic Consciousness.*

43. Milagros Ricourt and Ruby Danta, *Hispanas de Queens: Panethnicity in a New York City Neighborhood* (Ithaca, NY: Cornell University Press, 2002); and Michael Rosenfeld, "The Salience of Pan-national Hispanic and Asian Identities in U.S. Marriage Markets," *Demography* 38, no. 2 (2001): 161–75.

44. Much more research on interethnic marriage patterns is needed. We do not know, for example, what role location or time period might have played in who married whom. We might imagine, for example, that Mexican Americans in 1970s Chicago were more likely to marry interethnically (presumably because of the larger proportion of non-Mexican Hispanics living there at the time) than were their counterparts in Los Angeles. See Bergad and Klein, *Hispanics in the United States*, for an assessment of the broader, national trends in intermarriage.

45. Ricourt and Danta, *Hispanas de Queens.*

46. Ibid. See also Ana Maria Diaz-Stevens, "From Puerto Rican to Hispanic: The Politics of the Fiestas Patronales in New York," *Latino Studies Journal* 1, no. 1 (1990): 28–47.

47. Work on the rise of Asian American civic organizations suggests that variables on occupational segregation and competition are important indicators of panethnic organizing. See Dina Okamoto, "Institutional Panethnicity: Boundary Formation in Asian American Organizing," *Social Forces* 85, no. 1 (2006): 1–25.

48. Of course, much more research is needed to understand the parameters of Hispanic self-identification. There might be a self-selection process at work here, or it may be that these organizations help to foster more identification. Future studies that examine correlations between media consumption and panethnic identification, or organizational participation and identification, may help clarify these issues.

49. See NWX–US Department of Commerce, "Results of the 2010 Census Race and Hispanic Origin Alternative Questionnaire Experiment News Conference," George Washington University, August 8, 2012, 18.

50. See Edward Telles and Vilma Ortiz, *Generations of Exclusion: Mexican Americans, Assimilation, and Race* (New York: Russell Sage Foundation, 2008).

51. See Richard Alba and Tariqul Islam, "The Case of the Disappearing Mexican Americans: An Ethnic-Identity Mystery," *Population Research and Policy Review* 28, no. 2 (April 2009): 109–21; see also Peter Skerry, *Mexican Americans: The Ambivalent Minority* (Cambridge, MA: Harvard University Press, 1995).

52. See NWX–US Department of Commerce, "Results of the 2010 Census Race and Hispanic Origin Alternative Questionnaire Experiment."

53. This is not meant to discount, however, that a high percentage (upward of 30 percent and sometimes as high as 60 percent, depending on the form and the way that the question is phrased) do consider themselves to be racially white. Yet some of this might also have to do with expectations. Following historical precedent, many Latinos might choose the white racial option on census forms simply because they know that the bureau will often recategorize them as such. Respondents might not have this expectation, however, when filling out surveys or other noncensus forms that directly ask respondents whether Latinos are a distinct race. Nonetheless, more research is needed to clarify the issue further. See Luis R. Fraga, John A. Garcia, Rodney E. Hero, Michael Jones-Correa, Valerie Martinez-Ebers, and Gary M. Segura, *Latinos in the New Millennium: An Almanac of Opinion, Behavior and Policy Preferences* (New York: Cambridge University Press, 2012). See also Luis Ricardo Fraga, John A. Garcia, Rodney E. Hero, Michael Jones-Correa, Valerie Martinez-Ebers, and Gary M. Segura, *Latino Lives in America: Making It Home* (Philadelphia: Temple University Press, 2009); and Taylor et al., *When Labels Don't Fit.*

54. Leo Chavez, *The Latino Threat: Constructing Immigrants, Citizens, and the Nation* (Palo Alto, CA: Stanford University Press, 2008); and Nicholas DeGenova, "Introduction: Latino and Asian Racial Formations at the Frontiers of US Nationalism," in *Racial Transformations: Latinos and Asians Remaking the United States*, ed. Nicholas DeGenova, 1–22 (Durham, NC: Duke University Press, 2006).

55. Bergad and Klein, *Hispanics in the United States.*

56. See Nancy Denton and Douglas Massey, "Racial Identity among Caribbean Hispanics: The Effect of Double Minority Status on Residential Segregation," *American Sociological Review* 5, no. 5 (1989): 790–808; Tanya Hernandez, "Too Black to Be Latino/a: Blackness and Blacks as Foreigners in Latino Studies," *Latino Studies* 1, no. 1 (2003): 152–59; and Alison Newby and Julie Dowling, "Black and Hispanic: The Racial Identification of Afro-Cuban Immigrants in the Southwest," *Sociological Perspectives* 50, no. 3 (2007): 343–66.

57. Fraga et al., *Latinos in the New Millennium.*

CHAPTER 5

Arab and Muslim Americans: Brief Historical Perspectives

READING 11

Arabs and Muslims

Introduction

By Hamdi Elnuzahi

Arabs and Muslims immigrated to the United States as a result of encouragement from U.S.-funded missionary programs in the Middle East in the 19th century (Haddad, 2011). Two-thirds of Arab Americans in 2000 came from Lebanon, Syria, Egypt, and Palestine. Today they are among the most rapidly growing population in the United States. The professional-preference clauses within the 1965 Immigration and Naturalization Act increased immigration among both Muslims and Arabs. Arabs are an ethnic group, but Muslims are a religious group. Islam is a faith like Christianity, and the Arabic language is the single most unifying force among Arabs. Most American converts are from the African-American community.

On September 11, 2001, the terrorist attacks on the United States by Arabs and Muslims disconfirmed the Muslim communities in the following ways. Disconfirmation refers to communication patterns that devalue people like the Arabs and Muslims as American citizens (Floyd, 2016). The racist concept that all Muslims are terrorists negatively impacted all Muslims. As a result, people and institutions, such as schools, workplaces, and airports began to stereotype Muslims, leading to racial profiling. The negative feelings towards Muslims and their religion Islam is called Islamophobia. It is characterized by harassment, hate crimes and violence against Muslims. In response to the September 11, 2001 attacks, the U.S. Congress moved quickly to pass legislation to strengthen security controls. As a result, the Department of Homeland Security was created to coordinate domestic anti-terrorism efforts. Also, the USA Patriot Act (Uniting and Strengthening America by Providing Appropriate Tools Required to Intercept and Obstruct Terrorism Act of 2001) was passed to intercept and prevent terrorist attacks (Cainkar, 2009).

However, the contributions of Muslim communities were confirmed by President George W. Bush's speech: "Muslims make an incredibly valuable contribution to our country. Muslims are doctors, lawyers, law professors, members of the military, entrepreneurs, shopkeepers, moms and dads," he said at the Islamic Center of Washington on September 17, 2001. The words of President Bush recognized and acknowledged the contributions of all Muslims.

The video clip about Ms. Dalia Mogahed's powerful talk summarizes the disconfirmation and confirmation process that Muslims are experiencing during these polarizing times. According to Ms. Mogahed, "Muslims are like the canaries in the coal mines: We may be the first to feel the danger, but the toxic air will affect us all." She advises individuals and institutions to choose empathy over prejudice and discrimination against Arabs and Muslims.

References

Cainkar, Louis A. 2009. *Homeland Insecurity: The Arab American and Muslim American Experience after 9/11.* New York: Russell Sage Foundation.

Floyd, Kory. 2016. *Interpersonal Communication.* 3rd edition. New York: McGraw-Hill.

Haddad, Yvonne Yazbeck. 2011. *Becoming American? The Forging of Arab and Muslim Identity in Pluralist America.* Waco, Texas: Baylor University Press.

Mogahed, Dalia. 2016. "What It's Like to be Muslim in America." Ted Talks. https://www.ted.com/talks/dalia_mogahed_what_do_you_think_when_you_look_at_me

The speech President George W. Bush speech (September 17, 2001) gave at the Islamic Center of Washington D.C.

READING 12

Muslim in America

A trip to two of the most Islamic cities in the U.S.

By Shikha Dalmia

If Southeast Michigan's claim to fame is that it's the auto capital of America, its claim to notoriety—in certain circles, anyway—is that it's the Arab and Islamic capital too. Around 300,000 Muslims live in the area. Muslims make up less than 2 percent of the nation's population but more than 40 percent of two cities in the Metro Detroit region, Hamtramck and Dearborn.

The former, a 2-square-mile town of less than 30,000 people, triggered a national freak-out last November when it elected a 4-2 Muslim majority to its City Council. The punditocracy's lead Muslim-baiter, Pamela Geller, instantly predicted Shariah, terrorism, and persecution of Jews in Hamtramck's future. A Texas Republican councilman, Micky Garus, earnestly declared that the "end of Western civilization" was nigh.

There was a similar outcry in 2013, when Dearborn elected four Arab Americans, two of them Muslim, to its City Council. The Family Research Council's Jerry Boykin quickly claimed that radical Muslims had made Dearborn off-limits to Detroit police. Dearborn was, in fact, already outside the jurisdiction of Detroit police—not because of Muslim machinations but because Dearborn is not part of Detroit. The accusation prefigured former Louisiana Gov. Bobby Jindal's imaginary no-go zones in Europe, especially France, where central authorities have allegedly lost political control to local Muslims who allegedly shoo away all nonmembers of the faith.

It isn't just fringy sorts like Geller and Boykin who worry about Islamic assimilation. Mainstream center-right scholars such as National Review Institute's Andrew C. McCarthy and, to a lesser extent, center-left ones such as the Brookings Institution's Peter Skerry have similar concerns, albeit typically expressed in more temperate language.

The standard rap against Muslims is that they are fundamentally incapable of embracing liberal democratic values because Shariah—Islamic religious law—rejects the separation of religion and state and imposes regressive sexual norms, especially on women. Therefore, the argument goes, towns like Hamtramck and Dearborn will always be in tension with American values, incubating terrorists in the middle of the United States. In this view, Dearborn will become another Molenbeek, the Belgian city where many jihadi attacks have been hatched, including the recent ones in Brussels and Paris.

But if you set aside the lens of Molenbeek and look at life as it is actually lived in Hamtramck and Dearborn, an entirely different picture emerges. Molenbeek is the second-poorest borough in Brussels. It has been caught in a downward spiral of poor education, high crime, and nonexistent social mobility. In 2014, 27 percent of Molenbeek's working-age population, close to 50 percent of which is Muslim, was unemployed. The opposite cycle is unfolding in Hamtramck and Dearborn even though, remarkably enough, they are ensconced right next to Detroit, the closest thing to Molenbeek's depressive economy in America.

I have lived in Metro Detroit for 27 years, about 20 miles from both of these towns. Since December 2015, I have visited them dozens of times and talked to scores of people-politicians, reporters, shopkeepers, academics, imams. Both are vibrant, diverse, and hopeful communities with populations that, like Muslims across the country, seem fairly happy with life in the United States. (A 2011 Pew poll found that 56 percent of Muslim Americans were satisfied with the way things were going in the country, compared to 23 percent of the general public.) The Muslims of Dearborn and Hamtramck are indeed increasing their participation in political life, but that isn't a plot to turn the towns into little Shariahvilles—it's an effort to assimilate into American life.

Michigan's Muslim communities certainly have their troubles, but they aren't the insidious, subversive forces that Islamophobes imagine. They face the challenges of a community gradually adjusting to American life, generally successfully but with inevitable bumps in the road. Yes, Muslim attitudes on gay rights and censorship of religious speech are out of step with America's prevailing ethos of freedom. But they are no more heterodox than many minority populations before them, and those differences are hardly something a strong liberal polity can't handle.

Muslims in Dearborn and Hamtramck are increasing their political participation, but that isn't a plot to turn the towns into little Shariahvilles—it's an effort to assimilate.

A Tale of Two Cities

According to Sally Howell, a professor of Arab-American studies at the University of Michigan and the author of several books on Detroit's Arabs, Muslims in Hamtramck and Dearborn are assimilating very nicely. The median income of Detroit's Arab households, about half of whom are Muslim, is $31,700—on par with the region's median income of $32,824. Howell's 2003 Detroit Arab Americans Survey found that 25 percent of the area's Arabs report annual family incomes of $100,000 or more, compared to 16 percent of the general population. Among American-born Arabs (including Iraqi Christian Chaldeans), 94 percent have high school diplomas, 7 percent more than the general public. Identical percentages of both groups have college degrees, and over 31 percent of Arab Americans are self-employed, twice the figure for the general population.

And only 30 percent of Detroit's Arab Muslims go to mosque every month, compared to 66 percent of Arab Christians who attend church that often. Just 18 percent of the area's Muslims were active in their mosques, far less than the 47 percent of Arab Christians who were active in their churches. This is not what an incubator of zealotry looks like.

None of this means that terrorists could never sprout in the Metro Detroit Muslim community, any more than school shooters can't emerge from lily-white neighborhoods. But viewing them as uniquely problematic is unfair both to them and to America's assimilative capacity.

There are important differences between the two towns. Hamtramck's 11,000-strong Muslim population dates back only about two decades, and it consists of everyone from blue-eyed, light-skinned Bosnians to swarthy Bangladeshis. By contrast, Dearborn's community has 100-year-old roots and hails predominantly from the Middle East. Its Muslim population is almost three times bigger than Hamtramck's—more if you count Dearborn Heights, its companion city.

Because the Hamtramck community is newer, it has an air of innocence, as if it hasn't fully comprehended how much post-9/11 hostility there is toward Muslims in America. Its politics are primarily driven by economic security and ties to the old world. Dearborn's community is more settled, savvy, and middle-class, and it is acutely aware of the harsh national Klieg lights pointed at it. Its political participation is a complicated coping dance motivated not just by its economic interests but also the need to cooperate with anti-terrorism efforts without ceding civil or religious rights.

These two towns, 10 miles apart, give us snapshots of two points in the arc of Muslim assimilation in America.

Hamtramck

Thanks to Hamtramck's ridiculously low cost of living, it has long been a landing pad for new immigrants: Germans at the end of the 19th century, Poles three decades later, then other waves of Eastern Europeans and, since 1995, Muslims. No one visiting Hamtramck now can miss the strong Islamic imprint, given how dramatically the Muslim presence has altered the city's public spaces.

In the 1990s, Hamtramck embraced the New Urbanist approach to city planning, with mixed-use zoning and pedestrian-friendly design. By encouraging residents to walk more, planners pulled the new arrivals' customs outdoors, unintentionally making the Muslim presence more visible. It's almost impossible to cruise down Joseph Campau Road and Caniff Street, the city's two main drags, without seeing women pushing carts to grocery stores draped either in hijabs—headscarves—or in burqas, the head-to-toe black shroud that parts only at the eyes. Men with keffiyehs linger outside the kebab joints that flourish where Polish restaurants once stood. Muslim moms, children in tow, can be seen walking to the blingy Bangladeshi dress stores that have been elbowing out staid Polish boutiques.

There are about 35 bars in Hamtramck. That may sound like a lot, but there were 200 before Muslims started displacing Poles. Some of the former bars have been converted into mosques such as the Masjid Al-Iman Al-Ghazalli on Joseph Campau Street. They look like the poor cousins of Hamtramck's grand churches, especially the tall and majestic St. Florian that looms over the town. But what the mosques lack in grandness, they make up for in loudness when they blare the muezzin's summons ("Allah Hu Akbar") five times a day.

When the public call to prayer first came to Hamtramck in 2004, it became a flashpoint in the nation's culture wars—even bigger than the election that made the City Council majority-Muslim. Coverage of the vocal protests made it look like Hamtramck had become a cauldron of ethnic conflict. *Fox & Friends'* Pete Hegseth performed a typical hit job, finding an obligatory Polish American to say on camera that Muslims aren't "ready for Western culture yet."

The segment was neither the only nor the first to offer that kind of spin. Drive-by reporters come to the city, observe its altered appearance, ask loaded questions about tensions between Muslims and Poles, find out that one Muslim City Council member commented after getting elected, "now we'll show these Polish people," and dash out a piece confirming the narrative of ethnic tensions. (That comment, which every other Muslim council member condemned immediately, was a dig at a Polish opponent for making his religion an issue during the campaign.)

But Hamtramck's mayor, Karen Majewski, maintains that this narrative is profoundly misleading. For starters, she says, most of the people protesting the muezzin's call weren't locals but Christian fundamentalists sent from neighboring towns, some in Ohio. Greg Kowalski, a retired editor of the local Observer & Eccentric newspaper chain, confirms the same. Indeed, he says he was contacted by Christian attorneys in Chicago offering their services pro *bono* to stop the call. But Majewski insists the protesters didn't understand that the call was constitutionally protected speech; the council couldn't ban it any more than it could cut off the church bells that ring every hour. The council meeting that became the focus of protests was in fact never about banning the call; the aim was just to regulate its volume and timing.

Twelve years later, the call has become such a normal—even soothing—part of Hamtramck's auditory background that only visitors notice it anymore.

If anything, says Kowalski, a lifelong Hamtramck resident, Muslims have been far less aggressive in remaking the city compared to earlier European immigrants. The retiree, who volunteers at the Hamtramck Historical Museum, believes the current transition is far less contentious than the early-20th century conflict between the new Polish arrivals and the previously dominant Germans.

The two groups already had some bad blood between them from the old country. Germans, who outnumbered Poles 10-1 in 1900, pulled every trick in the book to prevent the Polish from gaining power, including stopping voting at 4 p.m., one hour before the Polish factory workers got off. They also held citywide elections for City Council rather than electing representatives by district—a system that still persists—to prevent Pole-heavy neighborhoods from getting a foothold in the local government.

Nothing that Hamtramck's Muslims have done to the city's 20-plus ethnic groups is nearly as nasty. The animosities within the Islamic community are probably fiercer than the divisions between Muslims and everyone else. East-Asian Bangladeshi Muslims (20 percent of Hamtramck's population) don't have much in common with Middle Eastern Yemeni Muslims (also 20 percent), who don't have much in common with European Bosnian Muslims (7 percent) and so on. Over the past two decades, strong disagreements between these groups, but also within them, have broken out. For example, various Bangladeshi factions, who tend to be the most politically active group, fought so hard over whose favorite icon from back home should be used when picking honorary names for streets that the whole project had to be dropped. If Hamtramck's politics show anything, it is the crudeness of viewing Muslims as a monolith whose religious identity trumps its linguistic, cultural, political, and economic interests.

Unlike the Germans and Poles before them, the city's Muslim council members don't appear to have any unified goal, religious or otherwise. They seem to disagree as much among themselves as other council members over city spending, what to do about vacant storefronts, road repairs, and how to attract new business to the city.

A council seat is a part-time position that pays only $3,000 a year—hardly a road to riches. But it's attractive as a stepping-stone to higher political office or higher status.

Consider Councilman Anam Miah, a likable first-generation Bangladeshi Muslim whose wife is African-American, He has a teenage son and a college-age daughter; the latter, dressed in tight jeans and a sweatshirt, was helping repaint her late grandfather's old house when I met them. Miah works at Flexible Products, an auto supplier in a ritzy Detroit suburb, where he is also president of the local United Steelworkers chapter. He is active in Michigan Democratic politics and clearly hopes to make a bid for state office someday. He is a practicing Muslim, but Shariah law doesn't mean much to him. "I don't understand or accept it," he says. "You don't have to practice Shariah to be a Muslim."

Status seems to be the motivating factor for 28-year-old Councilman Saad Almasmari, who came to America from Yemen in 2009, learned English by 2011, became naturalized in 2012, and obtained the most votes of any of the candidates last year. Since immigrating, he also got married, had three children, and opened an ice cream business. He sought his seat to signal to his family back in Yemen that he had truly arrived: "It shows them that I have everything in America."

The diverse political motivations and interests of the Muslim council members make it difficult for them to come together as a block, notes Kowalski. It also makes them similar to local politicians everywhere. One of the few times they did unite was over a barnyard animal ordinance two years ago. A burgeoning urban farm movement pushed the council to allow small barnyard animals in backyards. But this threatened local Muslim merchants, who control the live chicken business in town. They successfully lobbied some of the Muslim council members to make an exception in the final bill. The upshot is that people can now keep rabbits, ducks, and pigeons—but chickens are a no-no.

"You can tie [that debate] to religion if you want," mused Majewski when queried about the incident. "But it's really got more to do with internal Hamtramck politics." In other words, the grandest Muslim conspiracy in Hamtramck aimed to advance not Shariah law but old-fashioned low-stakes crony capitalism.

Hamtramck's diversity is the stuff of multi-culti dreams. Nearly 30 languages are spoken in Hamtramck's schools and each street is a mélange of different ethnicities and nationalities. (Besides Germans and Poles, the town is home to Ukrainians, Bosnians, Mexicans, Albanians, Indians, and more.) Down the block from Miah's house sits the Queen of Apostles Church. Right next door is a K-8 charter academy that advertises halal meals. Miah's neighbor is a Baptist minister, and across from him is a Polish guy who has lived there for six decades.

Hamtramck is poor—at least 50 percent of its population consists of recent immigrants who work in trucking, cabbing, or house cleaning or run small mom-and-pop stores—but it couldn't be more different from Jindal's imaginary European no-go ghettos. In the last few years it has become a trendy spot for hipsters priced out of Detroit's reviving downtown but who want good ethnic eateries, a cool bar scene, and cheap housing. (The average home here costs $50,000; an Albanian house painter told me that's a third of what a home costs in his country.)

Occasionally tensions do break out. Old-timers kvetch that their neighborhoods are transforming. But the real news is just how well everyone gets along, especially in a city where people are crammed in 20-foot-wide, two-story, two-family homes with just enough space to fit maybe two trashcans between houses.

The most vivid illustration of Hamtramck's ethos is the Al-Haramain International Food Market, the city's most popular shopping destination. In its cramped aisles, prim, older Polish ladies with coiffed hair, hipsters in skinny jeans or short skirts, and Muslim women in burqas literally rub shoulders—and carts. The store offers a greater variety of produce, spices, and meats than Whole Foods, but at Walmart prices. The only Islamic thing about it besides its Yemeni owners is that it doesn't sell pork or non-halal meat. That you can buy from Bozek's Polish market, right across the street.

Al-Haramain represents the live-and-let-live version of Islam that has established itself in America. "I don't see much radicalization among Muslims in Hamtramck," observes Andriy Zazulya, a Ukrainian student in his mid-20s who came to America with his family nine years ago. "They have the same aspirations as every other immigrant group here. And the immigrant bond that we all share is much stronger than any religious differences."

Dearborn

Arab Americans started flocking to Dearborn at the turn of the 20th century when Henry Ford announced that he would begin paying his workers $5 per day. Dearborn police literally ran a taxi service for Ford, waiting outside the train station to pickup arriving immigrants and driving them straight to his auto factories.

At first the influx was mostly Christian. But Muslim numbers ticked up every time war broke out in the Middle East. The first wave of refugees arrived during the 1975 civil war in Lebanon. By and large they stayed out of politics, mobilizing only when directly affected—like to defeat Dearborn's bid in the mid-'70s to level their homes on the south side of town to make room for an industrial park. Running for elections—considered dirty business where they came from—wasn't these immigrants' cup of tea. But they did vote.

It's rarely remembered today, but American Muslims were turning solidly Republican before 9/11 interrupted the process. That makes sense because Muslims are naturally conservative, argues Osama Siblani, a Lebanese-American engineer who founded the Dearborn-based *Arab American News* in 1984. George W. Bush was the community's clear favorite in the 2000 election, because he combined his conservatism with calls for a "humble" foreign policy and opposition to racial profiling. Siblani's paper gave Bush a ringing endorsement, and the Republican went on to win 71 percent of the national Muslim vote, prompting *Weekly Standard* editor Bill Kristol, no dove, to identify Siblani among the people Bush should thank for his victory.

But even before Donald Trump called for banning Muslims from the U.S. and Newt Gingrich laid out a proposal to require loyalty oaths, the GOP started to lose the Islamic vote. In the aftermath of the September 11 attacks, hawkish Republicans began to demonize Shariah and questioned Islam's compatibility with American values. And as some in the GOP rejected Muslims, they returned the favor. In the 2016 presidential primaries, 59 percent of Dearborn's Muslims voted for Bernie Sanders, a Jewish socialist. In Michigan, they helped fuel his upset victory over Hillary Clinton.

That's not the only political shift in the Islamic community. On the very day the hijackers flew their planes into the Twin Towers, Dearborn was holding primaries. Eleven Arab Americans were vying for mayor, City Council, the Board of Education, and other offices—the highest number to date. But the attack depressed Arab-American turnout, allowing opponents to capitalize on a surge of anti-Arab sentiment in a city with a long history of racial animus. Orville Hubbard, mayor of Dearborn from 1942 to 1978 (whose statue adorned the city square till 2015), was an unrepentant segregationist whose motto was "keep Dearborn clean." Originally directed at blacks, that sentiment paved the way for Michael Guido's successful 1985 mayoral campaign that made dealing with the city's "Arab problem" its central plank.

All of this was prodding Arab Americans to become more politically engaged at the turn of the millennium. Alas, September 11, 2001—the day they were poised to break through into local politics—became the day of their rout.

But after a period of retreat, the community remobilized. One issue that spurred action was a desire for more resources to help absorb refugees of the Iraq War, many of whom were clustering in East Dearborn and straining public services, especially schools. Dearborn authorities wanted to simply bus the kids to West Dearborn schools, but Siblani used his newspaper and his clout to campaign successfully for a $150 million millage to build three new schools in East Dearborn. Arabs also sought and won spots on school boards, campaigning to address the special needs of Muslim kids, such as halal lunches and bilingual education.

Rashida Tlaib—an attorney who in 2008 became the first Muslim woman elected to the Michigan legislature—recalls another challenge at that time: explaining some of the community's habits to the broader public. For example, many Arab families for decades had been turning their garages into living rooms and parking their cars on the streets. The local housing ordinance did nothing to prohibit this.

But over time, thanks partly to street overcrowding, tensions with neighbors and run-ins with the fire department increased. Arab Americans felt harassed and Dearborn authorities felt disrespected.

Matters likely would have blown up had Susan Dabaja, an Arab Muslim City Council member, not been in a position to intervene and diffuse the situation, notes Tlaib. Interestingly, some Ron Paul-supporting libertarians stepped in on the Arab-American side and lobbied against a proposed overly restrictive ordinance.

It is notable that all of Dearborn's Muslim City Council members, in contrast to their Hamtramck counterparts, have assumed American names such as Susan Dabaja, Mike Sareini, Robert Alex Abraham, and David Bazzy. They aren't the only ones. I met one second-generation Lebanese Christian businessman who assumed a milquetoast American name after 9/11, switching because he was afraid for his children and grandchildren. "I've read American history, and I know what happened to Japanese Americans in World War II," he shudders. The fear of internment camps haunts many Dearborn Arabs, Siblani affirms.

After 9/11, the feds illegally detained 1,400 Arab-American Muslims, many from Dearborn, sending shockwaves through the community. Despite that, about 4,000 of them voluntarily signed up as translators and agents for the CIA and FBI. Meanwhile, many Michigan Muslims used their familiarity with the Middle East to obtain lucrative defense contracts during the Iraq War, making veritable fortunes. But the biggest boon for Dearborn was, paradoxically, the PATRIOT Act. The feds used that law to crack down on Muslim charities sending money overseas for relief efforts out of suspicion that they were using philanthropy as a cover to fund militant outfits such as Hamas and Hezbollah. This spooked Dearborn Muslims into keeping their almsgiving closer to home.

As a result, outfits such as the Council on American-Islamic Relations, which fights for Arabs' civil rights, and the Arab Community Center for Economic and Social Services, which assists newly arriving Arab immigrants, experienced an explosive growth in their budgets. Donations to places of worship also jumped: More than a dozen mosques have been completed in Dearborn since 2001, including the $16 million Islamic Center of America.

Siblani believes that this growth is not entirely healthy. "It is like a steroid injection," he says. An influx of wealth within the community combined with rising Islamophobia outside, he argues, retarded the normal process of outward mobility. Dearborn has become a safe haven for Arab Muslims, so that even as they become more affluent, they don't necessarily move to tonier suburbs—or at least not ones too far from Dearborn. As a result, the town has become an enclave, observes Matthew Stiffler, a Lebanese Christian researcher at Dearborn's Arab American National Museum. Muslims can visit mosques, patronize Arabic-speaking doctors, send their kids to predominantly Arab public schools, and eat at halal restaurants without having to venture outside city limits.

Many conservatives see this and scream "Dearbornistan." But the city's Muslims say they have built parallel institutions as an act of self-protection, largely to avoid uncomfortable encounters with people who scream things like "Dearbornistan."

Although post-9/11 Islamophobia has in some ways driven American Muslims together, it has also divided them. The sectarian rift between Dearborn's Shiite majority (largely Lebanese) and its Sunni minority (much of it from Iraq) has significantly deepened and sometimes results in the vandalization of mosques on both sides. Americans chastise Muslims for not rising up in unison and issuing full-throated repudiations of "Islamic terrorism." But Shiites see Al Qaeda and ISIS—the worst 21st century terrorist groups—as Sunni terrorists, not "Islamic" terrorists. They don't think 9/11 or the San Bernardino and Orlando attacks have any more to do with them than the Catholic pedophilic priest scandal has to do with Protestants.

A generational divide has also opened. Dearborn's older Muslims, precisely because they are closer to their immigrant roots, have taken an accommodationist approach to the war on terror. The dilemma that Muslim leaders confronted after 9/11, the University of Michigan's Howell points out, is that they had to rely on the same authorities who were surveilling their community to defend it against a backlash. Many of the wealthier mosques, such as the Islamic Organization of North America (IONA), decided to deal with the situation by becoming completely transparent. They voluntarily started taping all their sermons and installed video cameras to record everyone who entered. They cultivated close ties with the FBI and CIA, even inviting the agency's representatives to community functions. Meanwhile, younger, college-educated, American-born Muslims are more likely to want to stand up to the authorities and defend their civil rights. Many of them condemn their elders as collaborators.

Minorities who feel under siege tighten their grip on their old ways. That's happening in Dearborn. Kaseem Ali—executive director of the Islamic Center of America, North America's biggest mosque—says that growing Islamophobia has renewed young Muslims' interest in their religion. Membership in the mosque has increased 30 percent since it reopened after renovations in 2004. And young Muslims are becoming more openly religious.

Tlaib, a 40-year-old divorced mother of two who now saunters around in pumps and a skirt, says she went through a religious phase. Although her Palestinian parents are fairly devout Muslims, they didn't demand religious fidelity from their children; one of her 14 siblings has become a Jehovah's Witness and another practices no religion at all. Yet in college, she started praying more and wearing the hijab. Indeed, the hijab is experiencing something of a revival among Michigan's Muslims—but not because the community is coming under the grip of some retrograde form of patriarchal Islam. Rather, women are donning it as a symbol of resistance to demands for mainstream conformity. Several Muslim men told me that they'd feel better if their wives ditched their headscarves to avoid harassment. But the wives themselves were digging in their heels, because they wanted to fight for the space to practice their faith on their own terms.

Broader America may see Dearborn's increasing insularity, mealy-mouthed condemnations of Islamic terrorism, backlash against the authorities, and resurgence of faith as symptoms of growing radicalization. But these are natural efforts to negotiate the terms of assimilation in a difficult environment. Allowing them to do so, says Howell, is more likely to forestall radicalization by reducing the sense of being under siege and making Muslims feel that they can effect change through normal democratic channels. The central paradox that American Muslims confront is that they are being challenged to assimilate in mainstream America, even as mainstream American has turned suddenly hostile to them.

Clash of Civilizations?

So Michigan isn't witnessing a clash of civilizations. But there are two potential tension points between the Muslims and other Americans, one involving sexual politics and the other involving religious speech. In both cases, the conflict doesn't involve American conservatives who oppose the Muslim presence but American progressives who support it.

The sexual issue is not the status of women. Women are certainly oppressed in many Muslim countries, but in America Muslim women are one of the most highly educated female religious groups, second only to Jewish women, according to a 2009 Gallup poll. Furthermore, 28 percent of Arab women work in professional occupations, compared to 17 percent of Arab men, according to Howell's survey. It is certainly true that some Muslim families prescribe regressive rules of interaction among the sexes. One man in Dearborn refused to shake my hand, allegedly out of respect for me. But that doesn't pose any more of a threat to fundamental American liberties than when certain observant Jewish men similarly refuse to greet women with a handshake, something they have been doing for years in America without causing political outcry. Like Christian puritanism, Muslim puritanism is a lifestyle choice. The crucial thing is that the moral high ground in the American Islamic community is on the side of educating and empowering women.

Not so on gay rights. Every true Islamic believer is required to oppose homosexuality, asserts IONA's Imam Steve Elturk, a lanky engineer who became a preacher after a nasty divorce and custody battle 20 year ago. Organizations such as the Institute for Social Policy and Understanding, a progressive Muslim outfit, are making the case for gay marriage to their fellow Muslims. But they are on the defensive in their community.

And then there is the issue of religious speech. Saeed Khan, a professor of Near Eastern and Asian studies at Wayne State University, maintains that Detroit mosques are moderating, not radicalizing, places; he says that you'd be hard pressed to find a single imam who would defend the violence against *Charlie Hebdo* for drawing cartoons of the prophet. But you would also be hard pressed to find believing Muslims who would defend the publication's right to do so.

Elturk, who has a son in the Marines, says that there is growing sentiment among Muslims that anti-apostasy laws don't represent the true teachings of the Koran. But he acknowledges that most Muslims, including him, believe in setting outside limits to free speech when it comes to religion. A 2012 Wenzel Strategies poll found that 58 percent of Muslim Americans believe criticism of Muhammad should not be protected under the First Amendment. If he were president, Elturk imagines, he would hold a multi-faith conclave to draw up red lines for every religion beyond which free speech rights would not be protected. "If non-Muslim Americans understood that Muslims love the prophet even more than their children and parents, they'd see why insulting him is unacceptable," he says. This betrays a fundamental inability to comprehend that such restrictions would eviscerate both free speech and the separation of church and state.

How threatening are these Muslim attitudes to bedrock liberal values? Given how small the Muslim presence in America is, not very. If this presence grows substantially, it will certainly affect the national conversation on religious speech and gay rights, just as the Catholic presence has affected the debate over abortion and reproductive rights—and the Jewish presence has affected the debate over Middle Eastern policy. But Muslims will not just influence the culture; they will be influenced by it. Islam in the West loses about a fourth of each Muslim-born generation. If Muslim numbers increase, interaction with the rest of America will splinter the community's already fraught cohesiveness. "There will be Democratic Muslims and Republican Muslims and civil libertarian Muslims and socialist Muslims and progressives and conservatives," Siblani predicts.

In other words, the American assimilation process will crunch them into a million pieces and then absorb them into the great body politic, just as it has for every other immigrant group. Nothing about Hamtramck and Dearborn suggests otherwise.

CHAPTER 6

Asian Americans: Brief Historical Perspectives

READING 13

Chinese Students and Critical Thinking in Education

By Lu Yan

Introduction

Studies have demonstrated concerns about Chinese students' low performance and even inadequacy in thinking critically and independently (Ip, Lee, Lee, Chou, Wootton, and Chang, 2000; Ku and Ho, 2010; Ten Dam and Volman, 2004; Yan and Berliner, 2009). While East Asian students value group solidarity/harmony more than expressing their personal opinions (Atkinson, 1997), their agreeableness and quietness in classrooms are interpreted rather as a lack of critical thinking spirit. Hofstede and Bond (1988) further stressed that, instead of seeking truth, East Asian students in classrooms are more interested in conversations that would not spark debate. Moreover, they are seemingly discouraged from having individual, creative, and innovative autonomy in their writings (Atkinson, 1997). Scholars have regarded Confucianism culture (Atkinson, 1997; Ten Dam & Volman, 2004; Paul, 1994) as the main reason for explaining Chinese students' seemingly weak critical thinking performance. For example, scholars criticize Chinese culture for valuing too much social hierarchy and group harmony, which unavoidably discourages people from questioning the pre-defined social order and authorities (Xing, 1995; Zhao, 2007). To some extent, therefore, Chinese teachers are seen as the authority figures and the knowers who have the knowledge all students come for (Hofstede & Bond, 1988; Lee, Lee, Makara, Fishman, and Hong, 2014). That is, to show their respect for teachers and maintain group harmony, students therefore usually stay quiet in classes and are mindful of others and their relative positions in groups (Lee and Carrasquillo, 2006; Sit, 2013).

Critical Thinking in American Education

Critical thinking, as an essential goal of American education, requires students to have the disposition and ability to seek the truth and eventually establish what to do and what to believe (Chiu, 2009). It involves six core skills: analysis, evaluation, explanation, interpretation, inference, and self-reflection (American Philosophical Association, 1990), as well as a "critical spirit" (Siegel, 1992).

Ennis (2011, p.15) further explains that ideal critical thinkers would: (a) care that their beliefs be true, and that their decisions be justified (e.g., be open-minded and willing to take others' opinions seriously); (b) care to understand and present a position honestly and clearly (e.g., be willing to be reflective about personal perspectives); and (c) care about every person (i.e., consider others' feelings and welfare). Through a process of repeated questioning, students skilled in these areas would be able to practice their critical thinking skills, cultivate their critical thinking spirit, and improve their critical thinking understanding and performance. Therefore, when questioning is the key to thinking critically, Chinese students who have been trained and educated within a culture and education system that promotes conformity over questioning, they seemingly lack critical thinking opportunities in their formal education.

To explore if Chinese students indeed have trouble understanding and applying critical thinking, I conducted the study summarized in this article to investigate how Chinese students perceive and experience critical thinking. Based on the research question, a phenomenological research approach was chosen to explain the individual participant's own meaning making of critical thinking, so as to provide an essence of the meaning of critical thinking that the participants perceived and experienced.

Creswell (2012) summarized a basic outline for carrying out phenomenological study:

> The purpose of a phenomenological approach is to emphasize and explore a single concept or idea as a phenomenon. Participants are a heterogeneous group who have all experienced the studied phenomenon/concept/idea. Bracketing the researcher out of the study by discussing personal experience with the phenomenon is important in a phenomenology study. Data is collected through interviews and analyzed from narrow to broader units and then on to detailed descriptions that essentially answer "what" the individuals have experienced and "how" they have experienced the phenomenon (pp. 78-79).

After IRB approval in 2017, 13 Chinese undergraduate students were selected as a convenient sample. They were enrolled in a large Midwestern university and were interviewed in their native language—Chinese (Mandarin). Their identities were kept confidential. Exploratory interviews were used to seek an understanding of their perceptions and experiences of critical thinking within their disciplines. Each interview lasted about 45 minutes and was audio recorded with the permission of the participant. To protect their privacy and confidentiality, pseudonyms that employed a numbered #C were used with their permission.

The following table shows their demographic information:

Table 13.1 Participants' Demographic Information

Participants	Major	Year in College	Gender
#C1	Mechanical Engineering	Senior	M
#C2	Food Science	Senior	F
#C3	Food Science	Senior	F
#C4	Computer Engineering	Junior	F
#C5	Mechanical Engineering	Senior	M
#C6	Computer Engineering	Junior	F
#C7	Civil Engineering	Junior	F
#C8	Civil Engineering	Junior	M
#C9	Food Science	Senior	M
#C10	Electrical Engineering	Senior	M
#C11	Civil Engineering	Senior	F
#C12	Software Engineering	Senior	M
#C13	Electrical Engineering	Senior	M

After all the 13 interviews were completed, I, as both a native Chinese and fluent English speaker, translated and transcribed the Chinese interviews into English. I then analyzed and interpreted the phenomenological data and categorized them into major themes/meaning units. Three themes of participants' perceptions and experiences of thinking critically emerged as follows: 1) as a way of thinking; 2) equals to problem solving most of the time; and 3) can be too confusing to grasp the true meaning.

Critical Thinking as a Way of Thinking

Nine out of the 13 participants mentioned their understanding of critical thinking as thinking from different/multiple perspectives. For example, participant #C9 was a senior in food science at the time when he was interviewed. He described critical thinking as:

> Thinking from multiple perspectives, noticing that everything has its positive sides and its negative sides. Keeping this in mind, then you would not say in certainty that this particular solution, for example, is right or wrong. In other words, everything is not 100% ... everything is relative. It is like Albert Einstein's

> Theory of Relativity. It is not absolute to say that an object is fast. There are always some objects are faster. We can only say that this object is faster than a relatively slow object. (Participant #C9 interview, 11/23/17)

Participants' #C2, #C3, and #C4 clearly gave their definition of critical thinking: "it is a comprehensive thinking" and "being able to look at things from multiple perspectives." Participant #7 also mentioned that critical thinkers are those who can think creatively and have good study habits. Participant #C10 defined critical thinking: "...your own independent thinking and understanding process, after which you compare your results with others." Participant #6 also thought of critical thinking as "more comprehensive thinking with creativity," but meanwhile she did not think she was "not good at critical thinking because I am from an exam-orientated educational background, and they call me 'exam machine.'" Another participant, #C5, mentioned that "one's critical thinking absolutely decides their independence." The less teachers say, the more you need to think from various perspectives." Overall, thinking and looking from a more comprehensive perspective [*quan mian si kao* 全面思考] is how the participants repeatedly defined critical thinking in their interviews.

Critical Thinking is Problem Solving

Seven of the 13 participants interchangeably used critical thinking and problem solving in their interviews. For example, participant #13 majored in electrical engineering (EE). He was finishing his senior project at the time of his interview. He emphasized his experience of critical thinking as problem solving. The first time he was asked to think critically in an assignment in his freshmen year, he did not know how to respond. "I remember I just did not know how to start. After getting the homework, it was very much inexplicable about what exactly the teacher wanted from me." After studying in his major for more than three years, he said he had a partial understanding of critical thinking, which is to utilize all resources to solve problems.

"The problems we [EE students] face after we graduate are very, very practical problems in the future. The more practical the problems, the more you need to have this critical-thinking skill," he said. He then shared with me one of his experiences doing these projects. He said that the goal of the project was to make a circuit design for a company. He and his teammates initially had two plans with plan A being the optimal one. They had to choose a valid location for the wire; it needed to be geologically valid—for example, neither on the bank of a river nor on private land. However, the initial location from their plan a on blueprint turned out not geologically valid. "So in this case," he explained, "we could erase the whole plan A and go to the alternative plan B, or we could just make minor changes in plan A, avoiding this particular location. But you need to keep in mind that it could be like a domino effect when you make changes in a plan. We also had to use the least amount of money from the company. Therefore, the critical thinking part needed to be applied at its finest.

When the problem involves the actual situation, you need to take care of different requirements in all aspects. That is to say that the final optimal solution is not necessarily the only solution you have."

Participant #8 also thought of critical thinking as problem solving but said, "You need to know where the problem is in the real world. You may choose not to say it out loud [in class], but you need to know where the problem/question is. And critical thinking is the tool to find out." Participant #6 also thought of critical thinking as problem solving, but she mainly used it in her studies [e.g., homework, projects, and exams] and so was not sure if it could be used in other areas of her life. "Maybe if you care enough," she said. Participant #2 regarded critical thinking as being able to solve problems in labs, lectures and his real-life situations.

Critical Thinking is Confusing

Five participants mentioned their frustration about not clearly knowing the definition. As a result, at beginning of the interviews, participants asked me what my opinion was on critical thinking.

I did not answer them because it would be leading them to my directions, but their frustrations and confusion were obvious. For example, participant #12 was a senior in software engineering at the time of his interview. To him, critical thinking was important to his education and future career, but he still thought the definition/explanation could be better and more clearly taught. Although some of his answers involved the aspects of using analysis and evaluation which are two of the six core skills mentioned earlier in this chapter, he still thought it was confusing:

> It would be helpful if I know for sure what critical thinking is. Then my questions would be different if I know the real meaning of this term [i.e., critical thinking]. My answers would be different too. I would know how to answer the questions based on the clear meaning of it [critical thinking]. In English class, for example, the teacher did not teach us what critical thinking is but only told us to think critically. (Participant #12 interview, 10/18/2017)

If critical thinking were not listed on a class syllabus, he said he would not want to initiate the thinking critically at all. Four other participants described their confusion similar as walking in a fog: "I may have a direction but really don't know where exactly I need to go to meet the teacher's expectations," said participant #8. Through mostly guessing and trial and error from doing homework, they thought they were still confused and hoped to get the definition clear and cut.

Discussion and Conclusion

The theme of thinking comprehensively from multiple perspectives is congruent with the disposition aspects from the report of American Philosophical Association (1990), and the work of Facione (2000; 2015), Halonen (1995) and Paul (1990; 1994), which all underscored the important aspects of exchanging and embracing with other minds/perspectives in critical thinking, and highlighted how it can help in reasoning and development of critical thinking skills. It is also consistent with the work from Garrison (1991), Quitadamo, Faiola, Johnson and Kurtz (2008), and Rowe, Harris, Koether, Shannon and Rose (2015) that stressed the importance of open-mindedness to embrace other perspectives and opinions in thinking critically.

The fact of participants understanding critical thinking as problem solving is partially consistent with the work from Pithers and Soden (2000), Afamasaga-Fuata'i (2005), Paul (1994), Durkin (2008, 2011), and Scollon (1999) that all stressed the overlapping skills between critical thinking and problem solving, and in fact, how critical thinking was often taught as problem solving in classrooms. While critical thinking is not equivalent to problem solving per se, as some participants may have understood in the study, there is an important relationship between the two. Problem solving is a means for achieving important goals during which we need to monitor our process continually and switch strategies if necessary (Martinez, 1998). It involves critical thinking but also engages with decision-making and questioning. Lack of clarity about the nature of critical thinking has caused it to be thought of as problem-solving (Kennedy, Fisher, and Ennis, 1991).

The finding of participants/students being confused about this concept is well documented in previous literature. Lacking the training, resources, and time to implement critical thinking, instructors often do not have the opportunities to show and teach it in their classrooms (Paul, Elder, and Bartell, 1997; Synder and Synder, 2008). As a result, students were rarely systematically taught about the concept and how to apply it to their disciplinary studies (Synder and Synder, 2008). That is, although students may understand the importance of thinking critically, they simply do not know how. Participants in the study expressed their disappointment for not getting it straightforwardly from their education, and wished they could know it better through their future experiences and projects. They shared a similar sentiment that, if they knew the definition clearly, they would know how to apply it better.

The study has its limitations. Because of the convenient sampling, the first limitation is the predominance of engineering participants—10 out of the 13 participants were from the field of engineering. Most of the engineering participants specifically mentioned problem solving as a key to their discipline studies. That is, participants in this study are not representative of the diversity of Chinese students regarding their disciplinary studies. As a result, engineering participants might have been overemphasized and represented in the interpretation of "problem solving" in all participants' experiences. In the future studies, therefore, having an even distribution of participants from different majors may reflect more fair implications regarding their understanding and experiences.

The second limitation is that I, as the researcher, translated the Chinese international students' interview transcripts. Although I am a native Chinese and fluent English speaker, in future studies, it is suggested to apply additional triangulation in data analysis and interpretations. For example, triangulating with other Chinese-speaking researchers would make a stronger contribution to translation accuracy and data analysis.

Overall, the Chinese participants showed their understandings and misunderstandings of critical thinking, which overlapped some of the ideas mentioned in previous literature on thinking critically. The results from this small-scale analysis did not really show that their understanding of critical thinking was "inadequate." I agree with what Durkin (2008) suggested: that, compared to their Western peers, Chinese students or East Asian students are only unfamiliar with the Western requirements and style of critical thinking rather than not knowing how to think critically.

References

Afamasaga-Fuata'i, Karoline. 2005. "Students' Conceptual Understanding and Critical Thinking: A Case for Concept Maps and Vee Diagrams in Mathematics Problem Solving." In M. Coupland, J, Anderson and T. Spencer (eds.), *Making Mathematics Vital.* Proceedings of the Twentieth Biennial Conference of the Australian Association of Mathematics Teachers (AAMT), January 17–21, 2005. (pp. 43–52). University of Technology, Sydney, Australia.

Atkinson, Dwight. 1997. "A Critical Approach to Critical Thinking in TESOL." *TESOL Quarterly, 31*(1), 71–94.

Chiu, Yi-Ching Jean. 2009. "Facilitating Asian Students' Critical Thinking in Online Discussions." *British Journal of Educational Technology, 40*(1), 42–57.

Creswell, John W. 2012. *Qualitative Inquiry and Research Design: Choosing Among Five Approaches.* Los Angeles, CA: Sage.

Durkin, Kathy. 2008. "The Adaptation of East Asian Masters Students to Western Norms of Critical Thinking and Argumentation in the UK." *Intercultural Education, 19*(1), 15–27.

Durkin, Kathy. 2011. "Adapting to Western Norms of Critical Argumentation and Debate." In L. Jin and M. Cortazzi (eds.), *Researching Chinese learners* (pp. 274–291). New York, NY: Palgrave Macmillan.

Ennis, Robert H. 2011. "The Nature of Critical Thinking: An Outline of Critical Thinking Disposition and Abilities. "University of Illinois. Retrieved from http://faculty.education.illinois.edu/rhennis/documents/TheNatureofCriticalThinki ng_51711_000.pdf

Facione, Peter. 1990. "Critical Thinking: A Statement of Expert Consensus for Purposes of Educational Assessment and Instruction." American Philosophical Association. ERIC Doc. No. ED 315–423.

Facione, Peter. 2000. "The Disposition Toward Critical Thinking: Its Character, Measurement, and Relation to Critical Thinking Skill." *Informal Logic, 20*(1), 61–84.

Facione, Peter. 2015. "Critical Thinking: What It Is and Why It Counts." *Insight Assessment.* Retrieved from http://www.insightassessment.com

Garrison, D. Randy. 1991. "Critical Thinking and Adult Education: A Conceptual Model for Developing Critical Thinking in Adult Learners." *International Journal of Lifelong Education, 10*(4), 287–303.

Halonen, Jane S. 1995. "Demystifying Critical Thinking." *Teaching of Psychology, 22,* 75–81.

Hofstede, Geert, and Bond, Michael Harris. 1988. "The Confucius Connection: From Cultural Roots to Economic Growth. *Organizational Dynamics, 16*(4), 4–21.

Ip, Wan Yim, Diana TF Lee, Iris FK Lee, Janita PC Chau, Yvonne SY Wootton, and Anne M. Chang. 2000. "Disposition Towards Critical Thinking: A Study of Chinese Undergraduate Nursing Students." *Journal of Advanced Nursing, 32*(1), 84–90.

Kennedy, Mellen, Michelle B. Fisher, and Robert H. Ennis. 1991. "Critical Thinking: Literature Review and Needed Research. In L. Idol and B. Fly Jones (eds.), *Educational Values and Cognitive Instruction: Implications for Reform* (pp. 11–40). Hillsdale, New Jersey: Lawrence Erlbaum.

Ku, Kelly YL, and Irene T. Ho. 2010. "Dispositional Factors Predicting Chinese Students' Critical Thinking Performance." *Personality and Individual Differences, 48*(1), 54–58.

Lee, Hye-Jung, Jihyun Lee, Kara A. Makara, Barry J. Fishman, and Young-Il Hong. 2014. "Does Higher Education Foster Critical and Creative Learners? An Exploration of Two Universities in South Korea and the USA." *Higher Education Research and Development, 34*(1), 131–146.

Lee, Kyung Soon, and Angela Carrasquillo. 2006. "Korean College Students in United States: Perceptions of Professors and Students." *College Student Journal, 40*(2), 442–456.

Martinez, Michael E. 1998. "What Is Problem Solving?" *The Phi Delta Kappan, 79,* 605–609.

Paul, Richard W. 1990. *Critical Thinking: What Every Person Needs to Survive in a Rapidly Changing World.* Rohnert Park, CA: Foundation for Critical Thinking.

Paul, Richard W., Linda Elder, and Ted Bartell. 1997. *California Teacher Preparation for Instruction in Critical Thinking: Research Findings and Policy Recommendations.* The Foundation for Critical Thinking: Dillon Beach, CA.

Paul, Richard. 1994. "Teaching Critical Thinking in the Strong Sense: A Focus on Self-deception, World Views, and a Dialectical Mode of Analysis." In K. Walters (ed.), *Re-thinking Reason: New Perspectives in Critical Thinking* (pp. 181–198). Albany, NY: State University of New York Press.

Pithers, Robert T., and Soden, R. 2000. "Critical Thinking in Education." *Educational Research, 42*(3), 237–249.

Quitadamo, Ian J., Celia L. Faiola, James E. Johnson, and Martha J. Kurtz. 2008. "Community-based Inquiry Improves Critical Thinking in General Education Biology. *CBE Life Sciences Education, 7,* 327–337.

Rowe, Matthew P., B. Marcus Gillespie, Kevin R. Harris, Steven D. Koether, Li-Jen Y. Shannon, and Lori A. Rose. 2015. "Redesigning a General Education Science Course to Promote Critical Thinking." *CBE-Life Sciences Education, 14*(3), 1–12.

Scollon, Suzanne. 1999. "Not to Waste Words or Students: Confucian and Socratic Discourse in the Tertiary Classroom." In E. Hinkel (ed.), *Culture in Second Language Teaching and Learning* (pp. 13–27). Cambridge, UK: Cambridge University Press.

Siegel, Harvey. 1997. *Rationality Redeemed? Further Dialogue on an Educational Ideal.* New York: Routledge.

Sit, Helena Hing Wa. 2013. "Characteristics of Chinese Students' Learning Styles." *International Proceedings of Economic Development and Research, 62*(8), 36–39.

Snyder, Lisa Gueldenzoph, and Mark J. Snyder. 2008. "Teaching Critical Thinking and Problem Solving Skills." *Delta Pi Epsilon Journal, 50,* 90–99.

Ten Dam, Geert, and Volman, Monique. 2004. "Critical Thinking as a Citizenship Competence: Teaching Strategies." *Learning and Instruction, 14,* 359–379.

Xing, Fan. 1995. "The Chinese Cultural System: Implications for Cross-cultural Management." *SAM Advanced Management Journal, 60*(1), 14–20.

Yan, Kun, and Berliner, David C. 2009. "Chinese International Students' Academic Stressors in the United States." *College Student Journal, 43*(4), 939–960.

Zhao, Yuqin. 2007. "Cultural Conflicts in an Intercultural Classroom Discourse and Interpretations from a Cultural Perspective." *Intercultural Communication Studies, 16*(1), 129–136.

READING 14

Asian Americans and the Shifting Politics of Race

Asian Americans as Victim and Success Stories

By Rowena Robles

Excerpter's note: In 1994 a group of students and their parents filed suit against the San Francisco Unified School District (SFUSD). They claimed its policy that required schools, such as Lowell High School, the premiere academic high school in the district, to enroll no more than a fixed percentage of students from a single racial group discriminated against Chinese American students based solely on their race.

The *Brian Ho, Patrick Wong & Hilary Chen v. SFUSD* lawsuit was waged by a group of Chinese Americans and effectively ended race-based school integration in the San Francisco Unifed School District. The Chinese American plaintiffs sued the San Francisco school district to contest the legal decision awarded to the National Association for the Advancement of Colored People (NAACP). It was the NAACP's original suit that resulted in the desegregation policy established in 1983, known as the San Francisco Unified School District's Consent Decree. The *Ho* lawsuit directly attacked one of the primary vestiges of the Civil Rights movement—the idea that all public school students are entitled to an equal education, from elementary to high school, regardless of race. More specifically, through desegregation, the Consent Decree has attempted to ensure that African Americans and other racial minorities are not relegated to "inherently unequal" public schools.

The *Brian Ho* lawsuit was evidence of political and public policy shifts away from an overt focus on race in education policy, as well as of how the Asian American supporters and plaintiffs of *Ho* have exploited this shift. Although *Ho* legally pointed to the dismantling of the Consent Decree, the main issue presented by the plaintiffs—that of race-based school assignments restricting the choice of Chinese American students[1]—was strengthened by a larger neoconservative project, namely the

Rowena Robles, "Asian Americans and the Shifting Politics of Race: Asian Americans as Victim and Success Stories," *Asian Americans and the Shifting Politics of Race: The Dismantling of Affirmative Action at an Elite Public High School*, pp. 57-70.

backlash against affirmative action and the rise of neoconservatism. *Ho* was not just a direct attack on the Consent Decree, it also "launche(d) a broad attack on race-based remedies."[2]

More generally, the *Ho* lawsuit demonstrated how far we have come as a nation from the civil rights movement that initiated African American struggles for social justice in the form of racial equality. Crenshaw states that,

> The image of a 'traditional civil rights discourse' refers to the constellation of ideas about racial power and social transformation that were constructed ... by ... the mass mobilization of social energy and popular imagination in the civil rights movements of the late fifties and sixties.[3]

This movement's victories and legal tenets, specifically "equal rights" and "equality of opportunity," were co-opted by a neoconservative movement to further its own agenda. This neoconservative agenda also incorporates a racial project in which the propagation of colorblindness, along with the idea of meritocracy, has worked to obscure the continuing significance of race in the debates around affirmative action, desegregation, and other race-conscious policies.

The Chinese students and parents behind the lawsuit contended that the goals and objectives of the Consent Decree never represented their particular group's interests, regardless of the fact that the desegregation mandate was designed to benefit all racial and ethnic groups. As the San Francisco Unified School District pointed out, "(the Decree) was not designed only to integrate African Americans with whites; the plan recognizes nine different racial and ethnic groups for desegregation purposes."[4] The *Ho* plaintiffs and supporters believed that they and other Chinese American public school students in San Francisco, were being discriminated against because of the stipulations of the 1983 Consent Decree.

The *Ho* plaintiffs embraced the Asian American Model Minority stereotype and articulated their cause through this racial myth. On the one hand, the dual construction of Asian Americans—as victims and as success stories—fit the agenda of the larger neoconservative political and social project. On the other, some Asian Americans also accepted this arguably positive racial construction. How did the plaintiffs' and supporters' framing of the case racially construct Chinese Americans, and how did they assert this racial construction? In a broader sense, how do the political sentiments of the Chinese American supporters of this case situate all other Asian Americans? The answers to these questions can be found in the way race, racial construction, and neoconservative politics meshed to produce the political and social climate in which the *Ho* lawsuit was filed.

A myriad of social and political factors come into play in a discussion of the *Ho* lawsuit. First, the Republican and neoconservative assault on affirmative action frames Asian Americans as a minority group that does not need racial considerations in admissions and is harmed by these policies. Second, the assertion of race by the *Ho* plaintiffs and supporters as the Model Minority fits squarely within the neoconservative propagation of colorblindness and meritocracy within education policy and politics. While these political catchphrases appear to be racially neutral, they still work to evoke race and construct African Americans and Latinos as undeserving beneficiaries of race-based policies, necessarily antithetical to the construction of Asian Americans as high-achieving victims of these policies. In this reading, I attempt to demonstrate how the Asian American supporters of the *Ho* lawsuit utilize a combination of racial stereotypes and neoconservative ideologies to further their cause within these highly politicized discursive contexts. While larger political and social forces racially construct minority groups such as African Americans and Latinos, the *Ho* plaintiffs and supporters demonstrate how Asian Americans possess the ability to transcend race—specifically negative racial stereotypes—and assert an arguably positive racial stereotype through the Model Minority Myth. In doing so, they effectively produce the simultaneous construction of victim and success story.

Situating Asian Americans within Traditional Civil Rights Goals and the New Neoconservative Ideology

The issues that underlie the lawsuit possess a larger history, involving both desegregation and affirmative action policies. The *Ho* plaintiffs, however, argued for colorblind policies that ensure meritocratic admissions and rearticulated recent history to situate the plaintiffs as both victims of past discrimination and victims of the policies addressing discrimination in the present. Ironically, their argument garnered widespread acceptance because they were Asian American and not white males crying reverse discrimination. The *Ho* lawsuit may not have been accepted judicially by the courts or socially by the public had not the tenor and meaning of equal rights and civil rights shifted in the larger political and social contexts. These shifts include the anti-affirmative action backlash as well as the growth and spread of neoconservative rhetoric, with the *Ho* lawsuit fitting squarely within and even complementing these political changes.

The success and widespread acceptance of the *Ho* lawsuit and the neoconservative and anti-affirmative action ideals it represents emerged within a context that is a turning point in the history of racial politics in the United States. Within this context, we can view the utilization of traditional civil rights demands for neoconservative ends. The *Ho* suit represents how the racist arguments of anti-affirmative action forces were changed to advocate an "end to discrimination" and a push for "equality of opportunity"—both rearticulated to demand an end to race-based policies such as affirmative action.

Although *Ho v. SFUSD* legally pointed to the dismantling of the Consent Decree and ending race-based desegregation, the main issue presented by the plaintiffs—that of race-based school assignment restricting the choice of Chinese American students[5]—was strengthened by the links between the backlash against affirmative action and the rise of neoconservatism. The politics of neoconservatism attempt to garner widespread support by simultaneously attacking anti-discriminatory policies such as affirmative action and advocating individual rights.[6] The cornerstone of this ideology rests on the "rearticulation of the meaning of racial equality as a matter of individual rather than group or collective concern."[7] In contrast, a basic tenet of the civil rights movement was group rights. Neoconservatives utilize the term, racial equality, yet envision racial equality to be the end of race-based policies. Instead, they put forth the belief that racial discrimination lies at the heart of these policies. The key in the political and legal strategy of the *Ho* plaintiffs was that by asserting a neoconservative stance, they were able to make the contradictory claims of being discriminated against while also taking an anti-affirmative action position.

The neoconservative stance propagated by the *Ho* plaintiffs and supporters both alludes to discriminatory treatment and encapsulates the larger backlash against affirmative action and other race-based policies. Their seamless merging of these contradictory ideals exemplifies the political strength of rearticulation. Michael Omi and Howard Winant define rearticulation by neoconservative forces as redefinitions of traditional civil rights ideals.

> The minority movements of the 1950s and 1960s ... definitively questioned (the) social assignment of identities and racial meanings. It was this questioning, this challenge, that the neoconservatives sought to confine and reorganize in their assault on affirmative action. They did this by limiting the meaning of racial discrimination to the curtailment of individual rights. ... The social logic of race was thus rendered opaque. ... [8]

This neoconservative assault on race-based policies has taken flight as the meanings of discrimination and equality have shifted to focus on the harm inflicted upon individuals as opposed to groups classified by race.

The neoconservative framing of race-based policies such as affirmative action, had been gaining momentum and garnering widespread support since the 1980s.[9] This political and social context created the space in which the *Ho* supporters were able to employ neoconservative language around racial equality and gain support. For example, the Chinese plaintiffs declared that "the justification for race-conscious assignment policies has ended."[10] The group believed that they were not being treated equitably or fairly and felt that this unfair treatment stemmed from the fact that they are Chinese. Lawrence Siskind, a San Francisco attorney and supporter of the lawsuit was quoted as stating, "A yellow skin can be a curse in San Francisco."[11]

In employing neoconservative definitions of racial discrimination, the *Ho* plaintiffs and supporters offered a convoluted version of equality that is widely accepted in the current political climate. The Chinese Americans involved in the *Ho* lawsuit claimed to "not (be) opposed to affirmative action."[12] The plaintiffs and supporters of the lawsuit, however, still put forth the racially coded language of neoconservative and anti-affirmative action forces and subliminally pointed to the undeserving beneficiaries of these policies—stereotypically framed as African Americans and Latinos. The *Ho* argument appeared to be one that included Chinese American students as a group, but it really focused on the individual rights of these students. Because they were actually arguing for the individual rights of Chinese American students, the contradictions in their argument lay in how they purported claims of discrimination against the group as a whole—an effective strategy for them politically but, in the end, detrimental to race-conscious policies.

The supporters of the *Ho* lawsuit simultaneously evoked racist and prejudicial treatment along with their rearticulated version of discrimination. This neoconservative version of racial equality confuses racist treatment with racial considerations in education policy. The supporters of *Ho* linked these racist experiences to the allegedly discriminatory aspects of the desegregation policy. The supporters and plaintiffs of the *Ho* suit directly appealed to the idea of being discriminated against—that they as minorities have experienced racial discrimination and now desire "equality." Lee Cheng, the vice-chair of the Chinese American Democratic Club's (CADC) Educational Reform Task Force, utilized his personal experiences to demonstrate this neoconservative rhetoric.

> "I grew up knowing a lot of racism," said Cheng, 23, (then) a UC Berkeley law student ... "I was beaten up as a kid, referred to as a chink, a Chinaman. But in school I was taught that the laws will treat everyone the same, that discrimination was being eliminated. ... Then my friends and I applied to public high school. We discovered that if you are Chinese, you have to do better than anyone else."[13]

Cheng equated desegregation, specifically Lowell High School's affirmative action policy, to that of discrimination. Several issues and concepts were combined here in order to affect a neoconservative tone that simultaneously evokes civil rights ideology—notably the elimination of what they perceive as racially discriminatory practices—and opposition to race-based policies.

For the supporters of the *Ho* lawsuit, racial discrimination was equated with the racial and ethnic caps imposed on all groups in order to achieve integrated schools. The CADC believed that these caps constituted discriminatory treatment. The *Ho* plaintiffs and supporters claimed that they have experienced racial discrimination firsthand, and equated the desegregation policy with racism. In comments made to a reporter, Daniel Girard, the attorney representing the (Ho) parents said, "Diversity doesn't justify racial discrimination in public assignments. ... Don't treat Chinese people differently and don't penalize them for being Chinese. Let's put an end to race-based assignments."[14] Girard alludes to racial discrimination in his statement while also denigrating race-based policies. In this statement, one can view how neoconservative "logic" situates the *Ho* plaintiffs as a racial minority group that is experiencing discrimination and that is being penalized in order to uphold desegregation policies. The underlying subtext is that Asian Americans are succeeding, yet are being penalized for this academic success.

Roland Quan, one of the leading members of the CADC, labeled the racial and ethnic ceilings imposed on all SFUSD schools as a form of dis crimination.

> "We're just trying to end discrimination against Chinese Americans by lifting the caps," Quan said. "Last year, 94 students were rejected from Lowell because of their race. How can you tell a student you can't get in because you were born Chinese? If you tell them they couldn't get in because there weren't enough seats, that's something else."[15]

Quan reframed the debate on affirmative action admissions to Lowell by completely removing the larger context of the desegregation Consent Decree and its goals. He, instead, emphasized the rejection of Chinese American students, while omitting their over-representation at Lowell and other San Francisco magnet high schools. He pointed to their race as the sole reason for rejection.

Again, the goals of the Consent Decree and desegregation policies were rearticulated and presented by the CADC as attempts to disenfranchise Chinese-American students. While the original intent of both desegregation and affirmative action policies was to provide historically underprivileged groups access to educational equality, the CADC stance jeopardized these goals. The neoconservative rearticulation of these policies has been a concerted effort of those groups whom these policies do not include, such as white males and presently some Asian American groups, to ensure prime public education for their children without a concern for the greater social good. In addition to equating the desegregation policy to discriminatory treatment, the CADC also considered the policy "racist" and "unequal." Cheng referenced the Civil Rights movement in his stance against the consideration of race in pupil assignments and puts forth that the maintenance of race in student assignments is a racist throwback to George Wallace.

> Right about now ... the disciples of preference appear ready to engage in a protracted campaign of trench warfare to maintain unequal, racist policies despite overwhelming public opposition to entitlements based on race. Vast amounts of resources and ... creativity, have and are being spent in attempts to overturn or circumvent limitations on the use of racial preferences.[16]

Those who supported desegregation and affirmative action were now "disciples of preference"[17]—not civil rights activists, progressives, or liberals. They were essentially cast as upholding racism through their endorsement of racial considerations, which Cheng labels racial preferences, and victimizing Chinese American students in doing so.

The dual construction of Asian Americans as success stories as well as victims of discriminatory treatment through race-based preferences is complex and multi-layered. Beginning in the 1980s, portrayals of Asian Americans as the Model Minority filled newspapers and magazines. These range from labeling them as the "New Whiz Kids" to highlighting prestigious colleges and universities that were composed largely of Asian American students.[18] In the mid 1990s, these stereotypic constructions began to change along with an upsurge in the backlash against affirmative action. Asian Americans became viewed as victims of their own success. Whereas before they were lauded and praised for their achievements, now their success was arguably threatened by policies such as affirmative action, effectively creating their dual construction as both success stories and victims.

Along with the strategic political construction of Asian Americans as the Model Minority, neoconservative rearticulations of equality and discrimination have opened up a space in which traditional calls for civil rights and equal access are no longer politically powerful. While the supporters of the *Ho* lawsuit demanded that race-based policies be ended in the district, the SFUSD and NAACP fought back, arguing that racial diversity and representation was still necessary. Unfortunately, the court did not view their calls for equal access as legally and politically viable, proving that those who continue to support civil rights law and advocacy must find new ways to do battle with those who oppose race-based policies.[19]

By asserting this political stance and racial identity, the supporters of *Ho* "launch(ed) a broad attack on race-based remedies."[20] The *Ho* plain tiffs and supporters believed that they were furthering their legal case, yet they were also perpetrating harm on other groups who had benefited from the racial considerations in desegregation and affirmative action policies and who were eventually harmed by the outcome. The assertion of the Model Minority Myth[21] worked to situate African American and Latino students as the antithesis of this stereotype—the underachieving and undeserving beneficiaries of affirmative action policies.

The Asian American Model Minority Stereotype as Racial Currency in a "Colorblind" Society

Interestingly and rather ironically, Asian Americans have been able to articulate race through the end of affirmative action policies and the ensuing incorporation of colorblindness, merit, and equality into educational policy debates. In contrast to African Americans and Latinos, who have been framed negatively as undeserving beneficiaries of these policies, Asian Americans have emerged with a positive stereotype. Further adding to the irony, the focus on the educational sector of society, the same site in which African Americans sought racial justice,[22] has enabled Asian Americans to assert themselves as the Model Minority.

This racial construct of the Model Minority Myth has gained its widespread currency because it functions within the American framework of meritocracy and equality. The *Ho* plaintiffs and supporters have been able to successfully play on a stereotype created by whites. This can be viewed in two ways. On the one hand, Asian Americans as a racial minority are able to exploit an arguably positive stereotype and be accepted into mainstream white society. In the acceptance of this stereotype, they also function as the good minority, in direct contrast to the other minorities who are framed by negative racial stereotyping. Asian Americans as the Model Minority get situated somewhere between black and white racial constructions.

The United States has historically and continues to operate within a simplistic paradigm of race. The black/white model of race relations informs historical as well as current battles around public policy, education, and politics.[23] Asian Americans, neither black nor white, are often constructed as "'near-white' or 'like Blacks.'"[24] This simplistic model of race and race relations and its fixity within the American mindset allows Asian Americans to transcend race to a certain extent. While the black/white racial paradigm remains fixed, Asian Americans, by virtue of the changeability and historical contexts of racial stereotypes, are situated and situate themselves at opposing ends of the model. Operating and shifting back and forth between the black and white ends of the U.S. racial paradigm, Asian Americans exist as both race-less and racially constructed at the same time. Okihiro presents a historical perspective on how Asian Americans have often traversed between black and white racial constructions in the United States—being framed as black when they immigrated as railroad workers and migrant farm workers, and then as white when larger numbers of professionals from Asia composed a great number of immigrants to the United States[25].

This dynamic nature of the racial construction of Asian Americans works to support the assertions of the Asian Americans involved in the *Ho* lawsuit. Michael Omi and Dana Takagi assert that, "Unlike 'black' and 'white' as racial categories, there is a greater fluidity to 'Asian American' that can be manipulated in particular ways to suit particular positions."[26] They theorize that the media and politicians hold the power to frame and construct Asian Americans as the Model Minority or as more white than black or other. I would add to Omi and Takagi by suggesting that some Asian Americans accept and assert the racial identity of the Model Minority, situating themselves at the white end of the racial paradigm. The widespread acceptance of the black and white model of race could also be viewed as allowing Asian Americans the currency of leaving the black side of the model in favor of the white. This perceived ability of Asian Americans to transcend negative racial stereotypes might even be considered a privileged position.

For the *Ho* plaintiffs, such racial transcendence situated them in a powerful position as well. The power of racial transcendence for Asian Americans was enabled by the elimination of explicit talk about race in all public policy issues, especially in regards to education. Meritocracy, a concept initiated by neoconservatives in their assault on affirmative action, opened up a space in which the Asian American Model Minority gained more acceptance. Neoconservatives have advocated the use of merit to take the place of racial considerations in education policy. Meritocracy works well with the stereotype of the Model Minority—diligent, hard working, and quintessentially apolitical. What is then discussed explicitly within the space in which race was eliminated is the merit and achievement that these Asian American students possess; but what is evoked is race. The Model Minority Myth works both to deflect the need for affirmative action programs (in support of merit) while simultaneously invoking race (in the attempts to garner a political and social backlash against affirmative action and integration). In other words, if merit connotes Asian-ness, then lack of merit connotes black-ness or Latino-ness, which shifts the blame from structural inequalities to underachieving minority groups.

The Dangers of Asserting the Model Minority Myth

In the *Ho* lawsuit, the framing of Chinese Americans as victims of a desegregation policy lay entirely in the hands of a group of Chinese parents and their children. Thus, while the *Ho* lawsuit advocated an end to racial preferences and the institution of colorblindness in admissions policies, the supporters and plaintiffs also effectively employed a discursive strategy in which Asian Americans, specifically Chinese Americans, were cast as victims and African Americans and Latinos[27] were framed as undeserving beneficiaries of the desegregation policy.

While Asian Americans can be seen as political tools for the purposes and goals of conservative and neoconservative politicians and their respective agendas, in the *Ho* example, they can be seen as actively negotiating the racial, political, and social terrain of United States society. By situating themselves as the Model Minority and a "class of innocents"[28] being unfairly harmed by race-conscious policies, the *Ho* plaintiffs and supporters engage in constructing and asserting their race. On the one hand, they are the Model Minority, immigrants or children of immigrants who have achieved educational and professional success. On the other hand, they are also a minority group who believes that they have not personally discriminated against other racial minority groups and, therefore, should not bear the brunt of desegregation and affirmative action policies.

Asian Americans have been able to transcend notions of fault or blame for racial discrimination and prejudice because they themselves are racial minorities. This lack of "fault" on their part, coupled with the Model Minority stereotype, allows Asian Americans to frame themselves as innocents, making the *Ho* lawsuit that much stronger. Additionally, this lack of fault allowed the plaintiffs and supporters of *Ho* to distance themselves from the negative ramifications of their lawsuit, political stance, and racial assertions. The dangers that the *Ho* plaintiffs and supporters initiated with their assertion of the Model Minority Myth include obscuring the need for race-preferential policies and possibly engendering inter-racial conflicts with other racial minority groups.

This power and privilege of racial framing and constructionism, as well as the acceptance of a socially and politically constructed racial stereotype in the form of the Model Minority, functions to situate Asian Americans such that they may be held in positive esteem. These positive depictions can also work to their detriment when utilized to further neoconservative politics as well as inter-racial divisions. While the *Ho* plaintiffs and supporters assert the arguably positive aspects of the Model Minority Myth, these positive aspects can also be re-framed such that they are, in the end, damaging to Asian Americans.

In Takagi's study on the Asian Admissions Crisis at some of the United States' premier universities, admissions officers were quick to point out that Asians were "good, but not exceptional students."[29] The power of framing Asian Americans as good or bad, as deserving or not of admissions, resided with the admissions offices and university officials. Also in Nancy Abelmann and John Lie's analysis of the Black and Korean conflict in the aftermath of the 1992 Los Angeles Riots, many Korean American merchants claimed that the media too often took the easy way out and portrayed them as greedy yet successful immigrant entrepreneurs.[30] The power of framing Asian Americans lay in the hands of the mainstream media and university admissions offices; these forces merely extended and re-constructed the Model Minority Myth, negatively in these cases, to suit their political purposes.

While racial constructionism for all racial and ethnic groups has historically lain in the hands of larger political and social forces,[35] Asian Americans have recently been more actively participating in the articulation of their own race. Some Asian Americans, because of their economic and educational achievements, believe that they are now able to dictate their own racial constructions. This is evident in the *Ho* plaintiffs' and supporters' conflation of their racial positionality with that of being a Model Minority. Buying into the Model Minority Myth lends itself to the belief in the American Dream and individual success and away from group empowerment. Situating oneself and one's ethnic group within the hierarchical social formation is one thing. But what if these attempts at positively defining one's positionality negatively affect that of other minority groups, such as Blacks and Latinos?

Since the birth of the Model Minority Myth, Asian Americans have often been pitted against other minority groups. The Model Minority Myth publicizes the academic and professional success of Asian Americans, and attempts to prove that the American Dream is attainable—that minority groups can succeed in the United States. Before the Model Minority Myth, Asians often vacillated between being framed as part of a "yellow peril" invading the United States and the extreme opposite—as a successful minority student and professional, often times "outwhit[ing] the whites" and making great contributions to United States' society.[32] This key paradox embedded within the Model Minority Myth works to prove the inaccuracy of the Myth, but still does not detract from the power of invoking and asserting the Myth.

Many Asian American scholars demonstrate the inaccuracy of the Model Minority Myth with discussions and studies of the high poverty rate, extensive employment stratification, and relatively lower incomes of Asian Americans.[33] Although these scholars definitively dispel the Myth, they do not take power away from the widespread acceptance of the Model Minority stereotype by whites, African Americans, Latinos, and, as in the *Ho* case, Asian Americans. While Asian Americans are placed close to the top of this racial hierarchy, we must also pay attention to who is placed below them and why. Stereotypes regarding whiteness, blackness, and Asian-ness were exploited in order for the *Ho* lawsuit to gain viability within the current political and social contexts, which do not support any race-preferential policies, yet they also cast a negative light on African Americans and Latinos who are never characterized as the Model Minority.

Gary Okihiro recognizes that the Model Minority Myth is more than a mere construction but also a reality. "The construct, importantly, is not merely ideology but is a social practice that assigns to Asian Americans, and indeed to all minorities, places within the social formations."[34] Okihiro illustrates the dangers in accepting any stereotypes, regardless of the positive light they might shed on certain groups, stating that Asians are positioned within an insidious circle, in which the Model Minority can also be equated with the Yellow Peril. "Asian workers can be 'diligent' and 'slavish,' 'frugal' and 'cheap,' 'upwardly mobile' and 'aggressive. ...'"[35] Beyond the stereotypical framings of Asian Americans, their own decisions regarding their personal and political positionality have engaged neoconservative Asian Americans into a hegemonic compromise, in which they are attaining academic and professional success at the expense of African Americans and Latinos.

Conclusions

In the case of the *Ho* lawsuit, the framing of Asians as victims of a desegregation policy lay entirely in the hands of a group of Chinese parents and their children. Thus, while the *Ho* lawsuit advocated an end to racial preferences and the institution of colorblindness in admissions policies, the supporters and plaintiffs also effectively utilized a discursive strategy in which Asians, specifically Chinese Americans, were cast as victims and African Americans and Latinos[36] were framed as undeservedly benefiting from a desegregation policy, which was framed by the plaintiffs as a racial preference policy. Omi and Takagi state that neoconservatives, what they term "the Right," frame Asian Americans as a minority group that has been wronged by racial preferences, "as the victims of affirmative action."[37] While the Right attempts to adhere to colorblindness and meritocracy in their quest to end all race-preferential policies, they also invoke race by utilizing Asian Americans. The complexity of this strategy comes across very simply—it is not just white men who are against affirmative action but some minority groups as well.

The discourse in the *Ho* lawsuit is emblematic of the larger national shifts away from support of affirmative action and any policy with racial or gender preferences. Stereotypes around whiteness, blackness, and Asian-ness are exploited in order for the *Ho* lawsuit to gain currency and viability within the current political and social contexts, which do not support any race-preferential policies. The *Ho* lawsuit has devised new arguments that are consonant with the current neoconservative political climate.

The danger lies not in the success of Asian-American individuals but how they are viewed and framed by other groups—most notably other minority groups, the media, and politicians. Anti-Asian sentiment, on the part of other minority groups, is brewing within the context of education. At U.C. Berkeley in the early 1990s, both African-American and Chicano/Latino students believed themselves to be stigmatized by their fellow Asian-American students. "(Some of them) saw Asian Americans as 'exclusionary,' 'isolationist,' and as wanting to distinguish themselves from the more pointedly stigmatized Chicano and Black students."[38]

Thus, while the *Ho* plaintiffs and supporters believe that they are dis criminated against and attempt to fight for their rights, the larger issue really surrounds other minority groups and the negative stereotypes attached to them through and because of the Asian Model Minority stereotype. The *Ho* case and its surrounding political and social contexts also serve to frame another emerging conflict—that of Black/Brown vs. Yellow.

DISCUSSION QUESTIONS

1. Discuss the harm done to other groups by asserting the Model Minority Myth as part of the *Ho* lawsuit arguments.
2. What are the achievements and consequences of Asian Americans racially construction themselves as the Model Minority?
3. What did the neoconservative movement gain from the *Ho* lawsuit and its arguments?

Notes

1. *Brian Ho, Patrick Wong, & Hilary Chen v. SFUSD*, p. 2.
2. Henry Der, *Preliminary Analysis of Brian Ho v. SFUSD,* Chinese for Affirmative Action, 9 September, 1994., 7.
3. Kimberle Crenshaw, Neil Gotanda, Gary Peller, and Kendall Thomas, "Introduction," in Kimberle Crenshaw, Neil Gotanda, Gary Peller, and Kendall Thomas, eds., *Critical Race Theory—The Key Writings that Formed the Movement,* (New York: The New Press, 1995), xiv.
4. San Francisco Unified School District, "Report on San Francisco School Desegregation plan to Judge William Orrick, United States District Court—Executive Summary," July 1992, 2.
5. *Brian Ho, Patrick Wong, & Hilary Chen v. SFUSD*, 2.
6. Michael Omi and Howard Winant, *Racial Formation in the United States—From the 1960s to the 1990s,* 2nd edition, (New York: Routledge, 1994), 130.
7. Omi and Winant, 130.
8. Omi and Winant, 131.
9. Edsall and Edsall chronicle the rise of neoconservative rhetoric through the politics of Ronald Reagan. The term "equality of opportunity" became a standard term that Reagan used to describe race-based policies. Edsall and Edsall observe that, 'The power of conservative egalitarianism—based on an idealized

concept of 'equal opportunity' and reinforced by free-market economic theory—is that it affirms basic American principles of equality while protecting, and in some cases reinforcing, the very unequal distribution of racial and economic benefits challenged by liberalism'. See Thomas Byrne Edsall with Mary D. Edsall, *Chain Reaction—The Impact of Race, Rights, and Taxes on American Politics,* (New York: W.W. Norton & Company, 1992), 147.

10. Gerard Lim, "Lawsuit Over Chinese American Enrollment: Class Warfare By the Bay," *AsianWeek,* 19 August, 1994.

11. Mamie Huey, "Chinese Americans Have Bone to Pick with Consent Decree," *Asian Week,* 27 January, 1995.

12. Elaine Woo, "Caught on the Wrong Side of the Line," *Los Angeles Times,* 13 July, 1995.

13. Woo, "Caught on the Wrong Side of the Line."

14. Nanette Asimov, "District's Long Struggle with Desegregation," *San Francisco Chronicle,* 19 June, 1995.

15. Alethea Yip, "Class-action Suit Sought on School Caps," *AsianWeek,* 6 October, 1995.

16. Lee Cheng, "Racialism Lives on in San Francisco Schools—SFUSD's New Assignment Plan Forces Race Mixing," *AsianWeek,* 7 October, 1999.

17. Cheng. "Racialism Lives On..."

18. Keith Osajima notes, "The articulation of successful Asians in the popular press carried ramifications that extended well beyond the Chinatowns and Japantowns of America." See Keith Osajima. "Asian Americans as the Model Minority: An Analysis of the Popular Press Image in the 1960s and 1980s." In *Reflections on Shattered Windows-Promises and Prospects for Asian American Studies,* eds. Gary Okihiro, Shirley Hune, Arthur Hansen and John M. Liu, (Washington State University Press: Pullman, 1988), 166.

19. Rowena Robles, "Articulating Race—Neoconservatve Renditions of Equality—An Analysis of the Brian Ho Lawsuit," AAPI Nexus, 2:1 (Winter/Spring 2004), 99.

20. Der, *Preliminary Analysis of Brian Ho,* 7.

21. Even though the plaintiffs and supporters of the *Ho* lawsuit are mostly Chinese Americans, the Model Minority Myth incorporates all Asian-American ethnic groups. Because they assert the Model Minority Myth, the assertion of race by the *Ho* plaintiff s and supporters may have worked inaccurately to include all Asian-American ethnic groups.

22. Through the *Brown* decision, the Supreme Court attempted to legislate racism as illegal and unconstitutional. The Supreme Court, along with the NAACP, believed that if schools could be desegregated, then so could the rest of society. David Kirp observes that, 'If the society as a whole cannot be integrated by law, it is thought, at least the schools can. Schools have also been regarded as a lever to more general social reform: integration in the schools just might catalyze wider change, brought about by a new

and more tolerant generation.' The NAACP sought to end legalized desegregation in public education, believing that it would lead to more widespread change throughout American society. See David Kirp. *Just Schools—The Idea of Racial Equality in American Education,* (Berkeley: University of California Press, 1982), 22.

23. Omi and Takagi describe how the black/white paradigm of race relations frames how Americans view race and race relations. They state that, "(t)he hegemonic 'black/white' paradigm of race relations has fundamentally shaped how we think about, engage, and politically mobilize around racial issues." See Omi and Takagi, *Situating Asian Americans,* 155.

24. Gary Okihiro, *Margins and Mainstreams—Asians in American History,* (Seattle: University of Washington Press, 1994), 33.

25. See Okihiro, *Margins and Mainstreams,* 34.

26. Omi and Takagi, *Situating Asian Americans,* 156.

27. Takagi, *Retreat from Race,* 176.

28. Alan Freeman utilizes the "fault concept" in describing groups, "innocents," who do not support school integration because these groups believe that they have never personally discriminated against certain groups and, therefore, should not bear the brunt of any race-conscious policies such as bussing or Affirmative Action. See Alan Freeman, "Legitimizing racial discrimination through antidiscrimination law: a critical review of Supreme Court doctrine," in *Critical Race Theory: the Key Writings that Formed the Movement,* eds. Kimberle Crenshaw, Neil Gotanda, Gary Peller, and Kendall Thomas, (New York: New Press, 1995), 30.

29. Takagi, *Retreat from Race,* 79.

30. See Nancy Abelmann and John Lie, *Blue Dreams: Korean Americans and the Los Angeles Riots* (Cambridge: Harvard University Press, 1995).

31. See Omi and Winant, *Racial Formation,* 65–69.

32. See Okihiro for a historical perspective on how Asian Americans have often traversed between black and white racial constructions in the United States. Okihiro, *Margins and Mainstreams,* 34.

33. Suecheng Chan demonstrates that newly-arrived Asian immigrant groups are not as successful as their Chinese and Japanese American counterparts who have been in the U.S. for several generations. She specifically points to the high rate of poverty and welfare dependency among Vietnamese refugees in attempts to counter the Model Minority stereotype. See Suecheng Chan, *Asians Americans—An Interpretive History,* (Boston: Twayne Publishers, 1991), 170. Paul Ong demonstrates that "despite high level(s) of education, APAs have not been able to translate their credentials into commensurate earnings and occupational status." Through an analysis of the intersections of income and education levels,

Ong shows that Asian Americans do not earn as much as their white counterparts even if they possess higher levels of education. See Paul Ong, "The Affirmative Action Divide," in *The State of Asian Pacific America-Transforming Race Relations*, ed. Paul Ong, (Los Angeles: LEAP Asian Pacific American Public Policy Institute and UCLA Asian American Studies Center, 2000), 329.

34. Okihiro, *Margins and Mainstreams,* 34.

35. Okihiro, *Margins and Mainstreams,* 170.

36. Takagi, *Retreat from Race,* 176.

37. Omi and Takagi, *Situating Asian Americans,* 157.

38. The Diversity Project, *Final Report*, November 1991, Institute of the Study for Social Change, Berkeley, November, 1991, 34.

CHAPTER 7

Social Movements: Brief Historical Perspectives

READING 15

The Origins and Causes of the Civil Rights Movement

By David Levering Lewis

If it is venturesome to suppose that anything analytically new may be offered as to the origins and causes of the Civil Rights Movement of the 1960s, it is equally true that the demography of this phenomenon is fundamental to its deepest comprehension. In this case, political demographics may truly be said to be racial destiny. In the two decades immediately following the outbreak of World War Two, almost three times as many Afro-Americans departed the South as had left during the Great Migration of the century's second decade—with 1,599,000 moving mostly North during the period 1940–1950, and 1,473,000 during the next ten years. The decade of the Sixties saw continued high migration, with some 1,380,000 more southern Afro-Americans outmigrating.

The political implications of this huge population shift were apparent to astute political observers as early as the 1928 presidential election, when the normally "solid" South divided its support between Herbert Hoover and Alfred E. Smith. For some Democrats, winning Afro-American voters in the urban North and East was seen as vital to garnering sufficient electoral votes to upset Hoover. Smith's campaign manager, the resourceful Mrs. Belle Moskovitz, persuaded him to offer the young assistant executive secretary of the National Association for the Advancement of Colored People (NAACP), Walter White, direction of the Smith-for-President Colored League. White and the NAACP leadership were assured that the Democratic standard bearer would adopt, publicly, a rhetoric of racial tolerance and, privately, a policy of seeking the counsel of and making federal appointments from the ranks of the civil rights establishment. Ultimately, white southern pressures forced Smith to renege. Walter White regretfully declined.[1] Nevertheless, about 20 percent of the Afro-American electorate voted for the Democrats, eight percent more than in previous elections.

Robert L. Vann, publisher of the Pittsburgh *Courier*, predicted that millions of his people would turn "the pictures of Abraham Lincoln to the wall" in the 1932 presidential election. With the unique exception, however, of Democratic Harlem, an even greater percentage voted for Hoover than before. What Walter White called the Afro-American's "chronic Republicanism" seemed fully reconfirmed with the rejection of Franklin D. Roosevelt. In fact, this was the last act in a drama of hidden attitudinal and political developments. The racial realignment was to come in the congressional elections two years later, when FDR's party won a majority of Afro-American voters for the first time in history. Howard University political philosopher Kelly Miller's pronouncement that the "Negro is no longer the wheelhorse of the Republican Party" fulfilled Robert Vann's prediction.

By 1936, the strategy pursued under Hoover to turn the southern GOP "lily white" was as dead as Prohibition—not to return until the Eisenhower Fifties. Alfred M. Landon wrapped himself in the mantle of Lincoln and Frederick Douglass, and Republicans inserted a fine-sounding civil rights plank in the national platform that year. Big city Democratic machines—Tammany in New York, Kelly-Nash in Chicago, Dickmann in St. Louis, Pendergast in Kansas City—lavished patronage on the black community. As Nancy Weiss shows, the Party effectively reminded Afro-Americans how well they had fared under FDR, after the misery caused by Hoover. "Let Jesus lead you, and Roosevelt feed you!" one popular slogan exhorted.[2]

Pat Watters and Reese Cleghorn observed of the years after 1934, "It was in this period that Negro votes and public policy at the presidential level became, in significant degree, cause and effect."[3] Northward migration reinforced the labor-urban-based wing of the Democratic Party, the wing in sympathy with the broader economic and social objectives of the New Deal. Southern Democrats in senior congressional positions not only meant disenfranchisement and segregation for Afro-Americans, but legislative obstructionism in the service of economic conservatism and regional parochialism. These were the Party satraps whom FDR finally publicly denounced as "feudal oligarchs" (Ellison Smith of South Carolina, Walter George of Georgia, Millard Tydings of Maryland, Martin Dies of Texas, Theodore Bilbo of Mississippi) and appealed directly but altogether unsuccessfully to their constituents to unseat some of them in the 1938 congressional elections. In matters of maximum importance to it, the South remained well in control of partisan and even national politics, but the emergence of countervailing forces within the Democratic Party was unmistakable.

As one of the key elements in this new coalition of power, Afro-Americans did, in fact, increase their advantages during the so-called Second New Deal (1936–1940). The new, more responsive Attorney General created the civil rights section in the Justice Department; the Department of Interior imposed racial quotas on WPA contractors; the Civilian Conservation Corps augmented Afro-American enrollment from 6 to 11 percent; other alphabet agencies recruited some 100 of the best and brightest Afro-American university graduates as midlevel bureaucrats (Ralph Bunche, William Hastie, Rayford Logan, et al.); finally, somewhat assuaging Afro-American anguish about his waffling over poll tax repeal and public silence about federal antilynching legislation, FDR delivered at Howard University his symbolic "no forgotten men and no forgotten races" speech. In 1940, the Democratic platform addressed itself directly for the first time to equal protection under law and due process rights for Afro-Americans.

By then, 48 percent of the Afro-American population was urban; and, although only about 23 percent of it resided outside the South, its concentration in key northern cities was imposing—13 percent of Philadelphia's total population; 13.5 percent of Detroit's; 13 percent of Indianapolis's; 8.3 percent of Chicago's (for a total of nearly 300,000); and 6.4 percent of New York's (477,000, a treble increase over the 1920 census). *Time* magazine had noted four years previously, if erroneously, "In no national election since 1860 have politicians been so Negrominded as in 1936."[4] More significantly, in 1941, Ralph Bunches *Journal of Negro Education* article, "A Critical Analysis of the Tactical Programs of Minority Groups," gave preliminary formulation to the crucial "balance of power" concept, to which NAACP publicist Henry Lee Moon devoted booklength treatment seven years later, and by which more than a generation of Afro-American policymakers and politicians have since been guided (sometimes overambitiously).[5]

Although isolation of any single election factor risks presenting a false picture, the reality that Afro-American votes were now potentially determinative in 16 non-South states with 278 electoral votes escaped no serious political strategist.[6] Thus, in the 1944 FDR-Dewey contest, Thomas E. Dewey would unquestionably have won if his percentage of Afro-American votes had been equivalent to Hoover's in 1932. Thus, once again, as at its historic 1936 national convention, the Democratic Party's presidential decisionmakers successfully calculated the risks of offending the South with Hubert Humphrey's strong 1948 civil rights plank. Four southern states went Dixiecrat, while Harry S. Truman narrowly defeated Dewey because, as historians August Meier and Elliott Rudwick state, 1948 was "the first election since Reconstruction in which the Negro's status was a major issue and in which his political power was a critical factor in the outcome."[7] Nevertheless, massive Afro-American support for Adlai Stevenson was irrelevant to the outcome four years later—a perfect object lesson in the limitations of the balance of power paradigm. Under Dwight D. Eisenhower, the Hoover strategy of winning the lily white South was again regnant. This devastating limitation aside—and it is the one by which Afro-Americans are currently bedeviled—" there had been," as Watters and Cleghorn affirm, "a revolution in the power to obtain results."[8]

A reductionist interpretation of postwar liberalism both distorts and disserves the considerable reserve of moral and constitutional principles by which that liberalism was powered. Fascism's doctrinal depravity, the solidarism of the war effort, and the trauma of the Holocaust deeply affected the collective American mind. There were not a few white southerners, and probably a majority of white northerners, who would have wished to say to the first sit-in students, as did the woman in the Greensboro Woolworth's, "you should have done this ten years ago."[9] George Fredrickson's *White Supremacy* has masterfully shown the potential for political and social inclusion of racial minorities that a constitutional commitment to egalitarian democracy can sustain and mobilize, even in the face of its longstanding nullification by formal and informal arrangements and compromises.[10] The official creeds of societies matter a great deal.

That said, it would be equally imperceptive to downplay the high degree of correspondence between the Afro-American's urbanization and outmigration from the South and the postwar mentality of racial meliorism. By 1950, the "power to obtain results" of Afro-Americans was running dangerously far ahead of the South's intellectual and institutional power to react constructively. Simultaneously, the racial attitudes in much of the rest of the nation were being transformed by that same potential power. Even the most casual reference to Tocqueville or Crane Brinton must have indicated a situation in which rising expectations and very slow social change presented the classic formula for upheaval, if not revolution—those flashpoint conjunctions which Ted Robert Gurr's work usefully assembles for our retrospective examination.[11] Was it not significant in this regard that the Carnegie Foundation, which had financed the massive study of an other evolving racial crisis (that arising from unrest among South Africa's Afrikaner poor), produced, through Gunnar Myrdal and his regiment of social scientists, the ultimate liberal conceptualization of and prescription for the American dilemma?[12]

The impact of *An American Dilemma* was so potent that it controlled racial thought and policy for at least a decade. For all its impressive sociological panoply and perdurable insights, the Myrdalian analysis was imbedded in Hegelian idealism. Right ideas would gradually transform wrong institutions; the American Creed would ultimately reify itself because the compounding tensions between high ideals and ignoble realities would compel white Americans to reexamine the racial status quo. "The moral dilemma of the American [is] the conflict between his moral valuations on various levels of consciousness and generality," Myrdal writes.[13] If, as I believe, Stanford Lymans contention is correct that the "entire body of Myrdal's argument is open to question" because of the explicit assumption that" 'higher values' generally win out in the long run over 'lower' ones," all this matters rather less than the transformative power that *An American Dilemma* attained principally by legitimizing debate about the dilemma.[14]

Its publication came in the same year as the Supreme Court, after a twelve-year toleration of the fiction that southern white primaries were privately organized occasions, found its rare Fifteenth Amendment voice in *Smith v. Allwright,* definitively striking down this major franchise impediment. Two years later, came the presidentially impanelled Committee on Civil Rights, whose eloquent, comprehensive report was ready for publication in late 1947. *To Secure These Rights* spoke in Myrdalese of the moral imperatives of the American Creed, but it introduced a significant new reason for its fulfillment: "The United States is not so strong, the final triumph of the democratic ideal is not so inevitable that we can ignore what the world thinks of us or our record."[15] Another blue-ribbon, presidential committee produced, in time for the 1948 election, a searing expose of the social consequences of segregated education and a recommendation that all forms of educational segregation end as soon as possible. Finally, Harry Truman gave Afro-Americans the long-awaited presidential rhetoric, calling on Congress in his State of the Union message to enact significant civil rights legislation.

In all of these developments there was the resonance of political demography; but neither the reality nor the prospect of Afro- American votes counting heavily in close elections would have sufficed alone to produce the civil rights advances ahead. By the early Fifties, demographics had also yielded impressive economic benefits. Despite severe employment dislocation caused by temporary dismantlement of defense industries and two punishing recessions in 1953–54 and 1957–58, Afro-Americans generally prospered in the score of years after the War. During the period 1947 to 1974, according to the U.S.

Census Bureaus global study, "the median income of Black families more than doubled," rising from 51 to 62 percent of white family income, with 51 percent becoming white collar.[16] During the late 1940 s and early 1950s, the black unemployment rate of less than 2 percent was at its lowest relative to the white rate (which it otherwise tends to double).[17] *Jet* and *Ebony,* and a number of mainstream popular magazines, ballyhooed the new black purchasing power, calculated to be larger than the gross national product of several European nations.

Rising incomes also meant a tripling of the college population, with prewar Afro-American invisibility at northern white universities giving way to dramatic increase.[18] Predictably, there was now a steady supply of "exemplary" Afro-Americans (athlete Jackie Robinson joining the Dodgers in 1947, poet Gwendolyn Brooks winning a Pulitzer and jurist William Hastie appointed to a federal judgeship in 1949, diplomat Ralph Bunche receiving the Nobel Peace Prize in 1950)—racial paragons whose lives rebutted inferiority stereotypes, on the one hand, and, on the other, diverted attention from the distressing Marxism of W.E.B. Du Bois, Paul Robeson, and Benjamin Davis, Jr. Thus, in the Myrdalian decade after 1944, that article of faith of such civil rights leaders as James Weldon Johnson, Charles S. Johnson, and Walter White that the race problem was essentially not so much institutional or even economic but, rather, a phenomenon of collective psychology, now seemed verified.[19] Many white and black civil libertarians began to believe that those rhetorical taboos—usually beginning, "Would you want your daughter ... ?"—might now be answered affirmatively, if the subject were Ralph Bunche, Jr., or Jackie Robinson, Jr.

In the case of the Supreme Court, the two taboo questions concerned housing and education. Richard Bardolph and Richard Kluger have amply documented the granite conservatism and infinite civil rights evasions of the Court during the administrations of FDR and Truman.[20] But New Deal and Fair Deal ideologies, reinforced by the Afro-American's increasingly credible political and economic presence, began the slow reversal of *Plessy v. Ferguson* in the late 1930's. The NAACP litigation strategy, conceived in 1931 during Nathan Margold's brief tenure as the first salaried legal counsel, produced, under Charles Hamilton Houston's inspired direction, a trickle and then a stream of Supreme Court victories. Beginning with *Missouri ex rel Gaines v. Canada,* the 1938 decision requiring University of Missouri Law School either to admit a single qualified applicant or build him a law school, continuing with the 1947 *Sweatt v. Painter* and 1948 *Sipuel v. Oklahoma* decisions, and climaxing with *McLaurin v. Oklahoma State Regents* in 1950, mandating truly equal professional school facilities, NAACP Lawyers had almost achieved their goal of making separate-but-equal higher education too expensive for the South.[21] In *McLaurin,* Chief Justice Fred M. Vinson's opinion had gone so far as to speculate on the possibility that separateness might be incompatible with equality. That same year, the NAACP filed its first public school segregation case before Judge J. Waties Waring of Charleston, South Carolina, contesting the educational policies in Clarendon County.

From one perspective, NAACP tactics simply made a virtue of necessity: litigation focusing on higher education raised constitutional issues whose validation involved, as a practical matter, only a finite cohort of Afro-Americans. From another perspective—that of class interests—the NAACP's tactics, as well as those of the National Urban League and other major civil rights organizations, betrayed a consistent elitism. Martin Kilson reminds us that, until the mid-1960's, "civil rights politics was largely a middle-class affair, and the Negro lower strata had little political relationship to civil rights politics."[22] However finite the cohort, white, law, dental, and business school admissions were bread- and-butter exigencies to the civil rights establishment and its dues-paying supporters.

To be sure, quality public-school education was one of their paramount concerns, but, to a considerable extent, E. Franklin Frazier's black bourgeoisie had carved out tolerable enclaves for its children either in the urban public school systems of the South or through private means there.[23] Furthermore, for much of the Afro-American civil rights rank and file, there was a vested interest in separate equality in public school education (principalships, teaching positions, the two-income-per-family necessity). In this regard, it is worth a good Marxist speculation about the surprising fact revealed by Kluger that it was Judge Waring of South Carolina who persuaded Thurgood Marshall to withdraw and amend the NACCP's petition so as to challenge head-on the constitutionality of racial segregation.[24] There were good reasons why just plain folk called it the "National Association for the Advancement of *Certain* People."

It was this "certain people" syndrome that had caused the NAACP to be roundly criticized by many of the younger Afro-American intellectuals during the Du Bois-sponsored 1933 Amenia Conference—particularly the Associations hostility to organized labor and relative indifference to economic issues.[25] Here again, migration north generated an important alliance. So long as most Afro-Americans remained in the South (the majority of them as peasant farmers), locked into the Republican Party, they remained irrelevant to the concerns of organized labor. The shift to the Democrats made a labor-black alliance at least a possibility; although, with the important exception of A. Philip Randolph of the Brotherhood of Sleeping Car Porters, Afro-American leadership during much of the Thirties regarded organized labor as the prime enemy. As Herbert Hill has shown, the racial exclusivity of the AFL was endemic and chronic, "from Gompers to benign William Green to the current era of sophisticated public relations under George Meany...."[26] But rampant mechanization of southern agriculture during the New Deal drove hundreds of thousands more unskilled Afro-Americans into northern industrial centers where fierce working-class white hostility to them as "scabs" was gradually attenuated, after the 1935 founding of the CIO, by a strategy of cooptation.

The collapse of such great labor strikes as Homestead in 1892 and the "Red Scare" steel strikes of 1919, as well as the 1927 United Mine Workers failure to organize the southern fields, was said to be attributable to black strike breakers.[27] With four out of five black workers unskilled, the Congress of Industrial Organizations John L. Lewis, Philip Murray, and David Dubinsky proclaimed the brotherhood of all and energetically set about organizing black coal miners, steel workers, and auto workers. The role of "SWOC" (the Steel Workers Organizing Committee) in cementing the new interracial alliance was crucial, SWOC funds flowed into the NAACP treasury, where they went to finance litigation and antilynch lobbying. In 1941, the longlived marriage of the NAACP and the United Automobile Workers occurred dramatically when patrician Walter White stood at the gate to Henry Ford's River Rouge plant with a bullhorn, exhorting black workers to join the union.[28] Weiss finds that CIO funds also struck a positive response from the deeply conservative National Urban League.[29]

While the American Federation of Labor remained as lily white as before, even its leadership soon found it useful to support rhetorically and financially the civil rights agenda, as well as to take such specific public relations steps as full admission of Randolphs Brotherhood of Sleeping Car Porters and official participation in Scottsboro and Angelo Herndon rallies.[30] Unskilled and skilled organized labor courted Afro-Americans for their own interests (interests largely coinciding with those of the Democratic Party), and Afro-Americans rallied to both from symmetrical motives. The very aggressive recruitment by communist unions of Afro-American membership and infiltration of Afro-American organizations, such as the National Negro Congress and Scottsboro defense groups, contributed a positive legacy of interracial activism. If, by 1940, the civil rights militancy of Harry Bridges's Marine Workers Industrial Union, Mike Quill's Transport Workers Union, and H. L. Mitchell's socialist-inspired Southern Tenant Farmers Union deadended in the debacle of the Popular Front, historians Harvard Sitkoff, Mark Naison, Nell Painter, Dan Carter, and Donald Grubbs *inter alia,* have shown how durably educative and energizing communist unionism could be.[31]

By the early 1950's, the cumulative impact of balance of power politics, rising incomes, federal court decisions, coalition with organized labor, and the string of exemplary racial "firsts," had primed much of the nation for an end to segregation. There was change even in the South, where *Smith v. Allwright* brought Afro-American registration from a mere 250,000 in 1944 to 1,008,614 by 1952—still only 20 percent of its voting age population there.[32] For a brief, incredible period, it seemed possible that gubernatorial politics might replicate Democratic presidential politics in Georgia and Alabama. In Georgia, former governor Ellis Arnall's protege, James Carmichael (candidate of urban, business, and progressive forces), polled more ballots than Eugene Talmadge in 1946, with the help of an overwhelming black vote—only to be denied office because of that state's infamous, rural-loaded "county unit" system.[33] In Alabama, populist Governor James Folsom opposed the Strom Thurmond Dixiecrats, courted "Nigra" votes, and stupefied white Alabamians with a 1949 Christmas message, declaring, "As long as the Negroes are held down by deprivation and lack of opportunity, all the other people will be held down alongside them."[34] Folsoms protege, George C. Wallace, later took the state in a different direction.

But Morton Sosna's "silent South" occasionally found its voice. Ralph McGill of the Atlanta *Constitution* and Virginius Dabney of the Richmond *Times-Dispatch,* while meticulously eschewing advocacy of racial integration, cautiously urged the abandonment of Jim Crow public transportation. The Chapel Hill sociologists, led by Howard W. Odum, and the Chapel Hill artists, influenced by Paul Green, expended much conscience-stricken passion, if not light, over the race problem. The Southern Regional Council, a gentlemanly, slightly interracial group of southern educators, debated, temporized, and finally, in 1951, authorized Arthur Fleming, its president, to state that it was "neither reasonable nor right that colored citizens of the United States should be subjected to the humiliation of being segregated by law." Of course, the loudest voice in the muted, Deep South was not a man's but Lillian Smiths whose novels and editorials in her *North Georgia Review* pricked the conscience of the white South. Fairly undetected, there were, as Aldon Morris's recent study reveals, highly significant civil rights developments occurring at the grass roots in numerous southern cities and towns. A new Afro-American leadership—ministerial and populist—was taking shape below the traditional oligarchic, white-black leadership configuration. Still, one had to have, as a reading of Sosna and Harry Ashmore indicates, the most restrained expectations for efficacious white southern liberalism in the 1950's.[35]

The stage was now set for decision in the five cases grouped as *Brown v. the Board of Education of Topeka, Kansas.* The sudden death of Chief Justice Vinson permitted the jurisprudentially radical reasoning—theories from sociology and psychology—leading to the Court's unanimous May 17, 1954 decision. In retrospect, the civil rights revolution appears to have been the inevitable consequence of *Brown.* "Revolution" here denotes social upheaval accompanied by collective citizen violence and extraordinary state intervention. Yet, at the risk of sinning counterfactually, it seems that the revolutionary character of civil rights might very well have been different—have been much more evolutionary—but for three interdependent factors. In order of ascending causal importance, those factors were: first, the internal politics of the Warren Supreme Court dictating, as the price of unanimity in *Brown,* a one-year stay of implementation and the enunciation of the anticlimactic, "all deliberate speed" doctrine; second, the collpase and supplanting of responsible southern white leadership in virtually every domain (religion, politics, business, education) by opportunists and extremists; and, third and decisively, the southern politics of the Eisenhower White House and the Presidents own race relations convictions.[36]

Eisenhowers well-known reactions—that Earl Warren's appointment had been a mistake and the decision foolish—and his refusal to endorse *Brown,* except in the negative sense of stating that it was law, was, as Ashmore, Kluger, Sitkoff, Anthony Lewis, and Steven Lawson among others have argued, calamitous.[37] It should be recalled that, for about two years after *Brown,* "all deliberate speed" meant just that in much of the South. About 700 of the 3000 southern school districts quietly desegregated, including, significantly, that of Hoxie township in rural Lawrence County, Arkansas. The governors of South Carolina and Virginia initially appealed for calm and promised dutiful compliance. "We will consider the matter and work toward a plan which will be acceptable to our citizens and in keeping with the edict of the Court," Virginia's governor promised.[38] If the white South was hardly enthusiastic about school desegregation and if, as the so-called 1956 Southern Manifesto attested, most of its leaders were plotting to retard implementation through legal casuistry and administrative procrastination, a course of outright white defiance and violence was probably not inevitable until Little Rock.

Here was the great political miscalculation. The Eisenhower White House, with its eyes on 1956, had no intention of forfeiting a large, grateful southern white vote, despite its secret deal with Democrat

Adam Clayton Powell to press for a civil rights act in exchange for the Harlem Congressmans endorsement of the President.[39] Ignorant of the Souths cultural and political atavisms, White House evasions and silences were bound to produce the very no-holds-barred crisis they hoped to avoid. Laissez-faire that had worked with Senator Joseph McCarthy was mistaken. Some 530 cases of recorded violence and reprisals against southern Afro-Americans were recorded between 1955-1958. The 1955 Interstate Commerce Commissions order banning segregation in interstate travel had no writ in the Deep South. School integration was nonexistent in Virginia, Georgia, Alabama, Louisiana, Mississippi, and South Carolina. In eight Deep South states, 45,845 fewer Afro-Americans registered to vote between 1956 and 1958 because of intimidation.[40]

But a primary contribution of the white South to the civil rights revolution was its assault upon the *NAACP.* Texas and Alabama's injunctions, Georgias annulment of tax exemption, Virginia's sedition acts, South Carolina's public employment prohibitions decimated the Association's chapters and made outlaws of the stalwarts. The Alabama NAACP could suppport Arthurine Lucy's successful admission to the University of Alabama; but it looked impotent when she was speciously expelled a few days later, while a local mob hooted. In this climate, Monroe County, North Carolina, NAACP chapter president Robert Williams, expelled by the national executive secretary for arming and drilling his members, was a predictable phenomenon. Little Rock, the South's 1957 redneck edition of Fort Sumter, was equally predictable. Scenting victory, Yale law professor Alexander Bickel wrote, "the southern leaders, or at least a sufficient number of them, sought to assure it by turning from litigation and agitation to direct action by the use of mobs."[41]

Meanwhile, Afro-American leadership was undergoing radical transformation. Southern Baptist preachers, conspicuous in the past for their civic parochialism and cautiousness, were leading desegregation boycotts—boycotts in which, for the first time, poor folk participated in large numbers. Audible above the din of demonstration was heard the baritone of a new leadership voice. "Give us the ballot," Martin Luther King, Jr., demanded from the Lincoln Memorial, during the May 1957 Prayer Pilgrimage to Washington:

> Give us the ballot and we will no longer have to worry the federal government about our rights. ... Give us the ballot and we will get the people judges who love mercy. Give us the ballot and we will quietly, lawfully, and nonviolently, without rancor or bitterness, implement the May 17, 1954, decision of the Supreme Court.[42]

The students who listened to Martin Luther King concluded that what was not given would have to be taken.

Notes

1. Cf., David Levering Lewis, *When Harlem Was in Vogue* (New York: Knopf, 1981), 205–6.

2. Nancy J. Weiss, *Farewell to the Party of Lincoln: Black Politics in the Age of FDR* (Princeton: Princeton University Press, 1983), 202.

3. Pat Watters and Reese Cleghorn, *Climbing Jacob's Ladder: The Arrival of Negroes in Southern Politics* (New York: Harcourt, Brace and World, 1967), 10.

4. Quoted in Harvard Sitkoff, *A New Deal for Blacks: The Emergence of Civil Rights as a National Issue—The Depression Decade* (New York: Oxford University Press, 1981), 91.

5. Ralph Bunche, "A Critical Analysis of the Tactical Programs of Minority Groups," *Journal of Negro Education*, IV (July 1935), 308–20; Henry Lee Moon, *Balance of Power: The Negro Vote* (Garden City: Doubleday, 1948).

6. Watters and Cleghorn, *Climbing Jacob's Ladder*, 21.

7. August Meier and Elliott M. Rudwick, *From Plantation to Ghetto*, (3rd ed.; New York: Hill and Wang, 1976), 279.

8. Quoted in Watters and Cleghorn, *Climbing Jacob's Ladder*, 12.

9. Quoted in Harvard Sitkoff, *The Struggle for Black Equality, 1954–1980* (New York: Hill and Wang, 1981), 70.

10. George M. Fredrickson, *White Supremacy: A Comparative Study in American and South African History* (New York: Oxford University Press, 1982), esp. chapter 6.

11. Crane Brinton, *Anatomy of a Revolution* (1938; reprint ed., New York: Vintage, 1965); Ted Robert Gurr, *Why Men Rebel* (Princeton: Princeton University Press, 1970). Alexis de Tocqueville, *L'Ancien Regime et la Revolution* (Paris, 1856).

12. Cf., seminal controversial essay by Ralph Ellison, "An American Dilemma: A Review," *Shadow and Act* (New York: Random House, 1964), 303–17.

13. Gunnar Myrdal, An *American Dilemma: The Negro Problem and Modern Democracy* (New York: Harper and Row, 1944), I, lxxi.

14. Stanford M. Lyman, *The Black American in Sociological Thought: A Failure of Perspective* (New York: Putnam, 1972), 113.

15. Albert P. Blaustein and Robert L. Zangrando, eds., *Civil Rights and the American Negro: A Documentary History* (New York: Trident, 1968), 379.

16. *The Social and Economic Status of the Black Population in the United States: An Historical View, 1790–1978* (Washington, D.C.: Government Printing Office, 1979), 379; William H. Harris, *The Harder We Run: Black Workers Since the Civil War* (New York: Oxford University Press, 1982), 127.

17. *The Social and Economic Status,* 61.

18. *Ibid.,* 93.

19. Cf., Lewis, *When Harlem Was in Vogue*, 93, and "Parallels and Divergences: Assimilationist Strategies of Afro-American and Jewish Elites from 1910 to the Early 1930s," *Journal of American History,* 73 (December 1984), 543–64, esp. 548–51.

20. Richard Bardolph, *The Civil Rights Record: Black Americans and the Law, 1849–1970 (New* York: Crowell, 1970); Richard Kluger, *Simple Justice: The History of Brown v. Board of Education and Black America's Struggle for Equality* (New York: Knopf, 1975).

21. Kluger, *Simple Justice,* 133–8, 274–84.

22. Martin Kilson, "Black Politics: A New Power," *Dissent,* 18 (August 1971), 333–45, 337.

23. Cf., Kluger, *Simple Justice,* 329; Constance McLaughlin Green, *The Secret City: A History of Race Relations in the Nation's Capital* (Princeton: Princeton University Press, 1967), 209–12; Mamie Garvin Fields with Karen Fields, *Lemon Swamp and Other Places: A Carolina Memoir* (New York: Free Press, 1983), chapters 3 and 4; August Meier and David L. Lewis, "History of the Negro Upper Class in Atlanta, Georgia, 1890–1959," *Journal of Negro Education,* 28 (Spring 1959), 128–39.

24. Kluger, *Simple Justice,* 304.

25. Sitkoff, *A New Deal for Blacks,* 251; B. Joyce Ross, *J. E. Spingam and the Rise of the* NAACP, *1911-1939* (New York: Atheneum, 1972), 182.

26. Herbert Hill, "The Racial Practices of Organized Labor: The Contemporary Record," in Julius Jacobson, ed., *The Negro and the American Labor Movement* (Garden City: Anchor, 1968), chapter 8, esp. 287.

27. Ray Marshall, "The Negro in Southern Unions," in Jacobson, ed., *The Negro and the American Labor Movement,* 138; Sitkoff, *A New Deal for Blacks,* 179.

28. August Meier and Elliott M. Rudwick, *Black Detroit and the Rise of the* UAW (New York: Oxford University Press, 1979), 100.

29. *Nancy J. Weiss, The National Urban League, 1910–1940* (New York: Oxford University Press, 1974), 291.

30. William H. Harris, *Keeping the Faith: A Philip Randolph, Milton P. Webster, and the Brotherhood of Sleeping Car Porters, 1925–37* (Urbana: University rtf Illinois Press, 1977), chapter 7.

31. Sitkoff, *A New Deal for Blacks,* chapter 6; Mark Naison, *Communists in Harlem During the Depression* (Urbana: University of Illinois Press, 1983); Nell Painter, *The Narrative of Hosea Hudson: His Life as a Negro Communist in the South* (Cambridge: Harvard University Press, 1979); Donald H. Grubbs, *Cry from the Cotton: The STFU and the New Deal* (Chapel Hill: University of North Carolina Press, 1971).

32. Watters and Cleghorn, *Climbing Jacob's Ladder,* 27.

33. *Ibid.,* 30.

34. Marshall Frady, *Wallace* (New York: World, 1968), 102.

35. Aldon Morris, *The Origins of the Civil Rights Movement: Black Communities Organizing for Change* (New York: Free Press, 1984); Morton Sosna, *In Search of the Silent South: Southern Liberals and the Race Issue* (New York: Columbia University Press, 1977); Harry Ashmore, *Hearts and Minds: The Anatomy of Racism from Roosevelt to Reagan* (New York: McGraw-Hill, 1982).

36. Kluger, *Simple Justice,* chapter 25; Steven F. Lawson, *Black Ballots: Voting Rights in the South, 1944–1969* (New York: Columbia University Press, 1976), chapter 6.

37. Anthony Lewis, *Portrait of a Decade: The Second American Revolution* (New York: Random House, 1964), chapter 4.

38. Quoted in *ibid.,* 29.

39. Maurine Christopher, *America's Black Congressmen* (New York: Crowell, 1971), 200.

40. Watters and Cleghorn, *Climbing Jacob's Ladder,* 28.

41. Lewis, *Portrait of a Decade,* 40.

42. David Levering Lewis, *King; A Biography* (Urbana: University of Illinois Press, 1978), 93.

READING 16

Contributions of African American Women in the Modern Civil Rights Movement

By Bruce A. Glasrud and Merline Pitre

African American women have played a significant role in the ongoing struggle for freedom and equality since the inception of this nation. Nowhere is this better illustrated than in the former Confederate states during the modern civil rights era, from 1954 to 1974. During the height of civil rights struggles, black women, like black men, were foot soldiers in sit-in, pray-in, and stand-in campaigns. They were crucial as grassroots and organizational leaders, stimulating mass participation in the movement. Women also served as chief sources for mobilization of people and capital within local communities. They organized black consumers, supported labor unions, and worked in politics and journalism. They particularly helped attack school segregation, coordinate lunch counter sit-ins, boycott buses, mobilize voter-registration drives, and establish communication networks. Yet during the era under study, black women were not typically quoted in the media or consulted by white politicians. Even in historians' accounts, the contribution of women remained obscure for a long time. As Charles Payne has argued, this historical invisibility did not match the historical reality.[1] What is now needed as a match for historical reality is a study that identifies, explores, and evaluates the roles and contributions of African American women in the modern civil rights movement throughout the South. *Southern Black Women in the Modern Civil Rights Movement* attempts to meet this need.

Even though black women performed prominent duties in the civil rights movement—bridge-building, organizing, protesting, participating, mobilizing, creating, energizing, and leading particular efforts—they seldom received credit either for their involvement or for their contributions. For example, no woman was a speaker during the 1963 March on Washington celebration, and only a few women were invited to sit nearby as Mahalia Jackson sang. But, despite the lack of public recognition, African American women set the stage for that moment—and for decades to follow—by their notable part in the eradication of the white-dominated, segregated Southern society. As Stephen

Tuck phrases it so well, "the activities of women were so obvious in Georgia protest that it would be a gross oversight to overlook them."[2] This observation was true not only of Georgia but of all the Southern states.

Studies of what happened at the state level are critical not only because of what black women accomplished but also because their activism, leadership, and courage demonstrated the militancy needed for a mass movement. Historians and sociologists have illuminated the ways in which blacks in urban centers, as well as in rural areas, interacted with major civil rights organizations and leaders. Yet we are still some distance from a convincing synthesis of national, or even regional, strategies and factors embodied in the history of the civil rights movement in this country. Our book is a major step toward that goal. Like Paula Giddings's *When and Where I Entered,* it makes clear that not all black women in the South entered the movement in the same way.[3] Some led demonstrations; others remained behind the scene. Most wanted integration; some promoted separate but equal. Many provided money; many, nurturing. Some gave up a career; others made a career of protests and demonstrations. The participants included high-profile women and women who acted without fanfare, even down playing the importance of their personal leadership, focusing instead on the success of a collective effort.

Southern Black Women in the Modern Civil Rights Movement focuses on the civil rights efforts of black females in the former Confederacy, devoting one chapter to each state. This approach is based on the assumption that white supremacy was most entrenched in those states. Local and state movement studies published in 1988 and 1990 transformed the field of civil rights by constructing narratives about a variety of women rather than focusing on a single national icon such as Rosa Parks. These studies pointed out that the transformation of America's black-white relations occurred differently in different locales. For example the strategies and methods used by Lulu B. White to eradicate Jim Crow in Texas were different from those used by Fannie Lou Hamer to end apartheid in Mississippi. Similarly, the factors in a city run by businessmen differed from those in a rural area dominated by people with farming interests.

It is generally agreed that the modern civil right movement spanned the years 1954 and 1974. We start with 1954, the year in which the US Supreme Court, in *Brown v. Board of Education of Topeka,* struck down segregated education, triggering years of struggle to integrate K-12 and university classrooms. The movement continued to grow. In 1955 a flurry of activity and agitation followed the lynching of fourteen-year-old Emmett Till in Mississippi and the unanimous acquittal of two white men charged in his death. And in December of that same year, Rosa Parks's refusal to yield her seat on a bus in Montgomery, Alabama, ignited a massive civil rights protest. We end two years following Barbara Jordan's 1972 election to the US House of Representatives. The year 1974 witnessed what Genna Rae McNeil refers to as a "nonrevolutionary social movement" on behalf of Joan Little. Sexually attacked by an ice-pick-wielding guard in a North Carolina prison, Little killed him. When she was tried, a massive "Free Joan Little" movement began, and in 1975 she was acquitted by a jury.[4] In 1974, Floridians unveiled a statue honoring a key state and national black leader, Mary McLeod Bethune.

We do not assert that the years 1954–74 were the only years to witness the civil rights revolution or that black women did not participate in earlier and later efforts to change and challenge white supremacy. We note only that these two decades were pivotal in the modern civil rights and black-power movements. In *Freedom's Daughters: The Unsung Heroines of the Civil Rights Movement from 1830 to 1970,* Lynne Olson thoroughly delineates the myriad efforts of women in the civil rights movement through one hundred forty years. She is not alone. Numerous authors have depicted black women's pre-1954 efforts to improve their status and that of their race vis-á-vis white supremacy in the South. One such collection, *Time Longer Than Rope: A Century of African American Activism, 1850–1950,* edited by Charles M. Payne and Adam Green, comprises a thoughtful group of articles.[5] However, we know of no study of the roles of black women in the modern civil rights and black-power movements during the key years 1954–74. *Southern Black Women in the Modern Civil Rights Movement* is written to fill this gap.

The story of women in the modern civil rights movement emerged as an area of concentration for research and teaching following the international conference "Women in the Civil Rights Movement: Trailblazers and Torchbearers, 1941–1965," hosted in 1988 by the Martin Luther King, Jr., Center for Nonviolent Social Change and by Georgia State University. At this event, scholars and activists spent a week reconstructing the activism of women. The papers presented at this conference, edited by Vicki L. Crawford, Jacqueline A. Rouse, and Barbara Woods and published by Indiana University Press in 1990 as *Women in the Civil Rights Movement: Trailblazers and Torchbearers, 1941–1965,* sparked the publication of memoirs, community studies, biographies, organizational studies, and autobiographical essays from black and white women (and men) who picketed, demonstrated, and went to jail for the cause of freedom and justice. This new body of literature introduced the issues of race, class, and gender to the movement.

Book-length studies of black women in the civil rights movement are becoming numerous. Seven years following *Women in the Civil Rights Movement,* Belinda Robnett's *How Long? How Long? African-American Women in the Struggle for Civil Rights* appeared. A sociological study, Robnett's work emphasized the relationship of gender to the civil rights struggle and developed a theory of bridge-building to explain the central role of black women in the civil rights efforts. Peter J. Ling and Sharon Monteith continued the emphasis on gender in their 1999 anthology, *Gender and the Civil Rights Movement.* As Ling and Monteith emphasized, "the civil rights movement was primarily concerned with race, but it was also about personal identity."[6]

Two influential books published in 2001 continued the study of black women and the civil rights movement. Lynne Olson's previously mentioned *Freedom's Daughters* discussed the modern civil rights era in connection with a long history of black women's activism. *Sisters in the Struggle: African American Women in the Civil Rights–Black Power Movement,* edited by Bettye Collier-Thomas and V. P. Franklin, moved the discussion to the years beyond 1970 by including the black-power movement in a signal collection of articles. As some of the essays note, the position of black and white women in the movement changed as a result of the goals and aspirations of the black-power movement.[7] For studies of white women in the struggle see Constance Curry, *Deep in Our Hearts: Nine White Women in the Freedom Movement,* and Gail S. Murray's collection, *Throwing Off the Cloak of Privilege: White Southern Women Activists in the Civil Rights Era.*[8]

Publication continued. In 2005, Jeanne Theoharis and Komozi Woodard edited *Groundwork: Local Black Freedom Movements in America,* which considered a much broader geographic scope than the Southern states. The editors pointed out the centrality of women in local black-freedom movements across the nation.[9] One other pivotal work should be included: in 1978, Sharon Harley and Rosalyn Terborg-Penn published *The Afro-American Woman: Struggles and Images.* This pioneering collection of excellent essays encompassed the earlier stages of the freedom struggle and provided a much-needed work for classes in women's history. Darlene Clark Hine and Kathleen Thompson later prepared an analytical study, *A Shining Thread of Hope: The History of Black Women in America.* Two other broad-based studies, *When and Where I Enter: The Impact of Black Women on Race and Sex in America,* by Paula Giddings, and *Too Heavy a Load: Black Women in Defense of Themselves, 1894–1994,* by Deborah Gray White, brought varied, albeit highly original, concepts to the study of black female history and its relationship to the civil rights movement.[10]

More local studies significantly increased our understanding of the centrality of black women in the Southern civil rights struggles. Five monographs of special importance are Shannon L. Frystak, *Our Minds on Freedom: Women and the Struggle for Black Equality in Louisiana, 1924–1967,* a thorough investigation of Louisiana women and civil rights. *Undaunted by the Fight: Spelman College and the Civil Rights Movement, 1957–1967,* by Harry G. Lefever, carefully tracks the emergence of a protest tradition in Spelman College. Merline Pitre's *In Struggle against Jim Crow: Lulu B. White and the NAACP, 1900–1957,* portrays a woman too often overlooked in regional as well as national studies. She belongs in the pantheon of prominent women. Cynthia Griggs Fleming's *In the Shadow of Selma: The Continuing Struggle for Civil Rights in the Rural South* concentrates on the rural areas of Alabama and the civil rights efforts largely conducted by women. Christina Greene turned our attention to a locality in North Carolina in *Our Separate Ways: Women and the Black Freedom Movement in Durham, North Carolina.*[11]

Memoirs or autobiographies and biographies allow us to understand some black women leaders of the civil rights movement. Memoirs include Dorothy Height's *Open Wide the Freedom Gates: A Memoir;* Daisy Bates's, *The Long Shadow of Little Rock: A Memoir;* Septima P. Clark's *Echo in My Soul;* Cynthia S. Brown's *Ready from Within: Septima Clark and the Civil Rights Movement;* Charlayne Hunter-Gault's *In My Place;* and Lulu Westbrooks-Griffin's *Freedom Is Not Free: Forty-five Days in Leesburg Stockade, A Civil Rights Story,* the brutal story of thirty young women locked in a filthy setting for their civil rights efforts.[12]

The outpouring of studies in recent decades regarding the modern civil rights freedom struggle continues to provide information about the role and contribution of women. African American females, we learn, were indispensable to the success of the struggle for racial equality in each of the former Confederate states. Local and state movement studies published in the 1980s and 1990s transformed the field of civil rights by constructing narratives about a variety of women rather than about a single prominent individual. These studies pointed out that the transformation of America's black and white relations occurred differently in different localities.

The purpose of this book is to depict black female civil rights action across all former Confederate states, not (as in other books on the topic) only five or six states. Nor is this book about only the stars; it is about black women generally and their contributions to civil rights throughout the South. It is intended for use in undergraduate and graduate classes in such fields as women's history/studies, civil rights, black studies/history, Southern history, and United States surveys. It will appeal to general readers with an interest in the modern civil rights struggle in the United States. And because it is based on both secondary and primary courses, it will be useful for the scholar.

Contributors to this volume, who come from across the South, have published books and articles about their topics. Together they identify general patterns and factors that distinguished civil rights activism in each state. They have supplemented previous scholarly investigations and, at the same time, have drawn attention to the roles played by African American women in the sustained protest effort. By reclaiming and retelling the contributions of black women to the civil rights movement, the contributors and their colleagues can view the past through a different lens. In the words of Glenda Gilmore, the time has come to "re-vision the southern political narrative from other angles" to "take into account the plethora of sources on African American and women's history."[13]

The organizational framework of *Southern Black Women in the Modern Civil Rights Movement* was developed purposefully. Each of the eleven states of the former Confederacy is discussed by a leading historian, who profiles one woman or more. The book is divided into two parts. Part I is titled "Professional and Organizational Leaders." Belinda Robnett describes a professional leader as one who had significant civil rights experiences prior to the movement activities and whose concerns transcend local issues. The chapters on Texas, Virginia, and Arkansas focus on individuals who fit this category. Each black female leader in those states worked with the NAACP in her efforts to destroy the legal basis for Jim Crow. Texas and Virginia blacks faced moderate resistance from whites. Blacks in Arkansas faced violent resistance, but with NAACP support and with Daisy Bates at their head, they pressed forward.

Part II, "Bridge Leaders and Foot Soldiers in the Deep South," treats North Carolina, South Carolina, Florida, Georgia, Alabama, Mississippi, Louisiana, and Tennessee, the eight states where white resistance was extreme. This violence served as a catalyst for bridge leaders and foot soldiers in their quest to change the status quo. According to Robnett, a bridge leader served as a liaison between organizations such as the Southern Christian Leadership Conference and the community the bridge leader strove to serve, and foot soldiers were local activists who worked in concert with community leaders.[14] Given the fact that the national civil rights movement had its roots in local movements, female foot soldiers and bridge leaders contributed immensely in bringing about an end to the Jim Crow system in their individual states and in the nation. A glimpse of the activities of black women in each state will be instructive.

According to Caroline Emmons, black women in the Virginia civil rights movements frequently have been overlooked because Virginia featured a supposedly "genteel" resistance, because key black women activists fought for civil rights accomplishments earlier than traditional dates, and (as elsewhere in the South) because men seemed to be leading and accomplishing advances. Virginia's black female leaders fit well the category of professional and organizational leaders, but black women in Virginia also effectively challenged segregation in public transportation, education, and other arenas. Generally the civil rights struggle in Virginia produced peaceful protests and resistance, but violence erupted in Danville. In every effort to halt the segregation of society, black women played a vital role. Virginia was at the center of early civil rights battles over educational access, teacher-pay equity, and integration in public transport. Important legal victories in Virginia, often with women as the plaintiffs, laid the groundwork for later struggles in the Deep South. Black females such as Irene Morgan and Barbara Johns, who were actively pursuing civil rights before the Montgomery bus boycott, help us understand not only how and why African Americans began to protest for greater equality but also the critical role played by women (and girls). This chapter, which examines the experience of African American women in the Virginia civil rights movement, offers further evidence that historians need to broaden their longitudinal (and geographical) boundaries when evaluating the history of the civil rights movement.

Yvonne Frear posits that African American women of Texas have been at the forefront of the civil rights movement since the 1940s. Lulu B. White, who would become the first female executive secretary of the NAACP in the South, was at the helm of the Houston chapter in 1944, when, in *Smith v. Allwright,* the US Supreme Court declared the Texas white Democratic primary unconstitutional. Nor was White instrumental in this endeavor only; she also encouraged blacks to vote and seek office. Among those heeding her advice was Hattie M. White, the second black and first black female to be elected to office in Texas since Reconstruction. Standing on Hattie White's shoulders would be Barbara C. Jordan, the first black from Texas to be elected to the US Congress since Reconstruction. Other black women throughout the Lone Star State, such as Juanita Craft, were organizers, mobilizers, and foot soldiers in the struggle against Jim Crow. They helped integrate universities and public facilities, and eventually they changed the landscape in Texas.

As Jeannie Whayne points out, black women contributed significantly to the civil rights struggle in Arkansas between 1940 and 1974, particularly in the struggle to achieve equal educational opportunities. They were at the forefront of the battle to equalize teacher salaries and to integrate professional schools. A professional leader and the most famous African American civil rights activist in Arkansas, Daisy Bates presided over the state chapter of the NAACP and counseled the "Little Rock Nine" as they integrated Central High School in 1957. In the early 1960s a group of black women played notable roles during SNCC's effort to end segregation practices and secure voting rights for African Americans in the Arkansas Delta.

In the Deep South—Florida, Alabama, Georgia, South Carolina, Mississippi, North Carolina, Louisiana, and Tennessee—civil rights activists faced intense prejudice and even violence. But in spite of confrontations and threats, black women participated extensively, as bridge leaders and as foot soldiers, in efforts to throw off Jim Crow.

Initially, Maxine Jones tells us, African American women in Florida supported black community efforts to eliminate such wrongs as lynching, injustice in the courts, and police brutality and to obtain the right to vote. Among these women, Mary McLeod Bethune was a leader. During the 1960s, black Florida women, serving as foot soldiers, still confronted Jim Crow, especially in the cities of Tallahassee, Jacksonville, and St. Augustine. Striving for improvements in education, transportation, politics, and economic opportunity, they moved closer to full citizenship—but not as close as others in those years of civil rights agitation.

In Alabama, Stefanie Decker notes, Rosa Parks's decision to sit in the front of a bus started the Montgomery struggle, but black women had long been preparing for such a challenge. Black men received media attention, but black women were a moving force during the march to Selma and in civil rights activities throughout southwestern Alabama. It was the women who led the integration of the University of Alabama, who supported the "Children's Crusade" in Birmingham, and who encouraged voter registration and protests. The women met vicious white opposition and retaliation, but they held the civil rights movement together. Women acted both as bridge leaders and as foot soldiers. In the late sixties and early seventies, black women also turned their attention to economic opportunity and achieved gains for themselves as well as their race. As Decker phrased it, they "dismantled the system of Jim Crow."

In negotiating the treacherous landscapes of segregation and racism in urban and rural Georgia, Clarissa Myrick-Harris discovered, African American women made profound contributions to the civil rights movement locally and nationally. United by a common purpose, these women—young and old—hailed from a range of socioeconomic backgrounds. Many worked behind the scenes as foot soldiers. Several, circumventing the undercurrent of sexism in the movement, became founders and leaders of organizations and institutions in the forefront of the fight for equality. This chapter explores the tradition and contexts of activism among black women in Georgia during four key phases of the struggle for social change in the state—beginning with the laying of the foundation in the 1940s.

W. Marvin Dulaney's judgment is that black women played a very important role in the civil rights movement in South Carolina. To win social and political justice, they participated in major lawsuits, such as *Elmore v. Rice* and *Briggs v. Elliott,* and in direct-action campaigns. In addition they served as bridge builders, and they established innovative programs to improve the lives of African Americans in the state. Women such as Septima Poinsette Clark, Modjeska Monteith Simkins, and

Elizabeth Waring challenged the status quo, worked with the NAACP and other organizations, and advanced the causes of social and political justice nationally.

In the early twentieth century, Mississippi, a rural Southern state, was dominated by poverty and a virulent white-supremacist mind-set. Beginning in the 1950s, both in spite of and because of the lynching of Emmett Till, the assassination of Medgar Evers, and the murder of at least three northern civil rights workers, the state produced an active group of civil rights participants. Black women, Tiyi M. Morris argues, engaged heavily in this effort. Black Mississippian bridge leader Fannie Lou Hamer epitomized their strength and leadership. She encouraged women not only to register to vote but also to take active roles in their communities. Black women did so, and they even challenged the national Democratic Party.

In North Carolina, as Dwonna Naomi Goldstone iterates, the physical and psychological strength of African American women, "served them both in leadership and behind-the-scenes roles in a civil rights movement that would not have been successful without them." In many organizations and events, the majority of participants were black women. In Greensboro many came from Bennett College (at one time more than half the student body had been jailed), and in Durham women assumed pivotal roles, serving as protesters, marchers, and canvassers. Black women fought job discrimination, work overloads, and racial harassment. They battled for school desegregation. North Carolina women produced a national civil rights leader, Ella Baker, and a leader for gender equality, Pauli Murray.

Shannon Frystak focuses on the significant role black women played in Louisiana's "long civil rights movement." Beginning in the 1920s, African American women foot soldiers not only fought for equality and citizenship in myriad ways; they also attained formal leadership positions in a movement largely overshadowed and dominated by men. They served as bridge builders. In the aftermath of the civil rights movement "proper," these same women continued their fight on behalf of Louisiana's black citizenry: in neighborhood associations, in War on Poverty initiatives, and in the world of politics.

Tennessee's civil rights movement, Bobby L. Lovett notes, involved women extensively. Long before the 1950s and 60s, and continuing into the twenty-first century, black women used social and civic clubs, benevolent societies, church auxiliaries, and professional training to promote black social and cultural uplift, agitate for racial equality, and gain woman's suffrage. Others assisted in the modern version of the civil rights movement, and provided support for black men. Through national and world exposure, athletes such as the Tennessee State University Tigerbelles helped sideline Tennessee's racial problems. A black woman led the effort to desegregate the higher education system. Women helped lead the political rights revolution. By 2006, women constituted 47 percent of blacks in the state legislature.

In this wide-ranging collection of essays, more than one truth stands out: African American women, many of whom had been marginalized within the large body of civil rights literature, were part of the defining national trajectory of the black liberation movement. Sources for mining African American women's history during the civil rights era have become more accessible. The use of gender as a system of analysis found its way into the emerging studies in the field of Southern history. And written histories have begun to shift toward a more balanced representation of black female reformers. It is also important to note that black women were not monolithic. They fought Jim Crow and segregation as professional and organizational leaders, as bridge leaders, and as foot soldiers. Without their efforts, the modern civil rights movement very likely would not have been as successful. Or successful at all.

Notes

1. Charles Payne, "Men Led, but Women Organized: Movement Participation of Women in the Mississippi Delta," in Vicki L. Crawford, Jacqueline Anne Rouse, and Barbara Woods, eds., *Women in the Civil Rights Movement: Trailblazers and Torchbearers, 1941–1965* (Bloomington: Indiana University Press, 1993), 1–12.

2. Stephen G. N. Tuck, *Beyond Atlanta: The Struggle for Racial Equality in Georgia, 1940–1980* (Athens: University of Georgia Press, 2001), 248.

3. Paula Giddings, *When and Where I Enter: The Impact of Black Women on Race and Sex in America* (New York: William Morrow, 1984).

4. Genna Rae McNeil, "'Joanne Is You and Joanne Is Me': A Consideration of African American Women and the 'Free Joan Little' Movement, 1974–75," in Bettye Collier-Thomas and V. P. Franklin, eds., *Sisters in the Struggle: African American Women in the Civil Rights–Black Power Movement* (New York: New York University Press, 2001), 276, n. 6.

5. Lynne Olson, *Freedom's Daughters: The Unsung Heroines of the Civil Rights Movement from 1830 to 1970* (New York: Simon and Schuster, 2001); Charles M. Payne and Adam Green, eds., *Time Longer Than Rope: A Century of African American Activism, 1850–1950* (New York: New York University Press, 2003).

6. Crawford, Rouse, and Woods, eds., *Women in the Civil Rights Movement;* Belinda Robnett, *How Long? How Long? African-American Women in the Struggle for Civil Rights* (New York: Oxford University Press, 1997); Peter J. Ling and Sharon Monteith, eds., *Gender and the Civil Rights Movement* (New York: Garland Publishing, 1999), 1.

7. Olson, *Freedom's Daughters;* Collier-Thomas and Franklin, eds., *Sisters in the Struggle.*

8. Constance Curry, ed., *Deep in Our Hearts: Nine White Women In the Freedom Movement* (Athens: University of Georgia Press, 2000); Gail S. Murray, ed., *Throwing Off the Cloak of Privilege: White Southern Women Activists in the Civil Rights Era* (Gainesville: University Press of Florida, 2004).

9. Jeanne Theoharis and Komozi Woodard, eds., *Groundwork: Local Black Freedom Movements in America* (New York: New York University Press, 2005).

10. Sharon Harley and Rosalyn Terborg-Penn, eds., *The Afro-American Woman: Struggles and Images* (Port Washington, N.Y.: Kennikat Press, 1978; reprint, 1997); Darlene Clark Hine and Kathleen Thompson,

A Shining Thread of Hope: The History of Black Women in America (New York: Broadway Books, 1998); Giddings, *When and Where I Enter;* Deborah Gray White, *Too Heavy a Load: Black Women in Defense of Themselves, 1894–1994* (New York: W. W. Norton, 1999).

11. Shannon L. Frystak, *Our Minds on Freedom: Women and the Struggle for Black Equality in Louisiana, 1924–1967* (Baton Rouge: Louisiana State University Press, 2009); Harry G. Lefever, *Undaunted by the Fight: Spelman College and the Civil Rights Movement, 1957–1967* (Macon, Ga.: Mercer University Press, 2005); Merline Pitre, *In Struggle against Jim Crow: Lulu B. White and the NAACP, 1900–1957* (College Station: Texas A&M University Press, 1999); Cynthia Griggs Fleming, *In the Shadow of Selma: The Continuing Struggle for Civil Rights in the Rural South* (Lanham, Md.: Rowman & Littlefield, 2004); Christina Greene, *Our Separate Ways: Women and the Black Freedom Movement in Durham, North Carolina* (Chapel Hill: University of North Carolina Press, 2005).

12. Dorothy Height, *Open Wide the Freedom Gates: A Memoir* (New York: PublicAffairs, 2003); Daisy Bates, *The Long Shadow of Little Rock: A Memoir* (Fayetteville: University of Arkansas Press, 1987); Septima Poinsette Clark, *Echo in My Soul* (New York: Dutton, 1962); Cynthia S. Brown, ed., *Ready from Within: Septima Clark and the Civil Rights Movement* (Navarro, Calif.: Wild Tree Press, 1986); Charlayne Hunter-Gault, *In My Place* (New York: Knopf, 1993); Lulu Westbrooks-Griffi n, *Freedom Is Not Free: Forty-Five Days in Leesburg Stockade, A Civil Rights Story* (Hamlin, N.Y.: Heirloom, 1998).

13. Glenda Gilmore, "But She Can't Find Her [V.O.] Key," *Feminist Studies* 25, no. 1 (Spring 1999): 137.

14. Robnett, *How Long? How Long?* 19–23, 150.

Selected Bibliography

Bates, Daisy. *The Long Shadow of Little Rock: A Memoir.* Fayetteville: University of Arkansas Press, 1987.

Brown, Cynthia Stokes, ed. *Ready from Within: Septima Clark and the Civil Rights Movement.* Navarro, Cal.: Wild Tree Press, 1986.

Clark, Septima Poinsette. *Echo in My Soul.* New York: Dutton, 1962.

Curry, Constance, ed. *Deep in Our Hearts: Nine White Women in the Freedom Movement.* Athens: University of Georgia Press, 2000.

Fleming, Cynthia Griggs. *In the Shadow of Selma: The Continuing Struggle for Civil Rights in the Rural South.* Lanham, Md.: Rowman and Littlefield, 2004.

Frystak, Shannon L. *Our Minds on Freedom: Women and the Struggle for Black Equality in Louisiana, 1924–1967.* Baton Rouge: Louisiana State University Press, 2009.

Greene, Christina. *Our Separate Ways: Women and the Black Freedom Movement in Durham, North Carolina.* Chapel Hill: University of North Carolina Press, 2005.

Lefever, Harry G. *Undaunted by the Fight: Spelman College and the Civil Rights Movement, 1957–1967.* Macon, Ga.: Mercer University Press, 2005.

Ling, Peter J., and Sharon Monteith, eds. *Gender and the Civil Rights Movement.* New York: Garland Publishing, 1999.

McNeil, Genna Rae. "'Joanne Is You and Joanne Is Me': A Consideration of African American Women and the 'Free Joan Little' Movement, 1974–75." In *Sisters in the Struggle: African American Women in the Civil-Rights-Black Power Movement,* edited by Bettye Collier-Thomas and V. P. Franklin, 259–79. New York: New York University Press, 2001.

Murray, Gail S., ed. *Throwing Off the Cloak of Privilege: White Southern Women Activists in the Civil Rights Era.* Gainesville: University Press of Florida, 2004.

Olson, Lynne. *Freedom's Daughters: The Unsung Heroines of the Civil Rights Movement from 1830 to 1970.* New York: Simon and Schuster, 2001.

Pitre, Merline. *In Struggle against Jim Crow: Lulu B. White and the NAACP, 1900–1957.* College Station: Texas A&M University Press, 1999.

Robnett, Belinda. *How Long? How Long? African-American Women in the Struggle for Civil Rights.* New York: Oxford University Press, 1997.

Theoharis, Jeanne, and Komozi Woodard, eds. *Groundwork: Local Black Freedom Movements in America.* New York: New York University Press, 2005.

Tuck, Stephen G. N. *Beyond Atlanta: The Struggle for Racial Equality in Georgia, 1940–1980.* Athens: University of Georgia Press, 2001.

READING 17

A League of American Citizens

By Craig A. Kaplowitz

The story of national Mexican American civil-rights policy has its origins in the years leading up to World War II. The history of Mexican Americans, of course, reaches back much further, but developments that would give shape to Mexican American efforts and policies through the civil rights era can be dated to the 1920s and 1930s. Mining and agriculture in the Southwest, which had been encouraged by technology and the railroads for over a generation by 1920, increased the population of both Anglos and Mexicans and brought big business and capital to the region, realigning any accommodation that had been achieved in the days of *rancheros*. The Mexican Revolution of 1910–1920 also contributed to changes in the region, pushing political refugees across the border and reawakening among Anglos the memory of the Alamo and U.S.–Mexican antagonism.

The nation-building efforts of the Progressive Era promoted America's civic nationalism, the idea of America as a place in which the inalienable rights of every human being is recognized and protected and in which hard work and determination are rewarded. But as Gary Gerstle has written, American civic nationalism "has contended with another potent ideological inheritance, a racial nationalism that conceives of America in ethnoracial terms, as a people held together by common blood and skin color and by an inherited fitness for self-government."[1] The tension between these two "nationalisms" animates much of the story of twentieth-century America; certainly the history of civil rights policy is the story of using the power and authority of the state, increasingly the national government, to mollify the tension. But as Gerstle's history makes clear, the growing federal power used to promote justice during the Progressive Era (or any era) could also deny or ignore justice. Progressive efforts led too easily into the restrictionism and hostility to newcomers and minorities, characteristic of the 1920s. While Mexicans remained free of legal restrictions on immigration, thanks to southwestern employers who desired their labor, anti-immigrant attitudes shaped their reception in American society.

Although they could be found at the many ends of the railroad lines by the start of World War II—especially in the Great Lakes region and the Pacific Northwest—Mexican Americans resided overwhelmingly in the Southwest, isolated from the centers of national power and largely ignored by national policy and politicians. Through the 1920s, their efforts to improve conditions focused on the local and state level. For Mexican Americans, national efforts would await the consolidation of self-help groups into sizable organizations reaching beyond local origins across state and regional lines. They would also await a national polity responsive to the claims of disadvantaged minorities and with a sufficiently strong executive to spur on or to circumvent the traditionally cumbersome Congress. The League of United Latin American Citizens (LULAC) was a creation of Tejanos (Texas Mexican Americans) and emerged from the particular history of South Texas; nevertheless, its influence in American national policy came through its reputation as a trans-regional organization that spoke as the voice of Mexican Americans across the Southwest and the nation and that engaged issues of national policy.

Mexican Americans in the Southwest

The history of the West has shifted from the story of the steady occupation of "virgin land" by whites from the East to one of a "legacy of conquest" in which races, cultures, and genders met, negotiated, and struggled.[2] Similarly, the history of the region now known as the American Southwest is far more complex than generally thought. What became the four states of California, Arizona, New Mexico, and Texas, while sharing common characteristics, has had diverse geographies, populations, and histories.[3] Even within Texas—and of particular importance for the history of LULAC—regional differences between Central, South, and West Texas shaped the Mexican American experience. The story of LULAC begins in South Texas but spreads across the state and region quickly.

For roughly fifty years after the annexation of Texas in 1845, residents of the area maintained what David Montejano has termed a "peace structure."[4] The old Mexican elite families, hoping to defend their long-standing land claims, to some extent accommodated and cooperated with new Anglo authorities. While the influx of Anglos into the new state brought competition and antagonism between the older residents—both Anglo and Mexican—and the newcomers, continued reliance on the open-ranch system allowed for accommodation to the changing social dynamics of the region. The first new settlers followed the established practice of large ranching estates and also maintained the paternalistic rancher-worker relationship. As the number of Anglos increased, Mexican land ownership decreased, and disputed property claims and competition bred conflict between new Anglo residents and Mexican elite families. As the old elite families began to lose their positions and their land, new Anglo settlers took over. For the individual families that lost their position, both Anglo and Mexican, this proved unfortunate. But for the Anglo population at large, this shift in power represented one Anglo elite being replaced by another. For Mexicans in the region, this shift represented a changing dynamic: as new Anglos gained positions of power, Mexicans lost such positions, and were relegated as a group to the status of sharecropper or laborer.[5]

While this loss of power by Mexican elites was smoothed somewhat by the maintenance of the open-ranch system, the final years of the nineteenth century brought change. For a variety of reasons, the ranching industry began to collapse. However, many of the technological changes of the late nineteenth century, most significantly new irrigation techniques, gave the arid Southwest a new lease on life as an agricultural region, and land-hungry farmers from the Midwest began to move into the Southwest. This infusion of farmers brought with it a focus on new business methods, replacing the largely paternalistic rancher-hand relationship with a wage-based owner-worker relationship. To old prejudices against Mexicans, represented by admonitions to "remember the Alamo," were added new ones that considered the Mexican a wage laborer, largely unskilled, lazy, and dirty. Once Mexican elite families no longer held positions of power, it became easy for Anglos to relegate Mexican Americans, who appeared ignorant of modern business practices, to an inferior social and economic class.[6]

The influx of Anglo farmers eager to make Texas a profitable agricultural region led to political and social changes that aggravated prejudices against Mexicans. In some areas, particularly areas close to the Mexican border, Mexican sojourners had little interest in American politics. However, Anglo politicians realized the potential of the Mexican vote to help secure lasting power, and Mexicans and Mexican Americans in some places became an important political resource. As Mario García has shown for El Paso, "American politicians, representing El Paso's business and professional class, supported through public jobs and patronage certain Mexican American politicos in return for their ability to organize and deliver Mexican votes." In these cases Mexicans were both "economically invaluable" and "a major political resource," although the benefits generally accrued to the Americanized middlemen, who received jobs and some political representation, rather than to the majority of Mexican-heritage residents.[7] Somewhat in contrast to that political picture, however, Mexican Americans, at least in the new agricultural regions of South Texas, tended to support the interests of the ranchers, both Mexican and Anglo, who offered the security of the old paternalistic relationship. In these areas the new class of commercial farmers undertook an effort, largely successful, to disfranchise Mexican Americans in areas of their greatest concentration.[8]

Among the social implications of the changes at the turn of the century was an altered relationship between employer and worker (generally, Anglo and Mexican). In the new world of wage labor, farmers expected Mexicans to engage in "sojourner pluralism."[9] These cheap laborers were welcomed to the United States with legal sanction (and, in many cases, extralegal sanction) but were expected to return home when the job ended. Increasingly, Anglos considered all workers of Mexican heritage to be temporary laborers. In the Winter Garden area of southwest Texas, where Lyndon Johnson briefly served as principal of a Mexican American school, one local Anglo quipped, "We don't want them to be associated with us, we want them for their labor." Throughout the region, segregation became more prevalent as growers hired more Mexican workers: custom-segregated churches, restaurants, cemeteries, and schools.[10]

To keep that source of labor, farmers cooperated to enact laws or to follow policies that limited competition, such as restrictive labor contracts or laws to keep non-Texans from recruiting farm workers in Texas. With their mobility limited with regard to farm jobs, some Mexicans migrated to cities to escape the harsh working conditions and limited options of Texas agriculture. The industrialization of southwestern cities, encouraged by the railroads, provided sufficient jobs to encourage Mexicans and Mexican Americans to move to growing urban areas. For example, in the 1900 El Paso city directory, 29 of 834 railroad employees had a Spanish surname, compared with 1,010 of 2,753 employees in 1920. Furthermore, shops, factories, construction companies, and other urban enterprises employed Mexicans and Mexican Americans through the first decades of the twentieth century. In San Antonio, Mexicans and Mexican Americans made up 25 percent of the city's population in 1900, 30 percent in 1910, and 37 percent in 1920 and worked in a variety of the city's growing industries. In Houston, the Mexican-heritage population grew from six thousand to fifteen thousand between 1920 and 1930. That increase of 150 percent was greater than the city's population growth as a whole during that boom decade. By 1940, Houston had twenty thousand Mexican and Mexican American residents.[11]

Even though workers of Mexican descent provided much of the labor that built the urban centers of the Southwest, the large numbers of new residents led some communities to plan the separation of Mexican residential areas. In others, agencies and individuals simply refused to rent or sell housing in new suburbs to the Spanish surnamed. The Mexican neighborhoods resulting from this form of discrimination suffered more than their share of health problems.[12] Because they depended more on local circumstances, with no state laws requiring separate facilities for people of Mexican heritage, the restrictions facing Mexicans and Mexican Americans were not as rigid as those for blacks in the Deep South. For example, one study noted that segregated schools were "desirable, but not absolutely essential," resulting (in general) in a less rabid racism than that aimed at blacks in Mississippi or Georgia. But those restrictions could be oppressive nonetheless, and in fact the local, less institutionalized source of discrimination could be more difficult to identify and combat.[13]

In that environment, education became a growing concern. State educators in Texas sought to use the public schools to socialize Mexicans to become good Americans. They hoped to instill the English language along with the values of patriotism, hard work, and personal hygiene. That effort emphasized a wholesale exchange: Mexicans must give up their native language and culture and adopt "American" traits. As state superintendent of public instruction Annie Webb Blanton stated in 1923, addressing those Texas Mexicans born in the United States, "If you desire to be one with us, stay, and we welcome you; but if you wish to preserve, in our state, the language and customs of another land, you have no right to do this." To accelerate the Americanization of students, the state adopted an English-only provision, which stipulated that English would be the only language of instruction in the public schools (other states having passed such laws against German and Italian). Through the early 1920s the state also worked out a policy to reach into private and parochial schools by holding their students to public-school standards, except when the student attended "a private or parochial school which shall include in its course a study of good citizenship, and shall make the English language the basis of instruction in all subjects."[14] Anglo private schools had nothing to fear from the legislation.

With the passage of the English-only law, state officials apparently thought their job complete. When combined with the Texas compulsory education law, the English-only provision meant that, in theory, all school children in Texas would be educated in English and would learn to be good citizens. The attitude of state school officials toward Mexican and Mexican American schoolchildren was patronizing, but they at least sought to educate all Texas schoolchildren. At the local level, however, problems facing Mexican American children proved more serious. Even though no laws prohibited Hispanic children from attending public schools, and in fact the compulsory education law required it, many local school districts managed to circumvent the laws and refused to educate Mexicans.

Historian Guadalupe San Miguel, Jr., has found three main ways that local school officials offered Mexican American children inadequate education. First, they either refused to enforce the compulsory education laws or were lax about them. This practice was most evident in rural areas, where a stable work force proved more desirable than an educated citizenry. Second, they misappropriated state education funds. Local school administrators counted Mexican American children among their school age population because the number of school age children in a district determined state funding for schools, regardless of enrollment. They would include in their count children of migrant farming families who for much of the school year would be living elsewhere. School officials then made little or no effort to enroll the Mexican and Mexican American children, or provided meager funds for a Mexican school, thus increasing available funds for the Anglo schools. Finally, local school officials overtly segregated Mexican American children from Anglo children. Some argued that the irregular attendance of children of migrant farm laborers disrupted classes for regularly attending children; Mexican American children were therefore taught in separate classrooms. Others insisted that poor knowledge of English among Mexican American schoolchildren made educating them together with Anglo children a disadvantage for all involved. The hypocrisy of this last argument was apparent when Hispanic students fluent in English were placed in segregated classes with Spanish-speaking children, but these justifications proved sufficient to keep the state at bay.[15] As Gilbert González suggests, although "there were no laws that mandated the practice of segregation, educators did invoke the state power granted to school administrators to adapt educational programs to the special needs of a linguistically and culturally distinct community." The result, in many cases, was segregation of students in Mexican schools or Mexican classrooms.[16]

Local and state circumstances were most significant for the Mexican American experience during the early twentieth century, but national and international developments had important implications as well. The industrial and technological change that reshaped the Southwest along with the rest of the country has already been considered. Furthermore, quick victory in the Spainish-American War at the turn of the century ushered in an era of nation building that continued through the 1910s and generally included Americanization efforts. Political cartoonists drew Uncle Sam coming to the rescue of Latin America and portrayed Latin Americans as children needing to be cleaned up with American help. Jane Addams's Hull House, the settlement house that ministered so importantly to the needs of poor immigrant families at the turn of the century, also assumed neighbors should gradually adopt

American middle-class values and tastes and offered cultural programs to that end. Israel Zangwell popularized the notion of America as a melting pot in his famous play. Americanization and nativism peaked during World War I, as sauerkraut became "Liberty Cabbage" and dissenting voices became suspect (and illegal). The culmination of this trend came after the war, as Congress saw fit to restrict immigration through legislation.[17]

The National Origins Act of 1924 limited new arrivals to the United States to 2 percent of the foreign-born of a given nationality based on the 1890 census. That act favored "old immigrants" from northern and western Europe at the expense of "new immigrants" from southern and eastern Europe. The law also excluded migrants from Asia, reinforcing existing limits to Chinese and Japanese immigration. But the demand of southwestern farmers for cheap agricultural labor proved strong enough to convince Congress to place no restrictions on arrivals from the Western Hemisphere. The demand for workers pulled, and the lingering effects of the Mexican Revolution pushed, many thousands of Mexicans to the United States. Immigration from Mexico peaked during the 1920s, when almost five hundred thousand documented immigrants crossed the boarder. In 1924, alone, eighty-nine thousand documented immigrants arrived from Mexico. Latin Americans (primarily Mexican Americans, but also including Puerto Ricans, Cubans, and others) were the fastest growing ethnic minority in the United States.[18]

The resulting status for Mexican Americans—owing to limits on immigration from Europe and Asia and to the increasing demand for labor in the Southwest—made this minority the focus of those Americans especially concerned about foreign influence in America. As Carey McWilliams noted in his path-breaking study *North from Mexico,* during the 1920s American scholars and writers flooded their books and journals with concerns about "the Mexican problem." McWilliams saw much of this focus encouraged by "the whole apparatus of immigrant-aid social work," involving social agencies and Americanization organizations that had to identify a target population after the National Origins Act of 1924 eliminated much of their "clientele."[19] The Latin American exemption from the restrictive immigration legislation resulted from the influence of southwestern employers rather than from a more favorable view of Mexicans, as compared with eastern Europeans and Asians, among white Americans. Indeed, during debate over the proposed 1924 act, nativists and labor unions (for different reasons) opposed the exemption for Latin American immigrants, sometimes with forecasts of the collapse of the American way of life should the exemption be approved.[20] As Clare Sheridan has argued, both restrictionists and immigration advocates proffered negative views of Mexican Americans to justify their positions:

> Pro-immigration groups considered Mexican workers a "safe" source of labor because they were docile, they could easily be deported, and because few of them desired naturalization. Anti-immigrant forces argued that the very characteristics that made Mexicans desirable laborers were liabilities for citizenship. They raised

the specter of a permanent Mexican presence in the United States not as citizens, but as a peon caste injurious to national character.[21]

Included in the national discussion of immigration and American culture, Mexicans and Mexican Americans continued to enjoy the welcome of southwestern employers (although to placate some critics Congress criminalized illegal entry for immigrants from the Western Hemisphere a few years later) while they also continued to face an ambivalent or hostile American civic culture.

Middle-Class Mexican Americans and the Rise of LULAC

Rural Mexicans and Mexican Americans through the 1920s remained dependent on local farmers for employment and income and faced a national culture indifferent or hostile to their presence. They had no means, certainly little political influence, by which to improve their working conditions and their children's education or to achieve desegregated public facilities. As Mexican Americans moved into the cities, however, a young middle class of Mexican American businessmen and professionals emerged to serve the growing Mexican American population.

The importance of a developing middle class in this context cannot be underestimated. In his synthesis of the immigrant experience in America, historian John Bodnar discusses the rise of an urban middle class among ethnic groups in the early twentieth century. Urban immigrant communities, rather than being homogeneous ethnic enclaves, were often as diverse as the country from which they came. "While most immigrants remained ordinary workers, the world of the urban immigrant was not only a working class world but one which included self-employed shopkeepers, fraternal officials, and other businessmen who fostered fragmentation by separating themselves from their humble moorings or mobilizing separate aggregations of newcomers to sustain their own power and prosperity."[22] Most often, the sectors of the economy open to ethnics included small artisan shops, family groceries, and the like. These businessmen relied on kinship ties and mutual assistance as much as on a drive for profit. Nevertheless, Bodnar concludes that a social distance often emerged in ethnic communities between workers and entrepreneurs, who were the first to move to new neighborhoods, often expanding their client base to decrease their dependence on the ethnic community.

These middle-class ethnics were often torn between their ties to community and their frustration with other ethnics who did not exhibit the progressive ideals with which they associated their own advance. Bodnar posits a community that struggled with the desire for mutual assistance and cooperation on one hand, and with the business class mentality of growing American cities on the other. According to historian Richard García, the Mexican American middle class in San Antonio developed "a sense of a status-consciousness as well as of its Mexican American ethnicity—a consciousness that reflected its dual Mexican and American historical and ideological reality, but that was not class conscious in a Marxist sense."[23] Because opportunities for ethnics were limited, and government services still largely nonexistent, ethnic groups such as Mexican Americans relied on internal group protection against unemployment, sickness, and death. Fraternal and mutual aid organizations developed, usually led by middle-class members of the group. These businessmen generally did not abandon those in the working class but maintained the ties of ethnic solidarity while promoting the value of Americanization, strengthening both their position as leaders of the ethnic community and, they hoped, the standing of the group as a whole in the new urban American setting.

This pattern of middle-class mobility and community affiliation fits with that identified by Alan Knight in post-revolutionary Mexico, where reformers invoked and celebrated *indigenismo,* the cultural and social world of the Indian peasants in Mexico, even while working to "civilize" them for the good of the whole. As Knight observes, many of the Mexican Americans arriving in U.S. cities around 1920 were political refugees from the Mexican Revolution and as newcomers might have had more reason to invoke ethnic heritage and culture while trying to shape the Mexican American community to fit (Mexican and American) middle-class standards.[24]

The influx of immigrants from Mexico and the heightened nativism of Anglos created a delicate situation for Mexican Americans, particularly those of the middle class. They were not sojourners, but citizens and residents who had achieved at least a modestly successful business in the urban areas of the Southwest and who intended to stay in the United States. As Bodnar suggests, they had benefited from the new business environment of American cities. Yet they also continued to face discrimination. By the 1920s this contradiction encouraged a generation of middle-class Mexican Americans toward calling for full inclusion in American society. Mexican American mutual aid societies (*mutualistas*), which had existed in local communities for decades, had called for an end to discrimination but never combined that call with efforts at integration into American political and social institutions. The older generations tended to identify more with Mexico than with the United States and had little desire to enter the mainstream of American life. For example, *mutualistas* often named themselves after Mexican heroes or Mexico itself, as in Houston's Benito Jaurez *mutualista* and its Mexico Bello (Beautiful Mexico) social club. Such groups kept ties with Mexican officials, receiving them when on business in Houston, and celebrated Mexican holidays.[25] George J. Sánchez also finds a relationship between Mexican leaders and the older Mexican American organizations. He notes the attention that reformers in Mexico paid to the Mexican-heritage community in Los Angeles. Elites in Mexico, who promoted nationalism after the Mexican Revolution in an attempt to control the mestizo and Indian populations, also explicitly targeted the Los Angeles Mexican-heritage community to create a Mexican national identity across national boundaries.[26] Up to the 1920s, such organizations focused on issues of work, sickness and death, and social affairs and encouraged members to cling to their primary identity as Mexican—at times a political identity but more often an ethnic or cultural one.[27]

The calls for change came from a more Americanized generation during the 1920s, many of whom had some access to Anglo education and some of whom had fought for the United States in World War I. According to historian Mario García, these middle-class Mexican Americans believed that they "had to learn the culture, language, and political system of the United States in order to effectively wage their political struggles and to integrate into the system." They also hoped to make the Mexican communities into Mexican American communities.[28] As a result of this emphasis in the years during and after World War I, new fraternal organizations rose up alongside the older Mexican American mutual-aid societies. Perhaps the first of these was the Order Sons of America (OSA), founded in 1921 in South Texas. The OSA was a nonpartisan group, but it sought a political agenda that included the right for Mexican Americans to serve on juries, to sue Anglos in court, and to use public facilities. Its efforts to raise the consciousness of Mexican Americans included voter registration drives and citizenship classes, not only to raise the quality of the Mexican American population but also to show Anglos that Mexican Americans were worthy of equality. Political scientist Benjamin Márquez notes that by "stressing American citizenship and the mastery of English, the [OSA] sought to reassure Texas Anglos that Mexican Americans could be trusted to be loyal and upstanding citizens."[29]

Another important early organization was the Sons of America, formed in San Antonio in 1921. The Sons undertook many of the same activities as the OSA and pursued the common goals of raising Mexican Americans' consciousness of their rights and responsibilities as citizens and of gaining equal rights. This group apparently suffered from internal personal rivalries, and several organizations splintered off during the 1920s.[30] By the end of the decade, leaders of several Mexican American organizations recognized the advantages of a united front, and in early 1929 twenty-five delegates and 150 nonvoting members attended a convention in Corpus Christi. The convention agreed to unite the represented groups and form a new statewide Mexican American organization.

In naming the new organization, members searched for a label that would not alienate either Anglos or Mexican Americans and would emphasize their determination that Mexican Americans were Americans first and foremost. They settled on "League of United Latin-American Citizens." A few years later the organization dropped the hyphen to accentuate further the Americanness of members. According to the organization's newspaper, the *LULAC News,* there existed only one kind of citizen in the United States "and that is the *American citizen,* and all other words used to describe that citizen of the United States are merely descriptive, participating of the qualities of an adjective and not of those of a noun."[31] The name reflected the goals of the organization, which included a commitment to "develop within the members of our race, the best, purest, and more perfect type of true and loyal citizen of the United States of America."[32] In the words of historian Guadalupe San Miguel, Jr., LULAC "proposed to integrate the community into the political and social institutions of American life," a change "from self-help and protective to assimilative activities." Rather than retreat into ethnic isolation, the organization sought to encourage Mexican Americans to "practice their citizenship by participating in the dominant political, economic, and social institutions of the land."[33]

The founding generation of LULAC already participated in those dominant institutions. They were members of what political scientist O. Douglas Weeks, an observer of LULAC's forming convention, called a "class of prosperous, educated citizenry whose living conditions and attitudes compare favorably with American standards."[34] The early leadership clearly fits the middle-class model suggested by Bodnar. The founders came from the business and professional classes, and initial members included businessmen, merchants, doctors, and lawyers, many of whom had come to America during the Mexican Revolution or belonged to elite Mexican American families.

The experiences of the first four LULAC presidents, all founding members, serve as examples of the middle-class roots of LULAC. Ben Garza had worked as a waiter and in the shipyards of Corpus Christi, Texas. After World War I he purchased a restaurant with several partners. The restaurant prospered, and Garza and a friend bought out the other partners. He eventually branched out into real estate, became a leader in the Order Sons of America, and was elected LULAC's first president. LULAC's second president, San Antonio native Alonso Perales, was born in 1898 in Alice, Texas. He was educated at a preparatory school in Washington, D.C., George Washington University, and the National University School of Law. After serving in World War I, Perales practiced law in Texas, served as assistant to the U.S. ambassador to the Dominican Republic in 1922, and was legal advisor to the U.S. electoral mission to Nicaragua in 1928. LULAC's third president, Manuel C. González, was born in Hidalgo, Texas, in 1899. He attended the University of Texas at Austin and became an attorney. González served as the head of the Knights of America and worked as legal advisor to the general counsel of Mexico in San Antonio. Judge J. T. Canales of McAllen, Texas, was a leading educator in South Texas. His LULAC presidency emphasized education for Mexican American children and developed the LULAC Scholarship Fund to help Mexican American students attend college.[35]

These leaders had a stake in American society. They formed LULAC after personal success in the fields of business, law, and education to help other Mexican Americans achieve the benefits of life in America. In addition, they sought to prove to Anglos that Mexican Americans could be productive citizens and could fulfill the responsibilities of citizenship. This emphasis on citizenship led to one of the most controversial decisions made by the group: LULAC's founders limited membership to United States citizens. This approach differed considerably from past Mexican American organizations, which had sought a united ethnic front and the assistance of the Mexican consulate by combining all people of Mexican heritage under one group. The decision to restrict membership was difficult but seemed the most pragmatic way to aid the entire Hispanic population of the Southwest. LULAC members believed that only as American citizens could they effectively press for reform in politics and society. Additionally, some members feared that the different political goals of Mexican nationals, many of whom expected to return to Mexico, would hamper the organization and confuse Anglos as to the group's intentions. By excluding noncitizens from membership, LULAC fully cast its lot with American society and distanced itself from reliance on the Mexican government for political protection.[36]

As we will see in more detail in later discussion, LULAC's long-term goal was to encourage and assist as many Mexicans as possible to become American citizens and to participate in the political system, thus strengthening the Mexican American voice. But the decision to restrict membership placed LULAC firmly within the American camp and defined the Southwest as primarily a political space. Recent work by David Gutiérrez on the borderlands—the American side of the border, the Mexican side of the border, and the "third space" of the borderlands in which residents do not consider themselves essentially a part of the United States or Mexico—brings into sharper relief the importance of the political statement that LULAC made in identifying and working for American solutions to the problems of the borderlands.[37] Despite the insistence on U.S. citizenship for it members, LULAC leaders did not restrict their activity to issues that affected only citizens (as we will discuss below and in chapter 2), and offered real benefits through the organization. In particular, historian Richard García notes LULAC's role in helping to forge a new mentality, one that could change "the 'homeless mind' of the immigrant generation into a 'Mexican American mind'" that could provide a basis from which to fight for civil rights.[38] LULAC leaders thus accepted Americanism, liberalism, and patriotism and reinforced (although they did not create) a division within the Mexican-heritage community in the United States. Their efforts would be on behalf of all people of Mexican heritage, but only American citizens would be plotting their course of action.

The founders further distanced themselves from Mexico when they made English the official language of the organization. Like the question of citizenship status for members, this step came not simply as a rejection of all things Mexican but as a practical measure. Actually, LULAC leaders called for bilingualism, arguing that Mexican Americans must, without forgetting their Spanish, become competent in the dominant language of the political and social institutions of the land. Speaking English would assist Mexican Americans in gaining equality, as well as in performing the responsibilities and obtaining the rights of citizenship. It was not a rejection of the use of Spanish. In fact, through the 1930s the *LULAC News* published bilingual editions to attract new members and to promote bilingualism. The organization also allowed some chapters to recruit and even conduct meetings in Spanish.[39]

In addition to questions about membership and language, the first LULAC leaders established a structure for the organization. LULAC's central governing body, the Supreme Council, consisted of two elected delegates from each local council. The Supreme Council would elect the president general and vice president general at its annual meeting, while the treasurer and secretary of the president's home council would hold the corresponding national office. The Supreme Council had final say on all matters of policy, including the creation of new local councils. Local councils would elect their own officers, and all officers and members had to subscribe to an oath to be loyal American citizens, to follow the laws of the United States, and to teach their children to be "good, loyal, and true American citizens." The group stirred interest among Mexican Americans, and by the end of 1929 LULAC had eighteen councils, primarily in southern Texas. By the early 1930s the organization began to spread across state borders, appointing organizers in New Mexico.[40]

The 1930s in America: LULAC's First Decade

LULAC's founding coincided with the emerging national awareness of the economic calamity that had been developing since the end of World War I. Farmers had been hit particularly hard and earlier than most other sectors of the economy. Overproduction and lower prices on the world market combined with drought across the "dustbowl" to strike every part of American agriculture. Subsequent crises in industry and other sectors of the economy required innovative responses, and the New Deal of President Franklin Roosevelt brought ideas and changes that have had a long life, collectively referred to as "New Deal Liberalism."

Located in Texas and the Southwest through the 1930s, LULAC councils were far from the centers of national political and economic power, but changes in the American system during the decade would have significance for the policy world that LULAC would enter after World War II. Although the Civil War had seen a rise in federal authority, the decades following the war saw many constraints on national public policy. States remained the most active governments, and even at that level many legislatures met infrequently and briefly and state executives had small budgets and small staffs (and some lacked a veto). At the federal level, Congress was the most significant branch but was slow and inefficient. Presidents were weak, with small executive staffs and limited control over departments. Among the most significant changes of the turn of the twentieth century, according to historian Peter Argersinger, was the "creation of nonpartisan commissions and regulatory agencies, staffed by experts committed to an overarching public interest." A concurrent change was the growth of the role of the president, under the exuberance of Theodore Roosevelt and his successors, which resulted in executive control over the processes of administration.[41] These Progressive Era changes resulted from concerns over industrialization and the power of corporations and represented an important, but only initial, aggrandizement of the executive branch.

The crisis of the 1930s further challenged and changed assumptions about the national government's role in society. Amid the freewheeling experimentation of New Deal programs, a common thread or organizing principle, according to historian David Kennedy, was security. "Job security, life-cycle security, financial security, market security—however it might be defined, achieving security was the leitmotif of virtually everything the New Deal attempted."[42] With the government actively seeking to provide security for Americans, the long-term expectations of government regarding security shifted. According to Alan Brinkley, by the late 1930s reformers turned from an older Progressive faith in using regulation to create an ideal society (temporary regulation to make regulation obsolete) toward an expectation that there would be a continuous role for the state to control conflict and create stability. Some continued to focus on regulation, but by the end of the decade a new focus emerged—fiscal policy on the part of the federal government to promote individual consumption rather than to assist production. By the post–World War II era, it was the government's responsibility to maintain full employment and to enhance purchasing power through welfare programs as much as to stabilize the economy through regulation of business.[43] Rather than simply regulate big businesses to ensure fair prices for consumers, as Teddy Roosevelt preferred, or keep businesses small to foster competition, as Woodrow Wilson preferred, the New Deal mixed the older regulation with new programs to protect the security of individual workers, epitomized by the Social Security Act and the protection of worker's rights to organize and bargain collectively in the National Labor Relations Act (commonly known as the Wagner Act). And to carry out this program Franklin Roosevelt orchestrated a reorganization of the executive branch that, in the words of political scientist Sidney Milkis, "cleared the way for unprecedented political responsibility and policy development to be centralized in the White House."[44] The new Executive Office of the President would become the driving force behind policy development—particularly on civil rights, an issue Roosevelt dealt with only obliquely—until imploding under the double burden of Vietnam and Watergate a full generation later.[45]

The New Deal ushered in the idea of an economic bill of rights, and its focus was not on social change or civil rights. But much of the New Deal did have social implications, including its funding of the arts and conservation programs as well as its small steps toward civil rights, such as the Indian Re-organization Act of 1934, which reversed the policy of forced assimilation of Native Americans. Policies for African Americans faced particularly difficult obstacles, including southern Jim Crow laws, northern ghettos, poll taxes and white primaries limiting their electoral influence. Particularly vexing was the filibuster and seniority system that kept Congress in the control of southern Democrats, whom Roosevelt needed in order to pass his economic programs. Nevertheless, the New Deal did result in important changes or signs of changing times: New Dealers joined with the National Association for the Advancement of Colored People to gain equal treatment for blacks under New Deal relief and recovery programs; the number of black federal employees tripled; Roosevelt appointed over a hundred blacks to administrative posts; the president met with a "black cabinet" of unofficial advisors; and he created a committee on fair employment practices. Most significantly, the New Deal raised black expectations of the federal government's actions, with important consequences for the future.[46]

In addition to the prevalent concerns it forced on all people on the margins, the Depression presented unique concerns to Mexican Americans, namely whether to repatriate to Mexico or to chance involuntary repatriation. Most repatriation programs, generally run by cities and states with large Mexican-heritage populations and with the cooperation of the Mexican government, were formally voluntary, but "encouragement" to leave could take many forms. America's tendency to fail to distinguish between Mexican immigrants and Mexican Americans meant that citizens of the United State were among those forced to board a train for Mexico. Children of immigrants—many of them citizens by virtue of birth in the United States—likewise were sent to Mexico, for the first time, with their repatriated parents.[47]

For Mexican Americans who stayed in the U.S., the New Deal offered somewhat less than it offered blacks, particularly in terms of recognition of problems and a voice in designing solutions. Indeed, scholars of Mexican American history are divided over the results of the New Deal. George Sánchez finds increased union activity among Mexican Americans during the 1930s, particularly a dressmakers' strike of 1933, a result of efforts to achieve the New Deal promises regarding wages and hours and the right to bargain collectively—part of Roosevelt's National Industrial Recovery Administration. In Sánchez's view, the New Deal encouraged political participation, ethnic cooperation, and involvement with the Democratic party—important changes in attitude for the future struggle for civil rights. Sánchez finds evidence that in Los Angeles the party tried to connect local union advances with Roosevelt's national policies. He also finds an increase in naturalization requests between 1934 and 1936, suggesting that Mexicans perceived a changed atmosphere in the U.S.[48] Other scholars of the Mexican American urban experience, particularly in the cities of the Midwest, tell a similar story. While Mexican Americans often lost jobs first and were replaced by Anglos, they joined and worked for unions through the 1930s, gaining a sense of the possibility for change within the system.[49] For agricultural workers in California, Devra Weber finds far fewer gains. Her study of cotton-farm workers suggests that exemption of agricultural employees from New Deal legislation, such as social security and the National Labor Relations Act, limited workers' expectation for change and that Mexican and Mexican American ambivalence toward the state discouraged much reliance on outside assistance. She concludes that the New Deal actually weakened the position of the cotton-farm workers in California by institutionalizing their position relative to farm owners.[50]

New Deal agencies did provide funds for projects in Mexican American neighborhoods. For example, the National Youth Administration (NYA) awarded a $100,000 grant to restore the old Mexican quarter in San Antonio. The city also received funding from the Federal Housing Authority, as did Austin (a segregated project proposal submitted by Congressman Lyn-don Johnson). LULAC petitioned for grants and received funding for projects, in particular a grant from the Works Progress Administration for a new recreation center in Albuquerque. LULAC actually took over sponsorship of the NYA in Albuquerque in 1939. Overall, LULAC became part of the New Deal coalition, supporting its bills and efforts. This is not to say that LULAC leaders accepted blindly everything the New Dealers proposed and set in motion. The organization could support the New Deal and still criticize the exclusion of farm workers from the Social Security and National Labor Relations acts.[51] Still, as Richard García argues, the decade of the 1930s and the New Deal response contributed one important element in LULAC's emerging Mexican American identity. Members of the organization had chosen American individualism, in the Jeffersonian tradition, but mixed with it "a sensitivity and an affinity to the Rooseveltian New Deal conservative revolution of pragmatic liberalism with its emphasis on pluralism, statism, centralization, and its sense of humanism."[52]

The crisis of the 1930s brought important changes to the American policy system, but those changes focused on the economic bill of rights of urban workers and the middle class. Without significant attention to civil rights or the plight of agricultural workers, the New Deal had a limited impact on Mexican Americans. The changes of the decade would be important for the postwar civil-rights struggle, but through the 1930s Mexican Americans as a whole had an ambivalent relationship to the U.S. government and the New Deal. Help could come in the form of grants, if groups had the information and resources necessary to apply, or in the right to bargain collectively, if one could join a union. In most cases, Mexican Americans continued to work at the state and local level if they hoped to improve their circumstances. For the newly created League of United Latin American Citizens, part of that work included forming its identity and ideology.

LULAC: Early Ideology and Activity

LULAC spent its first decade, in the words of Benjamin Márquez, "consolidating the group, engaging in political and community activities, and debating the fine points of the group's philosophy."[53] The major thrust of that philosophy was to create good, active American citizens. But Mexican Americans would never be productive citizens as long as they faced discrimination that limited the opportunities of individuals. According to LULAC, discrimination had two sources. First, many Anglos considered Mexican Americans to be second class citizens, at best, and throughout Texas kept Mexican Americans in subservient positions. Second, LULAC leaders placed some blame on Mexican Americans for failing to deserve equality. As beneficiaries, to some extent, of the American free enterprise system, many LULAC leaders and members believed in and promoted the qualities of an "American character" that they believed were partly responsible for their success, including individualism, a strong work ethic, and faith in progress. The organization held up successful middle-class Mexican Americans as models of the good American citizen. Mario García identifies a composite picture of such models: "American born, rising from poor backgrounds to achieve education, veterans of World War I or World War II, high school or college graduates, and professionally either a lawyer, teacher, physician, or government employee. In all, LULAC equated Americanism with middle-class success and believed that true leadership could emanate only from the middle class."[54]

To some Mexican nationals and Mexican Americans, as well as to some scholars, LULAC essentially adopted Anglo conceptions of respectability. David Montejano suggests that the "standards that the league expected of its exclusive membership were the highest standards of respectability—speak English, dress well, encourage education, and be polite in race relations.... In other words, the race ideas of Anglos—ideas of cleanliness, of beauty, of respectability—constituted much of the cultural ground on which segregationist policies were discussed and debated."[55] LULAC leaders would not have disagreed with such an assessment but would have objected to the pejorative tone that many such arguments assume (and perhaps to the argument that all such characteristics were simply Anglo). They reasoned that as members of the larger American society, a certain amount of acculturation was necessary and acceptable. Despite the complaints, then and now, that LULAC sold out, the organization was clear in its appreciation for its Mexican heritage and culture. Alonso Perales, founding member of LULAC, wrote in June 1929 that members of the new organization "solemnly declare once and for all to maintain a sincere and respectful reverence for our social origin of which we are proud" and that "our efforts to be rightfully recognized as citizens of this country do not imply that we wish to become scattered nor much less abominate our Latin heritage, but rather on the contrary, we will always feel for it the most tender love and the most respectful veneration."[56] Mario García argues that "LULACers, despite the insistence of later Chicano scholars to the contrary, hoped to achieve some functional balance between mainstream Anglo-American culture and the culture derived from their Mexican roots."[57] Their idea resembled not so much the melting pot of assimilation into American society as another idea gaining currency through the 1920s, a cultural pluralism such as that advocated by Horace Kallen.[58]

Efforts at Americanization, if not simply a rejection of ethnic identity, do reveal an awareness of class interests among LULAC leaders. The accommodation strategy offered by LULAC reinforced the virtues of middle-class status. LULAC sought not to revolutionize the American system, but rather to fine tune it to be more accessible to people of all backgrounds. In fact, they argued that discrimination was ultimately un-American, in that it worked against the functioning of a free-enterprise system. In the same vein, LULAC defended American capitalism against its foreign enemies during the 1930s, denouncing both fascism and Communism as antithetical to Americanism. As Márquez notes, "Because of their privileged yet precarious position, LULAC's membership had a stake in reforming rather than remaking American society. As a consequence they would be found proclaiming loyalty to the United States and its government even at a time when racism against Mexican Americans was rampant."[59]

In LULAC's view, the most able members of every ethnic group, in a society free of discrimination, would rise to high levels of achievement, while those lacking the proper qualities would remain near the bottom of the scale. The problem for Mexican Americans, in LULAC's opinion, was that they were held back by discrimination against the group as well as by a lack of initiative within the group. This belief led LULAC both to encourage Mexican Americans to prove the stereotypes false and to reform society so that it offered all individuals an equal opportunity to achieve, based on individual merit. Councils undertook programs as local circumstances warranted, but several standard practices emerged. Among the wide array of specific efforts undertaken by LULAC councils ran three main thrusts of activity: community education and encouragement, desegregation of public facilities, and improved education for Mexican American children. First and foremost, LULAC leaders concerned themselves with spreading the word. Because their ideology relied heavily on individual initiative, LULAC leaders refused to claim that Anglo prejudice was the exclusive cause of Mexican American disadvantage. Instead, they encouraged Mexican Americans to take advantage of what opportunities they had and to make themselves into citizens that the rest of society would have to respect. To this end, they traveled around Texas in groups called Flying Squadrons to organize new chapters and to promote the organization and its goals. They offered citizenship and English-language classes, held food and clothing drives, and worked with Boy Scouts and Girl Scouts. Through a combination of education and community service LULAC sought to promote the organization and to turn Mexican communities into Mexican American ones.[60]

LULAC also advocated participation in the political process. To avoid being labeled political agitators, the organization specifically avoided any overtly partisan activity. The group's founders repeatedly denied that LULAC was a political organization, and any LULAC member elected to public office became a "passive" member to prevent LULAC from becoming a political club.[61] The organization did, however, encourage its members to become active in politics on an individual basis. The goal was to replace the old machine politics—in which the Mexican American vote was, as they saw it, largely a commodity to be purchased—with a new, more democratic politics in which Mexican Americans voted as good citizens rather than as dutiful servants. LULAC went so far as to organize poll tax committees to encourage and help citizens pay the required taxes rather than lose the power of the ballot.[62]

While socializing the Mexican American population in the ways of mainstream America, LULAC also challenged the discrimination that society imposed on Mexican Americans. Custom and local practice, without the official imprimatur of state laws, determined segregation of public facilities for Mexican Americans, a civil rights challenge different from that faced by African Americans in the South. If segregation and discrimination were less systematic against Mexican Americans, offering perhaps more room to maneuver based on local circumstances, they also could be more difficult to pin down. Mexican Americans had no *Plessy v. Ferguson* court case or state Jim Crow laws to target at the regional and national level, to rally around, to draw to national attention, to use in making claims on society at large. For Mexican Americans living in areas of particularly harsh discrimination, the lack of national or state laws could make fighting for change more difficult, even if it allowed those living in other areas more opportunities than blacks had in the South.

Local LULAC councils worked to end discrimination based on local circumstances. As O. Douglas Weeks of the University of Texas noted in 1929, "The general status of the Mexican-American in each community is different, and the method of attack [against segregation] must, on that account, be altered to suit each situation."[63] The LULAC approach to desegregation was consistent: while willing to use legal action in the courts if necessary, LULAC leaders preferred to negotiate face-to-face to bring about change. William Flores, LULAC national president in 1944–45, remembered of the El Paso LULAC method of fighting discrimination:

> Now when we knew that we were on the right track and we knew that we had a good complaint, whether it was school or anything else, we then would see the big shots—they were actually politicians, that's what they were. And we went to them, a committee went to see them, and presented our facts and said, "We can prove our charges;" and they could fix it up just as easy as that. ... We threatened many times, "We'll go to the papers with this charge here if you won't listen to us. But I know that you can correct it." And they promised to correct it and they did so; and we were satisfied.[64]

Throughout the 1930s LULAC used this preferred method to desegregate public facilities, such as theaters, swimming pools, restaurants, and hospitals.[65]

In these desegregation efforts, LULAC emphasized that Mexican Americans were not a racial minority but were in fact white. This insistence resulted in part from self-identity and in part from pragmatism. Texas law segregated blacks and whites but did not specify segregation of Mexicans. LULAC lobbied for a white classification so Mexican Americans could vote in the Democratic primary elections. The organization did not lobby Congressman Lyndon Johnson in support of repealing the poll tax (Johnson was going to vote against repeal in any event) out of fear that they might lose that classification.[66] In several Texas cities the LULAC councils objected to any attempt to label Mexican Americans as "colored." Thus, in Wharton County, LULAC protested when officials returned poll tax receipts marked "colored" to Mexican Americans; in Corpus Christi LULAC fought the designations "American" (AM), "Mexicans" (M), "English-speaking Mexicans" (EM), and "Coloreds" (C) in the city directory. These objections did not question segregation itself, only the segregation of (white) Mexican Americans based on race status. LULAC did not necessarily protest the segregation of Mexican Americans who did not live up to an "American" standard, but rather opposed efforts to lump all Mexican Americans into an inferior category, particularly a "colored" category, based only on Mexican heritage. They bought into the racial nationalism identified by Gerstle, accepting the racial hierarchy that placed whites at the top and thus contributing to the subjugation of nonwhites in society.[67]

Educating Mexican American Children

Education, of all issues of discrimination and equal opportunity, was the most important issue for LULAC during its first decades. A number of obstacles impeded the education of Mexican American children. First, many children worked to contribute to the family's income. In particular, migrant farming families traveled seasonally, and children missed large portions of the school year. School facilities in agricultural areas operated according to farmers' needs for cheap labor, and farm children received only sporadic schooling. Furthermore, several studies during the 1920s found that Texas Mexicans, and agricultural workers in particular, remained indifferent to public education. By the late 1920s, however, particularly in small towns and cities, Mexican Americans began to complain about the poor education afforded their children. Most children of Mexican heritage faced at least some form of school segregation, and parents began to seek enforcement of compulsory school laws and equal educational facilities for their children.[68]

LULAC leaders saw education as a key to an active citizenry and took the lead in working for equal education for Mexican Americans. They started at home, working to increase the faith and interest in education among the Mexican American population. LULAC hoped to increase local Mexican American pressure on school authorities to provide better education, rather than to attack local schools directly and be viewed as an agency of outside agitation. To this end, members undertook public information campaigns to change what they viewed as the Mexican American community's problematic characteristics: an absence of education and a lethargic attitude. Guadalupe San Miguel, Jr., quotes one early LULAC member who suggested that some of the inadequate educational opportunity for Mexican Americans "is the result of the Latin American, who does not demand his rights nor does he try to find solutions to these problems which serve as obstacles for his children." LULAC members considered mastery of English as vital both in obtaining and in fulfilling the rights and responsibilities of citizenship. As one suggested, "If you talk English, you will think and act like Americans." By speaking to parent groups, starting parent-teacher associations, and establishing a scholarship fund for promising Mexican American students, LULAC promoted the use of English in the home and the value of education for Mexican American children. In addition, LULAC rejected the view that Mexican Americans were passive victims in the face of Anglo oppression. As one LULAC leader asserted, "If we, the Mexican American and the Mexican citizens raised in the United States, are to occupy the honorable place that we merit, it is indispensable to educate ourselves."[69]

While spreading the word to the Mexican American community, LULAC members also worked on a second approach to equal education—to change the prevailing practices of discrimination that resulted in inferior education for Mexican Americans. Some Mexican Americans in the early years of the century had favored separate schools for their children as advantageous both to learning English and to maintaining their Mexican culture. The newer generation of Mexican American leaders, however, viewed segregation as an impediment to education and to the self-respect of Mexican American children. Through a variety of means they sought to convince local school officials to educate Mexican American children with other white children. First, LULAC leaders used their standard practice of negotiation with local leaders to bring change. If negotiation failed, they encouraged community pressure, investigated and documented charges brought by parents, brought evidence to the attention of higher authorities, and publicized the differences between facilities for Mexicans and those for Anglos.

LULAC took these actions against the most egregious cases of discrimination and realized that good pedagogy might require the teaching of Mexican-heritage children separately from others for a time. Students who could not understand English, for example, could gain from separate English instruction through the second or third grade. When such practices continued well beyond the early grades, when schools assigned Mexican-heritage students to separate classes without regard for their English capability, or when schools treated Mexican-heritage students in ways different from their treatment of other white groups, then LULAC took action. As one parent noted, segregation "may be all right, on account of language. But the Bohemian and German and other non-English-speaking children go to the American school, and some Mexicans want their children to go there." LULAC agreed, and could not abide by segregation based only on Mexican heritage. Such segregation implied a racial distinction that LULAC refused to recognize. R. de la Garza, a founding member of LULAC, best expressed this view in an editorial in the *LULAC News* in 1931: "Let them segregate our children in the first grades until they have learned enough English to hold their own with other whites. If some of them are unclean, let them be placed in different schools until they have learned to be clean. *But we must battle segregation because of race prejudices*" (emphasis in original).[70]

When negotiation and local pressure proved insufficient to convince school districts to allow Mexican-heritage children to attend the same school as Anglos, LULAC took legal action. Its first legal challenge to segregation came in 1930, only one year after the founding of the organization. In *Independent School District v. Salvatierra,* LULAC lawyers helped Jesús Salvatierra and several parents who sought an injunction to prevent the Del Rio, Texas, school district from using bond monies to build new school facilities.[71] The parents argued that the new buildings would perpetuate the segregation of Mexican American children, who attended their own school through the third grade. They claimed that the school separated the children based on race, in violation of the equal protection clause of the Fourteenth Amendment of the U.S. Constitution. The local superintendent of schools argued that the school district separated the Mexican American children for instructional purposes. Migrant children, he suggested, arrived at school late in the fall, after the harvest. These children would be at a disadvantage if placed in classes already in progress. Similarly, he insisted that non-English-speaking children, regardless of age, benefited from their own school, where they could learn English at their own pace and develop their "innate talents."[72] His arguments did not convince the local trial court, which found the school district guilty of discrimination.

The Texas court of appeals, however, overturned the decision. The appeals court agreed that school districts could not segregate Mexican American children because of their heritage, but decided that the Del Rio school district segregated the children for educational reasons. The state supreme court refused to hear the case on appeal, but the decision retained at least some aspects of a moral victory. The Texas courts considered segregation of Mexican Americans illegal, but only if such segregation resulted from prejudice rather than pedagogy. This half-victory in the courts was time consuming and expensive. The young organization, which was founded in the opening year of the Great Depression, had insufficient funds to litigate consistently, and LULAC did not undertake another court case for over fifteen years. LULAC would most often return to its local, negotiation-based struggle against discrimination.[73]

Conclusion

LULAC's first decade, filled with depression and the coming of war, provided a difficult environment in which to develop an ideology and method for a new Mexican American organization. Nevertheless, during the 1930s LULAC experienced rapid growth. From nineteen councils located primarily in South Texas in 1929, the organization grew to thirty-seven by 1932 and on the eve of World War II had over eighty councils located in Texas, New Mexico, Arizona, and Kansas. After the war, the organization would experience a surge both in membership and activity and would extend its reach beyond Texas and the Southwest to engage national policy issues. The philosophy and tactics LULAC developed in its first decade foreshadowed the approach it would develop to deal with issues of federal policy. This middle-class organization would continue in its loyalty to the American free-enterprise system and in its emphasis on the responsibility of the individual, even while insisting that Mexican

Americans received unfair treatment in the mainstream of American society. At its inception, LULAC was somewhat ambivalent in placing blame for Mexican Americans' second-class status. Anglos treated Mexican Americans as inferior, but from their middle-class perspective LULAC leaders believed that many Mexican Americans were behaviorally inferior as well.

LULAC also articulated its opposition to characterizing Mexican Americans as anything other than white. Leaders founded their early efforts at desegregation on the lack of statutory grounds for segregation of (white) Mexican Americans, and this insistence would continue throughout the postwar period. While resistance to racial classification persisted, however, the group's leaders never demanded a complete rejection of Mexican heritage. They nevertheless implored Mexican Americans, already steeped in their Mexican heritage, to learn the language, customs, and norms of the larger American society. The group's leaders never claimed that all Mexican Americans were equally worthy of inclusion in the American mainstream. Worthiness had to be earned by the individual, and for LULAC the criteria remained distinctly middle-class. Without rejecting Mexican heritage, LULAC during its first decade leaned away from that heritage and toward Anglo middle-class values as a prerequisite to joining the American mainstream.

LULAC had relatively few opportunities to express its views on national issues. During its first decade it remained a regional, and primarily Texas, organization. Furthermore, the national policy environment did not fix its gaze on Mexican Americans or the Southwest. In its general approach to the economic crisis, however, the New Deal did attract the allegiance of Mexican Americans. Much like blacks, Mexican Americans received little specifically from the New Deal but expressed gratitude for efforts to help the poor, a large number of whom in the Southwest were of Mexican heritage. LULAC received funds to carry out New Deal projects, and Mexican Americans became Democratic voters. And, perhaps most significant, the American political system shifted in a way that would last through the 1960s. The rise of Franklin Roosevelt, and the increased power residing in the executive office of the president, had little impact on civil rights during the 1930s. But the policy initiative had shifted to the presidency, and future chief executives would wield that power in support of American civic nationalism, and at the expense of American racial nationalism. Those who gained the ear of the president and his advisors would gain important advantages in the policy stream.

Notes

1. Gary Gerstle, *American Crucible: Race and Nation in the Twentieth Century* (Prince-ton, N.J.: Princeton University Press, 2001), 4.

2. Henry Nash Smith, *Virgin Land: The American West As Symbol and Myth* (Cambridge, Mass.: Harvard University Press, 1950); Patricia Nelson Limerick, *Legacy of Conquest: The Unbroken Past of the American West* (New York: W. W. Norton, 1987).

3. Manuel G. Gonzales, *Mexicanos: A History of Mexicans in the United States* (Bloomington: Indiana University Press, 1999), chapter 4.

4. David Montejano, *Anglos and Mexicans in the Making of Texas, 1836–1986* (Austin: University of Texas Press, 1987), 34–41.

5. Montejano, *Anglos and Mexicans,* 50–74; Armando C. Alonzo, *Tejano Legacy: Rancheros and Settlers in South Texas, 1734–1900* (Albuquerque: University of New Mexico Press, 1998), 251–53.

6. Alonzo, *Tejano Legacy,* 198–200; Montejano, *Anglos and Mexicans,* 105.

7. Mario T. García, *Desert Immigrants: The Mexicans of El Paso, 1880–1920* (New Haven, Conn.: Yale University Press, 1981), 155. See also Arnoldo De León *The Tejano Community, 1836–1900* (Albuquerque: University of New Mexico Press, 1982), chapter 2.

8. Montejano, *Anglos and Mexicans,* 143–48.

9. Lawrence H. Fuchs, *The American Kaleidoscope: Race, Ethnicity, and the Civic Culture* (Hanover: Wesleyan University Press), 110–27.

10. Julie Leininger Pycior, *LBJ and Mexican Americans: The Paradox of Power* (Austin: University of Texas Press, 1997), 10–15.

11. M. García, *Desert Immigrants,* 65–72; Richard A. García, *Rise of the Mexican American Middle Class: San Antonio, 1929–1941* (College Station: Texas A&M University Press, 1991), 27–31; Arnoldo De León, *Ethnicity in the Sunbelt: Mexican Americans in Houston* (College Station: Texas A&M University Press, 2001), 23, 45; Mario Barrera, *Race and Class in the Southwest: A Theory of Racial Inequality* (Notre Dame, Ind.: University of Notre Dame Press, 1979), 86–87.

12. Montejano, *Anglos and Mexicans,* 167–68; M. García, *Desert Immigrants,* 127–46; R. García, *Rise of the Mexican American Middle Class,* 27–28, 38–41.

13. John Burma, "The Civil Rights Situation of Mexican Americans and Spanish Americans," in *Race Relations: Problems and Theory,* ed. Jitsuichi Masuoka and Preston Valien (Chapel Hill: University of North Carolina Press, 1961), 155–67; Gómez-Quiñones, *Chicano Politics,* 42, 76–80. Studies suggest that cities outside the Deep South, particularly with two or more substantial minority populations, tended to have more openings in their discriminatory systems even for blacks. See Kenneth Mason, *African Americans and Race Relations in San Antonio, Texas, 1867–1937* (New York: Garland, 1998) as compared with *Black Dixie: Afro-Texan History and Culture in Houston,* ed. Howard Beeth and Cary D. Wintz (College Station: Texas A&M University Press, 1992).

14. Cited in Guadalupe San Miguel, Jr., *"Let All of Them Take Heed": Mexican Americans and the Campaign for Educational Equality in Texas, 1910–1981* (Austin: University of Texas Press, 1987), 32, 36.

15. San Miguel, Jr., *"Let All of Them Take Heed,"* 54–58.

16. Gilbert G. González, *Chicano Education in the Era of Segregation* (Philadelphia: Balch Institute Press, 1990), 13. See also M. García, *Desert Immigrants,* 110–22.

17. Michael H. Hunt, *Ideology and U.S. Foreign Policy* (New Haven, Conn.: Yale University Press, 1987), 68, 86–88; Gerstle, *American Crucible,* chapters 1–3; Otis L. Graham and Elizabeth Koed, "Americanizing the Immigrant, Past and Future: History and Implications of a Social Movement," *The Public Historian* 15, no. 4 (fall 1993): 24–45.

18. John Higham, *Send These to Me: Immigrants in Urban America,* rev. ed. (Baltimore, Md.: Johns Hopkins University Press, 1984), 54–57; Leo Grebler, Joan W. Moore, Ralph C. Guzmán, *The Mexican-American People: The Nation's Second Largest Minority* (New York: Free Press, 1970), 65–66.

19. Carey McWilliams, *North From Mexico: The Spanish-Speaking People of the United States* (New York: Lippincott Company, 1949), chapter 11.

20. Matt S. Meier and Feliciano Ribera, *Mexican Americans/American Mexicans: From Conquistadors to Chicanos,* rev. ed. (New York: Hill & Wang, 1993), 125–27; Rudolfo Acuña, *Occupied America: A History of Chicanos,* 4th ed. (New York: Longman, 2000), 213–15.

21. Clare Sheridan, "Contested Citizenship: National Identity and the Mexican Immigration Debates of the 1920s," *Journal of American Ethnic History* 21, no. 3 (spring 2002): 3–35.

22. John Bodnar, *The Transplanted: A History of Immigrants in Urban America* (Bloomington: Indiana University Press, 1985), 117–18.

23. R. García, *Rise of the Mexican American Middle Class,* 53.

24. Alan Knight, "Racism, Revolution, and *Indigenismo:* Mexico, 1910–1940," in *The Idea of Race in Latin America, 1870–1940,* ed. Richard Graham (Austin: University of Texas Press, 1990), 71–113.

25. De León, *Ethnicity in the Sunbelt,* 31–34.

26. George J. Sánchez, *Becoming Mexican American,* chapter 5.

27. For accounts of early *mutualistas,* each with its own focus, see Roberto R. Calderón, "Union, Paz, Y Trabajo: Laredo's Mexican Mutual Aid Societies, 1890s" and Emilio Zamora, "Mutualist and Mexicanist Expressions of a Political Culture in Texas" in *Mexican Americans in Texas History,* ed. Emilio Zamora, Cynthia Orozco, Rodolfo Rocha (Austin: University of Texas State Historical Association, 2000).

28. Mario T. García, *Mexican Americans: Leadership, Ideology, and Identity, 1930–1960* (New Haven, Conn.: Yale University Press, 1989), 27–29; R. García, *Rise of the Mexican American Middle Class,* 254–56.

29. Benjamin Márquez, *LULAC: The Evolution of a Mexican American Political Organization* (Austin: University of Texas Press, 1993), 15–16.

30. M. García, *Mexican Americans,* 29.

31. *LULAC News,* Apr., 1940, cited in M. García, *Mexican Americans,* 35.

32. LULAC Constitution, cited in O. Douglas Weeks, "The League of United Latin-American Citizens: A Texas-Mexican Civic Organization," *Southwestern Political and Social Science Quarterly* 10 (Dec., 1929): 264. LULAC members often used the term "race" to describe people of Mexican heritage, just as they used it to describe those of Italian, Irish, or German heritage.

33. San Miguel, Jr., *"Let All of Them Take Heed,"* 69–71.

34. Weeks, "The League of United Latin-American Citizens," 258.

35. Alonso Perales, *LULAC: Fifty Years of Serving Hispanics* (Corpus Christi, Tex.: Bald-win Printing Co., 1978), 76–78; Carolyn Hernández, "LULAC: The History of a Grassroots Organization and Its Influence on Educational Policies, 1929–1983" (Ph.D. diss., Loyola University of Chicago, 1995), 51–53. The Knights of America was one of the Mexican American organizations that merged to form LULAC.

36. M. García, *Mexican Americans,* 31–32; San Miguel, Jr., *"Let All of Them Take Heed,"* 70; Weeks, "The League of United Latin American Citizens," 270–71.

37. David G. Gutiérrez, "Migration, Emergent Ethnicity, and the 'Third Space': The Shifting Politics of Nationalism in Greater Mexico," *Journal of American History* 86, no. 2 (Sept., 1999): 481–517.

38. R. García, *Rise of the Mexican American Middle Class,* 316–17.

39. Márquez, *LULAC,* 23; M. García, *Mexican Americans,* 32, 44–45.

40. Weeks, "The League of United Latin-American Citizens," 266–67; Cynthia E. Orozco, "Regionalism, Politics, and Gender in Southwestern History: The LULAC Expansion into New Mexico From Texas, 1929–1945," *Western Historical Quarterly* 29, no. 4 (winter 1998): 459–83.

41. Peter H. Argersinger, "The Transformation of American Politics, 1865–1910," in *Contesting Democracy: Substance and Structure in American Political History, 1775–2000,* ed. Byron E. Shafer and Anthony J. Badger (Lawrence: University Press of Kansas, 2001), 135, 136.

42. David M. Kennedy, *Freedom From Fear: The American People in Depression and War, 1929–1945* (New York: Oxford University Press, 1999), chapter 12 (quote from p. 365).

43. Alan Brinkley, "The New Deal and the Idea of the State," in *The Rise and Fall of the New Deal Order, 1930–1980,* ed. Steve Fraser and Gary Gerstle (Princeton, N.J.: Princeton University Press, 1989), 85–121.

44. Sidney M. Milkis, *The President and the Parties: The Transformation of the American Party System since the New Deal* (New York: Oxford University Press, 1993), 144.

45. For the creation and significance of the Executive Office of the President, see Fred I. Greenstein, "Change and Continuity in the Modern Presidency," in *The New American Political System,* ed. Anthony King

(Washington, D.C.: American Enterprise Institute, 1978), 45–53; and Milkis, *The President and the Parties,* chapter 6.

46. Kennedy, *Freedom from Fear,* 377–80; Harvard Sitkoff, *A New Deal for Blacks: The Emergence of Civil Rights as a National Issue* (New York: Oxford University Press, 1978).

47. Francisco E. Balderrama and Raymond Rodríguez, *Decade of Betrayal: Mexican Repatriation in the 1930s* (Albuquerque: University of New Mexico Press, 1995). See also Mark Reisler, *By the Sweat of Their Brow: Mexican Immigrant Labor in the United States, 1900–1940* (Westport, Conn.: Greenwood, 1976); and Emilio Zamora, *The World of the Mexican Worker in Texas* (College Station: Texas A&M University Press, 1993). For an interesting discussion of the New Deal as recording and reviving His-panic folk crafts, in an effort to "preserve" and "improve" Hispanic village life, see Suzanne Forrest, *The Preservation of the Village: New Mexico's Hispanics and the New Deal* (Albuquerque: University of New Mexico Press, 1989).

48. George J. Sánchez, *Becoming Mexican American: Ethnicity, Culture, and Identity in Chicano Los Angeles, 1900–1945* (New York: Oxford University Press, 1993), chapter 10.

49. Zaragosa Vargas, *Proletarians of the North: A History of Mexican Industrial Workers in Detroit and the Midwest, 1917–1933* (Berkeley: University of California Press, 1993), chapter 5; Juan R. García, *Mexicans in the Midwest, 1900–1932* (Tucson: University of Arizona Press, 1996), chapter 9; R. García, *Rise of the Mexican American Middle Class,* chapter 2.

50. Devra Weber, *Dark Sweat, White Gold: California Farm Workers, Cotton, and the New Deal* (Berkeley: University of California Press, 1994).

51. Pycior, *LBJ and Mexican Americans,* 26–38; Cynthia E. Orozco, "Regionalism, Politics, and Gender in the Southwest History: The LULAC's Expansion into New Mexico from Texas, 1929–45," *Western Historical Quarterly* 29, no. 4 (winter 1998): 459–83.

52. R. García, *Rise of the Mexican American Middle Class,* 301.

53. Márquez, *LULAC,* 17. This discussion of LULAC's ideology is drawn from Márquez, *LULAC,* 17–38, and M. García, *Mexican Americans,* 25–46.

54. M. García, *Mexican Americans,* 37.

55. Montejano, *Anglos and Mexicans,* 232.

56. Quoted in R. García, *Rise of the Mexican American Middle Class,* 260.

57. M. García, *Mexican Americans,* 43.

58. Horace M. Kallen, *Culture and Democracy in the United States* (New York: Boni & Liveright, 1924); For a thoughtful analysis of Kallen, which leads into his own answer to the question of his title, see Michael Walzer, "What Does It Mean to Be an American?" *Social Research* 57, no. 3 (fall 1990): 591–614.

59. Márquez, *LULAC,* 20.

60. R. García, *Rise of the Mexican American Middle Class,* 272–73.

61. Weeks, "The League of United Latin-American Citizens," 266.

62. M. García, *Mexican Americans,* 40–42; R. García, *Rise of the Mexican American Middle Class,* 266–72.

63. Weeks, "The League of United Latin-American Citizens," 270.

64. Oscar J. Martínez, interview with William Flores, Nov. 26 and Dec. 4, 1975, folder 18, box 3, Flores office files, LULAC papers, Benson Latin American Collection, University of Texas, Austin.

65. M. García, *Mexican Americans,* 46–53.

66. Pycior, *LBJ and Mexican Americans,* 34, 39.

67. Márquez, *LULAC,* 31–34. For a study of the process of Mexican Americans "becoming white" in Texas, see Neil Foley, *The White Scourge: Mexicans, Blacks, and Poor Whites in Texas Cotton Culture* (Berkeley: University of California Press, 1997).

68. González, *Chicano Education,* 94–112; San Miguel, Jr., *"Let All of Them Take Heed,"* 64–67.

69. San Miguel, Jr., *"Let All of Them Take Heed,"* 73–74.

70. M. García, *Mexican Americans,* 54–55; San Miguel, Jr., *"Let All of Them Take Heed,"* 75–76.

71. *Independent School District v Salvatierra,* 33 SW 2d 790 (Tex Civ App, 4th Dt 1930), cert. denied, 284 US 580 (1931).

72. Carolyn Hernández, "LULAC," 60–62; M. García *Mexican Americans,* 55–56.

73. San Miguel, Jr., *"Let All of Them Take Heed,"* 80–81; Hernández, "LULAC," 64–69.

READING 18

The Movement For Native Lives

Native Americans are killed by police at a rate higher than any other group

By Stephanie Woodard

Suquamish tribe descendant Jeanetta Riley, a 34-year-old mother of four, lay facedown on a Sandpoint, Idaho, street.

One minute earlier, three police officers had arrived, summoned by staff at a nearby hospital. Her husband had sought help there because Riley—homeless, pregnant and with a history of mental illness—was threatening suicide. Riley had a knife in her right hand and was sitting in the couple's parked van.

Wearing body armor and armed with an assault rifle and Glock pistols, the officers quickly closed in on Riley—one moving down the sidewalk toward the van, the other two crossing the roadway. They shouted instructions at her—to walk toward them, show them her hands. Cursing them, she refused. "Drop the knife!" they yelled, advancing, then opened fire.

They pumped two shots into her chest and another into her back as she fell to the pavement. Fifteen seconds had elapsed from the time they exited their vehicles.

That July evening in 2014, Riley became another Native American killed by police. Patchy government data collection makes it hard to know the complete tally. The *Washington* Post and the *Guardian* (U.K.) have both developed databases to fill in the gaps, but even these sometimes misidentify or omit Native victims.

To get a clearer picture, Mike Males, senior researcher at the Center on Juvenile and Criminal Justice, looked at data the Centers for Disease Control and Prevention (CDC) collected from medical examiners in 47 states between 1999 and 2011. When compared to their percentage of the U.S. population, Natives were more likely to be killed by police than any other group, including African Americans. By age, Natives 20–24, 25–34 and 35–44 were three of the five groups most likely to be killed by police. (The other two groups were African Americans 20–24 and 25–34.) Males' analysis of CDC data from 1999 to 2014 shows that Native Americans are 3.1 times more likely to be killed by police than white Americans.

Is it a gun, is it a knife / Is it a wallet, this is your life / It ain't no secret / No secret my friend / You can get killed just for living in your American skin

—BRUCE SPRINGSTEEN, "AMERICAN SKIN (41 SHOTS)"

Yet these killings of Native people go almost entirely unreported by mainstream U.S. media. In a paper presented in April at a Western Social Science Association meeting, Claremont Graduate University researchers Roger Chin, Jean Schroedel and Lily Rowen reviewed articles about deaths-by-cop published between May 1, 2014, and October 31, 2015, in the top 10 U.S. newspapers by circulation: the *Wall Street Journal, New York Times, USA Today, Los Angeles Times, New York Daily News, New York Post, Chicago Sun-Times, Denver Post, Washington Post* and *Chicago Tribune.*

Of the 29 Native Americans killed by police during that time, only one received sustained coverage—Paul Castaway, a Rosebud Sioux man shot dead in Denver while threatening suicide. The *Denver Post* ran six articles, totaling 2,577 words. The killing of Suquamish tribal member Daniel Covarrubias, shot when he reached for his cell phone, received a total of 515 words in the *Washington Post* and the *New York Times* (which misidentified him as Latino). The other 27 deaths received no coverage.

Compare this media blackout with the coverage of the next-most-likely group to be killed by police. The researchers found that the 10 papers devoted hundreds of articles to the 413 African Americans killed by police in that period, as well as to Black Lives Matter (BLM) protests and police violence more broadly. That's largely a testament to the power of the BLM movement, which exploded after the Aug. 9, 2014 killing of Michael Brown. When Minneapolis police killed both White Earth Ojibwe tribal member Philip Quinn, 30, and African-American Jamar Clark, 24, during the fall of 2015, Clark's story was well-reported, while Quinn's passing, like those of almost all other Native victims, was barely noted.

Nor did major media report on a spate of Native jailhouse deaths in 2015. The statistics on "death by legal intervention"—a term used by the CDC to describe fatalities at the hands of police—include those that occur in custody prior to sentencing. Whether the deaths are due to police action or neglect, the department is considered accountable. "When people are in custody, law enforcement has control of them and a responsibility for their welfare," Males explains.

A report commissioned by Alaska's Gov. Bill Walker found that Joseph Murphy, an Alaska Native veteran of the Iraq War, died of a heart attack in a holding cell in Juneau in August 2015, as jail staff yelled "fuck you" and "I don't care" in response to his pleas. According to the report, Larry Kobuk, identified in news articles as a 33-year-old Alaska Native, who had a heart condition known to his jailers, died in January 2015 while being held face down by four officers. Sarah Lee Circle Bear, a 24-year-old Sioux mother of two jailed in South Dakota, died after reportedly complaining of pain and being refused medical care. (At the Democratic National Convention, Sandra Bland's mother, Geneva Reed-Veal, who has become a vocal activist in the movement for black lives, pointed out that Circle Bear's death occurred during the same month her daughter died in police custody—July 2015.)

The list of 2015 deaths goes on: 53-year-old Choctaw medicine man Rexdale Henry, in a jail cell in Mississippi; Alaska Native Gilbert Joseph, 57, in Alaska; Yurok tribal member Raymond Eacret, 34, in California. On the Cheyenne River Sioux Tribe's reservation in South Dakota, an angry crowd marched on police headquarters after tribal member Phillip High Bear's mother alleged her 33-year-old son was beaten to death there. Protestors sang, drummed and shouted taunting references to the 1890 shooting death of Lakota spiritual leader Sitting Bull at the hands of Native police officers.

A larger narrative is at play: racial issues in the united states tend to be framed as black and white, while other groups are ignored.

Yet even this story received no coverage in the 10 largest papers. The Claremont researchers stress that they are not criticizing the important attention paid to the movement for black lives, but they note that a larger narrative is at play: Racial issues in the United States tend to be framed as black and white, while other groups are ignored.

But Native Americans' experiences of violence and discrimination in the United States often parallel those of African Americans. Federal investigations have found that on the borders of reservations, Native Americans are treated as second-class citizens by police and public agencies in ways that echo the experience of black Americans in towns like Ferguson, Mo.

Over the past 40 years, the U.S. Commission on Civil Rights (USCCR), an independent government agency, has held numerous hearings on discrimination in border towns surrounding reservations: in

The 'Justice for Jackie' movement emerged in response to the police killing of Jacqueline Salyers, 32, a mother of four.

New Mexico, near the Navajo reservation; in South Dakota, near the Sioux reservations; and, just this August, in Billings, Mont., near the Crow and Northern Cheyenne reservations.

Incidents aired even in recent hearings sound like tales from the pre-civil-rights Deep South. They ranged from denial of service in public places to police brutality to the failure to investigate murders. In Northern Plains states, USCCR members personally observed staff in restaurants and stores hassling or refusing to serve Natives. In South Dakota, the commission heard testimony about a police department that found reasons to fine Natives hundreds of dollars, then "allowed" them to work off the debt on a ranch. USCCR Rocky Mountain director Malee Craft described the situation as "slave labor."

This is the context for Native deaths at the hands of police.

The high rate of these killings is also a result of the comparative dearth of mental healthcare services for Native Americans, says Bonnie Duran, an Opelousas/Coushatta tribe descendent and an associate professor in the University of Washington School of Social Work. People threatening suicide and experiencing other mental health crises made up one-quarter of all those killed by cops in the first half of 2016, according to data collected by the *Washington Post*; they made up nearly half of the Native deaths examined by the Claremont researchers.

Distraught people in these situations—such as Riley or Castaway—can be particularly vulnerable. Commands from multiple officers in a quickly developing situation can be very difficult to parse, even for someone who isn't in crisis, says Jim Trainum, a former Washington, D.C., homicide detective.

"Attending to conflicting signals from multiple sources results in a huge cognitive demand," says Melissa Russano, a psychologist and criminal justice professor at Roger Williams University. "Split-second responses are required of the individual. You have to assess if and to what extent there is a threat, and that may create a certain level of panic."

As funding for mental healthcare continues to plummet, police are increasingly the first responders to mental health crises that they are untrained for and ill-equipped to handle.

In Native communities, the lack of mental healthcare services is particularly acute, according to an analysis of CDC data by the Suicide Prevention Resource Center (SPRC), and there's a critical shortage of Native professionals who understand cultural factors affecting patients. Data from the National Congress of American Indians illustrates this: In 2013, Indian Health Service per-capita expenditures were $2,849, compared to $7,717 per person for healthcare spending nationally. One indication of the situation's severity is the suicide rate for Natives, which in 2010 was 16.93 per 100,000, compared with 12.08 for the population as a whole, according to SPRC.

Mental health resources for Native Americans are even scarcer off-reservation, in the so-called urban-Indian communities, where about half of the Native population lives. There, clinics are funded at a lower rate, says Duran. This is also where the largest share of police killings occur: 79 percent, according to Chin.

Some police departments have responded by training officers in crisis intervention, which teaches them to slow down and find alternatives to the immediate application of lethal force, or by pairing officers with mental health professionals on calls that clearly involve such issues. Research is not yet conclusive about what works best, says Duran, but she stresses that the best solution is to address the problem at the root: Fund social services.

Native Lives Matter

The grassroots Native Lives Matter (NLM) movement is attempting to bring attention to the deaths, and to the larger social and economic oppression of Native Americans. Started in late 2014, the concept was inspired by Black Lives Matter, says one of the founders, Chase Iron Eyes, a Lakota attorney and Democratic candidate for Congress from North Dakota.

Neighboring South Dakota had been scrutinized by USCCR in a 2000 report, "Native Americans in South Dakota: An Erosion of Confidence in the Justice System." In the hearings that led up to the report, commissioners heard testimony about racial profiling during traffic stops, drunk drivers receiving light or suspended sentences for killing Natives, and, just as concerning to Natives, the white community's denial of the existence of racism toward Native people.

On Dec. 19, 2014, Iron Eyes and other Natives marched in Rapid City, S.D., to draw attention to police brutality against Natives. The next day, Rapid City police fatally shot a Native man, Allen Locke, who had attended the protest.

From the beginning, Iron Eyes says, NLM was intended to encompass numerous issues affecting Natives, from child welfare to incarceration disparities. The Native Lives Matter Facebook page and Twitter feed show the idea has proliferated across Indian country, with grassroots groups adopting the slogan as an umbrella term to advocate for environmental and social causes. "We don't own it; everyone has a right to it," says Iron Eyes.

Enter the Puyallup tribe (pronounced p-YAH-lup), an economically powerful, 4,000-member Northwest Indian nation with a successful casino, numerous tribal and individual fishing enterprises, and a real-estate portfolio of commercial and industrial properties. The tribe's reservation intersects the city of Tacoma, Wash., and members report the same kind of police harassment documented by USCCR in other border communities, such as being pulled over for "driving while Indian."

Now, the Puyallup are seeking to ensure that police are held accountable for their actions, no matter who the victim—Native or non-Native.

The Puyallup were catapulted into the issue of police violence on January 28. Shortly before midnight, Tacoma police officers approached a parked car. A convicted felon, Kenneth Wright, 36, who was wanted on drugs and weapons charges, was in the passenger seat; his pregnant girlfriend, 32-year-old tribal member Jacqueline Salyers, was the driver. Minutes later, one of the officers had shot Salyers in the head, and Wright had escaped into the night.

Almost immediately, relatives began to question the police account of the incident. They are now in the process of conducting their own investigation. There is no video record: Tacoma officers used no body or dash cams at the time, a police surveillance camera overlooking the street allegedly malfunctioned during the event, and police apparently destroyed three security cameras on a nearby house during their investigation.

The city of Tacoma, however, freely provided *In These Times* with hundreds of pages of witness statements, detectives' reports, 911 calls, logs of police-vehicle movements, scene photographs and more, assembled for its internal investigation.

According to the official account, Scott Campbell, the officer who shot Salyers, said that while on patrol, he recognized Wright and, behind the wheel, saw "a Native American female that appeared to be around 30 years of age." His partner, Aaron Joseph, stopped their cruiser across the street.

The two officers challenged Salyers and Wright to put their hands up. According to Campbell, Salyers then accelerated the car toward him; he says he shot at her to save his life.

Of the eight shots discharged, four hit Salyers. No shots hit Wright, who, when apprehended weeks later, told investigators he had ducked down.

After the gunfire, the officers took cover. Campbell told police investigators that he hid behind the bed of a pickup truck with his pistol pointed toward Salyers' vehicle. From this spot, he observed Wright "climbing around in the front of the vehicle [and] attempting to retrieve something from the rear of the vehicle," screaming "you fucking killed her" and other accusations, clambering over the "apparently shot female," exiting the car on the drivers side and running away, armed with a rifle.

James and Steve Rideout (R), return to the Tacoma street where their niece Jacqueline Salyers was shot, trying to figure out how it happened.

The police account raises a number of questions. Why did Campbell believe shooting the driver would stop a car that was in gear and underway? Why would an officer duck, pistol in hand, and watch while a dangerous wanted criminal laboriously armed himself and escaped into a residential neighborhood? In what would undoubtedly be a dangerous and quickly changing situation, why didn't the officers call for back-up or first look for a way to get Salyers, a bystander, out of the car?

About half an hour later, two officers removed Salyers from her vehicle—dragged her, according to a witness from the neighborhood—and put her in a patrol car. According to Tacoma Police Department spokesperson Loretta Cool, "The suspect, in the area with a rifle, would dictate moving to a safer location to administer medical aid." Cool declined to comment further, citing the possibility of a lawsuit.

Once in the new location, Salyers was dragged back out of the patrol car and onto the pavement, where Campbell performed chest compressions. Medics arrived and Salyers was pronounced dead. At some point, her right arm was broken, but not by a bullet; her family discovered this while preparing her for burial.

Based on the Tacoma Police Department's internal investigation and the medical examiner's report, the county prosecutor found the shooting justified. A review board later affirmed these findings, announcing on August 16 that "Campbell's use of deadly force was reasonable and within department policy." Salyers' family strenuously objects to that conclusion.

Corey Kanosh, an unarmed 35-year-old Paiute man, died in the Utah desert on Oct. 15, 2012. Police, believing the car in which he was a passenger to be stolen, chased it to a stop. After Corey got out of the car, police shot him and left him overnight. In the morning, he was pronounced dead.

Pregnant, homeless and threatening suicide, 34-year-old Suquamish tribe descendent **Jeanetta Riley** was shot and killed by Sandpoint, Idaho police on July 8, 2014, seconds after they exited their vehicles. Riley was holding a knife, and her shooting was ruled justified.

On Dec. 30, 2014, just one day after attending a Native Lives Matter protest, **Allen Locke** was shot and killed by a police officer in his Rapid City, S.D., home. A police investigation found the shooting justified because the 30-year-old Lakota man was holding a knife.

Rexdale Henry, a 53-year-old Choctaw medicine man, was arrested in Philadelphia, Miss., fora minor traffic violation and outstanding tickets. On July 14, 2015, he was found dead in his jail cell. Henry's cellmate was charged with his murder, but the details of the death are unclear.

After telling jailers that she was in excruciating pain, **Sarah Lee Circle Bear**, 24, was found dead in her Aberdeen, S.D., holding cell on July 5, 2015. Police later said the Lakota woman died from a meth overdose, but her family notes that she had been in police custody for two days before she died.

Mah-hl-vlst Goodblanket, 18, a member of the Cheyenne and Arapaho tribes, was Tasered twice and shot seven times in his Clinton, Okla., home by police on Dec. 21, 2013. His mother had called the police to request help keeping her son safe during a mental health episode.

'Everyone is welcome'

The killing horrified residents of the multi-ethnic Tacoma neighborhood. Gary Harrison, a 48-year-old African-American veteran, was awakened by the gunfire. The shooting happened right in front of his home. "I saw [Jackie's] car and so many police, for blocks around," he recalls. Two of his housemates told the others, "They shot Jackie." He had known the young woman. "She always had a smile for you," he says, eyes bright with tears.

At Salyers' funeral, her mother, Lisa Earl, 53, called for justice—not only for her daughter, but for everyone impacted by excessive use of force by law enforcement. Her tribe took up the challenge under the banner "Justice for Jackie, Justice for All."

Following her killing, Salyers' relatives met weekly at the Puyallup Little Wild Wolves Youth/Community Center, where Earl works, to mourn and to plan a March 16 two-mile protest march from the tribal headquarters to Tacoma's federal courthouse. Nearly 300 people turned out. Family and tribal members were joined by other Tacoma residents who had lost loved ones to police shootings and citizens involved with other issues, such as workers' rights and the environment. In May, family

On April 21, 2015, Lakewood, Wash., police shot and killed 37-year-old **Daniel Covarrubias**, when they mistook his cell phone for a gun. The shooting of the Suquamish man, a descendant of Chief Seattle, was later ruled justified. His family is calling for an independent investigation.

When **Christina Tahhahwah**, a Comanche woman with bipolar disorder, refused to leave her grandparents' house in Lawton, Okla., police took her to jail—instead of to the hospital, as her family wished. The next day, Nov. 14, 2014, she was found hand-cuffed to her cell door and unresponsive.

On March 27 in Winslow, Ariz., a police officer shot and killed **Loreal Tsingine**, a 27-year-old Navajo woman who had been holding medical scissors. Fellow police have said that in training, the officer was unable to control his emotions and was too quick to use his weapon.

Denver police officers claim that they shot 35-year-old **Paul Castaway** four times on July 12, 2015, because he had come "dangerously close" with a long knife. But a video shows the Rosebud Sioux man holding the knife only to his own neck. Family say he was having a schizophrenic episode and needed assistance, not violence.

Raymond Eacret, a 34-year-old Yurok tribal member, died in a Humboldt County, Calif., jail on June 26, 2015. Officers say that he hanged himself with a makeshift noose, but Eacret's mother says that her son's body looked as if it had been brutally beaten first.

Philip Quinn's family called St. Paul, Minn., police multiple times on Sept. 24, 2015, for help containing the 30-year-old, whom they said was psychotic and suicidal. Police shot and killed the White Earth Ojlbwe man as he ran toward them with a screwdriver.

members joined tribal council member Tim Reynon on a trip to Washington, D.C., to press the Department of Justices Office of Tribal Justice for an independent investigation of the shooting. At press time, no decision had been made whether to undertake one.

As time went by, others in the region—both Native and non-Native—who had lost friends and relatives to police killings began attending the family's gatherings, which continue regularly. They recount their stories in a traditional Puyallup talking circle (during which participants express themselves in turn and without interruption), then share a meal. Each person is in a different phase of their grieving, says James Rideout, 45, Lisa Earl's brother. "They are in such tender moments."

On the evening of June 20, *In These Times* attended one of the meetings. As participants filtered into the community center, they hugged, exchanged bits of gossip and found places in a circle of chairs. They were Native, black, white and Latino, young and old, united by concern about friends, family and neighbors lost in encounters with the police. The scent of cooking crab—gathered by Rideout in the Puget Sound earlier that day—wafted over the gathering, as participants told stories of tragedy and survival.

Andre Taylor, 48, spoke about what he called the "execution" of his brother, Che Taylor, an African American shot to death at age 46 in Seattle earlier this year. Silvia Sabon, a 53-year-old Tlingit tribal member, described the death of a 23-year-old Latino family friend, Oscar Perez-Giron, whom she says was killed on a bus platform by police challenging his lack of a ticket. African-American mother Crystal Chaplin, 52, said that in May 2015, Olympia, Wash., police shot both of her sons, Andre Thompson, then 23, and Bryson Chaplin, then 21, in the back. Both survived, but Bryson was paralyzed.

In a shooting that garnered national attention, **John T. Williams**, 50, was shot on Aug. 30, 2010 by a Seattle police officer who clalmed—agalnst witness testimony—that the Nuu-chah-nulth man had lunged at him with a knife. A proposed police reform bill in Washington state bears his name.

When jailed in Anchorage, Alaska, on Jan. 27, 2015. **Larry Kobuk**, 33, told the attending nurse he had a heart condition. Officers placed him face down in his jail cell and forcibly removed his clothes as he yelled that he couldn't breathe. Within minutes, he was unresponsive; he never regained consciousness.

On Dec. 16, 2012, at a travel plaza 35 miles north of Las Vegas, tribal police from the Moapa Band of Palutes Tasered and then shot to death **Marcus Lee**, a 28-year old father of four. Lee, who was killed in front of one of his sons, was wanted on several warrants. The FBI cleared the officers involved in the shooting.

Wichita, Kansas police officers shot **Karen Day-Jackson**, 45, a mother of three and grandmother of 11, on July 10, 2012. Police say the Eastern Shawnee woman came at them with a knife, stabbing herself In the chest and yelling "shoot me."

"Everyone is welcome [at the meeting]," says Sabon. "It doesn't matter what color you are. We are all going through the same thing."

Not alone

Though the family and tribal community have acknowledged the Native Lives Matter movement, the thrust of the Puyallup's efforts has been ecumenical. This approach makes sense culturally to the Puyallup. Their name for themselves in their language connotes "generous and welcoming behavior to all people who enter our lands."

"When the police killings happened to people who didn't have a tribe to back them up, they were alone, on their own out there," says Rideout. "When our tribe took a position on this issue, we realized we had an opportunity to take care of them all, to bring them along with us."

In addition, says tribal council member Reynon, a tribe can be effective in a ways an individual advocate or advocacy group cannot. "We have a trust relationship with the federal government, so we are a sovereign nation with the full weight of the United States behind us. We also have the recognition and respect of local governments."

The Puyallup tribe supports a Washington state ballot initiative that seeks greater police accountability for lethal use of force. The bill that the initiative would put before the legislature is named for John T. Williams. He is one of few Natives whose death-by-cop, in Seattle in 2010, received more coverage. Then 50, he was shot by an officer who first claimed Williams lunged at him with a knife, though eyewitnesses contradicted this. The shooting was termed unjustified, but the officer never faced criminal penalties.

"With the ballot initiative, we want to build a model for this issue that can be replicated around the nation," says Chester Earl, 42, Salyers' cousin. "On January 28, our family was made part of a circle of families throughout the nation who are living with this issue."

Puyallups have joined individuals and groups statewide, like the NAACP, that are collecting signatures; 250,000 are needed by the end of 2016 to put the measure before the legislature.

When Seattle Mayor Ed Murray announced that he backed the bill, a Seattle Police Department representative said, "We support the mayor's position on the initiative, so by default, we support it." It appears to be the only police department in the state to issue a positive response to the potential change.

In another development, state legislative leaders have appointed Reynon to a new Joint Legislative Task Force on Deadly Force and Community Policing, a committee drawn from community groups as well as law enforcement. The bill establishing the task force acknowledges the danger police are often placed in as they protect the community, but it also seeks ways to reduce violent interactions between law enforcement and the public.

"We have to find a solution that works for everyone," says Reynon. "It will mean change, and change is never easy."

For Salyers' family, it's been a painful process. "We never asked to be a part of this," Rideout says. "We always want to stress the good narratives, our children succeeding. But now that we are involved, we must ensure that nothing like this ever happens again."

At the spot where Jacqueline Salyers' body lay on the pavement Puyallup tribal members have held candlelight vigils.

Justice for Jackie ... and Jennie

Tribal involvement means the possibility of real and lasting change to Ramona Bennett, a Puyallup elder in her late seventies. "People and movements may fade, but a tribe doesn't go away," says Bennett, a former tribal chairwoman and long-time activist who was gassed, clubbed, shot at and arrested during 1970s "fish-ins" to demand recognition of treaty-guaranteed fishing rights.

The Puyallup have long been easy victims in Tacoma, Bennett says. Traditionally, they lived in communal longhouses, but late-19th-century presidential proclamations and Congressional actions broke up the reservation and forced tribal members to move to isolated cabins on separate plots. "Fishing and trapping were outlawed, so the men went out at night, making the cabins very dangerous," says Bennett. "White men would come, kick the doors in, rape and murder the [women] and throw their bodies on the railroad tracks, where they'd be called 'railroad accident deaths.' ... We discovered in our tribal enrollment office a stack of 'railroad death' documents from 1912 to 1917." Among them was one that recorded the death of Bennetts grandmother Jennie.

The Justice for Jackie, Justice for All effort will succeed, Bennett believes. "But I'm still out for justice for Jennie ... a girl who has been dead for 104 years."

This story was reported and written with the support of the Fund for Investigative Journalism and the Leonard C. Goodman Institute for Investigative Reporting.

READING 19

Coming Together

The Asian American Movement

By Yen Espiritu

Arriving in the United States, nineteenth-century immigrants from Asian countries did not think of themselves as "Asians." Coming from specific districts in provinces in different nations, Asian immigrant groups did not even consider themselves Chinese, Japanese, Korean, and so forth, but rather people from Toisan, Hoiping, or some other district in Guandong Province in China or from Hiroshima, Yamaguchi, or some other prefecture in Japan. Members of each group considered themselves culturally and politically distinct. Historical enmities between their mother countries further separated the groups even after their arrival in the United States. Writing about early Asian immigrant communities, Eliot Mears (1928:4) reported that "it is exceptional when one learns of any entente between these Orientals." However, non-Asians had little understanding or appreciation of these distinctions. For the most part, outsiders accorded to Asian peoples certain common characteristics and traits that were essentially supranational (Browne 1985: 8–9). Indeed, the exclusion acts and quotas limiting Asian immigration to the United States relied upon racialist constructions of Asians as homogeneous (Lowe 1991: 28).

Mindful that whites generally lump all Asians together, early Asian immigrant communities sought to "keep their images discrete and were not above denigrating, or at least approving the denigration of, other Asian groups" (Daniels 1988: 113). It was not until the late 1960s, with the advent of the Asian American movement, that a pan-Asian consciousness and constituency were first formed. To build political unity, college students of Asian ancestry heralded their common fate—the similarity of experiences and treatment that Asian groups endured in the United States (Omi and Winant 1986: 105). In other words, the pan-Asian concept, originally imposed by non-Asians, became a symbol of pride and a rallying point for mass mobilization by later generations. This chapter examines the social, political, and demographic factors that allowed pan-Asianism to take root in the 1960s and not earlier.

Ethnic "Disidentification"

Before the 1960s, Asians in this country frequently practiced ethnic disidentification, the act of distancing one's group from another group so as not to be mistaken and suffer the blame for the presumed misdeeds of that group (Hayano 1981: 162). Faced with external threats, group members can either intensify their solidarity or they can distance themselves from the stigmatized segment. Instead of uniting to fight anti-Asian forces, early Asian immigrant communities often disassociated themselves from the targeted group so as not to be mistaken for members of it and suffer any possible negative consequences (Hayano 1981: 161; Daniels 1988: 113). Two examples of ethnic disidentification among Asians in this country occurred during the various anti-Asian exclusion movements and during World War II. These incidents are instructive not only as evidence of ethnic disidentification but also as documentation of the pervasiveness of racial lumping. Precisely because of racial lumping, persons of Asian ancestry found it necessary to disassociate themselves from other Asian groups.

Exclusion Movements

Beginning with the first student laborers in the late nineteenth century, Japanese immigrants always differentiated themselves from Chinese immigrants. Almost uniformly, Japanese immigrants perceived their Chinese counterparts in an "unsympathetic, negative light, and often repeated harsh American criticisms of the Chinese" (Ichioka 1988: 191). In their opinion, the Chinese came from an inferior nation; they also were lower-class laborers, who had not adapted themselves to American society. In 1892, a Japanese student laborer described San Francisco's Chinatown as "a world of beasts in which ... exists every imaginable depravity, crime, and vice" (cited in Ichioka 1988: 191).

Indeed, the Japanese immigrants were a more select group than their Chinese counterparts. The Japanese government viewed overseas Japanese as representatives of their homeland. Therefore, it screened prospective emigrants to ensure that they were healthy and literate and would uphold Japan's national honor (Takaki 1989: 46).

More important, Japanese immigrants distanced themselves from the Chinese because they feared that Americans would lump them together. Aware of Chinese exclusion, Japanese immigrant leaders had always dreaded the thought of Japanese exclusion. To counteract any negative association, Japanese immigrant leaders did everything possible to distinguish themselves from the Chinese immigrants (Ichioka 1988: 250). For example, to separate themselves from the unassimilable Chinese laborers, some Japanese immigrant leaders insisted that their Japanese workers wear American work clothes and even eat American food (Ichioka 1988: 185). In 1901, the Japanese in California distributed leaflets requesting that they be differentiated from the Chinese (tenBroek, Barnhart, and Matson 1970: 23).

However, under the general rubric Asiatic, the Japanese inherited the painful experiences of the Chinese.[1] All the vices attributed to the Chinese were transferred to these newest Asian immigrants (Browne 1985). Having successfully excluded Chinese laborers, organized labor once again led the campaign to drive out the Japanese immigrants. In 1904, the American Federation of Labor adopted its first anti-Japanese resolution. Charging that the Japanese immigrants were as undesirable as the Chinese, the unions' resolution called for the expansion of the 1902 Chinese Exclusion Act to include Japanese and other Asian laborers. By mid-1905, the labor unions of California had joined forces to establish the Asiatic Exclusion League (Hill 1973: 52–54; Ichioka 1988: 191–192).

Since the Japanese immigrants considered themselves superior to the Chinese, they felt indignant and insulted whenever they were lumped together with them. In 1892, a Japanese immigrant wrote in the *Oakland Enquirer* that he wished "to inveigh with all my power" against American newspapers that compared the Japanese to "the truly ignorant class of Chinese laborers and condemned them as bearers of some mischievous Oriental evils" (cited in Ichioka 1988: 192). Instead of joining with the Chinese to fight the anti-Asian exclusion movement, some Japanese leaders went so far as to condone publicly the exclusion of the Chinese while insisting that the Japanese were the equals of Americans (Daniels 1988: 113). Above all else, Japanese immigrant leaders wanted Japanese immigration to be treated on the same footing as European immigration (Ichioka 1988: 250,.

In the end, Japanese attempts at disidentification failed. With the passage of the 1924 Immigration Act, Japanese immigration was effectively halted. This act contained two provisions designed to stop Japanese immigration. The first barred the immigration of Japanese wives even if their husbands were United States citizens. The second prohibited the immigration of aliens ineligible for citizenship. Because the Supreme Court had ruled in 1922 that persons of Japanese ancestry could not become naturalized citizens, this provision effectively closed the door on Japanese and most other Asian immigration (U.S. Commission on Civil Rights 1986: 8–9). The Japanese immigrants felt doubly affronted by the 1924 act because it ranked them, not as the equals of Europeans, but on the same level as the lowly Chinese, the very people whom they themselves considered inferior (Ichioka 1988: 250). Thus, despite all their attempts to disassociate themselves from the Chinese, with the passage of the act, the Japanese joined the Chinese as a people deemed unworthy of becoming Americans. Little did they foresee that, in less than two decades, other Asian groups in America would disassociate themselves from the Japanese.

World War II and Japanese Internment

Immediately after the bombing of Pearl Harbor, the incarceration of Japanese Americans began. On the night of December 7, the Federal Bureau of Investigation (FBI) began taking into custody persons of Japanese ancestry who had connections to the Japanese government. Working on the principle of guilt by association, the security agencies simply rounded up most of the Issei (first-generation) leaders of the Japanese community. Initially, the federal government differentiated between alien and citizen Japanese Americans, but this distinction gradually disappeared. In the end, the government evacuated more than 100,000 persons of Japanese ancestry into concentration camps, approximately two-thirds of whom were American-born citizens. It was during this period that the Japanese community discovered that the legal distinction between citizen and alien was not nearly so important as the distinction between white and yellow (Daniels 1988: ch. 6).

Like the Japanese, the Chinese understood the importance of the distinction between white and yellow. Fearful that they would be targets of anti-Japanese activities, many persons of Chinese ancestry, especially in the West, took to wearing buttons that proclaimed positively "I'm Chinese." Similarly, many Chinese shopkeepers displayed signs announcing, "This is a Chinese shop." Some Chinese immigrants even joined the white persecution with buttons that added "I hate Japs worse than you do" (Daniels 1988: 205; Takaki 1989: 370–371). The small Korean and Filipino communities took similar actions. Because of Japan's occupation of Korea at the time, being mistaken as Japanese particularly angered Koreans in the United States. Cognizant of Asian lumping, the United Korean Committee prepared identification cards proclaiming "I am Korean." During the early months of the war, women wore Korean dresses regularly to distinguish themselves from the Japanese (Melendy 1977: 158; Takaki 1989: 365–366). Similarly, persons of Filipino ancestry wore buttons proclaiming "I am a Filipino" (Takaki 1989: 363).

Given the wars between their mother countries and Japan, it is not surprising that the Chinese, Koreans, and Filipinos distanced themselves from the Japanese. But their reactions are instructive not only as examples of ethnic disidentification but also as testimonies to the pervasiveness of racial lumping. Popular confusion of the various Asian groups was so prevalent that it was necessary for Chinese, Filipinos, and Koreans to don ethnic clothing and identification buttons to differentiate themselves from the Japanese. Without these *visible* signs of ethnicity, these three Asian groups would probably have been mistaken for Japanese by anti-Japanese forces. As Ronald Takaki (1989: 370) reported, Asian groups "remembered how they had previously been called 'Japs' and how many whites had lumped all Asians together." But there are also examples of how Asian groups united when inter-Asian cooperation advanced their common interests.

Inter-Asian Labor Movements

The most notable example of Inter-Asian solidarity was the 1920 collaboration of Japanese and Filipino plantation laborers in Hawaii. In the beginning, plantation workers had organized in terms of national origins. Thus, the Japanese belonged to the Japanese union and the Filipinos to the Filipino union. In the early 1900s, an ethnically based strike seemed sensible to Japanese plantation laborers because they represented about 70 percent of the entire work force. Filipinos constituted less than 1 percent. However, by 1920, Japanese workers represented only 44 percent of the labor force, while Filipino workers represented 30 percent. Japanese and Filipino union leaders understood that they would have to combine to be politically and economically effective (Johanessen 1950: 75–83; Takaki 1989: 152).

Because together they constituted more than 70 percent of the work force in Oahu, the 1920 Japanese–Filipino strike brought plantation operations to a sudden stop. Although the workers were eventually defeated, the 1920 strike was the "first major interethnic working-class struggle in Hawaii"

(Takaki 1989: 154).[2] Subsequently, the Japanese Federation of Labor elected to become an interethnic union. To promote a multiethnic class solidarity, the new union called itself the Hawaii Laborers Association (Takaki 1989: 154–155).

Although the 1920 strike was a de facto example of pan-Asian cooperation, this cooperation needs to be distinguished from the post-1960 pan-Asian solidarity. The purported unifying factor in 1920 was a common class status, not a shared cultural or racial background (Takaki 1989: 154). This class solidarity is different from the large-scale organization of ethnicity that emerged in the late 1960s. For most Asian Americans, the more recent development represents an enlargement of their identity system, a circle beyond their previous national markers of identity. True, like working-class unions, panethnic groups are interest groups with material demands (Glazer and Moynihan 1963; Bonacich and Modell 1980). However, unlike labor unions, panethnic groups couch their demands in ethnic or racial terms-not purely in class terms. In other words, their ethnicity is used as a basis for the assertion of collective claims, many but not all of which are class based.

Social and Demographic Changes: Setting the Context

Although Asians in the United States have long been engaged in political action, their efforts never drew public attention until the 1960s (Chan 1991: 171). Prompted by broader political struggles and internal demographic changes, college students of Asian ancestry spearheaded the Asian American movement. Critical to its development was the mobilization of American blacks. Besides offering tactical lessons, the civil rights and the Black Power movements had a profound impact on the consciousness of Asian Americans, sensitizing them to racial issues (Uyematsu 1971). The anticolonial nationalist movements in Asia also stirred racial and cultural pride and provided a context for the emergence of the Yellow Power movement (P. Wong 1972). Influenced by these broader political struggles, Americans of Asian ancestry united to denounce racist institutional structures, demand new or unattended rights, and assert their cultural and racial distinctiveness. Normal urban issues such as housing, education, and social welfare began to take on ethnic coloration.

While important, these broader societal developments alone do not explain why the Asian American movement became panethnic. To understand this development, we first need to understand the underlying social and demographic factors that allowed pan-Asianism to take root in the 1960s but not earlier. Before World War II, pan-Asian unity was not feasible because the predominantly foreign-born Asian population did not share a common language. During the postwar years, increasing intergroup communication and contact facilitated the emergence of a pan-Asian consciousness. The breakdown of economic and residential barriers during the postwar period provided the first opportunity for an unprecedented number of Asian Americans to come into intimate, sustained contact with the larger society—and with one another.

TABLE 19.1 Chinese and Japanese American Foreign-Born Population in the United States, 1860–1940

Year	Chinese		Japanese	
	Number	Percentage Foreign-Born	Number	Percentage Foreign-Born
1900	80,853	90	24,057	99
1910	56,596	79	67,655	94
1920	43,107	70	81,383	73
1930	44,086	59	70,477	51
1940	37,242	48	47,305	37

Source. U S. Bureau of the Census (1943: tables 4 and 6).

From an Immigrant to a Native Population

Before 1940, the Asian population in the United States was primarily an immigrant population (see Table 19.1). Immigrant Asians faced practical barriers to pan-Asian unity. Foremost was their lack of a common language. Old national rivalries were another obstacle, as many early Asian immigrants carried the political memories and outlook of their homelands. For example, Japan's occupation of Korea resulted in pervasive anti-Japanese sentiments among Koreans in the United States. According to Brett Melendy (1977: 155), "Fear and hatred of the Japanese appeared to be the only unifying force among the various Korean groups through the years." Moreover, these historical enmities and linguistic and cultural differences reinforced one another as divisive agents.

During the postwar period, due to immigration restrictions and the growing dominance of the second and third generations, American-born Asians outnumbered immigrants. The demographic changes of the 1940s were pronounced. During this decade, nearly twenty thousand Chinese American babies were born. For the first time, the largest five-year cohort of Chinese Americans was under five years of age (Kitano and Daniels 1988: 37). By 1960, approximately two-thirds of the Asian population in California had been born in the United States (Ong 1989: 5–8). As the Asian population became a native-born community, linguistic and cultural differences began to blur. Although they had attended Asian-language schools, most American-born Asians possessed only a limited knowledge of their ethnic language (Chan 1991: 115). By 1960, with English as the common language, persons from different Asian backgrounds were able to communicate with one another (Ling 1984: 73), and in so doing create a common identity associated with the United States.

Moreover, unlike their immigrant parents, native-born and American-educated Asians could muster only scant loyalties to old world ties. Historical antagonisms between their mother countries thus receded in importance (P, Wong 1972: 34). For example, growing up in America, second-generation Koreans "had difficulty feeling the painful loss of the homeland and understanding the indignity of fapanese domination" (Takaki 1989: 292). Thus, while the older generation of Koreans hated all fapanese, "their children were much less hostile or had no concern at all" (Melendy 1977: 156). As a native-born fapanese American community advocate explained, "By 1968, we had a second generation. We could speak English; so there was no language problem. And we had little feelings of historical animosity" (Kokubun interview].

As national differences receded in subjective importance, generational differences widened. For the most part, American-born Asians considered themselves to have more in common with other American-born Asians than they did with foreign-born compatriots.[3] According to a third-generation Japanese American who is married to a Chinese American, "As far as our experiences in America, I have more things in common than differences with a Chinese American. Being born and raised here gives us something in common. We have more in common with each other than with a Japanese from Japan, or a Chinese from China" (Ichioka interview). Much to their parents' dismay, young Asian Americans began to choose their friends and spouses from other Asian groups. Eui-Young Yu (1983: 47) related that second- and third-generation Koreans "identify and intermingle as much with other Asian minorities as with fellow Koreans, especially with the fapanese and Chinese." Similarly, Stephen Fugita and David O'Brien (1991: 146) reported that the Sansei (third-generation) were much more likely than the Nisei (second-generation) to see themselves as Asian Americans. This muting of cultural and historical divisions distressed their parents, who, more often than not, had supported these divisions for most of their lives. As a young Chinese American asserted:

> My parents mean well and I try to respect them, but they do not understand what it's all about. We have buried the old hatreds between Chinese and Japanese, and my friends and I must go beyond our parents' "hang ups." My mother is upset because I'm engaged to a Japanese girl but she knows she can do nothing about it. (Cited in Weiss 1974: 235)

The Watershed of World War II

Before World War II, Asian immigrant communities were quite distinct entities, isolated from one another and from the larger society. Because of language difficulties, prejudice, and lack of business opportunities elsewhere, there was little chance for Asians in the United States to live outside their ethnic enclaves (Yuan 1966: 331). Shut out of the mainstream of American society, the various immigrant groups struggled separately in their respective Chinatowns, Little Tokyos, or Manilatowns. Stanford Lyman (1970: 57–63) reported that the early Chinese and Japanese communities in the western states had little to do with one another—either socially or politically. Although statistical data do not exist, ethnographic accounts confirm the ethnic homogeneity of each early Asian immigrant community. For example, according to a study of New York's Chinatown in the 1890s, "The entire triangular space bounded by Mott, Pell, and Doyers Streets and Chatham Square is given to the exclusive occupancy of these Orientals" (cited in Yuan 1966: 323). Within these enclaves, diversity among Asian nationalities was more salient than commonality.

Economic and residential barriers began to crumble after World War II. The war against Nazism called attention to racism at home and discredited the notions of white superiority. The fifteen years after the war was a period of largely positive change as civil rights statutes outlawed racial discrimination in employment as well as housing (Daniels 1988: ch. 7). Popular attitudes were also changing. Polls taken during World War II showed a distinct hostility toward Japan: 74 percent of the respondents favored either killing off all Japanese, destroying Japan as a political entity, or supervising it. On the West Coast, 97 percent of the people polled approved of the relocation of Japanese Americans. In contrast, by 1949, 64 percent of those polled were either friendly or neutral toward Japan (Feraru 1950).

During the postwar years, Asian American residential patterns changed significantly. Because of the lack of statistical data,[4] a longitudinal study of the changing residential patterns of Asian Americans cannot be made. However, descriptive accounts of Asian American communities indicate that these enclaves declined in the postwar years. Edwin Hoyt (1974: 94) reported that in the 1940s, second-generation Chinese Americans moved out of the Chinatowns, Although they still came back to shop or to see friends, they lived elsewhere. In 1940, Rose Hum Lee found twenty-eight cities with an area called Chinatown in the United States. By 1955, Peter Sih found only sixteen (Sung 1967: 143–144). New York's Chinatown exemplifies the declining significance of Asian ethnic enclaves. In 1940, 50 percent of the Chinese in New York City lived in its Chinatown; by 1960, less than one-third lived there (Yuan 1966: 331). Similarly, many returning Japanese Americans abandoned their prewar settlement in old central cities and joined the migration to suburbia (Daniels 1988: 294). in the early 1970s, Little Tokyo in Los Angeles remained a bustling Japanese American center, "but at night the shop owners [went] home to the houses in the suburbs" (Hoyt 1974: 84).

Although single-ethnic communities were still the norm, residential segregation between Asian nationalities declined in the postwar years. Formerly homogeneous, the ethnic enclaves started to house other Asian groups—as well as non-Asian groups. In 1957, driving past 7th and H streets in Washington, D.C., Betty Lee Sung (1967: 142–143) reported, "I passed the length of Chinatown before I suddenly realized that the place was almost deserted. The faces that I did see on the street were not Chinese but Filipinos." In 1970, due to the influx of Japanese and Filipinos, there was a proposal to rename Oakland Chinatown "Asiantown" (Sano 1970). Multigroup urban centers also emerged. Paul Wong (1972: 34) reported that since the early 1960s, Asian Americans of diverse national origins have moved into the suburbs outside the major Asian communities such as Berkeley or San Mateo, California. Although a small proportion of the local population, these Asian Americans tended to congregate in pockets; consequently, in some residential blocks a majority of the residents were Asian Americans.

TABLE 19.2 Mean Segregation Indices for Chinese and Japanese Americans in 822 U.S. Suburbs, 1960,1970, and 1980

Ethnic Groups	1960	1970	1980	Change. 1960–80
Chinese–White	38.83	31.45	28.22	–10.61
Chinese–Black	54.02	50.42	49.43	–4.59
Japanese–White	34.00	22.16	26.77	–7.23
Japanese–Black	48.62	48.46	45.97	–2.65
Chinese–Japanese	39.11	27.70	24.97	–14.14

Source: Lam (1986: tables 1, 2, and 3)

Moreover, recent research on suburban segregation indicates that the level of segregation between certain Asian American groups is often less than that between them and non-Asians. Using Standard Metropolitan Statistical Area (SMSA) data[5,] for 1960, 1970, and 1980, Frankie Lam (1986) computed indices of dissimilarity (ID)[6] among Chinese, Japanese, black, and white Americans in 822 suburbs. As indicated in Table 19.2, from 1960 to 1980 the level of segregation between Chinese and Japanese Americans was much less than that between these two groups and blacks and, in one case, less than that between these groups and whites. But the actual level of segregation is only one issue. The decline of segregation over time is another. From 1960 to 1980, Chinese segregation from the Japanese shows a more pronounced decline (–14.14) than that of Chinese or Japanese from whites (–10.61 and –7.23 respectively) and from blacks (–4.59 and –2.65 respectively).[7] Though not comprehensive, these studies together suggest that Asian residential segregation declined in the postwar years.

As various Asian groups in the United States interacted, they became aware of common problems and goals that transcended parochial interests and historical antagonisms. One recurrent problem was employment discrimination. According to a 1965 report published by the California Fair Employment Practices Commission, for every $51 earned by a white male Californian, Japanese males earned $43 and Chinese males $38—even though Chinese and Japanese American men had become slightly better educated than the white majority (Daniels 1988: 315). Moreover, although the postwar period marked the first time that well-trained Chinese and Japanese Americans could find suitable employment with relative ease, they continued to be passed over for promotion to administrative and supervisory positions (Kitano and Daniels 1988: 47). Asians in the United States began to see themselves as a group that shared important common experiences: exploitation, oppression, and discrimination (Uyematsu 1971).

Because inter-Asian contact and communication were greatest on college campuses, pan-Asianism was strongest there (P. Wong 1972: 33–34). Exposure to one another and to the mainstream society led some young Asian Americans to feel that they were fundamentally different from whites. Disillusioned with the white society and alienated from their traditional communities, many Asian American student activists turned to the alternative strategy of pan-Asian unification (Weiss 1974: 69–70).

The Construction of Pan-Asian Ethnicity

Although broader social struggles and internal demographic changes provided the impetus for the Asian American movement, it was the group's politics—confrontational and explicitly pan-Asian—that shaped the movement's content. Influenced by the internal colonial model, which stresses the commonalities among "colonized groups," college students of Asian ancestry declared solidarity with fellow Asian Americans—and with other Third World[8] minorities (Blauner 1972: ch. 2). Rejecting the label "Oriental," they proclaimed themselves "Asian American." Through pan-Asian organizations, publications, and Asian American studies programs, Asian American activists built pan-Asian solidarity by pointing out their common fate in American society. The pan-Asian concept enabled diverse Asian American groups to understand their "unequal circumstances and histories as being related" (Lowe 1991: 30].

From "Yellow" to "Asian American"

Following the example of the Black Power movement, Asian American activists spearheaded their own Yellow Power movement to seek "freedom from racial oppression through the power of a consolidated yellow people" (Uyematsu 1971: 12). In the summer of 1968, more than one hundred students of diverse Asian backgrounds attended an "Are You Yellow?" conference at UCLA to discuss issues of Yellow Power, identity, and the war in Vietnam [Ling 1989: 53). In 1970, a new pan-Asian organization in northern California called itself the "Yellow Seed" because "Yellow [IS] the common bond between Asian-Americans and Seed symboliz[es] growth as an individual and as an alliance" (Masada 1970). This "yellow" reference was dropped when Filipino Americans rejected the term, claiming that they were brown, not yellow (Rabaya 1971: 110; Ignacio 1976: 84). At the first Asian American national conference in 1972, Filipino Americans "made it clear to the conferees that we were 'Brown Asians'" by forming a Brown Asian Caucus (Ignacio 1976: 139–141). It is important to note, however, that Filipino American activists did not reject the term "yellow" because they objected to the pan-Asian framework. Quite the contrary, they rejected it because it allegedly excluded them from that grouping (Rabaya 1971: 110).

Other community organizers used the term "Oriental" to define their organizations and service centers. In Southern California, the Council of Oriental Organizations (COO) became the political base for the diverse Asian American communities. In 1968, COO lobbied for federal funding to establish the Oriental Service Center in Los Angeles County, serving Chinese, Japanese, Filipinos, and Koreans. But Asian American activists also rejected *Oriental* because the term conjures up images of "the sexy Susie Wong, the wily Charlie Chan, and the evil Fu Manchu" (Weiss 1974: 234). It is also a term that smacks of European colonialism and imperialism: *Oriental* means "East"; Asia is "east" only in relationship to Europe, which was taken as the point of reference (Browne 1985). To define their own image and to claim an *American* identity, college students of Asian ancestry coined the term *Asian American* to "stand for all of us Americans of Asian descent" (Ichioka interview). While *Oriental* suggests passivity and acquiescence, *Asian Americans* connotes political activism because an Asian American "gives a damn about his life, his work, his beliefs, and is willing to do almost anything to help Orientals become Asian Americans" (cited in Weiss 1974: 234).

The account above suggests that the creation of a new name is a significant symbolic move in constructing an ethnic identity. In their attempt to forge a pan-Asian identity, Asian American activists first had to coin a composite term that would unify and encompass the constituent groups. Filipino Americans' rejection of the term "yellow" and the activists' objection to the cliche-ridden *Oriental* forced the group to change its name to Asian American, The history of the Sansei Concern, a UCLA student group, provides a telling example. In the summer of 1968, as we have seen, Sansei Concern organized the "Are You Yellow?" conference. At the end of the conference, in an effort to incorporate other Asian subgroups, Sansei Concern changed its name to Oriental Concern. In 1969, reflecting its growing political sophistication, the group changed its name once more to Asian American Political Alliance, a name adopted by a group of activists at the University of California at Berkeley the year before [Ling 1989: 53). It is noteworthy that while *Yellow, Oriental,* and *Asian American* connote different ideologies, all three terms signify panethnicity.

Pan-Asian Organizations

Influenced by the political tempo of the 1960s, young Asian Americans began to join such organizations as the Free Speech Movement at the University of California at Berkeley, Students fora Democratic Society, and the Progressive Labor Party. However, these young activists "had no organization or coalition to draw attention to themselves as a distinct group" (P. Wong 1972: 33). Instead, they participated as individuals—often at the invitation of their white or black friends (Chin 1971b: 285; Nakano 1984: 3–4). While Asian American activists subscribed to the integrationist ideology of the 1960s and 1970s social movements, they also felt impotent and alienated. There was no structure to uphold their own identity. As an example, when the Peace and Freedom Party was formed on the basis of black and white coalitions, Asian American activists felt excluded because they were neither black nor white (P. Wong 1972: 34; Yoshimura 1989: 107).

In the late 1960s, linking their political views with the growth of racial pride among their ranks, Asian Americans already active in various political movements came together to form their own organizations (Nakano 1984: 3–4). Most of the early pan-Asian organizations were college based. In 1968, activists at the University of California, Berkeley founded one of the first pan-Asian political organizations: the Asian American Political Alliance (AAPA). According to a co-founder of the organization, its establishment marked the first time that the term "Asian American" was used nationally to mobilize people of Asian descent (Ichioka interview), AAPA was formed to increase the political visibility and effectiveness of Asian American activists:

> There were so many Asians out there in the political demonstrations but we had no effectiveness. Everyone was lost in the larger rally. We figured that if we rallied behind our own banner, behind an Asian American banner, we would have an effect on the larger public. We could extend the influence beyond ourselves, to other Asian Americans. (Ichioka interview)

AAPA differed from the traditional Asian cultural groups on most college campuses in two primary ways: its political activism and its pan-Asian emphasis. Reflecting the various political movements from which its members had come, AAPA took progressive stands against the war in Vietnam and in support of other Third World movements (Ichioka interview). Espousing a pan-Asian framework, AAPA brought together young Chinese, Japanese, and Filipino American activists (Nishio 1982: 37).[9] Shortly after AAPA was formed at the University of California at Berkeley, a sister organization was established at San Francisco State College (now University). Like its Berkeley counterpart, San Francisco State AAPA "was a vehicle for students to share political concerns in a pan-Asian organization" (Umemoto 1989: 17). AAPA's influence also spread to Southern California as Asian American students formed similar organizations on the UCLA and California State University, Long Beach campuses (Ling 1984; Yoshimura 1989).

Pan-Asian organizations also mushroomed in other parts of the country. In 1969, through the initiative of West Coast students, Asian American organizations began to form on East Coast campuses. For example, in New York, young Asian Americans organized Asian Americans for Action, or Triple A. At Columbia University, Asian Americans involved in white radical politics came together to found their own Asian American Political Alliance. Students at Yale prepared and taught a course on "Asians in America" (Chin 1971*b*: 285). Similarly, in the Midwest, the civil rights, antiwar, and United Farm Workers movements drew Asian Americans together. Out of these political gatherings emerged a group of Asian American activists who subsequently formed Madison's Asian Union, Illinois' Asian American Alliance, and Minneapolis' Asian American Political Alliance (*Rice Paper* 1975).

Not only did pan-Asian organizations reinforce the cohesiveness of already existing networks, but they also expanded these networks. By the mid-1970s, *Asian American* had become a familiar term (Lott 1976: 30). Although first coined by college activists, the pan-Asian concept began to be used extensively by professional and community spokespersons to lobby for the health and welfare of Americans of Asian descent. In addition to the local and single-ethnic organizations of an earlier era, Asian American professionals and community activists formed national and pan-Asian organizations such as the Pacific/Asian Coalition and the Asian American Social Workers (Ignacio 1976: 162; Kuo 1979: 283–2.84), Also, Asian American caucuses could be found in national professional organizations such as the American Public Health Association, the American Sociological Association, the American Psychological Association, the American Psychiatric Association, and the American Librarians Association (Lott 1976: 31), Commenting on the "literally scores of pan-Asian organizations" in the mid-1970s, William Liu (1976: 6) asserted that "the idea of pan-Asian cooperation [was] viable and ripe for development."

Asian American Studies

On college and university campuses, the most important legacy of the Asian American movement was the institutionalization of Asian American studies.[10] Beginning in 1968, under the slogan of self-determination, Asian American and other U S. Third World students fought for an education more relevant and accessible to their communities. Reflecting the larger national struggle over cultural hegemony, these students demanded the right to control their educational agenda, to design their own programs, and to evaluate their instructors (Umemoto 1989; 3–4), In 1968, after the most prolonged and violent campus struggles in this country's history, Asian American studies programs were established at San Francisco State College (now University) and at the University of California at Berkeley. These campus struggles emboldened students at other colleges to fight for ethnic studies courses, programs, and departments and forced college administrations to heed such demands (Murase 1976*a*: 205–209). In succeeding years, Asian American Studies programs were established on major campuses throughout the country.[11] Since 1968, the field has progressed from experimental courses to degree programs. For example, UC Berkeley and UCLA now offer B.A. and M.A. degree programs in Asian American Studies respectively (Nakanishi and Leong 1978: 6).

Although varied in their curriculum development and course offerings, Asian American Studies programs built, and continue to build, an Asian American heritage, putting courses and reading selections together and expounding similarities—as well as differences—in the experiences of Asian peoples in the United States. Indeed, the curriculum was designed to help students "know who they are as Asian Americans" (Contemporary Asian Studies Division 1973: 38). Clearly part of the heritage being created hinges on Asian Americans' shared history of racial discrimination. Many courses stress an Asian American identity and experience, yielding highly emotional discussions on subjects dealing with discrimination, alienation, and racism (Weiss 1974: 241). Such an emphasis is evident in the following statement of curriculum philosophy for Asian American Studies:

> Throughout much of America's history, Asians in this country have been the victims of contempt and exploitation. Often they were singled out as scapegoats in periods of severe economic depression, such as the nation-wide anti-Chinese agitations and riots in the 1870's and 1880's, and Asian Americans were regarded as enemies during times of international conflicts, particularly the Second World War and the Korean War. (Contemporary Asian Studies Division 1973: 35)

This statement links together the experiences of Chinese, Japanese, and Korean Americans; in so doing, it calls attention to their collective identity.

Table 19.3 Percentage of Studies on Specific Asian Groups for Bibliographies and Publications Released during the 1970s and 1980s

Ethnic Group	Total Number	Percentage of Total Studies for Century	Percentage Published 1970s–80s
Asian	208	15	37
Chinese	460	33	23
East Indian	53	4	17
Filipino	96	7	26
Japanese	514	37	18
Korean	32	2	75
Pacific Islander	8	0.6	75
Southeast Asian	6	0.4	83

Source: Asians in America (1983: vii).

Also, Asian American scholars began to reinterpret Asian history in the United States to bring out what is common to all Asian Americans. These histories highlight a record of violence against Asians, who were denied the rights of citizenship, forbidden to own land, interned in relocation camps, and forced to live in poverty-stricken enclaves (Jensen and Abeyta 1987: 406). For example, in discussing discriminatory Jaws and informal acts perpetrated against Chinese, Korean, Filipino, and Japanese immigrants, Lowell Chun-Hoon (1975: 47) concluded that "what is significant (about this exploitation) is that all of these varied Asian groups, each representing a separate country and unique culture, encountered a similar or identical pattern of racial oppression and economic exploitation." Also, Asian Americans were treated increasingly as a single unit of analysis in academic studies. A survey of studies on Asian groups in the United States indicates that works dealing with "Asians" increased dramatically during the 1970s and 1980s (see Table 19.3). Articles published in these decades represent 37 percent of such articles published in this country, "almost three times as many works" as might have been expected (*Asians in America* 1983: viii).

Along the same lines, in addition to explaining specific group experiences, Asian American writers have turned their attention to those experiences shared by the various Asian peoples. In the 1971 publication *Roots: An Asian American Reader,* the autobiographies and poems that appear in the "identity" section "express the increasing commitment of Asian Americans to redefine and articulate their individual and collective identity. While they reflect a wide range of backgrounds and responses to American society, there can be found a common level of experience with which all Asians in America can identify" (Tachiki 1971: 4).This new direction enlarged the context of Asian American writing, and led to the use of the term "Asian American literature" (E. Kim 1982). As Jesse Hiraoka (1986: 95) stated, the overriding objective "became that of establishing an Asian American heritage in terms of the arrival and stay of the Asians in the United States, and the changes that occurred as they consolidated their presence in American society."

In sum, Asian American Studies provides an institutional means to reach more Asian American students and to create "an Asian American awareness expressing a unity of all Asians, Chinese, Japanese, Filipino, Korean, Samoan, and Hawaiian" (E. Wong 1971: 248). Its by products—the Association for Asian American Studies, national conferences, research centers, and publications—further stimulate pan-Asian solidarity because they provide a forum for Asian Americans to discuss common problems and experiences.[12] In these settings, "the experiences of different Asian groups were compared and recognized as historically intertwined" (Ling 1989: 73).

Asian American News Media

The 1960s and 1970s also saw the rapid growth of a pan-Asian news medium directed toward the largest possible Asian audience, covering both ethnic and panethnic developments and concerns (see Table 19.4). Ethnic publications are important because they promote ethnic ideology and keep alive ethnic symbols and values, heroes, and historical achievements. It is the very business of the ethnic media to be concerned with the events and progress of the ethnic group (Breton 1964: 201). Until the late 1960s, most of the Asian newspapers and periodicals were concerned primarily with local and single-ethnic issues.

Pan-Asian periodicals came out of the Asian American movement, the efforts of Asian American student organizations on university campuses across the country. In fact, "these newspapers, pamphlets, and magazines were the lifeblood of the movement" (Quinsaat 1976: 267). While the traditional ethnic press continued to be important, its neglect and disdain of such political issues as civil rights, the Vietnam war, and ethnic studies prompted young dissidents to launch their own publications. Much of their journalism was committed to the empowerment of the Asian American people.

Although not always successful, some publications attempted to formulate a pan-Asian perspective rather than any singular ethnic outlook (Quinsaat 1976). In 1969, five ucla students put up $100 each to launch the monthly publication *Gidra,* the first and most widely circulated pan-Asian publication. In all, during its five years of publication, about two hundred individuals participated in producing *Gidra* (Murase 1976*b*). On the East Coast, *Getting Together,* a New York Chinatown newspaper, expounded Asian American issues from a militant orientation; its stated purpose was to "further advance the just causes of Asian people in this country" (Chin 1971*a* 30; *Getting Together* 1972: 1). These movement periodicals covered both ethnic and panethnic concerns. For example, the first issue of *Getting Together* included the following stories: "Chinatown and Its Problems," "Serving the People," "Yellow Power," and "Concentration Camps in the USA." Emphasizing its Chinese American as well as Asian American identity, the staff of *Getting Together* wrote, "We are not a bunch of 'do-gooders' out to save somebody else; we only know that our freedom and happiness are tied-in with the freedom and happiness of every Chinese and every Asian person" (cited in Chin 1971*b*: 286). Initiated in 1971 by

Table 19.4 Partial Listing of Asian American Periodicals, Late 1960s–Early 1970s

Publication	Place of Publication
AACTION	Philadelphia, Pa
AASA	California State University at Northridge
AASA	Cornell University, Ithaca, N.Y.
Aion	San Francisco
Amerasia Journal	Yale University, New Haven, Conn. (now UCLA)
Ameri-Asia News	Forest City, Fla.
Asian American for Equal Employment Newspaper	New York City
Asian Expression	California State University at Dominguez Hills
Asian Family Affair	Seattle, Wash.
Asian Spotlight	College of San Mateo, Calif.
Asian Student, The	Berkeley, Calif.
Asian Student	City College of New York
Asian Student Voice	San Francisco State
Bridge: An Asian American Perspective	New York City
Crosscurrents	Los Angeles
East Wind	Los Angeles
Eastern Wind	Washington, D C.
Getting Together	New York City Chinatown
Gidra	Los Angeles
Jade: The Asian American Magazine	Los Angeles
Pacific Ties	Los Angeles
Rice Paper	Madison, Wis.
Rodan	San Francisco

Source. Compiled by author.

the Yale Asian American Students Association, *Amerasia Journal* (now housed at UCLA) became the only national scholarly publication devoted exclusively to the study of the experience of Asians in America.

Besides functioning as a source of news for young Asian American activists, these media efforts also forged pan-Asian consciousness. Through articles, poetry, and photographs in a variety of publications, and by meeting together, these young Asian Americans across the country began to communicate with one another and to share their frustrations and their dreams. From these efforts, they began "to formulate their own values, establish their own identities and sense of pride, and create a new 'culture' which they can truly call Asian American" (Chin 1971*a*: 29). In the final issue of *Gidra,* Mike Murase (1976*b*: 319) described the solidarity that emerged from this collective experience:

> It has been an experience in sharing—in giving and receiving—in a sisterly and brotherly atmosphere. It has meant a chance to work for something we really believe in. It has meant a chance to express ourselves in a variety of ways .... It has meant working with people who care about people, and genuinely feeling the strength that can only come out of collective experience.[13]

By the mid-1970s, due to inadequate manpower and funding, many of the movement publications had folded. In their place came slicker and more business-minded publications. The transition from radical to "bourgeois" journalism reflects broader changes in pan-Asian political consciousness in the last two decades—from the confrontational to the more orthodox. For example, founded in the late 1980s, both *Rice* and AsMm were nationally distributed magazines geared toward young and upper-income Asian American professionals.[14] Among the pan-Asian newspapers, *Asian Week,* published in San Francisco since 1979, has been the most stable. According to the weekly's managing editor, the management team decided to name the newspaper *Asian Week* instead of the proposed *Chinese Week* to "reflect the widespread acceptance of the pan-Asian concept" (Andersen interview). In recent years, some single-ethnic newspapers have also broadened their scope to cover additional Asian communities. For example, in the mid-1980s, *East/West* dropped its subtitle "A Chinese American Newspaper" and devoted more space to national Asian American issues. A content analysis of the longstanding Japanese American publication *Pacific Citizen* indicates that, from 1955 to 1985, the newspaper became more pan-Asian. As Table 19.5 indicates, the surge in Asian articles coincided with the Asian American movement of the late 1960s.

Although varied in their successes, these pan-Asian journals testify to the salience of a generalized Asian American readership. They are also important because they bring the news of the entire Asian American population to the various Asian American subgroups. In so doing, they enlarge the scope of Asian American awareness and dialogue beyond the boundaries of province and nationality.

Table 19.5 Number of Pacific Citizen Articles Covering Asian Stories, April, August, and December 1955–85

Year	April	August	December	Total
1955	0	0	1	1
1960	0	0	0	0
1965	1	0	0	1
1970	12	5	8	25
1975	2	2	1	5
1980	4	4	4	12
1985	12	5	7	24

Source: Compiled by author from *Pacific Citizen,* 1955–85 An Asian story is defined as one that covers a non-Japanese Asian group or one that covers all Asian groups. Only the first issue of each month was examined.

An Asian American Perspective: In Quest of Identity

Although an offshoot of the mass struggles of the late 1960s, the Asian American movement was not only a political movement but one that emphasized "race," as that term is conventionally understood. Like their non-Asian peers of the time, young Asian American activists joined in the struggles against poverty, war, and exploitation. However, they often viewed these struggles from an Asian American perspective, emphasizing race and racism directed against Asian Americans. This racial perspective bound them to other Asian groups as well as to other minorities, while separating them from whites. The importance of race (or racial ideology) is most evident in Asian American participation in and interpretation of the antiwar, New Left, and women's movements.

Antiwar Movement

The antiwar movement united Asian Americans along racial lines. For many Asian American activists, the American invasion of Vietnam involved more than the issues of national sovereignty or imperialism; it also raised questions of racism directed against Asian people (Kwong 1987: 148). Watching the images of war on the evening television news, "an increasing number of Asian American college and high school students realized with a shock that the 'enemy' whom American soldiers were maiming and killing had faces like their own" (Chan 1991: 174). Seeing unarmed, unresisting civilians napalmed in Vietnam angered young Asian Americans and stirred them to protest the prevailing assumption that Asian lives were cheap. To emphasize the racist nature of the war, Asian American protesters discarded the popular slogans "Give peace a chance" and "Bring the GIs home," and touted their own "Stop killing our Asian brothers and sisters" and "We don't want your racist war" (P. Wong 1972: 35–36). According to Asian American antiwar activists, the slogan "Bring our boys home" clearly proclaimed that the primary concern was to avoid American, not Vietnamese, casualties (*Bridge* 1973: 3).

As Asian people fighting in an Asian country, Asian American G.I.s were particularly repulsed by the atrocities committed against the Vietnamese people:

> For some G.I.'s in Vietnam, there are no Vietnamese people. To them the land is not populated by people but by "Gooks," considered inferior, unhuman animals by the racist-educated G.I. Relieved in his mind of human responsibility by this grotesque stereotype, numerous barbarities have been committed against these Asian peoples, since "they're only 'Gooks.'" (Nakamura 1971: 24)

Because of their racial similarity to the "enemy," Asian American G.I.s also endured anti-Asian racism. Many Asian Americans complained that their superior officers and fellow G.I.s lumped them together with other Asian groups: regardless of their ethnic background, Asian American soldiers were indiscriminately called Gook, Jap, Chink, or Ho Chi Minh. An Asian American G.I. related that, upon entering basic training, he was called a "Gook" and was made to stand in front of his platoon as an example of "what the enemy looked like" (Yoshimura 1971). The "Gook" stereotype "portrays Koreans, Vietnamese, Cambodians, Laotians, and other Asians as subhuman beings who do not value individual human life and who all look like the treacherous Chinese Communist enemy" (Tachiki 1971: 2–3). The stereotype angered and ethnicized Asian American G.I.s. As a former American G.I. of Japanese ancestry related, "I became ethnicized when I was in Vietnam. I saw how whites were treating the Vietnamese, calling them Gooks, running them over with their trucks. I figured I am a Gook also" (Watanabe interview).

At times, the race question alienated Asian Americans from the majority of the antiwar protesters. An Asian American activist recounted the tension in the antiwar camp:

> In the early stage, there was a debate on what would be the main slogan. One slogan was "Bring the GIs home." The white component felt that this would unite the greatest amount of concern. But the Asian community felt that this slogan ignored what the U.S. was doing over there in Asia. Asian Americans were the only group that pushed the question of racism toward Asians. They wanted to know why the U.S. was involved in Asia in World War II and in Vietnam now. (Omatsu interview)

In 1971, the Asian American contingent refused to join the main antiwar march in Washington, D.C. because the coordinating committee failed to adopt the contingent's antiracist statement for the march. On other occasions, the contingent's appeals "were met with hostility and rejection" (P. Wong 1972: 34–36). When Asian Americans did take part in the white-dominated marches, they passed out their own leaflets, which denounced racism and imperialism. A Japanese American antiwar protester described the Asian flavor of the Asian American contingent:

> I marched in the April 24 [antiwar] demonstration in San Francisco with the Asian contingent. That was everybody: Filipinos, Chinese, Koreans, and Japanese. We marched together, waving red books and carried the People's Chinese flag, a Pathet Lao flag, some North Korean flags, Vietnamese flags, and a Chinese flag—and it was good. (Sumi 1971: 259)

In sum, Asian American emphasis on race and racism differentiates their antiwar protest from that of whites. In characterizing the Vietnam war as a racist act against Asians, Asian American activists proclaimed racial solidarity not only with each other but also with the Vietnamese people, their "Asian brothers and sisters" (*Bridge* 1973: 3). In the process, pan-Asian political consciousness became transnationalized, encompassing the political struggles not only in America but also in Asia. As an Asian American activist stated, "As long as there are U.S. troops in Asia, as long as the U.S. government and the military wage wars of aggression against Asian people, racism against Asians will serve the interest of this country. Racism against them is often racism against us" (Yoshimura 1971: 29).

New Left Movement

In the late 1960s and early 1970s, a significant number of Asian Americans also became active in New Left activities and organizations such as the Free Speech Movement (FSM), Students for a Democratic Society (SDS), the Weathermen, and the Progressive Labor Party. Asian American Marxist organizations grew out of these New Left activities (Nakano 1984: 2–3). Diverging from the Old Left emphasis on the working class as the leading revolutionary stratum, the New Left sought to organize people across class lines. The New Left also looked away from the Soviet Union and to the Vietnamese National Liberation Front and the People's Republic of China as new models of socialism. It was the New Left's version of socialism and the movements growing admiration for Asian countries that influenced the thinking of Asian American Marxists (Liu and Cheng 1986: 144–145).

As in the antiwar movement, the Asian American New Left separated itself from the dominant New Left movement over the issues of racism and national oppression. It was over these questions that Asian American working people acquainted themselves with Marxism—a Marxism that emphasized race as well as class (Liu and Cheng 1986: 148). Influenced by the call for national liberation by the Black Power movement and Asian socialist countries, Asian American Marxists added racial self-determination to their revolutionary agenda (Nakano 1984: 4–5). For many Asian American community activists, there was no contradiction between a Marxist–Leninist approach and the prominence given to race. Because race constitutes such a fundamental category in American society, Asian Americans (and other racial minority groups) often view class issues from a racial perspective (Lipsitz 1988: 235). For example, the ethnic consciousness of the Red Guard in San Francisco's Chinatown "usually supersedes and sometimes clashes with their alleged attachment to a class-oriented ideology" (Lyman

1973: 29).[15] The centrality of race is evident in the following call for Marxist–Leninist organizing in the Asian American communities:

> The situation in the Asian communities is so deplorable that a Marxist-Leninist Party must begin to take firm root among the people. It is necessary that this party does not alienate the people or create any factions among the budding Asian American movement as we do not even make up 1% of the total population of America. The purpose of this party is to educate the people on the fact that the Asian communities in America are included in the genocidal American foreign policy in Asia. (Hing 1970: 9–10)

In contrast, other white-dominated groups like the Revolutionary Union (now the Revolutionary Communist Party) considered the national oppression question to be of secondary importance to the "bread and butter" issues that affected all workers (*East Wind* 1979: III).

Varied in their understanding and application of Marxism, Asian American Marxist organizations struggled over the relative importance of nation building and party building. Despite their desires for revolutionary change and socialism, the issue of national liberation continued to be the guiding principle for many Asian American community groups. This position is evident in the following statement issued by the I Wor Kuen (IWK),[16] the largest revolutionary organization in the Asian American community in the 1970s:

> Our organization, like many others in America, arose as a response to national oppression and racial discrimination, and as part of the growing anti-imperialist movement in the 1960s. We formed as an Asian organization because, in 1968–69, the national oppression and corresponding national struggles of Third World peoples was the sharpest in the nationwide progressive movements. Furthermore, the bankruptcy of the Communist Party, USA and Progressive Labor Party, among others, especially in relation to the national question, made joining their ranks out of the question. (I Wor Kuen 1974: 6–7)

The IWK also combined the goal of racial self-determination with the goal of socialism. For example, in 1969, the organization issued a twelve-point program and platform that included demands for self- determination for Asian Americans and Asians as well as the establishment of a socialist party (Liu and Cheng 1986: 147).

In 1972, in an attempt to apply Marxism to the national question, the Marxist-oriented organization East Wind adopted the "Asian nation" line. Echoing the separatist call in the black community, East Wind declared that as a racially oppressed minority, Asian Americans were entitled to form their own nation. Although East Wind dropped the Asian nation line in 1975, it continued to stress the importance of national liberation (Nakano 1984: 10–12). On the other hand, organizations such as the New York-based Asian Study Group advocated party building and criticized other Asian American revolutionary groups for their preoccupation with "band-aid" social service programs (Nakano 1984: 14–17). Many of these differences remained unresolved, eventually dissolving friendships as well as organizations (Ling 1984).

In short, as in the antiwar movement, Asian American Marxists added a racial perspective to the New Left movement. This racial perspective bound them to other Asian Americans as it separated them from other non-Asian components. Just as women in other social movements were identifying barriers that restricted their roles, Asian American women activists began to challenge sexism and introduce gender-related issues into the Asian American movement.

Women's Movement

Although Asian American women had been involved in each stage of the Asian American movement, they were often restricted to such subordinate tasks as taking minutes, typing, making coffee, and answering phones. The small number of Asian American women who achieved leadership positions in the movement found themselves called "bossy" and "unfeminine" (*Rodan* 1971; Ling 1989: 53). Asian American feminists who challenged Asian American sexism were often cast as betraying Asian American nationalism—as assimilationists (Lowe 1991: 31).

Sexist oppression prevailed even in the most revolutionary Asian American organizations. For example, the San Francisco–based Red Guards initially claimed that women's worth was only in staying at home and in producing children (Nakano 1984: 13). Along the same lines, the Marxist-oriented I Wor Kuen championed forsaking monogamy to liberate relations between men and women and to build collective solidarity. In actuality, this sexual liberation was "a cover for degeneracy and the most blatant forms of male supremacy and the oppression of women" (cited in Nakano 1984: 13). Rebelling against the sexual oppression of women in the Asian American movement, an angry Asian American poet wrote:

> so you come to me for a spiritual piece
> my eyes have the ol' epicanthic fold
> my skin is the ideologically correct color
> a legit lay for the revolutionary
> well, let me tell you, brother
> revolution must be total
> and you're in its way
> yeah, yeah, I'm all sympathy
> your soul and your sexuality has

been fucked over by Amenka
well, so has mine
so has ours
we chronic smilers
asian women
we of the downcast almond eyes
are seeing each other
sisters now, people now
asian women. (T, Tanaka 1971)

Frustrated with male chauvinism, Asian American women began meeting separately from men to discuss feminist concerns. Their collective anger was nurtured by the progressive ideology of the women's movement of the late 1960s. Although they borrowed heavily from the general women's movement, Asian American women seldom joined these middle-class, white-dominated organizations. Like black, Chicana, and Native American women, Asian American women felt alienated and at times exploited by these women's organizations.

In its early development, the women's movement was in fact insensitive to the issues of minority and lower-class women (Ling 1989). In contrast, Asian American and other Third World feminists emphasized the "triple oppression" concept: their gender was inextricably linked to their race and class. As an Asian women's studies instructor reflected, "The writings of white middle-class women on 'women's lib' ... failed to speak relevantly to Asian American women. Many Asian women faced discrimination not only as women, but also on the basis of race, cultural background or low socio-economic status" (Chen 1976: 235). In the provocative "Yellow Prostitution," an Asian American feminist chastised Asian women who tried to be white:

> It is not enough that we must "kow tow" to the Yellow male ego, but we must do this by aping the Madison Avenue and Hollywood version of *White* femininity. All the peroxide, foam rubber, and scotch tape will not transform you into what you are not ... Whether this is a conditioned desire to be white, or a desperate attempt to attain male approval, it is nothing more than Yellow Prostitution. (Gil 1968)

Because "their ethnic identity was a critical component of their feminism" (Ling 1989: 52), Asian American feminists refused to advocate a non-Asian alliance—despite the fact that white feminists could offer important resources and shared similar concerns. Distancing themselves from the general feminist movement, Asian American women organized their own movement. For Asian American women activists, the ideology of feminism had to be incorporated into the larger identity of being Asian American. According to Susie Ling (1989: 63), "The Asian Women's Movement's umbilical cord was still very much attached to the larger Asian American Movement." Asian American women chose two major paths of activism: they worked within the Asian American community or within Marxist–Leninist groups. In 1971, Asian American women m Los Angeles organized Asian Sisters to address the drug problems of young Asian American women. It was one of the first social service projects for Asian American women by Asian American women. In 1972, they established Little Friends Playground to provide childcare for the community (Ling 1989). The Marxist-Leninist groups that Asian American women were involved in remain Asian American-oriented today (Ling 1984: 209). Asian American women were also concerned with the social conditions of their Asian sisters in China and Vietnam. For example, in 1971, the Los Angeles Asian women's movement sent delegates to the Vancouver Indochinese Women's Conference to express their solidarity with these women (Ling 1989: 55).

The Limits of Pan-Asianism

Although pan-Asian consolidation certainly has occurred, it has been by no means universal. For those who wanted a broader political agenda, the pan-Asian scope was too narrow and its racial orientation too segregative (P. Wong 1972: 33; Lowe 1991: 39). For others who wanted to preserve ethnic particularism, the pan-Asian agenda threatened to remove second- and third-generation Asians "from their conceptual ties to their community" (R. Tanaka 1976: 47). These competing levels of organization mitigated the impact of pan-Asianism.

Moreover, pan-Asianism has been primarily the ideology of native- born, American-educated, and middle-class Asians. Embraced by students, artists, professionals, and political activists, pan-Asian consciousness thrived on college campuses and in urban settings. However, it barely touched the Asian ethnic enclaves. When the middle-class student activists carried the enlarged and politicized Asian American consciousness to the ethnic communities, they encountered apprehension, if not outright hostility (Chan 1991: 175). Conscious of their national origins and overburdened with their day- to-day struggles for survival, most community residents ignored or spurned the movement's political agenda (P. Wong 1972: 34). Chin (1971*b*: 287) reported that few Chinatown residents participated in any of the pan-Asian political events. Similarly, members of the Nisei-dominated Japanese American Citizens League "were determined to keep a closed mind and maintain their negative stereotype" of the members of the Asian American Political Alliance (J. Matsui 1968: 6). For their part, young Asian American activists accused their elders of having been so whitewashed that they had deleted their experiences of prejudice and discrimination from their history (Weiss 1974: 238). Because these young activists were not rooted in the community, their base of support was narrow and their impact upon the larger society often limited (P. Wong 1972: 37; Nishio 1982: 37).

Even among those who were involved in the Asian American movement, divisions arose from conflicting sets of interests as subgroups decided what and whose interests would be addressed.

Table 19.6 Asian American Studies Instructors in the United States by Ethnic Group, 1973

Ethnic Group	Total	Doctorate	Master's	Bachelor's or less	Don't Know
Chinese	27	1	10	12	4
Filipino	9	1	1	4	3
Japanese	33	6	14	6	7
Korean	3	1	1	1	0
White	5	4	0	0	1
Don't Know	5	0	1	0	4

Source: Chun-Hoon, Hirata, and Moriyama (1973 85) Chun-Hoon, Hirata, and Moriyama (1973) sent about twenty-five questionnaires to select institutions across the country. The table is based on the eight responses received

Oftentimes, conflicts over material interests took on ethnic coloration, with participants from smaller subgroups charging that "Asian American" primarily meant Chinese and Japanese American, the two largest and most acculturated Asian American groups at the time (Ignacio 1976: 220; Ling 1984: 193–195). For example, most Asian American Studies progtams did not include courses on other Asian groups, but only on Chinese and Japanese. Similarly, the Asian American women's movement often subsumed the needs of their Korean and Filipina members under those of Chinese and Japanese women (Ling 1984: 193–195). Chinese and Japanese Americans also were the instructors of Asian American ethnic studies (see Table 19.6), directors and staff members of many Asian American projects,[17] and advisory and panel members in many governmental agencies (Ignacio 1976: 223–224).

The ethnic and class inequality within the pan-Asian structure has continued to be a source of friction and mistrust, with participants from the less dominant groups feeling shortchanged and excluded. As discussed in subsequent chapters, the influx of the post-1965 immigrants and the tightening of public funding resources have further deepened the ethnic and class cleavages among Asian American subgroups.

Conclusion

The development of a pan-Asian consciousness and constituency reflected broader societal developments and demographic changes, as well as the group's political agenda. By the late 1960s, pan-Asianism was possible because of the more amicable relationships among the Asian countries, the declining residential segregation among diverse Asian groups in America, and the large number of native-born, American-educated political actors. Disillusioned with the larger society and estranged from their traditional communities, third- and fourth-generation Asian Americans turned to the alternative strategy of pan-Asian unification. Through pan-Asian organizations, media, and Asian American

Studies programs, these political activists assumed the role of "cultural entrepreneurs" consciously creating a community of culture out of diverse Asian peoples.[18] This process of pan-Asian consolidation did not proceed smoothly nor did it encompass all Asian Americans. Ethnic chauvinism, competition for scarce resources, and class cleavages continued to divide the subgroups. However, once established, the pan-Asian structure not only reinforced the cohesiveness of already existing networks but also expanded these networks. As later chapters indicate, although first conceived by young Asian American activists, the pan-Asian concept was subsequently institutionalized by professionals and community groups, as well as government agencies. The confrontational politics of the activists eventually gave way to the conventional and electoral politics of the politicians, lobbyists, and professionals, as Asian Americans continued to rely on the pan-Asian framework to enlarge their political capacities.

Notes

1. On the other hand, due to the relative strength of Japan in the world order, Japanese immigrants at times received more favorable treatment than other Asian immigrants. For example, in 1905, wary of offending Japan, national politicians blocked an attempt by the San Francisco Board of Education to transfer Japanese students from the public schools reserved for white children to the "Oriental" school serving the Chinese (Chan 1991: 59).

2. Although many Korean laborers were sympathetic to the 1920 strike, because of their hatred for the Japanese, they did not participate. As the Korean National Association announced, "We do not wish to be looked upon as strikebreakers, but we shall continue to work in the plantation and we are opposed to the Japanese in everything" (cited in Melendy 1977: 164).

3. The same is true with other racial groups. For example, American-born Haitians are more like their African American peers than like their Haitian parents (Woldcmikael 1989: 166).

4. Ideally, residential patterns should be analyzed at the census tract level. However, this analysis cannot be done because Asians were not tabulated by census tracts until the 1980 census.

5. The units of analysis used by Lam (1986) were 822 suburbs with a population m 1960 of 10,000 or more located within the 212 smsa that could be identified in 1970 as well as in 1980.

6. The Index of Dissimilarity (ID) is the leading measure of residential segregation. The index of dissimilarity ranges from 0 to 1 (some researchers prefer 0 to 100) and reflects the percentage of a group that would have to move to obtain equivalent proportional distributions. In general, values of dissimilarity above .600 are considered high, while those under .300 are low; values from

7. .300 to 600 indicate a moderate level of residential segregation (Denton and Massey 1988; 804).

8. The 1980 census provided a first-time opportunity to examine the census tract separation of Asian subgroups. Analyses of the 1980 data show a relatively high level of residential segregation among Asian subgroups. In selected areas in Southern California, the level of segregation between Asian subgroups is (in some cases) as high as that between each group and non-Asians (Hodge, Arsdol, Ko, and Gorwaney 1986: table 2; White 1986: table 1). In the absence of longitudinal data, these findings do not necessarily invalidate the claim made in this section that residential segregation among Asian subgroups has declined over time. Moreover, this section is concerned primarily with the immediate postwar period, when the majority of the Asian population was native born. In 1980, the Asian population was, once again, an immigrant population (73 percent foreign born). Rapid growth through immigration promotes the formation of new ethnic-specific enclaves, thereby reducing contact with other Asian groups as well as with non-Asians (Massey and Denton 1987: 821).

9. During the late 1960s, in radical circles, the term *third world* referred to the nation's racially oppressed people.

10. According to Yuji Ichioka, potential members were drawn from the Peace and Freedom Party roster: "We went down the list and picked out identifiable Asian names, aapa participants were younger people in their twenties and thirties. They were more Americanized. All American-born. We felt we had to do something because we were part of American society. We were not new immigrants" (Ichioka interview).

11. I thank Jesse Hiraoka for sharing his thoughts with me on this subject.

12. A 1978 survey identified the following longstanding Asian American Studies programs in the United States: California State Universities at San Francisco, Fresno, Sacramento, and Long Beach; Universities of California at Berkeley, Santa Barbara, Davis, and Los Angeles; University of Southern California; University of Washington; University of Colorado; City College of New York; and the University of Hawaii. Harvard, Yale, Columbia, and Princeton offered courses once but never established programs (Nakanishi and Leong 1978),

13. As stated in the 1991 program of the Association for Asian American Studies Conference, one of the purposes of the association is to promote "better understanding and closer ties among the various groups within the Asian American community."

14. In 1990, some of the former *Gidra* staff reunited to publish a twentieth-anniversary issue of the paper. Reflecting the ethnic diversity of the Asian Pacific American population in the 1990s, the 128-page publication included many articles on and by the post-1965 Asian immigrants and refugees.

15. The publication of *Rice* magazine was suspended in 1989.

16. For example, the Red Guards accepted an invitation to guard a meeting of the Chinese Contractors' Association against a threatened assault by the Teamsters who sought to organize Chinatown's heavily exploited seamstresses (Lyman 1973: 29).

16. IWK later merged with the August Twenty-Ninth Movement (atm) and changed its name to the League for Revolutionary Struggle.

17. For example, the staff of the movement publication *Gidra* were predominantly Japanese Americans.

18. For a discussion of the role of "cultural entrepreneurs," sec Cornell (1988*b*).

References

Blauner, Robert. 1972. *Racial Oppression in America.* New York: Harper & Row.

Bonacich, Edna, and John Modell. 1980. *The Economic Basis of Ethnic Solidarity: A Study of Japanese Americans.* Berkeley: University of California Press.

Breton, Raymond. 1964. "Institutional Completeness of Ethnic Communities and the Personal Relations of Immigrants." *American Journal of Sociology* 70: 193–205.

Bridge. 1973. "Editorial: What Price 'Peace with Honor.'" 2 (4): 3.

Browne, Blaine T. 1985. "A Common Thread: American Images of the Chinese and Japanese, 1930–1960." Ph.D. dissertation, University of Oklahoma.

Chan, Sucheng. 1991. *Asian Americans: An Interpretive History.* Boston: Twayne.

Chen, May Ying. 1976. "Teaching a Course on Asian American Women." Pp, 234–239 in *Counterpoint: Perspectives on Asian America,* edited by Emma Gee. Los Angeles: UCLA Asian American Studies Center.

Chin, Rocky. 1971*a*. "Getting beyond Vol. 1, No. 1: Asian American Periodicals." *Bridge* 1 (2): 29–32.

———. 1971b. "NY Chinatown Today: Community in Crisis." Pp. 282–295 in *Roots: An Asian American Reader,* edited by Amy Tachiki, Eddie Wong, and Franklin Odo. Los Angeles: UCLA Asian American Studies Center.

Chun-Hoon, Lowell. 1975. "Teaching the Asian-American Experience; Alternative to the Neglect and Racism in Textbooks." *Amerasia Journal* 3(1): 40–59.

Chun-Hoon, Lowell, Lucie Hirata, and Alan Moriyama. 1973. "Curriculum Development in Asian American Studies; A Working Paper." Pp. 83–90 in *Proceedings of the National Asian American Studies Conference II: A Tool of Change or a Tool of Control?,* edited by George Kagiwada, Joyce Sakai, and Gus Lee. Davis: University of California, Davis Asian American Studies Center.

Contemporary Asian Studies Division, University of California, Berkeley. 1973. "Curriculum Philosophy for Asian American Studies." *Amerasia fournal* 2(1): 35–46.

———. 1988*b*. "Structure, Content, and Logic in Ethnic Group Formation." Working Paper series, Center for Research on Politics and Social Organization, Department of Sociology, Harvard University.

Daniels, Roger. *Asian America: Chinese and Japanese in the United States since 1850.* Seattle: University of Washington Press.

Denton, Nancy A., and Douglas S. Massey. 1988. "Residential Segregation by Socioeconomic Status and Generation." *Social Science Quarterly* 69 (4): 797–817.

Feraru, Arthur N. 1950. "Public Opinions Polls on Japan." *Far Eastern Survey* 19 (10): 101–103.

Getting Together. 1972. 3–17 March, p. 1.

Gil, Dinora. 1968, "Yellow Prostitution." *Gidra,* April, p, 2.

Glazer, Nathan, and Daniel Patrick Moynihan. 1963. *Beyond the Melting Pot: The Negroes, Puerto Ricans, lews, Italians, and Irish of New York City.* Cambridge, Mass.: M.I.T. Press.

Hayano, David M. 1981. "Ethnic Identification and Disidentification: Japanese-American Views of Chinese-Americans." *Ethnic Groups* 3 (2): 157–171.

Hill, Herbert. 1973. "Anti-Oriental Agitation and the Rise of Working-Class Racism." *Society* 10 (2): 43–54.

Hing, Alex. 1970. "The Need for a United Asian American Front." *Aion* I (1): 9–11.

Hiraoka, Jesse. 1986. "Asian American Literature." Pp. 93–97 in *Dictionary of Asian American History,* edited by Hyung-Chan Kim. New York: Greenwood Press.

Hodge, Robert W., Maurice D. Van Arsdol, Jr., Chyong-Fang Ko, and Namtara Gorwaney. 1986. "New Patterns of Ethnic Residential Segregation in Los Angeles." Paper presented at the International Sociological Association, XI World Congress of Sociology, New Delhi, India, 18–23 August.

Hoyt, Edwin P. 1974. Asians *in the West.* New York: Thomas Nelson.

Ichioka, Yuji. *The Issei: The World of the First Generation fapanese Americans, 1885–1924.* New York: Free Press.

Ignacio, Lemuel F. 1976. *Asian Americans and Pacific Islanders (Is There Such an Ethnic Group?)* San Jose: Pilipino Development Associates.

I Wor Kuen. 1974 "The National Question & Asian Americans." *IWK Tournal* 1 (August).

Jensen, Richard J., and Cara J. Abeyta. 1987. "The Minority in the Middle: Asian-American Dissent in the 1960s and 1970s "*Western Journal of Speech Communications* 51: 402–416.

Johanessen, Edward L. H. 1950. *The Labor Movement in the Territory of Hawaii.* M.A. thesis, University of California, Berkeley.

Kim, Elaine H. 1982. *Asian American Literature: An Introduction to the Writings and Their Social Context.* Philadelphia: Temple University Press.

Kitano, Harry H. L., and Roger Daniels. 1988. *Asian Americans: Emerging Minorities.* Englewood Cliffs, N.J.: Prentice-Hall.

Kuo, Wen H. 1979. "On the Study of Asian-Americans: Its Current State and Agenda." *Sociological Quarterly* 20 (Spring): 279–290.

Kwong, Peter. 1987. *The New Chinatown.* New York: Hill & Wang.

Lam, Frankie. 1986. "Suburban Residential Segregation of Chinese and Japanese Americans, 1960, 1970, and 1980." *Sociology and Social Research* 70 (4): 263–265.

Ling, Susie Hsiuhan. 1984. "The Mountain Movers: Asian American Women's Movement in Los Angeles." M.A. thesis, University of California, Los Angeles.

______. 1989. "The Mountain Movers: Asian American Women's Movement in Los Angeles." *Amerasia Journal* 15(1): 51–67.

Lipsitz, George. 1988. *A Life in the Struggle: Ivory Perry and the Culture of Opposition.* Philadelphia: Temple University Press.

Liu, John M., and Lucie Cheng. 1986. "A Dialogue on Race and Class: Asian American Studies and Marxism." Pp. 139–163 in *Left Academy: Marxist Scholarship on American Campuses,* edited by Bertell Oilman and Edward Vernoff. New York: Praeger.

Liu, William. 1976. "Asian American Research: Views of a Sociologist." *Asian Studies Occasional Report,* no. 2,

Lott, Juanita Tamayo. 1976. "The Asian American Concept: In Quest of Identity." *Bridge,* November, pp. 30–34,

Lowe, Lisa. 1991. "Heterogeneity, Hybridity, Multiplicity: Marking Asian American Differences." *Diaspora* 1: 24–44.

Lyman, Stanford M. 1970. *The Asian in the West.* Reno and Las Vegas. Desert Research Institute, University of Nevada.

______. 1973. "Red Guard on Grant Avenue: The Rise of Youthful Rebellion in Chinatown." Pp. 20–44 in *Asian Americans: Psychological Perspectives,* edited by Stanley Sue and Nathaniel Wagner. Palo Alto, Calif.: Science and Behavior Books.

Masada, Saburo. 1970. "Stockton's Yellow Seed." *Pacific Citizen,* 9 October. Massey, Douglas S., and Nancy A. Denton. 1987. "Trends in the Residential Segregation of Blacks, Hispanics, and Asians, 1970–1980." *American Sociological Review* 52 (December): 802–825.

Matsui, Jeffrey. 1968. "Asian Americans." *Pacific Citizen,* 6 September.

Mears, Eliot Grinnell. 1928. *Resident Orientals on the American Pacific Coast.* New York: Arno Press.

Melendy, H. Brett. 1977. *Asians in America: Filipinos, Koreans, and East Indians.* Boston: Twayne.

Murase, Mike. 1976*a*. "Ethnic Studies and Higher Education for Asian Americans." Pp. 205–223 in *Counterpoint: Perspectives on Asian America,* edited by Emma Gee. Los Angeles: UCLA Asian American Studies Center.

______. 1976*b*. "Toward Barefoot Journalism." Pp. 307–319 in *Counterpoint: Perspectives on Asian America,* edited by Emma Gee. Los Angeles: UCLA Asian American Studies Center.

Nakamura, Norman. 1971. "The Nature of G.I. Racism." Pp. 24–26 in *Roots: An Asian American Reader,* edited by Amy Tachiki, Eddie Wong, and Franklin Odo. Los Angeles· UCLA Asian American Studies Center.

Nakamshi, Don T., and Russell Leong. 1978. "Toward the Second Decade: A National Survey of Asian American Studies Programs in 1978." *Amerasia Journal* 5(1): 1–19.

Nakano, Roy. 1984. "Marxist Leninist Organization in the Asian American Community: Los Angeles, 1969–79." Unpublished student paper, UCLA Asian American Studies Center.

Nishio, Alan. 1982. "Personal Reflections on the Asian National Movements." *East Wind,* Spring/Summer, pp. 36–38.

Omi, Michael, and Howard Winant. 1986. *Racial Formation in the United States: From the 1960s to the 1980s.* New York: Routledge and Kegan Paul.

Ong, Paul. 1989. "California's Asian Population: Past Trends and Projections for the Year 2000." Los Angeles: Graduate School of Architecture and Urban Planning.

Pacific Citizen, 1985. "Asian Students Retain Minority Status," December.

Quinsaat, Jesse. 1976, "Asians in the Media: The Shadows in the Spotlight." Pp. 264–268 in *Counterpoint: Perspectives on Asian America,* edited by Emma Gee. Los Angeles: UCLA Asian American Studies Center.

Rabaya, Violet. 1971. "I Am Curious (Yellow?)." Pp. 110–111 in *Roots: An Asian American Reader,* edited by Amy Tachiki, Eddie Wong, and Franklin Odo. Los Angeles: UCLA Asian American Studies Center.

Rice Paper. 1975. 1 (2): (whole issue).

Rodan. 1971. "Asian Women as Leaders." 1 (9).

Sano, Roy. 1970. "Asiantown in Oakland." *Pacific Citizen,* 4 August.

Sumi, Pat. 1971. "An Interview with Pat Sumi." Pp. 253–264 in *Roots: An Asian American Reader,* edited by Amy Tachiki, Eddie Wong, and Franklin Odo. Los Angeles: UCLA Asian American Studies Center.

Sung, Betty Lee. 1967. *Mountain of Gold: The Story of the Chinese in America.* New York: Macmillan.

Tachiki, Amy. 1971, "Introduction." Pp. 1–5 in Soots; *An Asian American Reader,* edited by Amy Tachiki, Eddie Wong, and Franklin Odo. Los Angeles: UCLA Asian American Studies Center,

______. 1989. Strangers *from a Different Shore: A History of Asian Americans.* Boston: Little, Brown.

Tanaka, Ron. 1976. "Culture, Communication, and the Asian Movement in Perspective." *Journal of Ethnic Studies* 4 (1): 37–52.

Tanaka, Tomi. 1971. "From a Lotus Blossom Cunt." P. 109 in Roots. *An Asian American Reader,* edited by Amy Tachiki, Eddie Wong, and Franklin Odo. Los Angeles: UCLA Asian American Studies Center.

tenBroek, J., E. N. Barnhart, and F W. Matson. 1970. *Prejudice, War, and the Constitution.* Berkeley: University of California Press.

Umemoto, Karen. 1989. "'On Strike!' San Francisco State College Strike, 1968–69: The Roots of Asian American Students." *Amerasia Journal* 15 (1):

U.S. Bureau of the Census. 1943. *Sixteenth Census of the U.S., 1940.* Vol. 2: *Characteristics of the Population.* Washington, D.C.: U.S. Government Printing Office.

Uyematsu, Amy. 1971. "The Emergence of Yellow Power in America." Pp. 9–13 in *Roots: An Asian American Reader,* edited by Amy Tachiki, Eddie Wong, and Franklin Odo. Los Angeles; UCLA Asian American Studies Center.

Weiss, Melford S. 1974. *Valley City:* A *Chinese Community in America.* Cambridge, Mass.: Schenkman.

White, Clay. 1986. "Residential Segregation among Asians in Long Beach: Japanese, Chinese, Filipino, Korean, Indian, Vietnamese, Hawaiian, Guamanian, and Samoan." *Sociology and Social Research* 70 (4): 266–267

Woldemikael, Tekle Mariam. 1989. *Becoming Black Americans: Haitians and American institutions in Evanston, Illinois.* New York: AMS Press.

Wong, Eddie. 1971. "Introduction." Pp. 247–250 in *Roots: An Asian American Reader,* edited by Amy Tachiki, Eddie Wong, and Franklin Odo. Los Angeles: UCLA Asian American Studies Center.

Wong, Paul, 1972. "The Emergence of the Asian-American Movement." *Bridge* 2(1): 33–39.

Yoshimura, Evelyn. 1971. "G.I.'s and Asian Women." Pp. 27–29 in *Roots: An Asian American Reader,* edited by Amy Tachiki, Eddie Wong, and Franklin Odo. Los Angeles: UCLA Asian American Studies Center.

______. 1989. "How I Became an Activist and What It All Means to Me." *Amerasia Journal* 15 (1): 106–109.

Yu, Eui-Young. 1983. "Korean Communities in America: Past, Present, and Future." *Amerasia Journal* 10 (2): 23–51.

Yuan, D. Y. 1966. "Chinatown and Beyond: The Chinese Population in Metropolitan New York." *Phylon* 23 (4): 311-332.

Interviews

Andersen, Patrick, 5 January 1990, telephone interview.

Ichioka, Yuji, 2 May 1988, Los Angeles.

Kokubun, Kei, 16 June 1989, Gardena, Calif.

Omatsu, Glenn, 30 November 1989, Los Angeles.

Watanabe, Mike, 19 July 1989, Los Angeles.

READING 20

The Current State of Same-Sex Marriage

An Analysis of the Federal and State Income Tax Consequences

By Alisha M. Harper and Elizabeth Breathitt

The headline "DOMA Found Unconstitutional" filled newspapers following the U.S. Supreme Court's decision in *U.S. v. Windsor* (133 S.Ct. 2675, 2013). What the headlines failed to note is that *Windsor* struck down only one section of the Defense of Marriage Act (DOMA). In October 2013, *The CPA Journal* published "Marital Status after DOMA: Exploring the Practical Tax Implications," by Mark Jackson, Sonja Pippin, and Richard Mason, which noted the potential implications of *Windsor* at the federal level: the issues of filing status, tax rates, various deductions, and the earned income credit.

This article expands on the earlier one by analyzing the federal and state income tax effect of *Windsor* on same-sex married couples. The analysis begins with the historical background and enactment of DOMA, then moves on to show the income tax impact (numerical effect) on same-sex couples filing federal and state income tax returns while DOMA's definitions of "marriage" and "spouse" were in effect. The *Windsor* decision struck down the definitions section of DOMA, leaving intact each state's right to determine whether it will recognize a legal same-sex marriage. The article concludes with a breakdown of the various state edicts post-*Windsor* and an examination of the impact on same-sex couples filing federal and state income tax returns.

Background

On May 7, 1996, HR 3396, a bill to define and protect the institution of marriage, was introduced to the U.S. House of Representatives Committee on the Judiciary. The bill was introduced in response to a case making its way through the Hawaii court system, *Baehr v. Lewin* (852 P.2d 44, Haw., 1993). *Baehr* involved three couples that were denied applications for marriage by the Hawaiian Department of Health based on a Hawaiian law that forbade same-sex marriage (Haw. Rev. Stat. section 572–1). The couples filed suit in state court challenging the constitutionality of the law. The trial court granted the state's motion for judgment on the pleadings; this ruling was reversed and the case

Alisha M. Harper and Elizabeth Breathitt, "The Current State of Same-Sex Marriage," *The CPA Journal*, vol. 85, no. 1, pp. 48-55.

remanded by the Supreme Court of Hawaii (*Baehr*, 852 P.2d at 74). The Hawaii Supreme Court determined that the denial of a license to same-sex couples discriminated on the basis of sex and placed the burden on the state to "overcome the presumption that HRS section 572-1 is unconstitutional" (*Baehr*, 852 P.2d at 74).

Before the remanded case came to trial, HR 3396 was introduced to address the implications of allowing same-sex marriage in Hawaii (or any other state). First, would the Full Faith and Credit Clause of the U.S. Constitution require states that do not recognize same-sex marriage to nonetheless recognize the marriage of same-sex couples who legally obtained a marriage license in Hawaii? Second, federal law (both statutes and regulations) is replete with the words "marriage" and "spouse"; however, neither of these terms was defined at the time.

Better known as the Defense of Marriage Act, HR 3396 addressed both of these concerns. The bill proposed to amend Chapter 115 of Title 28 of the United States Code (USC) by adding section 1738C, which provides:

> No State, territory, or possession of the United States, or Indian tribe, shall be required to give effect to any public act, record, or judicial proceeding of any other State, territory, possession, or tribe respecting a relationship between persons of the same sex that is treated as a marriage under the laws of such other State, territory, possession, or tribe, or a right or claim arising from such relationship.

This provision was clearly designed to allow states that did not recognize same-sex marriage to disregard the marriage of same-sex couples who legally obtained a marriage license in another state.

The second implication was addressed by a proposed addition of section 7 to Chapter 1 of Title 1 USC to read as follows:

> In determining the meaning of any Act of Congress, or of any ruling, regulation, or interpretation of the various administrative bureaus and agencies of the United States, the word "marriage" means only a legal union between one man and one

woman as husband and wife, and the word "spouse" refers only to a person of the opposite sex who is a husband or a wife.

The full U.S. House of Representatives approved HR 3396 without amendment on July 12, 1996; the Senate passed it on September 10, 1996, and President Bill Clinton signed it into law on October 26, 1996 (P.L. 104–199).

Federal versus State Laws

Internal Revenue Code (IRC) section 1 sets forth the tax rates applicable for individuals. The tax rate of each individual taxpayer is dictated by income level and filing status. Although the actual income tax rates remain the same for each filing status, the progression to an increased rate is based on taxable income (e.g., see http://www.irs.gov/pub/irs-drop/rp-13-35.pdf).

A taxpayer's personal and dependency exemption amounts, as well as the ability to claim various deductions and credits, are based on income level, filing status, or both.

IRC section 6013 permits a husband and wife to make a joint return [IRC section 6013(a)], but only if they are legally married as of the close of the tax year (IRC section 7703). DOMA specifically forbade same-sex couples from using this filing status. Legally married taxpayers who choose not to file jointly must file separately [IRC section 1(d)]. Head of household filing status can be used by individuals who are unmarried and maintain a household for a dependent [IRC section 2(b)], but individuals who are unmarried and do not have any dependents must use the single filing status [IRC section 1(c)].

The majority of state revenue systems use a piggyback approach, pulling from federal adjusted gross income as the starting point for the state income tax calculation. Additionally, like federal law, certain state income tax rates are dictated by filing status and income level.

DOMA defined "marriage" and "spouse" for purposes of federal law only. The states were left to their own devices in handling same-sex marriage. For example, several states passed laws recognizing same sex-marriage (Connecticut, New Hampshire, New York, Vermont, and Washington, as well as the District of Columbia). In others, state courts mandated that same-sex couples be granted the same protections and benefits as heterosexual couples (California, Iowa, and Massachusetts). The definition of "marriage" and "spouse" in these states included same-sex couples. Still other states recognized that same-sex couples should be granted the same tax benefits and filing options as heterosexual couples (Illinois). Other states, however, maintained that same-sex marriages were unconstitutional and would not be recognized (Arkansas, Kansas, Louisiana, and Mississippi). This is by no means a comprehensive list, and only shows the widely varying tax treatment of same-sex couples at the state level.

Case Study: 2012 Tax Return

To show the difference in actual tax, assume Julie and Ann Smith were legally married in Vermont in June 2010. They were legal residents of New York for the entire tax year 2012. Prior to *Windsor*, and while DOMA's definitional section was in effect, federal law did not recognize Julie and Ann's marriage. If Julie and Ann had no children, for purposes of filing their 2012 federal income tax return, Julie and Ann each were required to file as single. New York, however, did recognize Julie and Ann's Vermont marriage as valid for 2012; thus, for purposes of filing their New York State income tax return, Julie and Ann were required to elect either married filing jointly (MFJ) or married filing separately (MFS).

High-Income Scenario

Placing Julie and Ann in a high-income scenario shows that their single status was more beneficial at the federal level. For example, assume Julie and Ann had the following income and expenses for 2012:

Exhibit 20.1 Definition of Marriage, State by State

State	Guidance	Date Issued	Income Tax Effect
Alabama	Tax Guidance: Alabama Income Tax Filing Status for Same-Sex Couples	12/05/2013	Each individual must file separately as single or head of household (if qualified); allocate the federal income tax liability shown on a federal joint return to each individual, based on the ratio of the individual's separate federal AGI to combined federal AGI.
Arizona	*Connolly v. Roche*	12/27/2013	Arizona District Court ruled that Arizona's ban on same-sex marriage is unconstitutional. A stay of this decision has not been issued, although an appeal to the Ninth Circuit Court of Appeals was filed on Nov. 17, 2014.
Arkansas			Does not recognize same-sex marriage. The District Court for the Eastern District of Arkansas ruled that Arkansas's ban on same-sex marriage is unconstitutional. This case has been appealed to the Eighth Circuit Court of Appeals.
California	California Franchise Tax Board Notice 2008-5	06/20/2008	Taxpayers married to another individual of the same sex are required to file either a joint return or a MFS return if they are married as of the last day of that taxable year.
Colorado	Colorado Department of Revenue Information Regarding IRS Ruling on Same-Sex Marriage and Tax Filing Status	09/12/2013	Both federal and Colorado income tax returns must have the same filing status (same-sex couples may file MFJ for federal and state).

State	Guidance	Date Issued	Income Tax Effect
Connecticut	Attorney General Opinion 2008-18	10/28/2008	Parties in a same-sex marriage must be given the same tax treatment as those in a civil union or other marriage.
Delaware	Civil Marriage Equality and Religious Freedom Act of 2013	07/01/2013	Beginning in 2012, Delaware began allowing those in a recognized civil union to file jointly. Effective July 1, 2013, same-sex couples can marry in Delaware.
District of Columbia	D.C. Code Ann. Section 47-1805.01	03/03/2010	Married same-sex individuals may file either a joint return or separate returns on a combined form.
Georgia	Georgia Informational Bulletin IT 2013-10-25	10/25/2013	Each individual must file separately as single or head of household (if qualified); recomputed federal AGI as if a single or head of household federal return were filed.
Hawaii	Hawaii Department of Taxation Announcements 2013-26	12/23/2013	Act 1, Second Special Session Laws of Hawaii 2013, recognizes marriages between individuals of the same sex.
Idaho	*Latta v. Otter*	10/15/2014	The Ninth Circuit Court of Appeals ruled that Idaho's ban on same-sex marriage is unconstitutional. On October 15, 2014, the Ninth Circuit issued an order dissolving the stay currently pending on same-sex marriages. A petition for writ of certiorari has been filed seeking Supreme Court review.
Illinois	750 ILCS 75/1	06/01/2011	Under the Illinois Religious Freedom Protection and Civil Union Act, partners in a civil union must file joint Illinois income tax returns as married couples beginning January 2012.
Indiana	*Baskin v. Bogan*	10/07/2014	The Seventh Circuit Court of Appeals ruled that Indiana's ban on same-sex marriage is unconstitutional. The matter was appealed to the Supreme Court, which on October 6, 2014, denied review. The Seventh Circuit's opinion became the governing law in Indiana on October 7, 2014, when a mandate was issued that the court's opinion take effect.
Iowa	Iowa Tax Treatment of Same-Sex Marriages	06/11/2009	Beginning with tax year 2009, same-sex spouses should file Iowa income tax returns as married persons, either jointly or separately.

Income	Julie	Ann
Wages	$225,000	$240,000
Taxable interest	$5,400	$500
Dividends	$6,000	$6,000
Capital gain	$5,000	$5,000
Schedule K	$5,600	$3,500
Expenses	**Julie**	**Ann**
State income taxes	$22,500	$28,000
Real estate taxes	$4,750	$4,750
Home mortgage interest	$9,000	$9,000
Charitable contributions	$2,500	$2,500
Tax preparation	$750	$750
Investment expense	$2,350	$2,350
Safe deposit box	$50	

For 2012, Julie and Ann's total federal tax bill would have been as follows:

- Single/Single: $113,704
- Married Filing Jointly: $127,760
- Married Filing Separately: $128,740

Filing as single saved Julie and Ann a total of $14,045 in federal income taxes because this kept them in the 33% marginal tax bracket. Combining their income on a joint return would increase their marginal tax rate to 35%.

New York State tax rates range from 4% to 8.82%. The brackets are based on three filing statuses: MFJ, single or MFS (same rate), and head of household. Julie and Ann's New York State income tax using married filing jointly filing status resulted in $33,018 of income taxes. For both MFS and single, the total income tax number is $32,694 ($324 less). As with the federal return, combining Julie and Ann's income on a single return resulted in a greater marginal tax rate.

Alternatively, if Julie and Ann had lived in Kentucky in 2012, their total state income tax would have remained the same regardless of filing status ($26,848). Kentucky has only one tax rate schedule that applies regardless of filing status. When a taxpayer's taxable income exceeds $75,000, the taxpayer is subject to a 6% tax rate. In this high-income scenario, Julie and Ann's filing status would be irrelevant. Michigan, a state with a flat tax rate structure, would also result in a total tax amount unaffected by filing status ($21,411). Both Kentucky and Michigan required that Julie and Ann file as single for the 2012 tax year.

If the analysis of Ann and Julie's tax situation had included a dependent child, the end result for federal income tax purposes would have remained the same. The tax savings as single/head of household would still be $14,056. The only change in the federal return would involve a $600 credit for child and dependent care expenses.

In addition, the state income tax numbers for Michigan and Kentucky would remain constant regardless of filing status. However, New York recognizes a different rate structure for head of household filing status. If Julie had a dependent child, Julie and Ann would have been in a better tax position had Julie been allowed to file as head of household and Ann allowed to file as single. The state income tax amount for MFJ was $32,949. The total state income tax amount for MFS was $32,625, a savings of $324. The total state income tax amount for single/head of household was $32,182, a further savings of $443.

Middle-Income Scenario

Placing Julie and Ann in a middle-income scenario shows that joint status was more beneficial for federal tax purposes. For state and local income tax purposes, however, MFS or single/head of household were still the preferable status. For example, assume Julie and Ann had the following income and expenses:

Income	**Julie**	**Ann**
Wages	$55,000	$25,000
Taxable interest	$5,400	$500
Dividends	$6,000	$6,000
Capital gain	$5,000	$5,000
Schedule K	$5,600	$3,500
Expenses	**Julie**	**Ann**
State income taxes	$6,500	$2,800
Real estate taxes	$2,250	$2,250
Home mortgage interest	$6,000	$6,000
Charitable contributions	$2,500	$2,500
Tax preparation	$750	$750
Investment expense	$2,350	$2,350
Safe deposit box	$50	–

For 2012, Julie and Ann's total federal tax would have been as follows:

- Single/Single: $9,482
- Married Filing Jointly: $7,630
- Married Filing Separately: $9,482

The ability to file MFJ would have saved Julie and Ann a total of $1,852 in federal income taxes.

Julie and Ann's New York State tax using MFJ status resulted in $5,490 of income taxes. For MFS and single status, the total income tax was $216 less, $5,274. As noted previously, New York required Ann and Julie to file either MFJ or MFS in 2012.

Alternatively, if Julie and Ann had resided in Kentucky in 2012, Julie and Ann would have saved only $3 by filing MFS or single (their total state income tax for MFS combined was $4,802; their total state income tax for filing singly was $4,799). Although Michigan has a flat tax rate structure, Julie and Ann would have saved $510 by filing MFS or single for 2012. By combining their incomes on a joint return, Julie and Ann would have lost the Michigan property tax credit (which is phased out once "total household resources" exceed $50,000). Julie and Ann's total state income tax for MFJ was $4,740; their total state income tax for MFS and single was $4,230. Both Kentucky and Michigan required that Julie and Ann file as single for 2012. This resulted in neither a benefit nor a burden to Julie and Ann because their total tax amounts for single versus MFS were the same.

The federal tax benefit of MFJ status increased if the analysis of Ann and Julie's tax situation included a dependent child. The total tax savings for MFJ increased to $3,171, compared to MFS and single/head of household filing status.

- Single/Single: $8,511
- Married Filing Jointly: $5,340
- Married Filing Separately: $8,511

In this scenario, the taxpayers' combined income using MFJ status caused the taxpayers to lose the additional child tax credit (IRC section 24). The tax savings using MFJ rates, however, still resulted in a higher total refund: $6,160 for MFJ, compared to $3,981 for MFS and single/head of household.

The most advantageous filing status for state and local income tax purposes changes depending on the state. For Julie and Ann, New York's requirement to file as MFJ or MFS resulted in additional taxes due. Filing as single/head of household would have been preferable, with a tax savings of $136 (MFJ state tax was $5,424; MFS state tax was $5,209), and single/head of household state tax was $5,073; this is, again, attributable to the reduced rate applicable for head of household filing status. In addition to the actual tax effect, combining their incomes on a joint New York return reduced Julie and Ann's child tax credits by $566. For MFS and single/head of household, the credits were $881; the credits for MFJ were $315.

The analysis for Michigan showed a tax savings of $510 for MFS and single/head of household as a result of the loss of the property tax credit for MFJ combined income. The analysis of Kentucky showed a total tax of $4,669 for single/head of household filing status and MFS, a tax savings of $13 over MFS on a combined return. Again, Michigan and Kentucky's requirement that Julie and Ann file as single for the 2012 tax year resulted in neither a benefit nor a burden to them, because their total taxes for single/head of household versus MFS were the same.

Exhibit 20.1 Definition of Marriage, State by State (Continued)

State	Guidance	Date Issued	Income Tax Effect
Kansas	*Kitchen v. Herbert*	10/06/2014	See the discussion of *Kitchen v. Herbert* under Utah. The Tenth Circuit's opinion became the governing law in Kansas on October 6, 2014, when a mandate was issued that the court's opinion take effect.
Kentucky	*Bourke v. Beshear*	11/06/2014	The Sixth Circuit Court of Appeals issued an opinion in consolidated cases from Kentucky, Michigan, Ohio, and Tennessee concluding that each state's ban on same- sex marriage was constitutional. On January 16, 2015, the Supreme Court agreed to review the cases. Separate returns must be filed.
Louisiana	Louisiana Revenue Information Bulletin 13-024	09/13/2013	Taxpayers must file a separate Louisiana return as single, head of household, or qualifying widow, as applicable.
Maine	Maine Tax Alert, vol. 23, no. 3	01/01/2013	Same-sex couples who are legally married on the last day of tax years ending on or after December 29, 2012, must file individual income tax returns for those tax years as MFJ or separate.
Maryland	Md. Code. Ann. Tax-Gen. section 10-807	07/01/2013	Married couples who file a joint federal income tax return must file a joint Maryland income tax return.
Massachusetts	Massachusetts Technical Information Release 04-17	07/07/2004	Case law recognizing same-sex marriage decided in 2004; same-sex spouses file as married, jointly or separately.
Michigan	*Bourke v. Beshear*	11/06/2014	The Sixth Circuit Court of Appeals issued an opinion in consolidated cases from Kentucky, Michigan, Ohio, and Tennessee concluding that each state's ban on same-sex marriage was constitutional. On January 16, 2015, the Supreme Court agreed to review the cases. Separate returns must be filed.
Minnesota	Minnesota Tax Information for Same-sex Married Couples	09/05/2013	Use the same filing status as federal (MFJ or MFS for federal and state).
Mississippi	Mississippi Individual Income Tax FAQs—Same-sex Marriage	12/01/2013	Must file as single, or head of household, if qualified.

State	Guidance	Date Issued	Income Tax Effect
Missouri	Executive Order 13-14	11/14/2013	Married individuals (including same-sex couples legally married in a state that authorizes such marriages) who file a joint federal income tax return must file a combined state income tax return.
Montana	*Rolando v. Fox*	11/19/2014	The U.S. District Court for the District of Montana, Great Falls Division, ruled that Montana's same sex marriage ban is unconstitutional. An appeal to the Ninth Circuit has been filed, but no stay prohibiting same-sex marriage is in effect.
Nebraska	Nebraska Revenue Ruling 22-13-1	10/24/2013	Individuals in a same-sex marriage are not allowed to file Nebraska individual income tax returns using MFJ or MFS but must instead file as single, or head of household, if qualified.
New Jersey	N.J. Admin. Code section 18:35-1.6, "Civil Unions"	03/03/2008	All state gross income tax benefits, protections, and responsibilities of spouses apply in like manner to civil union partners. Same-sex marriage recognized October 21, 2013.
New Mexico	*Kitchen v. Herbert*	10/06/2014	See the discussion of *Kitchen v. Herbert* under Utah. The Tenth Circuit's opinion became the governing law in New Mexico on October 6, 2014, when a mandate was issued that the opinion take effect.
New York	*Marriage Equality Act*	07/21/2011	Law recognizing same-sex marriage enacted in 2011; same-sex spouses file as married, jointly or separately.
North Carolina	*Bostic v. Schaefer*	10/06/2014	See discussion of *Bostic v. Schaefer* under Virginia. The Fourth Circuit's opinion became the governing law in North Carolina on October 6, 2014, when a mandate was issued that the opinion take effect.

DOMA Found Unconstitutional

Following the *Windsor* decision, headlines claimed that the Supreme Court had ruled DOMA unconstitutional (e.g., Reilly, Ryan J.; Siddiqui, Sabrina, "Supreme Court DOMA Decision Rules Federal Same-Sex Marriage Ban Unconstitutional," *Huffington Post,* http://www.huffingtonpost.com/2013/06/26/supreme-court-doma-decision_n_3454811.html; Savage, David G., "Gay Marriage Ruling: Supreme Court Finds DOMA Unconstitutional," *Los Angeles Times,* http://articles.latimes.com/2013/jun/26/news/la-pn-doma-supreme-court-ruling-20130626). This is true, but only in part.

The *Windsor* decision involved only section 3 of DOMA, the definitions of "marriage" and "spouse" for federal law. The Court clearly noted in the opening paragraphs of its opinion that section 2, which allows states to refuse to recognize same-sex marriage, "has not been challenged here."

The states continue to be split on whether the definition of marriage includes only a man and woman or includes same-sex couples. This split is evident in the statements issued following the decision in *Windsor* addressing filing status for state income tax purposes. *Exhibit 20.1* notes the position of each state with an income tax (as well as the District of Columbia).

The state tax situation remains in flux. The decision of the U.S. Supreme Court on October 6, 2014, not to hear cases appealed from the Fourth, Seventh, and Tenth Circuit Courts of Appeal means that the decision of those courts is the law of the land for states within their jurisdiction. The Fourth, Seventh, and Tenth Circuits have all concluded that state bans on same-sex marriage are unconstitutional. As a result, Colorado, Kansas, Illinois, Indiana, Maryland, New Mexico, North Carolina, Oklahoma, South Carolina, Utah, Virginia, West Virginia, Wisconsin, and Wyoming are required to permit and recognize same-sex marriage.

The states continue to be split on whether the definition of marriage includes only a man and a woman or includes same-sex couples.

The lifting of the stay prohibiting same-sex marriages in Idaho by the Ninth Circuit Court of Appeals on October 15, 2014, means that Idaho same-sex marriages are currently recognized as valid. In addition, rulings from the district courts in Alaska, Arizona, and Montana finding same-sex marriage bans unconstitutional are not currently subject to stay. Thus, Alaska, Arizona, and Montana same-sex marriages are also currently recognized as valid. In Florida, cases have been appealed to the Eleventh Circuit Court of Appeals for decision. The stay preventing same-sex marriage in Florida expired on January 5, 2015. A second motion to extend the stay was filed on December 15, 2014, in light of the Sixth Circuit's opinion, but no order has been issued on this second motion.

As of the time of publication, only 12 states can refuse to recognize same-sex marriages. As a result of the ruling from the Sixth Circuit Court of Appeals upholding the ban on same-sex marriages in states within its jurisdiction, stays prohibiting same-sex marriage that remain in place, or lack any final court determination, in Alabama, Arkansas, Georgia, Kentucky, Louisiana, Michigan, Mississippi, Nebraska, North Dakota, Ohio, Tennessee, and Texas continue to prohibit same-sex marriage and prohibit recognition of any same-sex marriage as valid. The decisions of the Sixth Circuit Court of Appeals as well as a case out of Louisiana have been appealed to the U.S. Supreme Court. On January 16, 2015, the Supreme Court agreed to review the decision of the Sixth Circuit Court of Appeals that upheld same-sex marriage bans in Kentucky, Michigan, Ohio, and Tennessee. Until the Supreme Court issues a final ruling, the law applicable for these jurisdictions should be assessed individually for any further updates.

Exhibit 20.1 Definition of Marriage, State by State (Continued)

State	Guidance	Date Issued	Income Tax Effect
North Dakota	Guideline-Income Tax Filing by Individuals in a Same-Sex Marriage	09/27/2013	Each individual must file separately as single or head of household (if qualified); individuals who file a joint federal income tax return must complete a worksheet to show the amount of income allocable to each individual, and determine federal AGI used by each individual.
Ohio	*Bourke v. Beshear*	11/06/2014	The Sixth Circuit Court of Appeals issued an opinion in consolidated cases from Kentucky, Michigan, Ohio, and Tennessee concluding that each state's ban on same-sex marriage was constitutional. On January 16, 2015, the Supreme Court agreed to review the cases. Separate returns must be filed.
Oklahoma	*Kitchen v. Herbert*	10/06/2014	See the discussion of *Kitchen v. Herbert* under Utah. The Tenth Circuit's opinion became the governing law in Oklahoma on October 6, 2014, when a mandate was issued that the opinion take effect.
Oregon	Oregon Family Fairness Act	01/01/2008	Legally registered domestic partners are subject to the same tax statutes and regulations as married filers. In 2013, Oregon began recognizing same-sex marriages in other states.
Pennsylvania	*Whitewood v. Wolf*	05/20/2014	A federal judge struck down Pennsylvania's ban on same-sex marriage. The ruling did not come with a stay attached, and the Governor announced he would not appeal the decision.
Rhode Island	Marriage Equality Law	08/01/2013	Same-sex marriage was legalized as of August 1, 2013, and legally married couples as of December 31, 2013, file as married, jointly or separately.
South Carolina	*Bostic v. Schaefer*	10/06/2014	See discussion of *Bostic v. Schaefer* under Virginia. The Fourth Circuit's opinion became the governing law in South Carolina on October 6, 2014, when a mandate was issued that the opinion take effect.

State	Guidance	Date Issued	Income Tax Effect
Tennessee	*Bourke v. Beshear*	11/06/2014	The Sixth Circuit Court of Appeals issued an opinion in consolidated cases from Kentucky, Michigan, Ohio, and Tennessee concluding that each state's ban on same-sex marriage was constitutional. On January 16, 2015, the Supreme Court agreed to review the cases. Separate returns must be filed.
Utah	*Kitchen v. Herbert*	10/06/2014	The Tenth Circuit Court of Appeals concluded that Utah's ban on same-sex marriage is unconstitutional. The matter was appealed to the Supreme Court who on October 6, 2014, denied review. The Tenth Circuit's opinion became the governing law in Oklahoma on October 6, 2014, when a mandate was issued that the opinion take effect.
Vermont	An Act to Protect Religious Freedom and Recognize Equality in Civil Marriage	09/01/2009	Same-sex marriage legalized as of September 1, 2009; Vermont recognized the right of those in civil unions to file as MFJ or MFS beginning in 2001.
Virginia	*Bostic v. Schaefer*	10/06/2014	The Fourth Circuit Court of Appeals concluded that Virginia's ban on same-sex marriage is unconstitutional. The matter was appealed to the Supreme Court, which on Oct. 6, 2014, denied review. The Fourth Circuit's opinion became the governing law in Virgina on Oct. 6, 2014, when a mandate was issued that the opinion take effect.
Washington	Referendum 74	02/13/2012	Referendum 74 upheld marriage rights for same-sex couples, which had been passed into law by the legislature and governor.
West Virginia	*Bostic v. Schaefer*	10/06/2014	See discussion of *Bostic v. Schaefer* under Virginia. The Fourth Circuit's opinion became the governing law in West Virginia on October 6, 2014, when a mandate was issued that the opinion take effect.
Wisconsin	*Baskin v. Bogan*	10/07/2014	See discussion of *Bostic v. Bogan* under Indiana. The Seventh Circuit's opinion became the governing law in Wisconsin on October 7, 2014, when a mandate was issued that the court's opinion take effect.

Case Study: The 2013 Tax Return

Returning to the example of Julie and Ann Smith above, the Windsor decision has had an impact on their tax situation for the next year.

High-Income Scenario

Placing Julie and Ann Smith in the high-income scenario reveals that the Windsor decision and subsequent IRS guidance would create a losing situation for the 2013 tax year. Julie and Ann's itemized deductions for MFJ and MFS status would be partially phased out as a result of their income levels; Julie and Ann's personal exemptions would be fully phased out [IRC section 68(b); IRC section 151]. In addition, new taxes imposed in 2013 would increase their total tax liability. In sum, Julie and Ann would owe additional federal income taxes of $16,763 in 2013. The comparison shows a total federal income tax of $128,564 for Julie and Ann using MFJ status; $128,565 for MFS; and $111,801 for single. Even with the addition of a dependent, the comparison would remain the same, reduced by the $600 child and dependent care credit.

For state income tax purposes, the 2013 analyses remain the same. As a result of its flat rate tax structure, Michigan's requirement that same-sex couples continue to file as single would have no impact on the state income taxes paid by Julie and Ann. Kentucky's low progressive rate structure would also result in no impact. New York's rate structure, however, creates a difference in filing status. If Julie and Ann have no dependents, the total tax numbers for married filing separately and single are the same (less than married filing jointly). It is only when a dependent is added to the scenario that Julie and Ann lose at the New York state level, as a result of the rate structure applicable to head of household filing status.

Middle-Income Scenario

In the middle-income scenario, Julie and Ann could take advantage of the tax benefits bestowed by MFJ status for federal income tax purposes. For 2013, this would result in a tax savings of $1,852 if Julie and Ann had no dependents and $2,748 if Julie and Ann had one dependent.

For state income tax purposes, the benefit or burden to Julie and Ann would depend upon their state of residence and the tax rate structure. In Michigan, the taxpayers paid less tax by filing as single or head of household because Michigan's property tax credit would be eliminated if Julie and Ann were permitted to combine their income for MFJ status. However, as noted previously, this benefit also remains if Julie and Ann are permitted to file as MFS.

In Kentucky, a state with a low progressive tax rate structure, Julie and Ann would pay $4 less as MFS or single than MFJ. Even with a dependent, Julie and Ann would save only $14 by choosing single/head of household or MFS filing status versus MFJ. States with a higher progressive tax rate structure and more varied brackets, such as New York, result in Julie and Ann paying more income tax if the state requires MFJ status when a dependent is involved. Without a dependent, Julie and Ann would pay the same amount of tax (less than MFJ), whether they are required to file as MFS or single.

An Evolving Issue

From strictly a federal income tax perspective, the *Windsor* decision is a blessing to middle-income same-sex married couples, especially those with dependents. For 2013, these couples could take advantage of MFJ status and the attendant tax savings. In addition, the IRS is allowing, but not requiring, same-sex married couples to file amended returns for 2012 and 2011 claiming MFJ status for prior years (see http://www.irs.gov/uac/Answers-to-Frequently-Asked-Questions-for-Same-Sex-Married-Couples). Hypothetical middle-income taxpayers Julie and Ann would be advised to seize this opportunity to amend their prior year's returns and claim a refund. For high-income same-sex married couples, however, the *Windsor* decision results in a substantial tax burden, as demonstrated by the above case study.

A recent study published by the Williams Institute shows that the majority of same-sex couples fall into the middle-income scenario. The median annual household income for same-sex couples when both couples "are in the labor force" is $94,000. For same-sex couples where only one individual is in the labor force, median household income is $60,000 (Gary J. Gates, *Same-Sex and Different-Sex Couples in the American Community Survey: 2005–2011,* Williams Institute).

The impact on same-sex couples at the state level depends on the filing status and income of the taxpayers. States with a flat rate structure result in neither a benefit nor a burden. Even in states in which credits are phased out by income level, such as Michigan's property tax credit, taxpayers pay the same total tax regardless of filing status.

In states with a single, low progressive rate structure, the impact of filing status is minimal. In Kentucky, for example, when the taxpayers' income level exceeds a threshold amount, the income tax rate is essentially a flat rate structure. In the middle-income scenario, the taxpayers are still better off in a status other than MFJ. Moreover, because there is only one rate structure, the tax for MFS versus single or head of household are the same.

The impact on same-sex couples at the state level depends on the filing status and income of the taxpayers.

The above analysis shows that their filing status is only really significant in a state like New York. Even then, there is no benefit or burden between MFS and single, which entails tax savings over MFJ, because the brackets for MFS and single are the same. It is only when a dependent is involved that there will be an increased tax liability due to the loss of the head of household filing status and rate.

Although marriage is a matter generally left within the purview of the states (*Maynard v. Hill,* 125 U.S. 190, 1888), the power of the states to regulate it is subject to certain constitutional guarantees (*U.S.*

v. Windsor, 133 S. Ct. 2884, 2013). In *Loving v. Virginia* (388 U.S. 1, 1967), the U.S. Supreme Court struck down a statute adopted by the state of Virginia prohibiting interracial marriage. In *Loving,* the Court discussed racial classifications and equal protection in terms of race. However, the Court made two broad statements regarding the "freedom to marry" and "basic civil rights" in terms of marriage that would support it once again striking down state marriage laws.

On January 16, 2015, the Supreme Court agreed to review the decision of the Sixth Circuit Court of Appeals that upheld same-sex marriage bans in Kentucky, Michigan, Ohio, and Tennessee. The Court's prior decision to deny review of same-sex marriage cases out of the Fourth, Seventh, and Tenth Circuits, which had struck down same-sex marriage bans, represents further evidence the Court may once again strike down state marriage laws. Until the Supreme Court issues a final ruling, most likely by the end of its session in June, the laws governing the marriage ban remain in place, and taxpayers are left with a state-by-state analysis for this filing season.

READING 21

Black Lives Matter and the Struggle for Freedom

By Brian P. Jones

In late April 2016, at a town hall-style event in London, President Obama complained about the rising movement against the state-sanctioned murder of black people often referred to as Black Lives Matter. Activists, he admonished, should "stop yelling" and instead push for incremental change through the official "process." "Once you've highlighted an issue and brought it to people's attention and shined a spotlight," the President remarked, "and elected officials or people who are in a position to start bringing about change are ready to sit down with you, then you can't just keep on yelling at them."[1] The spectacle of the first black president scolding black activists in the context of a rising rate of police murder (as of this writing, the police have killed 630 individuals, at least 155 of them black, nationwide in 2016) speaks volumes about the state of black politics today.[2]

For those trying to understand the emergence of a new black movement—or, perhaps more accurately, a new phase of a longer, older movement—on the watch of the first black president, Keeanga-Yamahtta Taylor's new book, *From #BlackLivesMatter to Black Liberation* is an essential starting point. In lucid prose, free from jargon and pretense, she renders important historical lessons about how we got to this point, and lays out forceful arguments for the kinds of vision and strategy that can guide the future of this movement.

Anti-black racism in this country has taken many forms, whether pseudo-scientific, psycho-cultural, or both, but what has remained unchanged throughout U.S. history is the need for a system of exploitation and oppression to locate the "problem" with black people themselves. Pathologizing black people is, Taylor writes, "as old as the nation itself." Thomas Jefferson insisted that black people's apparent inferiority was not the result of being enslaved; it was, he claimed, "nature, which has produced the distinction." So, too, in our time, Taylor argues, the widespread ideas about black inferiority—even if no longer couched in "natural" terms—are just as insidious. More than two centuries after Jefferson, liberals love to believe that programs such as the Harlem Children's Zone and KIPP charter schools, promising to teach "middle class norms" to black children, can "solve" poverty. But just as Jefferson's ideas served to rationalize slavery, today's "culture of

Brian P. Jones, "Black Lives Matter and the Struggle for Freedom," *Monthly Review*, vol. 68, no. 4, pp. 1-8.

poverty" trope "politically narrates the necessity of austere budgets while sustaining-ideologically at least—the premise of the 'American Dream.'"[3]

Such ideological props are even more essential in times of acute crisis. When millions of Americans lost their homes in the aftermath of the 2008 economic crisis, half of the collective wealth of African Americans was wiped out. "The 'middle-class norms' of homeownership," Taylor writes, "could not stop Black people's wealth from disappearing into thin air after banks fleeced them by steering them toward sub-prime loans." In 2016, notions of "culture" and "personal responsibility" pervade mainstream discourse on black poverty, providing a rationale for inequality, just as much as they did three hundred years ago.[4]

The sharpest edge of American racism, of course, is the U.S. criminal justice system. In 2014, after police officer Darren Wilson fatally shot eighteen-year-old Michael Brown in Ferguson, Missouri, and left his body lying in the street for four hours, Brown's neighbors and friends took to those same streets to protest. They were soon joined by many thousands of residents from the surrounding area, who faced down tanks and riot police day after day, night after night. The protests forced the U.S. Department of Justice to conduct an investigation of the police, which uncovered what local black people had known for years: a pattern of intense police surveillance and harassment of black residents, driven by a strong financial incentive. The police department was essentially shaking down Ferguson residents for petty offenses on a regular basis, and these tickets and summonses amounted to roughly 23 percent of the town's revenue.[5] In a majority-black community, the nearly all-white Ferguson police force were steeped in the "culture of poverty" framework. During the federal inquiry, "several officials" explained to investigators that black people were issued more citations and tickets because of a "lack of personal responsibility."[6]

Sadly, it is not an exaggeration to extrapolate from Ferguson to the nation. This is the age of "mass incarceration," as Michelle Alexander has termed it.[7] Today the United States is by far the world's leading jailer, with approximately 2.3 million people locked away in cages; almost one million of those are African American.[8] Cash-strapped cities that struggle to fund schools and social services regularly write blank checks for police brutality. Chicago, for example, paid $50 million in 2014 alone to settle police misconduct cases, and devoted more than half a billion dollars to that purpose over the last decade.[9] Taylor, like Alexander and others, sees the rise of mass incarceration as a response to the civil rights and Black Power movements of the mid-twentieth century. The ideological corollary of mass incarceration is so-called "colorblindness," which "has become the default setting for how Americans understand how race and racism work." While mass incarceration tries to physically restrain black movements, the logic of colorblindness does so ideologically:

> It is repeatedly argued that the absence of racial insult means that racial discrimination is not at play. Indeed, the mere mention of race as a possible explanation, or as a means of providing greater context, risks accusations of "playing the race

> card"—a way of invoking race to silence disagreement. This is deployed to hide or obscure inequality and disparities between African Americans and whites. It has helped to elevate and amplify politics that blame Blacks for their own oppression.[10]

These developments are all contingent and contested—that is, they are the result of a *struggle.* Taylor effectively contrasts the rhetoric of the first black president with that of Lyndon Johnson, a white president from the South. While Obama has fairly consistently hewed to the ideology of "personal responsibility," readers will be struck by the degree to which Johnson emphasized the need to overcome *systemic* racism. The difference is not to be explained by their personal proclivities, but by the ability of mass movements to shift the national political context and its assumptions. "The entire dynamic of the black struggle pushed mainstream politics to the left during this period," Taylor argues, "as evidenced by the growth of the welfare state and the increasing number of mainstream voices that identified racism as a problem."[11]

Taylor shows that leading figures and organizations in the 1960s and '70s moved towards systemic, structural critiques of racism and U.S. society. Dr. King said that the black movement was "forcing America to face all of its interrelated flaws—racism, poverty, militarism, and materialism"; Huey Newton declared that "only by eliminating capitalism and replacing it with socialism would all black people be able to practice self-determination and thus achieve freedom."[12] At their height, these black freedom movements successfully transformed the political landscape of U.S. politics. In their official report, social scientists brought together under the Johnson administration to investigate the riots sweeping U.S. cities concluded, in remarkably unambiguous language, that white people had created the problems plaguing black people. "What white Americans have never fully understood-but what the Negro can never forget," they wrote, "is that white society is deeply implicated in the ghetto. White institutions created it, white institutions maintain it, and white society condones it."[13]

One of the most important changes to the landscape of the historic black freedom struggle has been the rise of a black political elite. When twenty-five-year-old Freddie Gray was murdered by Baltimore police—a cell phone video showed him being "disappeared" into a police van, emerging hours later with his spinal cord cut nearly in half—the city erupted in protest. However, "this was no Ferguson." "What distinguishes Baltimore from Ferguson and North Charleston [where a black man, Walter Scott, was gunned down by a white police officer two weeks before Freddie Gray was murdered in Baltimore] is that the black political establishment runs the city," Taylor writes. "African Americans control virtually the entire political apparatus." Black elected officials were quick to condemn the mostly black demonstrators. Mayor Stephanie Rawlings-Blake and President Obama both condemned them as "criminals" and "thugs." Just like the white-dominated political establishment in Ferguson, Baltimore's black political establishment did not hesitate to call out city and state troops to clear the protesters off the streets. "When a Black mayor, governing a largely Black city, aids in the mobilization of a military unit led by a black woman to suppress a black rebellion, we are in a new period of the Black freedom struggle."[14]

How did it come to this? Taylor's fluency with history is useful here. She takes us through the high hopes the left invested in the election campaigns of the first black mayors of Cleveland, Camden, and Philadelphia, the rise of the Congressional Black Caucus, and the thousands-strong national convention of black activists and elected officials held in Gary, Indiana, in 1972. Tragically, the rise of thousands of highly placed black elected officials since that time—primarily in the Democratic Party—has coincided with the decline of mass-movement organizing and the rise of mass incarceration. These politicians swept into office promising radical change, but have instead become reliable custodians of the system. The black political class "has no *fundamental* political differences with the status quo in the United States insofar as it does not directly impede their ability to participate freely in the nation's governing and business institutions." Mass movements made their careers possible, expanded the political horizons, and created the impetus for reform. But when those movements receded, so did the pressure for real change:

> It was the Black insurgency that created the conditions that allowed Black elected officials to become viable politically. But the more the movement on the streets waned, the greater the distance between ordinary Black people and the black officials claiming to represent them. Added to that dilemma were the constraints of governing in a time of budget cuts and austerity that compelled Black officials to act in fiscally conservative ways—just as their base was in desperate need of robust spending and resources.[15]

The chapters that follow are filled with political and theoretical in-sights—about the nature of the police, the new organizations that have arisen to challenge police murders, and the strategic challenges ahead. To call this book theoretically rich may puzzle readers accustomed to equating "theory" with vague abstractions and impenetrable prose. Taylor takes the opposite approach, laying out sophisticated ideas in blunt, forceful, and sometimes biting sentences. Her analysis of the police is concise and provocative:

> The racism of the police is not the product of vitriol; it flows from their role as armed agents of the state. The police function to enforce the rule of the politically powerful and the economic elite; this is why poor and working-class communities are so heavily policed. African Americans are overrepresented among the ranks of the poor and the working class, so police overwhelmingly focus on those neighborhoods, even as they direct their violence more generally against all working-class people, including whites. But the police also reflect and reinforce the dominant ideology of the state that employs them, which also explains why they are inherently racist and resistant to substantive reform. In other words,

> if the task of the police is to maintain law and order, then that role takes on a specific meaning in a fundamentally racist society.[16]

Likewise, Taylor is attuned to the finer points of the U.S. race-class dialectic, often describing it in terms that are counterintuitive to today's activists. For example, she notes that pathologizing black people and "naturalizing" black inequality have deleterious effects for white people:

> The intractability of Black conditions becomes seen as natural as opposed to standing as an indictment of the system itself, while the hard times befalling ordinary whites are rendered almost invisible. For example, the majority of poor people in the United States are white, but the public face of American poverty is Black. It is important to point out how blacks are overrepresented among the poor, but ignoring white poverty helps to obscure the systemic roots of all poverty.[17]

Taylor contests popular usage of the concept of "whiteness," arguing that it misrepresents the behavior of elite and ruling class people of color. "[W]hen 'acting white' is invoked to explain the actions of reactionary nonwhite political actors, like Supreme Court justice Clarence Thomas," she writes, "it is being used to transpose class and race, further distorting the existence of class differences." She continues,

> In this way, "whiteness" is an adaptation of the American left to the myth that the United States is a classless society. Nonwhite people in positions of power are accused of "performing whiteness" instead of exercising their class power—as if Clarence Thomas or Barack Obama are acting in ways they do not wholly intend to. Moreover, it invariably collapses important distinctions among whites into a common white experience that simply does not exist.[18]

The murder of Trayvon Martin and the acquittal of his killer, George Zimmerman, was a turning point in the development of this new phase of the black struggle. The first black president warned against letting our "passions" get the better of us, lecturing that "we are a nation of laws." But what does such talk really mean, Taylor asks, given the dramatically different treatment meted out to African Americans in the criminal justice system? "George Zimmerman benefited from this dual system," she writes. "He was allowed to walk free for weeks before protests pressured officials into arresting him." And, adding insult to injury: "He was not subjected to drug tests, though Trayvon Martin's dead body had been … . Obama's call for quiet, individual soul-searching was a way of saying that he had no answers." In the days and weeks that followed, activists sensed the need to concretize new efforts to challenge U.S. racism, and accordingly they created new organizations. Patrisse Cullors and Opal

Tometi teamed up with Alicia Garza to turn the online hashtag Garza began using after Zimmerman's acquittal—#BlackLivesMatter—into a national organization. In Chicago, youth organizers created Black Youth Project 100, and in Florida, where Martin was murdered, Umi Saleh and friends formed the Dream Defenders.[19]

In the book's final chapters, Taylor assesses the ideas and debates that have animated these and other leading activists and organizations, which have collectively come to be called the Black Lives Matter movement. Noting, for example, activists' frequent references to "state violence," she argues that use of this language "strategically pivots away from a conventional analysis that would reduce racism to the intentions and actions of the individuals involved." Many of the people and organizations she highlights are "intersectional" in their approach to organizing. "In other words, they start from the basic recognition that the oppression of African Americans is multidimensional and must be fought on different fronts."[20] The highly decentralized, multifaceted nature of organizing in this movement has been a source of strength—allowing space for new leadership, particularly that of black women, and new organizations to grow.

At the same time, however, some activists raise the model of disruptive actions by small groups to a political principle. Taylor argues instead that genuine liberation requires transcending capitalism, which in turn means building a movement that can, at some point, collaborate in highly coordinated ways on a large scale. She quotes historian Barbara Ransby: "If we think we can all 'get free' through individual or uncoordinated small-group resistance, we are kidding ourselves." And if our goal in the long term is to achieve a *mass* movement, in the short term, she writes, decentralized and "leaderless" organizing can make it harder for new people to join. As Taylor cautions, "at a time when many people are trying to find an entry point into anti-police activism and desire to be involved, this particular method of organizing can actually narrow opportunities for the democratic involvement of many in favor of the tightly knit workings of those already in the know."[21] Other important debates she takes up include the role of private foundations and philanthropy in contemporary activism and the importance of formulating and fighting for winnable demands, while keeping our eyes on the proverbial prize of black liberation.

Black liberation is essential to the liberation of *all* people, and impossible without it. While the black elite are steadily working to preserve the status quo, working-class and poor people of all races have an interest in challenging the status quo. The nationwide fight for a $15 hourly minimum wage, spearheaded by low-wage service workers, should be a focus of anyone who cares about black life in the United States. "Twenty percent of fast-food workers are Black," Taylor writes, "and 68 percent of them earn between $7.26 and $10.09 an hour .... Twenty percent of Walmart's 1.4 million workers are African American, making it the largest employer of Black Americans. There is a logical connection between the low-wage workers' campaigns and the Black Lives Matter movement."[22]

On May Day 2015, union activists around the country rallied under the banner of Black Lives Matter, and Taylor notes that the International Longshore and Warehouse Union Local 10 "conducted a work stoppage that halted the flow of millions of dollars' worth of goods and prevented them from being loaded onto cargo ships. This was the first time a major union had initiated a work stoppage in solidarity with the Black Lives Matter movement." Others, however, regard gestures of solidarity or connection with suspicion. When activists wanted to highlight racism against Arabs and Muslims by using the hashtag #MuslimLivesMatter, some in the Black Lives Matter movement objected that the phrase amounted to an "appropriation" of a cause that rightfully belonged to black people. Taylor disagrees. "It is one thing to respect the organizing that has gone into the movement against police violence and brutality," she argues, "but quite another to conceive of Black oppression and anti-Black racism as so wholly unique that they are beyond the realm of understanding and, potentially, solidarity from others who are oppressed."[23]

Ultimately, *From #BlackLivesMatter to Black Liberation* argues that black liberation requires an intersectional movement for black lives that aspires to challenge the structures of capitalism itself and the U.S. state that upholds it. The historic dynamic of the black freedom struggle has been to raise these large issues again and again, to "force America to face all of its interrelated flaws." The last great wave of black struggle was crushed with co-optation on one hand and repression on the other. The next, coming wave will inevitably grapple with similar questions, but in new and changing conditions. Taylor's short but powerful and provocative book is a vital read for those wrestling with how to understand the rise of this phase of the black struggle, and where it can and should go from here. Black people will no doubt lead any movement for black liberation, but in the long run, Taylor reminds us, the question of black liberation should be an urgent concern for all people fighting for genuine freedom, justice, and equality. "The aspiration for Black liberation cannot be separated from what happens in the United States as a whole," she concludes. "Black life cannot be transformed while the rest of the country burns."[24]

Notes

1. Michael D. Shear and Liam Stack, "Obama Says Movements Like Black Lives Matter 'Can't Just Keep on Yelling,'" *New York Times,* April 23, 2016.

2. "The Counted: People Killed by the Police in the US," *Guardian,* http://the-guardian.com; Julia Craven, "Here's How Many Black People Have Been Killed by the Police This Year. Too Many," *Huffing ton Post,* July 7, 2016, http://huffington-post.com.

3. Keeanga-Yamahtta Taylor, *From #BlackLivesMatter to Black Liberation* (Chicago: Haymarket, 2016), 23–25.

4. Ibid., 28.

5. Michael Martinez, "Policing for profit: How Ferguson's fines violated rights of African-Americans," CNN, March 6, 2015, http://cnn.com.

6. Taylor, *From #BlackLivesMatter to Black Liberation,* 49.

7. Michelle Alexander, *The New Jim Crow: Mass Incarceration in the Age of Colorblindness* (New York: New Press, 2012).

8. National Association for the Advancement of Colored People, "Criminal Justice Fact Sheet," http://naacp.org.

9. Taylor, *From #BlackLivesMatter to Black Liberation,* 129.

10. Ibid., 72.

11. Ibid., 1,45,47.

12. Judson L. Jeffries, *Huey P. Newton: The Radical Theorist* (Jackson, MS: University Press of Mississippi, 2002), 69–70.

13. Taylor, *From #BlackLivesMatter to Black Liberation, 76,* 78, 80.

14. Ibid., 103–04, 106.

15. Ibid., 108.

16. Ibid., 49.

17. Ibid., 210–11.

18. Ibid., 150–151.

19. Ibid., 151.

20. Ibid., 167.

21. Ibid., 175–76.

22. Ibid., 183.

23. Ibid., 185, 187.

24. Ibid., 193–94.

READING 22

MeToo to #MeToo: What's in the Name?

By Sherrise Truesdale-Moore

Sexual violence has been one of the most pervasive features of the American legal system (Muraskin, 2005), and the present-day outcry among women against sexual violence shows signs that they are no longer remaining silent about this issue. The #MeToo Movement is a sure sign that women are now standing up against male patriarchy, and the days of women sitting idle, tolerating actions of men, while rape, domestic violence, and sexual harassment are ignored are no longer.

MeToo a Safe Space for Women of Color

The MeToo Movement was originally founded to create a safe space for women of color to talk about sexual violence. Having courage and vision, Tarana Burke, in 2007, founded MeToo in Alabama to give women of color a voice to be heard about their experiences with sexual violence (Douglas, 2018). This is a significant contribution because women of color are particularly vulnerable to sexual violence. In the United States, half (49.5%) multiracial women, 45.6% of American Indian/Alaska Native women, 38.9% of non-Hispanic White women, 35.5% of non-Hispanic Black women, 26.9% of Hispanic women, and 22.9% of Asian/ Pacific Islander women experienced some form of sexual violence during their lifetime (Smith, et. al., 2017). Women of color may also encounter a criminal justice system that has historically exercised disparate treatment between "European American perpetrators and perpetrators of color or between European American victims and victims of color" (Smith, et. al. 2017).

African American women, in particular, have had a history of violence against their bodies, which has led to their overrepresentation within the criminal justice system (Battle, 2016; Baker, 2005). Since the days of slavery, African American women have been criminalized and lynched for defending themselves against domestic violence, rape, and other forms of violence (Battle, 2016; Baker, 2005; Truesdale & Lewis, 2016). Even after emancipation, the vulnerability of African American women being subjected to sexual violence was not improved during the postbellum period; in fact, it was greater (Broussard, 2013). Davis (1981) stated:

> The sexual abuse they had routinely suffered during the era of slavery was not arrested by the advent of emancipation. As a matter of fact, it was still ruled that colored women were looked upon as the legitimate prey of white men—and if they resisted white men's sexual attacks, they were frequently thrown into prison to be further victimized by a system which was a return to another form of slavery (as cited in Baker, 2005, p. 411).

Unfortunately, the 21st century has not shown much progress toward improving the circumstances of African American women against sexual violence. Marissa Alexander, for example, is an African American woman who was defending herself from an abusive husband by shooting warning shots. Alexander was prosecuted by Angela Corey for aggravated assault with a lethal weapon and received a mandatory minimum sentence of 20 years in prison. After much controversy, an appellate court ordered a new trial, but this time the prosecutor, Angela Corey, pursued a sixty-year sentence if found guilty. Alexander pleaded guilty and was given credit for three years already served, and she was placed on house arrest for two years. She was required to wear an ankle monitor, allowed to attend classes, take her children to school, and attend medical appointments (Marissa Alexander Justice Project, 2018). Another familiar example is the Clarence Thomas United States Supreme Court confirmation hearings, regarding sexual harassment allegations by Anita Hill, a law professor who had previously worked under Clarence Thomas at the United States Department of Education and the Equal Employment Opportunity Commission (Abramson, 2018; Muraskin, 2005).

#MeToo Transcends Race and Class

By 2017, the MeToo Movement had transformed into something more; within ten years, it became the #MeToo Movement, transcending race and class by recognizing that sexual violence among women persists in all racial groups and classes. In the U.S., about one in three women (36.3%) and nearly one in six men (17.1%) experienced some form of contact sexual violence during their lifetime (Smith, et. al., 2017). Alyssa Milano sparked a conversation on twitter when she posted: "If all the women who have been sexually harassed or assaulted wrote 'Me too' as a status, we might give people a sense of the magnitude of the problem" (Ohlheiser, 2018). Ashley Judd, Gwyneth Paltrow, Heather Graham, and other celebrities shared their stories, which ignited a whirlwind of stories by women, giving rise to the idea that all races and classes were affected by this issue in a very profound way (Ohlheiser, 2018).

The Washington Post examined the tweeted conversations of the #MeToo Movement; it revealed two significant peaks in conversations from the years 2013–2018. The first was small, indicating when an Access Hollywood audio recording of Donald Trump making sexually lewd comments in 2005 was publicized during the 2016 presidential campaign. The second peak was very significant; the research team collected more than 96 million tweets from 2010 through the end of 2017 that spoke about sexual harassment. These tweets were identified by searching for keywords and hashtags that were entirely or partially about sexual harassment and abuse (Ohlheiser, 2018).

Criticism Surrounding the #MeToo Movement

One of the biggest criticisms among supporters of the #MeToo Movement is that for decades victims of sexual harassment and sexual assault were almost never believed or given the benefit of doubt, which led to no recourse of action, but rather accusations hurled toward the victims of making up the stories, exaggerating the offense, and/or purposefully trying to ruin the accuser's reputation or career (Sirota, 2018). According to Mantler, Schellenberg, and Page (2003), situational variables and characteristics of the victim are often considered when judgments are made about blame and responsibility, and the sentiments that are projected become key factors in assigning the blame, judgments about the controllability of the event, and responsibility for the occurrence of the event. How the blame is pronounced will attribute to the response, actions, and judgments for appropriate punishments.

Previous research has shown several factors associated with disbelief, including familiarity of the assailant, victim-police interaction, the gender of the victim, and the sexual orientation of the victim. In general, the victim's familiarity with the assailant typically renders the victim blameworthy and the assailant is blamed less. This is not the case if the assailant is a stranger (Stephens and Sinden, 2000; Stormo, et. al., 1997). On the other hand, if the victim was inebriated due to intoxication or was high, then more blame will be placed on the victim (Stephens and Sinden, 2000; Stormo, et. al., 1997). Considering child sexual abuse in the case of analyzing gender and belief, research has shown that there are gender differences in measuring credibility—females compared to males report that children were less likely to lie, less likely to confuse reality with imagination, and more likely to have good memories. The factors of disbelief are exceptionally poignant when examining the interactions between the victim and police. Research has revealed that in many cases police officers have conveyed messages doubting the seriousness of the offense or discounted the victim's appeal for the police officer's help, threatening to arrest both parties or simply brushing off the incident, which ultimately humiliates the victim (Stephens and Sinden, 2000). In the case of sexual orientation, violence is viewed as a justification by the assailant because the experience of an advance is justified through retaliation of an unwanted advancement (Wall, 2000).

On the other hand, non-supporters of the #MeToo Movement argue that blatant belief without due process is problematic. Under the 14th Amendment of the United States Constitution every person, including aliens, are guaranteed equal protection under the law, which means that in the case of being accused of sexual violence or harassment, the accused is protected against any conviction until facts have proven that he or she is guilty. The United States Supreme Court case, In re Winship, 397 U.S. 358 (1970), made this point clear by deciding that the presumption of innocence is a constitutional principle binding on all the states. Supporters of the #MeToo Movement argue that this does not apply when the accusations are about a job interview, which was the case involving Circuit Court Judge Brett Kavanaugh, who was seeking confirmation to the United States Supreme Court in 2018. Judge Kavanaugh was accused of sexual assault by Dr. Christine Blasey Ford, a psychology professor at Palo Alto University. She testified at the Senate confirmation hearing that Judge Kavanaugh sexually assaulted her when they were teenagers at a party during their high school years, which Judge Kavanaugh vehemently denied. In a survey conducted by the National Public Radio/Marist poll, college-educated white women said they believed Ford over Kavanaugh by 66% to 26% and African-American women believed her by 73% to just 5%. However, white women without college degrees were not so supportive of Dr. Ford, indicating only 33% said they believed Ford, while others were divided closely between them or unsure (Brownstein, 2018). Many opponents of Judge Kavanaugh's confirmation argued that this was not about due process, but about his character, arguing his character was significantly flawed and thus he should not hold a permanent seat as justice to the United States Supreme Court (Livni, 2018; CNN, 2018).

Finally, some African American women have criticized the #MeToo Movement by arguing that the movement has been made all about celebrities and politicians, particularly white women and men, rendering the experiences of women of color faceless and invisible (Black Women's Roundtable, 2017). This is troubling since the Me Too Movement was originally intended to make them visible. Women of color experience high rates of sexual violence, yet the faces of #MeToo are typically white actresses like Alyssa Milano and high-profile accused celebrities like Harvey Weinstein, Matt Lauer, and Bill Cosby (Morales, 2018).

African American women have had a long history in civil rights, and their contributions have been largely ignored (Dastagir, 2018). If we are to make the most of the Me Too/#MeToo Movement, then all people, regardless of color, men included, must contribute to the fight of this cause. Every face must be visible. Donna Brazile, an African American woman, a political strategist and former interim chairwoman of the Democratic National Committee, explains the faces of activism in the best way. She states:

> Black women are taking an active role in beginning what I call the next phase of the black political movement, which is to prepare for a century in which the minority citizens of today will become the majority citizens of tomorrow. Black women are going to lead that way, but we're not going to be alone. We're going to bring as many people with us because in moving the country forward, we can leave no one behind (Dastagir, p. 1, 2018).

References

Abramson, Jill 2018. "The Forgotten Testimonies against Clarence Thomas." *Intelligencer*. Retrieved on October 15, 2018 from http://nymag.com/intelligencer/2018/02/the-forgotten-testimonies-against-clarence-thomas.html

"About Marissa Alexander." 2018. Marissa Alexander Justice Project. Retrieved on October 15, 2018 from https://marissaalexander.org/

Baker, David. 2005. "Systemic White Racism and the Brutalization of Executed Black Women in the United States." In Roslyn Muraskin (4th Ed.) *It's a Crime: Women and Justice* (pp. 333–343). Pearson Publishing: Upper Saddle River.

Battle, Nishaum T. 2016. "From Slavery to Jane Crow to Say Her Name: An Intersectional Examination of Black Women and Punishment." *Meridians: Feminism, Race, Transnationalism 15*(1), 109–136. doi: 10.2979/meridians.15.1.07

Black Women's Roundtable salutes trailblazer Tarana Burke, founder of the "Me Too" movement, and others. (2017, December 14). New York Amsterdam News, p. 33. Retrieved from https://search.ebscohost.com/login.aspx?direct=true&db=aph&AN=128329272

Broussard, Patricia. 2013. "Black Women's Post-Slavery Silence Syndrome: A Twenty-first Century Remnant of Slavery, Jim Crow, and Systemic Racism—Who Will Tell Her Stories?" *Journal of Gender Race & Justice, 16*, 373–421.

Brownstein, Ronald. 2018. "There Is Still a Huge Divide on Gender Roles in the U.S." *CNN Politics*. Retrieved on October 15, 2018 from https://www.cnn.com/2018/10/09/politics/us-divide-gender-roles-kavanaugh-women-college/index.html

Dastagir, Alia. 2018. "Unsung Heroes of the Civil Rights Movement Are Black Women You've Never Heard of." *USA Today*. Retrieved on February 19, 2018 from https://www.usatoday.com/story/news/nation/2018/02/16/unsung-heroes-civil-rights-movement-black-women-youve-never-heard/905157001/

Douglas, Deborah. 2018. "Black Women Say #MeToo." *The New York Times Upfront* (winter). pp. 5–6.

Fox, Lauren. Devine, Curt, Brownstein, Scott, and Perez, Evan. 2018. "Kavanaugh's Yale Classmates Say They've Struggled to Connect with FBI. *CNN Politics*. Retrieved on October 15, 2018 from https://www.cnn.com/2018/10/03/politics/kavanaugh-yale-classmates-fbi-investigation/index.html

Hauser, Christine. 2017. "Florida Woman Whose 'Stand Your Ground' Defense Was Rejected Is Released." *New York Times*. Retrieved on October 15, 28 from https://www.nytimes.com/2017/02/07/us/marissa-alexander-released-stand-your-ground.html

In re Winship, 397 U.S. 358 (1970).

Livni, Ephrat. 2018. "'Innocent until proven guilty' doesn't apply to job interviews." *Quartz*. Retrieved on October 15, 2018 from https://qz.com/work/1401422/brett-kavanaugh-confirmation-innocent-until-proven-guilty-doesnt-apply-to-job-interviews/

Mantler, Janet, Schellenberg, Glen, and Page, Stewart. 2003. "Attributions for Serious Illness: Are Controllability, Responsibility, and Blame Different Constructs?" *Canadian Journal of Behavioural Science, 35*, 142–152.

Morales, Valerie. 2018. "The Invisible Victims of #Metoo." *Huffington Post.* Retrieved on October 15, 2018 from https://www.huffingtonpost.com/entry/opinion-morales-metoo-black-brown-women_us_5a833de2e4b-0cf06751f4396

Muraskin, Roslyn. 2005. "Sexual Harassment and the Law: Violence against Women." In Roslyn Muraskin (4th Ed.) *It's a Crime: Women and Justice* (pp. 333–343). Pearson Publishing: Upper Saddle River, New Jersey.

Ohlheiser, Abby. 2018. "How #Metoo Really Was Different, According to Data. *The Washington Post* (January 22). Retrieved on October 15, 2018 from https://www.washingtonpost.com/news/the-intersect/wp/2018/01/22/how-metoo-really-was-different-according-to-data/?noredirect=on&utm_term=.027faabab4f9.

Sirota, Marcia. 2018. "It's Time to Start Believing Victims of Sexual Assault." *Huffington Post.* Retrieved October 15, 2018 from https://www.huffingtonpost.ca/marcia-sirota/its-time-to-start-believing-victims-of-sexual-assault_a_23347029/.

Smith, Sharon, Chen, Jieru, Basile, Kathleen. C., Gilbert, Leah, Merrick, Melissa, Patel, Nimesh, Walling, Margie, and Jain, Anurag. (2017). *The National Intimate Partner and Sexual Violence Survey (NISVS): 2010–2012 State Report.* Retrieved on October 15, 2018 from https://www.cdc.gov/violenceprevention/pdf/NISVS-StateReportBook.pdf

Stephens, B. Joyce, and Peter G. Sinden. (2000). "Victims' Voices: Domestic Assault Victims' Perceptions of Police Demeanors." *Journal of International Violence, 15*(5), 534–547.

Stormo, Karla J., Alan R. Lang, and Werner GK Stritzke. 1997. "Attributions about Acquaintance Rape: The Role of Alcohol and Individual Differences." *Journal of Applied Psychology. 27*, 279–305.

Truesdale, Sherrise and Lewis, Jacqueline. 2016. "Revisiting Empathy: Counseling African American Women in Corrections." Paper presented at the American Society of Criminology, New Orleans, LA. U.S. Const. amend. XIV

USA Today Special Edition, 2018. Retrieved from https://issuu.com/studiogannett/docs/blackhistorymonth_2018

Wall, Barry W. 2000. "Criminal Responsibility, Diminished Capacity, and the Gay Panic Defense." *Journal of the American Academy of Psychiatry and the Law, 28*, 454–459.

READING 23

The Collective Power of #MeToo

By Sarah Jaffe

You never can tell where a social movement is going to come from. They're built of a million injustices that pile up and up, and then, suddenly, spill over. I've spent years covering movements, trying to explain how one incident becomes the spark that catches, turning all those individual injustices into an inferno.

When the *New York Times* ran a story about Harvey Weinstein's repulsive—and long—history of sexual harassment and assault in October last year, no one knew what it would start. But soon a wave of people, most of them, though not all of them, women, began to wield their stories like weapons in a battle that, for once, they seemed to be winning. Well, if not winning, then at least drawing some blood. When #Metoo began to circulate on Facebook I was beyond cynical; I was actually angry that the men around me might be shocked to learn that yes, it had happened to me, it had happened to almost every woman I know. Yet #Metoo defeated my cynicism and became something else: a watershed moment in contemporary feminism, one that has made sexual violence into big news.

Like so many movements that appear spontaneous, the #Metoo moment is built on the work of longtime organizers. Tarana Burke has worked for decades with young women of color who survived sexual violence, and in 2006 she named her campaign "me too" as an expression of solidarity. But when she found the words trending on social media last year she worried that they were being used for something that she did not recognize as her life's work. Burke's "me too" campaign was designed to support survivors, to get them resources and help them heal; despite #Metoo hinging on survivor stories, it has, Burke noted in a recent interview, been more focused on outing the actions of perpetrators.

This focus is to some degree a reaction to a system designed to fail survivors of violence and harassment. Under the existing legal system, "justice" for sexual violence requires convincing first the police and then a court of law that what was done to you actually happened, and then that it counts as a crime. In a case of workplace harassment, the situation is similar: the person being harassed must come forward and lodge a complaint with HR (if her company has it) or her boss (if it doesn't).

In the exceedingly likely scenario that the person harassing her is in fact her superior, she likely has no one to report to who does not have every incentive to side with the boss.

This is how we got to the moment when sexual harassment stories are big news. The structures of the legal system and the workplace did not change. Instead, tens of thousands of women said yes, me too. Then, rather than wait for men to absorb that knowledge and decide whether to change or not, they started naming names. And making lists. And talking to each other.

That's how organizing starts, after all. It starts with people talking about the conditions of their lives, realizing that they are common, and that they want them to change. It starts with enough people joining the conversation that they begin to believe that they can win. And despite the individualizing tendency of the tales of horror flowing through the press, many of those stories became public through organizing work. The whisper network has long been a form of organizing for the powerless, sharing information quietly, person-to-person, even if it often left out exactly the people who were the most vulnerable, those who had the fewest connections. The now-infamous "Shitty Media Men" list, begun by journalist Moira Donegan, turned the whisper network into a spreadsheet, where women could add layers to each report. The crowd-sourced google document, which collected women's anonymous stories of more than seventy men in media in the few hours it was live, was designed to collectivize the incomplete information that individuals receive based on their social networks.

I refused to look at the list when I learned of its existence—I still refuse to. Not that I blame anyone for reading to try to protect themselves, or in the case of hiring editors, for trying to learn more about the people working for them. But for me not looking was a tiny refusal of the work that is constantly forced back upon women, the work that the backlash writers—recycling the bad arguments they've been making since the 1990s at least—keep demanding that we do. *Protect yourself. Yell louder. Stop complaining, you should have known better.* Bullshit.

The viral hashtag that spread across social media asked not just about workplace harassment, but sexual assault in general. The discussion surrounding it has been broad and sprawling. But the common denominator has been, as sociology professor Christy Thornton noted, "In our culture, part of what it means to be a powerful man is to have unfettered access to women's bodies," or the bodies of others who are less powerful—transgender and queer people, and people of color are especially vulnerable to such sexual violence. The movement's opponents or even just those made slightly uncomfortable by its breadth keep attempting to narrow its parameters. But the wide scope is the point. The movement is not just about Hollywood, just about the worst of the worst, or even just about the workplace. It is a rejection of a core piece of patriarchal power—and the beginnings of imagining what a society without that power looks like.

It feels to many feminists now, in this second year of trump, that it is not the time to accept petty reforms and good-enough moments. Why should we compromise, when our opponents refuse to?

Things are rotten, and there is a significant number of people who are willing to defend the indefensible as the powerful pass it into law. Against such opponents, who care nothing for our lives, why play nice?

As Charlotte Shane wrote at *Splinter* in January,

> If this past year taught us anything, it was how profoundly every system one might have hoped to improve with mere reform, every institution one might have trusted to "do the right thing," every politician who'd been positioned as a beacon of integrity, will never come to our rescue. Parity and justice and restitution are not priorities of our existing structures because those structures were designed to maintain hierarchies that make justice and parity and restitution impossible.

One of the things that it has seemed hardest for the opponents or even just the confused sideline-sitters to grasp is that people are not calling for perpetrators to go to jail. Perhaps one of the deepest assumptions of the #Metoo movement is that the society we live in provides us no real options for justice. The court system does not work for survivors and Hr is a tool of the boss. The tools we need do not exist yet, so we must build from the ground up.

In fact, the thing I have heard the most from survivors (and we are all survivors, aren't we, that was the point of saying "me too") is that they want acknowledgment of what happened. If the perpetrator was in a position of power over them at work, they might want him fired. Since so much of the #Metoo conversation has revolved around workplace harassment and assault, powerful men have faced investigations and even lost jobs. Some of those were prestigious jobs those men assumed they had worked uniquely hard to win, and a perk of which was access to women's bodies.

Women's bodies—and women's work—are considered rewards for proper male behavior. The women themselves aren't supposed to find this unpleasant. Some men treated women as just another tray of canapés at a party—think of Al Franken's record of ass-grabbing. Others seemed to glory in the horror they created—Harvey Weinstein, whose story broke the floodgates open, or Matt Lauer and the button he had installed to lock his office door from the inside.

The stories are mostly not about dating, yet the backlashers worry that #Metoo will ruin dating. The men are not going to jail, but the backlashers constantly argue that they should not go to jail. They persist in using legal definitions for what, as Tressie McMillan Cottom noted, is a conversation about norms. "When we require a perfect victimless norm before we will consider the possibility of the improved lives of women," she wrote, "we are making an affirmative case about our values."

The norms #Metoo revealed are often called "rape culture," but I prefer the term "patriarchy" despite, or perhaps because of, its old-fashionedness. I write about systems, and "rape culture" is just a piece of the whole, an answer that seems only to provoke more questions. Rape culture exists to ensure a culture of male dominance, which takes many forms. By naming patriarchy, I hope that we

At the 2018 Women's March in Washington, D.C. Photo by John M. via Flickr.

can begin to understand the way the threads of power and dominance leak into every corner of our lives. Then we can see that violations are not purely or even mostly about sex, but instead reinforce a structure that offers power to a few by pretending to offer rewards to many. Patriarchy spreads the lie that there are rules we can follow that will keep us safe—that if we wear the right clothes, say no loudly enough, walk away, don't laugh at men, work hard, no harm will come to us.

There are not.

Well-intentioned men are now afraid that they have done harm, or that they will be accused of having done what they did not realize was harm. Because even when they are not bosses, when they might have had little tangible power over others, they have had the power of *not being required to learn* to read the people around them. That, after all, has been women's job, whether or not it is done for pay.

The reason for telling stories about men we thought were "good" is not to permanently etch their names into some list of "shitty men," though the lack of real justice means those lists are often all we get. The reason is for us to understand deep in our bones that there are no "good" and "bad" men or "good" and "bad" people. To repair the harms done is going to take change from all of us. We can't just pat ourselves on the back for not being as bad as Weinstein.

The scariest part of #Metoo is the realization, as Tarana Burke notes, that "more often than not, the reality is we live in the gray areas around sexual violence." there is a spectrum of abuses of power, some tiny and some huge, that all add up to a world where women's voices, women's work, and women's sexual desires are ignored or devalued. What most of us who've told stories want is for that to stop happening. It is a huge demand, perhaps unrealizable in our lifetimes, one that is bigger than any perpetrator outed in the media: It is not a demand for men to go to jail. It is a demand for men to do the work of learning.

What does justice and accountability look like when the perpetrator is your boss?

We asked ourselves that a lot this year, and by this "we," I mean a specific group of women who worked alongside me at the online news website AlterNet and had been harassed by the organization's executive director Don Hazen. Because while we—a group of journalists—knew better than most that getting a story published in the media often doesn't change anything, we realized that if there was going to be a moment to topple an abusive boss, this was it.

And so we organized. We discussed, we planned, and we supported each other. We wondered if our stories were sympathetic enough, because we all knew how the media loves a perfect victim and how commentators will tear you apart if you don't fit that mold. We verified one another's stories and we talked, a lot, about what we wanted to happen. We wanted him out of a position of power over others, that was for sure, but what else? What did justice look like? Just having the story told is not justice but it can be wielded, occasionally, as a tool to help get there.

My former coworker Kristen Gwynne told Rebecca Traister, "[e]ven if the people who did target me were punished, I still feel like I deserve some sort of compensation. I don't want them to release a public apology—I want them to send me a check."

This comment stuck with me. When famous men are accused, some of them will release a public apology for us to hem and haw over, to try to decide if we can forgive someone with whom our only interaction has been consuming their performance on television. But really, it's not for me to forgive Louis CK or Kevin Spacey or Aziz Ansari. Such forgiveness would only serve to make me feel better about watching their films or TV shows, as if I could consume anything with clean hands.

Restorative and transformative justice hinges on the notion of community; that accountability can happen within and with the support of the people around us. Yes, famous people feel like they're part of our community, but they aren't, not really. And your boss? Most of us didn't want to repair or restore a relationship with our boss—we wanted him to no longer have power to affect our lives. What we want repaired is the damage to our work. Maybe part of what such restoration looks like, as Gwynne said, is a check.

A flyer from the Wages for Housework movement in the 1970s, on the cover of a new collection, declares "the women of the world are serving notice!" It lists demands for which women want wages, including "every indecent assault." Such assaults, in this framework, are part of a broader picture of exploitation that assumes that housework is a woman's role, that they are "naturally" subservient to men, and that sees this exploitation replicated in the paid workplace. The women of the Wages for Housework movement wanted to be able to refuse that work—the flyer says "if we don't get what we want we will simply refuse to work any longer!"—but they also fought for concrete support in the here and now, for abuses that have happened and are happening. Those assaults in the workplace, then, should be *compensated.*

The question of wages for assaults can seem strange, like putting a monetary value on violence, but in fact such compensation can take many forms. In the wake of the Movement for Black Lives, the framework of reparations is back in the public consciousness, as a way to try to acknowledge and make up for systematic, rather than individual, oppression. Late in 2017 I sat down with raj Patel and Jason W. Moore to talk about their new book, *A History of the World in Seven Cheap Things.* We discussed their use of the idea of reparations, which Patel described thus: "reparations are necessarily a collective process that demand revolutionary organizing, jolting the imagination with the historical memory of what happened, the challenge of accountability, and the invitation to dream a society that ceases the crimes on which capitalism is based." What, he asked, would reparations for patriarchy look like?

Reparations remains a fraught topic in the United States even though campaigns for reparations exist and even succeed. Organizers won reparations for police torture in Chicago—a plan that included not just cash for survivors but also recovery services, counseling, and importantly, that the story would be taught in public schools.

What would such a framework look like for sexual violence? For harassment? How do we come up with demands that move beyond naming and shaming?

Part of the challenge of talking about sexual harassment in the media is that stories are always told based on news value. As a reporter who has covered labor issues for years I can tell you that until recently, stories of sexual harassment at a call center or a restaurant or of home healthcare workers did not garner a lot of attention. It usually took famous perpetrators and photogenic, famous victims for these stories to crack the media.

But something changed this time. It started, I think, with a letter from 700,000 women farmworkers of the Alianza Nacional de Campesinas, published in *Time* magazine, that expressed solidarity with the Hollywood women who had come forward. "Even though we work in very different environments, we share a common experience of being preyed upon by individuals who have the power to hire, fire, blacklist and otherwise threaten our economic, physical and emotional security."

Those women hit on the thing that has been at the core of these seemingly endless revelations: the power of the boss. Sexual harassment is just one of the many tools used to keep women compliant and their labor cheap. It drives women out of prestigious occupations and terrorizes them in subsistence occupations. It doesn't matter how hard you "lean in" if someone keeps leaning *on* you. As my former colleague Sarah Seltzer wrote, the problem was never us. "If unadorned sexism, exploitation, and harassment are the biggest problem white-collar women face, then it turns out women across most industries are actually up against some of the same enemies."

Suddenly it wasn't about being the perfect victim or being the perfect, upwardly mobile worker. The media rippled with stories of hotel housekeepers, restaurant workers, domestic workers. Women at a Ford plant in Chicago told stories to the *New York Times* of being called "Fresh meat!" on the shop floor, and of complaints to the union going unheard.

While some unions, like UNITE HERE, have made campaigns against sexual harassment central to their work and connected the dots explicitly to the Weinstein case—Chicago members wore "No Harveys in Chicago" shirts to celebrate the passage of an ordinance granting hotel housekeepers panic buttons to wear on the job—the labor movement itself has not been immune to sexual harassment. High-up officials at SEIU and at the AFL-CIO itself have stepped down after harassment allegations, including the leader of the Fight for $15 campaign in New York, Kendall Fells. "Sexual harassment is a reason women organize," Kate Bronfenbrenner, Director of Labor Education research and a Senior Lecturer at Cornell University's School of Industrial and Labor relations noted. "But it can be a reason women don't organize."

While unions grapple with how to handle this moment, famous women are learning what solidarity looks like. Tarana Burke walked the red carpet at the golden globes alongside Michelle Williams; other movie stars brought Ai-Jen Poo of the National Domestic Workers Alliance and Saru Jayaraman of restaurant Opportunities Centers United as their dates.

Five years ago in this magazine I wrote of the problems with feminism's obsession with cracking glass ceilings and "having it all." In the year following Hillary Clinton's second failed attempt at breaking "the biggest glass ceiling," we have learned that even the women we thought had it all had instead been trapped in their own personal hells. And perhaps, just perhaps, we have learned that feminism will not trickle down from the top.

Rather than advice on how to work harder and get ahead, it seems that the issue that unites women across a broad number of workplaces is being abused by more powerful men. And rather than leading from the top, famous and powerful women are accepting leadership from those at the bottom. They are putting some money where their mouths are, too. The time's Up fund, administered by the National Women's Law Center, began with over $13 million in donations from film stars and aims to provide legal support for those facing harassment. Their launch letter read:

> To every woman employed in agriculture who has had to fend off unwanted sexual advances from her boss, every housekeeper who has tried to escape an assaultive guest, every janitor trapped nightly in a building with a predatory supervisor, every waitress grabbed by a customer and expected to take it with a smile, every garment and factory worker forced to trade sexual acts for more shifts, every domestic worker or home health aide forcibly touched by a client, every immigrant woman silenced by the threat of her undocumented status being reported in retaliation for speaking up and to women in every industry who are subjected to indignities and offensive behavior that they are expected to tolerate in order to make a living: We stand with you. We support you.

Of course, the time's Up page links to LeanIn.org as a trusted partner organization. The progress away from such top-down, work-harder ideology is still incomplete.

Still, it is beginning to feel like a sea change in feminism has come, not from one wealthy woman almost but not quite getting elected president, but rather, from a rippling of anger that spread from woman to woman for a thousand reasons that are at once individual and deeply familiar. It even came from a few men sharing their stories. And it has brought us to this place, where we are talking, finally, about structural barriers—the way sexual harassment and violence shape women's lives at work and away from it, the way class hierarchies are brutally maintained—in a way that emphasizes the breadth and depth of the problems. Perhaps next we will grapple with the breadth and depth of the change we will need to begin to solve them.

READING 24

Black Women Say #MeToo

The #MeToo Movement Gives Women of Color a Space to Share Struggle

By Deborah Douglas

The #MeToo movement continues to astonish as the window of relevance on reckoning with America's deep-seated sexual harassment ethos shows no sign of shutting soon. But more than a platform to launch Oprah Winfrey's much hoped-for presidential campaign, the value proposition of #MeToo may lie in presenting a bigger platform for the everyday Black woman.

"For Black women who have a history of violence against our bodies, from forced rape, sterilization and interpersonal violence from people who say they love us, there's a long history and thread we can follow," said Monica Simpson, executive director of Sister Song Inc., an Atlanta-based reproductive justice organization.

#MeToo offers a language and safe space to talk about sexual violence, Simpson said of the hashtag originally created by activist Tarana Burke. As such, Black women can't be afraid to tell their stories, she said.

"We have to be unapologetic about putting our voices out there. Stop censoring ourselves," Simpson said. "Black women have a history of wanting to keep our stories hidden. The experiences we've been shamed about, whether it's because of the Black church or respectability politics, we've been positioned to hold our pain and trauma."

For activist Bree Newsome, the #MeToo movement goes to the core of who we are as Americans and how sexual violence against Black women was codified by law, which allowed the legal rape of the Black woman and sale of her children. This is why the movement needs to include voices and concerns of marginalized women to keep the story straight, she said.

The primary call to action is to listen to Black women, said Newsome. Though the Hollywood women's #TimesUp initiative includes among its founders African-American showrunner Shonda Rhimes, Burke originally created the #MeToo program in 2006 to support Black and Brown girls who survived sexual violence.

"There's this real fixation with trying to make #MeToo about the public shaming of celebrities," Newsome said. "Tarana was never about focusing on high-profile men.

"There's a real fixation with trying to make #MeToo about public shaming of celebrities."

I take issue with folks who are continuing to frame it that way."

Nicole Burrowes, a professor in the African and African Diaspora Studies department at the University of Texas at Austin, agreed and noted that Burke embraced both women of color survivors and #SayHerName—Professor Kimberlé Crenshaw's call to pay heed to Black women and girls killed by police as part of the same struggle of Black men killed by law enforcement.

#MeToo, Burrowes said, is "a struggle that says we won't tolerate individual behavior, nor the wider system, that renders our bodies—and our very lives—disposable, violable and invisible."

CHAPTER 8

Migration/Immigration: A Case Study on the United States

READING 25

Theoretical Perspectives on Immigration

By Kebba Darboe

Why Do People Migrate?

Migration is the movement of people from one geographic location to another for various reasons, for example, in search of food, shelter, or freedom. Therefore, migration, of the three population processes (including fertility and mortality), is the most controversial. While migration is as old as humanity itself, theories about migration are fairly new. One of the early scholars on modern migration is Ravenstein, who in the 1880s based his "Laws of Migration" on empirical migration data (Tobler, 1995). In addition, international migration or immigration is a relatively recent phenomenon because "it was only in the early 20th century that the system of nation-states, passports, and visas developed to regulate the flow of people across borders," (Martin and Widgren, 2002, p. 3). An international migrant is defined by the United Nations as a person outside his or her country of citizenship for over a year or more, regardless of the reason for migration or the legal status of the person (Koser, 2010).

Three Major Waves of Immigration to the United States

Politics matters in migration theory because migration laws and policy directly influence migration flows, for instance, the right to cross a border legally (Green, 2002). The United States of America, despite being a nation of immigrants and descendants of immigrants, has periodically restricted immigration. The United States policy responses to immigration have varied from one period to another. First, 1) a laissez-faire policy was implemented from 1780 to 1875, followed by 2) a qualitative restrictions policy from 1875 to 1920. During this period the 1882 Chinese Exclusion Act was passed and suspended Chinese immigration until it was repealed in 1943. Next, 3) a quantitative restrictions policy was implemented in 1921. The Johnson-Reed Act was passed in 1924 and created a new national-origins quota system favoring immigrants from northern and western Europe. Then 4) the 1960s Civil Rights Movement struggles led to the passage of the 1965 amendments to the

Immigration and Nationality Act, which eliminated the race-based admission criteria and instituted ones that favor immigrants from Africa, Asia, Latin America, and skilled people (Brunner and Colarelli, 2010). Later, 5) President Reagan signed the Immigration Reform and Control Act of 1986, which granted amnesty to undocumented immigrants and instituted sanctions for employers who hire undocumented workers (Gimpel and Edwards, Jr., 1999); and 6) following the terrorist attacks of September 11, 2001, the United States Congress passed and President Bush signed on October 26, 2001 into law the Patriot Act (Uniting and Strengthening America by Providing Appropriate Tools Required to Intercept and Obstruct Terrorism Act of 2001), which gives the federal government broad powers to indefinitely detain suspected terrorists (USA Congressional Digest, 2003).

The attacks on September 11 intensified anti-immigration policy, and "on November 25, 2002, the Homeland Security Act of 2002 became law," which led to the creation of a new Department of Homeland Security (King III, 2009, p. 152). The Immigration and Nationalization Service merged with the new department, and its responsibility was divided between the United States Citizenship and Immigration Services (USCIS), which now oversees legal immigration and enforcement of laws preventing illegal entrance, and Immigration and Customs Enforcement (ICE), which holds responsibility for deporting undocumented immigrants. The aforementioned policy responses always informed immigration debate.

Immigrants entered the United States through two receiving ports: Ellis Island, New York, and Angel Island, California. Ellis Island received immigrants from eastern and southern Europe between 1892 and 1954 (Desforges and Maddern, 2004, p.437). Similarly, Angel Island received immigrants from the Pacific shores between 1910 and 1940 (Barde and Bobonis, 2006, p. 103). Today, international airports are the receiving ports, for example, New York, Chicago, Los Angeles, etc. Further, Portes and Rumbaut (2006) point out that, "immigration is a transformative force, producing profound and unanticipated social changes" (p. xv). The push-pull conceptual framework can be applied to all immigrants; for instance, the push factors for immigrants from Ireland were poverty and potato famine, and they were pulled to the United States because of economic opportunities and freedom.

According to McLemore, Romo, and Baker (2001) there were three immigration streams to the United States during the Agrarian and Industrial Revolution periods and each had different characteristics. The first immigration stream came in the early nineteenth century and included the Irish, Germans, Norwegians, and Swedes. From 1890 to 1924, the second immigration stream came from southern and eastern European countries, for example, Italy, Spain, Portugal, Greece, and Poland. Their languages and religion were further removed from the English as compared to the first stream of immigrants. From 1946 to present, the third immigrant stream or new immigration came mainly from Asia, Latin America, Africa, and refugees.

Demographic changes: The Browning and Beiging of America

To date, white Americans are the dominant majority. Since 1965, however, America has experienced a population increase due to the liberalization of immigration policy. As a consequence, the complexion of America is "browning" because a large number of immigrants are coming from Asia and Latin America. According to Pew Foundation projections, white Americans will not be a majority by 2055 (Chua, 2018, p. 167). Additionally, Asians are outnumbering Hispanics as the largest group of new immigrants. As a result, "browning" is being replaced by "beiging" (Chua, 2018, p.167).

This rapid demographic change is laced with cultural, economic, and political anxieties. For instance, according to the Public Religion Research Institute post-election survey, "52 percent of Trump voters said that they feel like the country has changed so much...feel like strangers in their own land," (Chua, 2018, p.170). In summary, Dr. Chua challenges us to cross the chasm between groups, not by denying our differences, but celebrating them. Ralph Ellison, in his book *Invisible Man*, states that "America is woven of many strands; I would recognize them and let it so remain ... . Our fate is to become one, and yet many—This is not prophecy, but description" (Ellison, p. 567–568, 1994).

Does International Migration Lead to Development or Underdevelopment?

This study answers the preceding question through two competing theoretical approaches. Neoclassical economic perspective contends that migration leads to development in both the sending and receiving countries. This theoretical approach is one dimensional because it views economic factors as the main cause of migration. Conversely, cumulative causation theory perspective contends that migration leads to underdevelopment and exploitation in the sending countries. The migration-development theories include neoclassical economic, new economics of migration, dual labor market theory, and network theory. On the other hand, migration-underdevelopment theories include institutional theory, world systems, and theory of cumulative causation. The migration-development and underdevelopment dynamics guide the theoretical explanations of immigration.

Theoretical Perspectives on Immigration

The theoretical perspectives through the push-pull conceptual framework explain the dynamics of migration-development and underdevelopment. Lee (1966) elaborates on the 19th century geographer Ravenstein's laws of migration and advances a new analytical framework for migration called "push-pull factors," (Stark, and Taylor. 1991). As shown in Figure 25.1, the push-pull and intervening factors conceptual framework guides theoretical explanations of international migration. What is the difference between emigration and immigration? Emigration means leaving one's country of origin; for example,

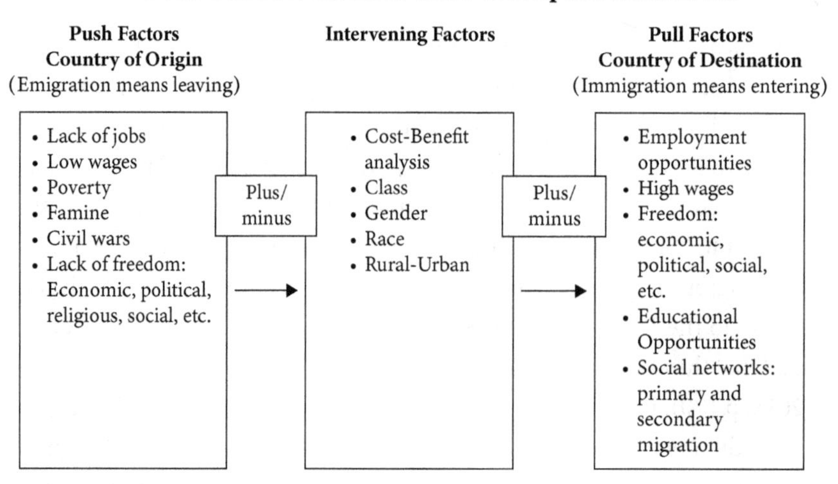

Figure 25.1 Push-Pull Factors: A Modified Conceptual Framework

Christopher emigrated from Gambia to the United States in 2001. Conversely, immigration means entering the country of destination; for example, Joseph and Angel immigrated to the United States in 2005.

Migration theories can be categorized according to their level of analysis; for example, micro-level theories focus on individual migration decisions. On the other hand, the macro-level theories focus on aggregate migration trends. However, the meso-level is in between the micro and macro level and focuses especially on the household or community level and can explain both causes and perpetuation of migration. Thomas Faist (2000), a sociologist, emphasizes the meso-level of migration and points out that social relations and social capital in households, neighborhoods, communities, and formal organizations help migrants in their migration decision-making and adaptation processes. On a meso level also, social capital, institutions, and networks can help or hinder migration.

The push-pull framework is a descriptive model listing different factors that affect positively or negatively (plus/minus) the migration decision-making process. Applying the logic of cost-benefit analysis, people decide to migrate, for instance, if the benefits are greater, such as employment opportunities, than the costs, like lack of jobs and low wages. Arguably, more non-white males from low socioeconomic status and developing economies migrate. However, today many new immigrants are well educated people and women. Through social networks both primary and secondary migration can happen. Primary refers to first place of destination; for example, Joseph immigrated to New York in 2005. After some time, Joseph relocated to Minnesota in 2006—secondary migration.

References

Barde, Robert, and Bobonis, G. J. 2006. "Detention at Angel Island." *Social Science History*, *30*(1), 103–136.

Brunner, Lawrence, and Colarelli, Stephen. M. 2010. "Immigration in the Twenty-First Century: A Personnel Selection Approach." *Independent Review*, *14*(3), 389–413.

Chua, Amy. 2018. *Political Tribes: Group Instinct and the Fate of Nations*. New York: Penguin Press.

Desforges, Luke. and Maddern, Joanne. 2004. "Front Doors to Freedom, Portal to the Past: History at the Ellis Island Immigration Museum, New York." *Social & Cultural Geography*, *5*(3), 437–457. doi:10.10SO/1464 9.160420002S28U.

Ellison, Ralph. 1994. *Invisible man* (Modern Library ed.). New York: Modern Library.

Faist, Thomas. 2000. "The Crucial Meso-Level." In T. Hammer, G. Brachman, K. Tamas and T. Faist, *International Migration, Immobility and Development*. Oxford: Berg Publishers.

Gimpel, James G. and James R. Edwards, Jr. 1999. *The Congressional Politics of Immigration Reform*. Boston: Allyn and Bacon

Green, Nicole W. 2002. *CQ's Vital Issues Series: Immigration, University of Michigan*. Washington, D.C.: Congressional Quarterly Inc.

King III, Charles B. 2009. "The Department of Homeland Security: An Organization in Transition." *Joint Force Quarterly*, *55*, 152–159.

Koser, Khalid. 2010. "Introduction: International Migration and Global Governance." *Global Governance*, *16*(3), 301–315.

Martin, Philip and Jonas Widgren. 2002. "International Migration: Facing the Challenge." *The Population Reference Bureau*, *57*(1), 1–43.

McLemore, S. Dale, Harriett D. Romo, and Susan Gonzalez Baker. 2001. *Racial and Ethnic Relations in America* (6th ed.). Boston: Allyn & Bacon

Portes, Alejandro, and Rubén G. Rumbaut. 2006. *Immigrant America: A Portrait*. 3rd edition. Los Angeles: University of California Press.

Stark, Oded, and J. Edward Taylor. 1991. "Migration Incentives, Migration Types: The Role of Relative Deprivation." The Economic Journal, 101(4), 1163–1178.

Tobler, Waldo. 1995. "Migration: Ravenstein, thornthwaite, and Beyond." *Urban Geography*, *16*(4), 327–343.

USA Patriot Act. 2003. *Congressional Digest*, *82*(4), 110.

READING 26

Key Findings About U.S. Immigrants

Pew Research Center, Washington, D.C.

By Gustavo López, Kristen Bialik and Jynnah Radford

The United States has more immigrants than any other country in the world. Today, more than 40 million people living in the U.S. were born in another country, accounting for about one-fifth of the world's migrants in 2016. The population of immigrants is also very diverse, with just about every country in the world represented among U.S. immigrants.

Pew Research Center regularly publishes statistical portraits of the nation's foreign-born population, which include historical trends since 1960. Based on these portraits, here are answers to some key questions about the U.S. immigrant population.

How many people in the U.S. are immigrants?

The U.S. foreign-born population reached a record 43.7 million in 2016. Since 1965, when U.S. immigration laws replaced a national quota system, the number of immigrants living in the U.S. has more than quadrupled. Immigrants today account for 13.5% of the U.S. population, nearly triple the share (4.7%) in 1970. However, today's immigrant share remains below the record 14.8% share in 1890, when 9.2 million immigrants lived in the U.S.

What is the legal status of immigrants in the U.S.?

Most immigrants (76%) are in the country legally, while a quarter are unauthorized, according to new Pew Research Center estimates based on census data adjusted for undercount. In 2016, 45% were naturalized U.S. citizens.

Some 27% of immigrants were permanent residents and 5% were temporary residents in 2016. Another 24% of all immigrants were unauthorized immigrants. From 1990 to 2007, the unauthorized immigrant population tripled in size—from 3.5 million to a record high of 12.2 million. During the

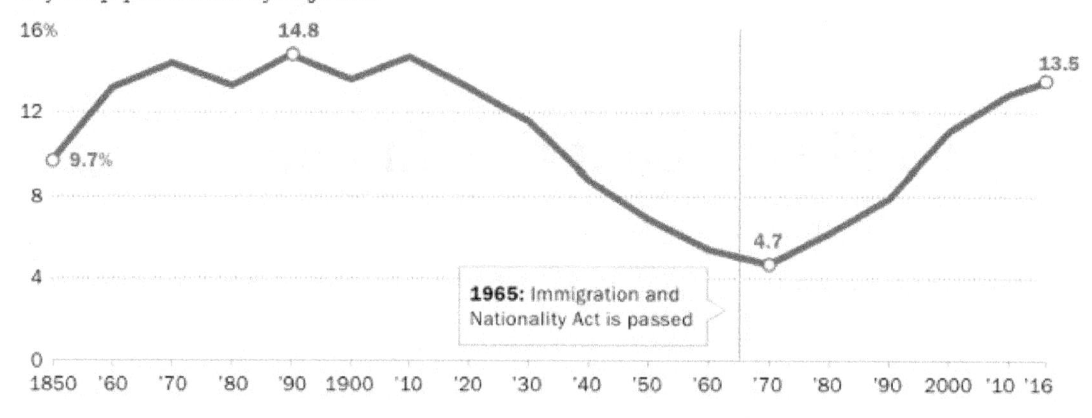

Immigrant share of U.S. population nears historic high

Source: U.S. Census Bureau, "Historical Census Statistics on the Foreign-Born Population of the United States: 1850–2000" end Pew Research Center tabulations of 2010 and 2016 American Community Survey IPUMS).
Pew Research Center

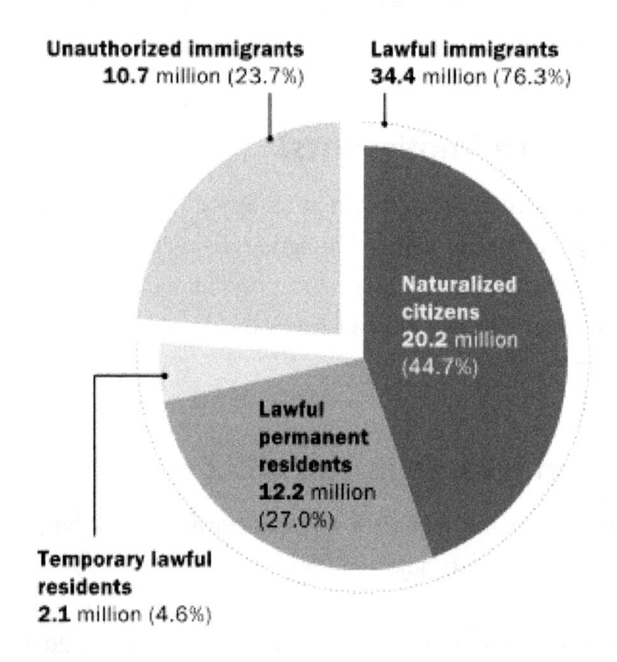

Unauthorized immigrants are a quarter of the U.S. foreign born population

Note: Figures for the total and subgroups differ from published U.S. Census Bureau totals because census data have been augmented and adjusted to account for undercount of the population. All numbers are rounded; see Methodology for rounding rules. Unauthorized immigrants include some with temporary protection from deportation under Deferred Action for Childhood Arrivals (DACA) and Temporary)' Protected Status (TPS).
Source: Pew Research Center estimates based on augmented U.S. Census Bureau data. See Methodology for details.
"U.S. Unauthorized Immigrant Total Dips to Lowest Level in a Decade"
Pew Research Center

Great Recession, the number declined by 1 million and since then has leveled off. In 2016, there were 10.7 million unauthorized immigrants in the U.S., accounting for 3.3% of the nation's population.

The decline in the unauthorized immigrant population is due largely to a fall in the number from Mexico –the single largest group of unauthorized immigrants in the U.S. Between 2007 and 2016, this group decreased by more than 1 million. Meanwhile, there was a rise in the number from Central America.

Do all lawful immigrants choose to become U.S. citizens?

Not all lawful permanent residents choose to pursue U.S. citizenship. Those who wish to do so may apply after meeting certain requirements, including having lived in the U.S. for five years. In fiscal year 2017, 986,851 immigrants applied for naturalization. The number of naturalization applications has climbed in recent years, though the annual totals remain below the 1.4 million applications filed in 2007.

Generally, most immigrants eligible for naturalization apply to become citizens. However, Mexican lawful immigrants have the lowest naturalization rate overall. Language and personal barriers, lack of interest and financial barriers are among the top reasons for choosing not to naturalize cited by Mexican-born green card holders, according to a 2015 Pew Research Center survey.

Where do immigrants come from?

Mexico is the top origin country of the U.S. immigrant population. In 2016, 11.6 million immigrants living in the U.S. were from there, accounting for 26% of all U.S. immigrants. The next largest origin groups were those from China (6%), India (6%), the Philippines (4%) and El Salvador (3%).

By region of birth, immigrants from South and East Asia combined accounted for 27% of all immigrants, a share equal to that of Mexico. Other regions make up smaller shares: Europe/Canada (13%), the Caribbean (10%), Central America (8%), South America (7%), the Middle East (4%) and sub-Saharan Africa (4%).

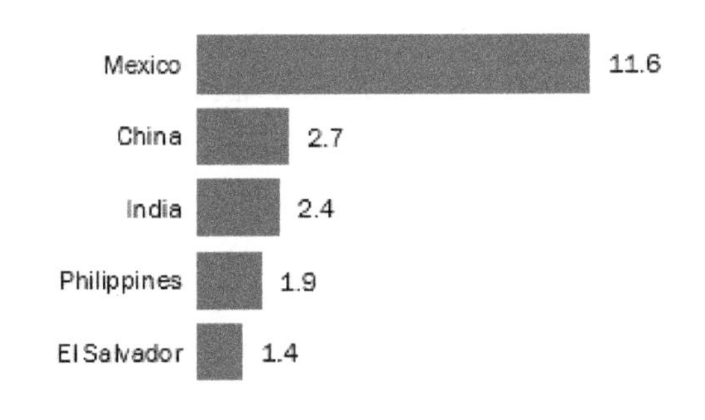

Mexico, China and India are top birthplaces for immigrants in the U.S.
Note: China includes Taiwan, Hong Kong.
Source: Pew Research Center tabulations of 2016 American Community Survey (1% IPUMS).
Pew Research Center

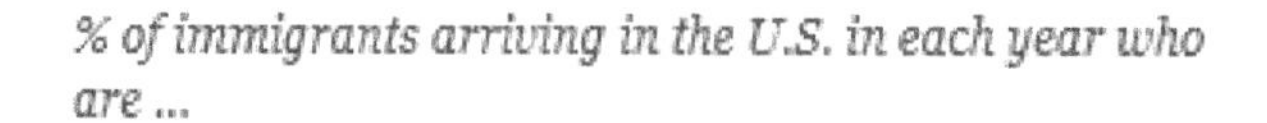

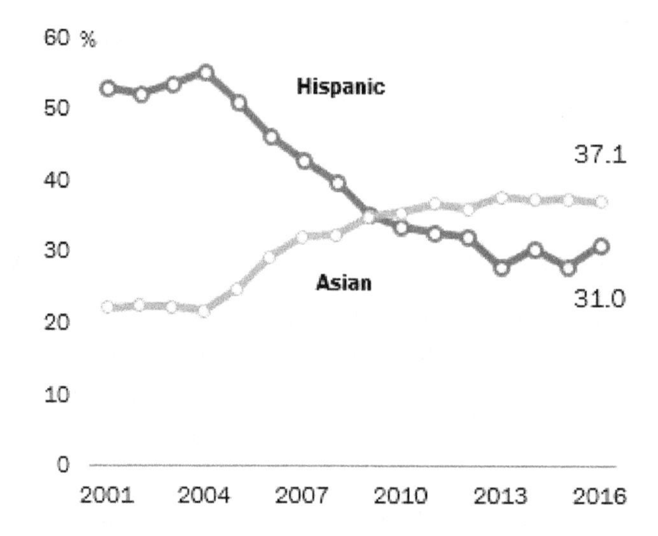

Among new immigrant arrivals, Asians outnumber Hispanics

Note: Figures for 2001 to 2005 are based on the household population and do not include arrivals residing in group quarters. 2016 figure represents only arrivals between Jan.1 and April 1, 2016. Figures reflect only immigrants who are residing in the U.S. as of April I, 2016. Race and ethnicity based on self-reports. Asians include only single-race non-Hispanics. Hispanics are of any race.
Source: Pew Research Center tabulations of 2001–2016 American Community Surveys (IPUMS).
Pew Research Center

Who is arriving today?

More than 1 million immigrants arrive in the U.S. each year. In 2016, the top country of origin for new immigrants coming into the U.S. was India, with 126,000 people, followed by Mexico (124,000), China (121,000) and Cuba (41,000).

By race and ethnicity, more Asian immigrants than Hispanic immigrants have arrived in the U.S. each year since 2010. Immigration from Latin America slowed following the Great Recession, particularly from Mexico, which has seen net decreases in U.S. immigration over the past few years.

Asians are projected to become the largest immigrant group in the U.S. by 2055, surpassing Hispanics. Pew Research Center estimates indicate that in 2065, Asians will make up some 38% of all immigrants; Hispanics, 31%; whites, 20%; and blacks, 9%.

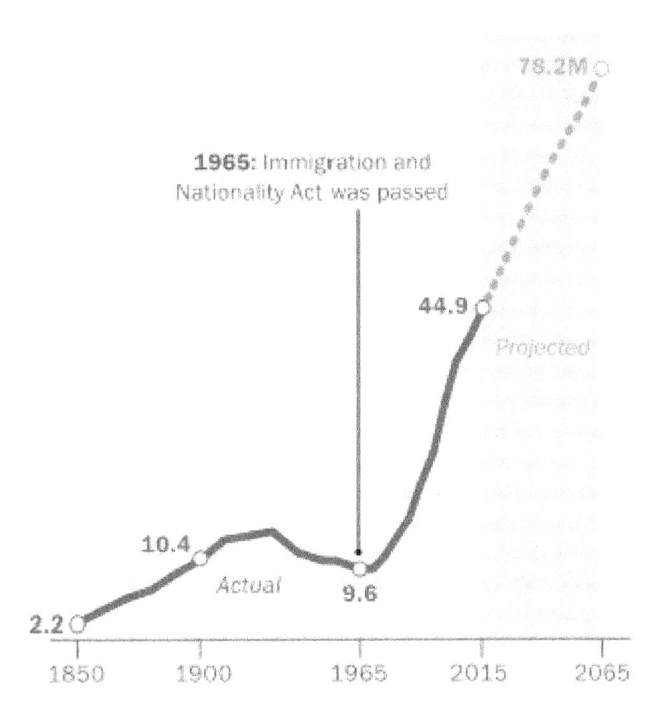

U.S. foreign-born population reached 45 million in 2015, projected to reach 78 million by 2065

Source: Gibson and Jung (2006) for 1850 to 1890. Edmonston and Passel (1994) estimates for 1900–1955; Pew Research Center estimates for 1960–2015 based on adjusted census data; Pew Research Center projections for 2015–2065.
Pew Research Center

Is the immigrant population growing?

New immigrant arrivals have fallen, mainly due to a decrease in the number of unauthorized immigrants coming to the U.S. The fall in the growth of the unauthorized immigrant population can partly be attributed to more Mexican immigrants leaving the U.S. than coming in.

Looking forward, immigrants and their descendants are projected to account for 88% U.S. population growth through 2065, assuming current immigration trends continue. In addition to new arrivals, U.S. births to immigrant parents will be important to future U.S. growth. In 2016, the percentage of women giving birth in the past year was higher among immigrants (7.4%) than among the U.S. born (5.9%). While U.S.-born women gave birth to over 3 million children that year, immigrant women gave birth to more than 750,000.

How many immigrants have come to the U.S. as refugees?

Since the creation of the federal Refugee Resettlement Program in 1980, about 3 million refugees have been resettled in the U.S.—more than any other country.

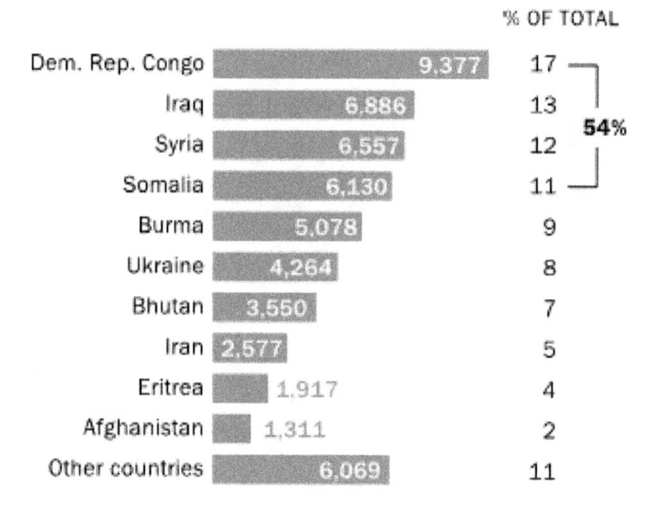

More than half of U.S. refugees in 2017 were from D.R. Congo, Iraq, Syria and Somalia

Note: Data do not include special immigrant visas and certain humanitarian parole entrants.
Source: U.S. State Department's Refugee Processing Center accessed Aug. 30, 2018.
Pew Research Center

In fiscal 2017, a total of 53,716 refugees were resettled in the U.S. The largest origin group of refugees was the Democratic Republic of the Congo, followed by Iraq, Syria, Somalia, and Burma (Myanmar). Among all refugees admitted in that fiscal year, 22,861 are Muslims (43%) and 25,194 are Christians (47%). California, Texas and New York resettled nearly a quarter of all refugees admitted in fiscal 2016. [...]

READING 27

DACA has Shielded Nearly 790,000 Young Unauthorized Immigrants from Deportation

By Jens Manuel Krogstad

Nearly 790,000 young unauthorized immigrants have received work permits and deportation relief through the federal government's Deferred Action for Childhood Arrivals program since it was created five years ago by President Barack Obama, according to the latest data released by U.S. Citizenship and Immigration Services.

The program, known as DACA, was created through an executive action Obama signed in August 2012.

It gives unauthorized immigrants who came to the U.S. before age 16—a group sometimes called "Dreamers"—a chance to stay in the U.S. to study or work, provided they meet certain conditions such as being enrolled in high school or having a high school degree or GED equivalent, and not having a serious criminal conviction. Those approved for the program are given a work permit and protection from deportation for two years, and these benefits can be renewed.

Number of DACA renewal applications accepted, in thousands

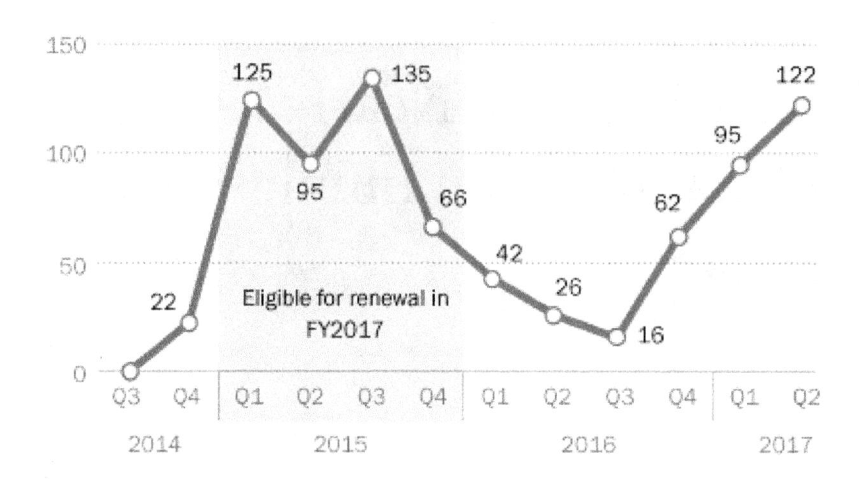

Many 'Dreamers' have extended deportation relief and work permits in fiscal 2017

Notes: Totals are applications approved for renewal of Deferred Action for Childhood Arrivals program benefits, which can be renewed every two years.
Source: U.S. Citizenship and Immigration Services.
Pew Research Center

Since 2012, about 800,000 such renewals have been issued. Requests for renewals have increased significantly each quarter since spring 2016—from about 16,000 in the third quarter of fiscal 2016 to about 122,000 in the second quarter of fiscal 2017—as an increasing number of program participants have become eligible to renew their benefits for another two years. Halfway through fiscal 2017, more than 200,000 unauthorized immigrants have renewed their benefits so far. (The latest government data include the first two quarters of fiscal year 2017, through March 31; the full fiscal year ends Sept. 30.) [...]

READING 28

Zero Tolerance for Illegal Immigration

An Urgent Policy Need

By Donald Mann

Summary Statement

NPG's primary concern with immigration, both legal and illegal, is that it is the driving force behind America's population growth. Our population grew by some 33 million in the decade of the 90s, and is on track to grow even more in this decade. The Census Bureau's current estimate is that U.S. population, now approaching 300 million, will reach 420 million by the middle of the century and still be growing rapidly. If present trends are allowed to continue, substantially more than two thirds of that environmentally devastating growth will be due to post-2000 immigrants and their descendants.

Our immigration policy should be an integral part of a national population policy aimed at reducing our U.S. population over time to a sustainable level of not more than 150 million and then stabilizing it there. To halt, and eventually reverse, our population growth we need to:

1. Halt illegal immigration, which increases the national population by 400,000 to 500,000 each year.
2. Reduce to near zero the present population of aliens living here unlawfully, estimated at 10–15 million.
3. Reduce legaland quasi-legal immigrationdrastically from the present 1.1 million each year to not more than 200,000—a level favored by public opinion. A 2003 poll for NPG found that 58 percent of respondents favored keeping yearly immigration at 300,000 or less with the majority of those favoring a limit of 100,000. (Curbs on legal immigration are examined in a separate NPG Forum Paper.)

Donald Mann, "Zero Tolerance For Illegal Immigration: An Urgent Policy Need (An NPG Internet Forum Paper)," pp. 1-12.

Ending the flow of illegal immigrants and reducing to near zero the pool of 10–15 million now settled here demands far tougher penalties for illegal entry and illegal presence and their consistent and timely application. Higher fines and, for persistent offenders, mandatory jail terms must be applied to illegal entry and presence, but also to a range of abuses and violations that support the process: document fraud; knowingly hiring or harboring illegals; abuse of asylum and open-ended temporary protection; automatic citizenship for U.S.-born children of illegal aliens; and delays and obstructions to deportation.

Sanctions on employers of unlawful aliens must be backed up by a secure computerized process for verifying job applicants' legal status. But verification should not be limited to the hiring process. Detection and deterrence of illegal aliens should be an ongoing process using checks of legal status for common everyday transactions in banking and finance, medical care, school and college enrollment, licensing, housing, and access to vital documents.

The cooperation of state and local governments, particularly the police, in removing illegal aliens should be required by law. Vigorous federal, state and local efforts in carrying out these measures will deter prospective illegals abroad and convince many of those already here to opt for "self-deportation." Local government "sanctuary policies" to shield violators should be penalized as harboring under federal law. Amnesties in whatever form must be discarded as an option in immigration management.

Bringing illegal entry and presence down to zero will serve other interests: curbing crime and terrorism; raising labor standards and job opportunities for citizens; easing crowding in low income housing and schools; and reducing social service costs. But its overriding importance remains in reducing the population growth that is now degrading America's environment and progressing toward a smaller and more sustainable population.

Section One

Most Americans Favor Tougher Action

What measures are needed to halt illegal immigration and compel settled illegal aliens to leave the U.S.? Clearly, our present policy, to the extent it is applied at all, is not working. Formal deportations number only about 160,000 a year, most of whom are criminals or terrorists. An estimated 500,000 aliens who have received deportation orders are running loose in the U.S. Many of those actually deported return to the U.S., a felony which U.S. attorneys lack time or willingness to prosecute. About 1.3 million are caught each year by ICE (Immigration and Customs Enforcement) at or near the border, and until recently either released on their own recognizance if non-Mexican, or given voluntary departure back to Mexico with no penalties.

The sanctions enacted against willful employers of illegal aliens have all but been abandoned by our Federal government. A patchwork of ongoing partial amnesty programs and other loopholes legalizes some 180,000 illegal aliens a year.

A 2005 Government Accountability Office (GAO) report found that ICE man-hours spent on worksite enforcement fell from an already inadequate 240 in 1999 to just 90 in 2003. Other enforcement indicators such as arrests of persistent violators, employer fine notices, and worksite arrests declined even more steeply. While Washington blamed changed priorities after 9/11, the cutbacks started almost two years before 9/11 when the economic boom of the late 1990s sparked employer complaints of labor shortages.

Without consistent detection and tough penalties for illegal employment and illegal presence, it will remain next to impossible for the border patrol to halt the influx of millions of illegal aliens. One of the reasons for this futility is obvious. There is now no effective penalty for crossing our borders illegally. In 99 percent of the cases a Mexican illegal alien now apprehended at our border is simply recorded, fingerprinted, checked for criminal history and prior attempted entry, and then transported back across the border to Mexico. Once across, he or she is free to try again. Many do, often the same night.

Eventually, those who persist do succeed. That is why there are two to three million illegal border crossings each year, with over 500,000 new illegal aliens who settle each year. The entire system, if it were not tragic, would be almost comical. It is a very elaborate, expensive game known to the Border Patrol as "catch and release." Illegal aliens have no trouble calculating that the benefits of succeeding outweigh the risks of capture.

Washington's leniency and indifference deeply trouble more and more Americans. A national poll commissioned by NPG and carried out in March 2003 by Roper ASW found that more than 60 percent of Americans agree that:

- Congress should set a goal of halting completely the annual settlement of new illegal entrants, currently estimated at 500,000 to 600,000.
- Congress should set a goal of reducing the estimated 10 million to 15 million resident illegal immigrants to near zero.
- Congress should make penalties for illegal presence here so severe that no illegal immigrants would come here or remain here. Our legislators should enact such tough measures as mandatory fines and prison terms for anyone found to be here illegally, or attempting to enter illegally, followed by deportation and a permanent ban on return.

The entire Roper poll can be found at: www.npg.org.

Rising Congressional Support for Reform

Nothing less than the above goals and implementation measures must be at the core of a national policy of zero tolerance for illegal immigration. Moved by public opinion, Congress itself and a rising number of state legislatures have seriously considered a number of bills to deter illegal immigration.

In December 2005, the House of Representatives passed HR 4437, the *Border Protection, Anti-Terrorism and Illegal Immigration Control Act*, which authorizes the toughest countermeasures for illegal immigration in modern memory. Among its key measures, HR 4437, which faces serious opposition in the Senate:

- Makes illegal presence in the U.S. a felony, raising the maximum prison term from six months to one year or more. Ends the practice of "catch and release" with a citation of illegal aliens.
- Mandates 700 additional miles of high-tech border barriers.
- Empowers and further assists and trains state and local police to enforce immigration laws; denies federal assistance funds for handling illegal immigrants to those state and local governments that bar employees from cooperation with USCIS (U.S. Customs and Immigration Service).
- Extends the definition of "harboring" illegal aliens to cover some services provided by private charitable and social service agencies.
- Raises civil or criminal penalties on a wide range of immigration fraud and abuse—such as alien smuggling, document fraud, marriage fraud, establishment of shell companies, failure to depart as ordered and persistent hiring of illegals.
- Ends many of the loopholes, frivolous appeals, extra layers of judicial review and other delays to prompt deportation. Sets minimum sentences for those reentering the U.S. after deportation and for the smugglers who bring them.
- Phases in a mandatory federal computerized system linked to employers by phone, online, or point of sale devices using USCIS and Social Security data to verify work eligibility of prospective new hires. Requires reverification of longstanding employees.
- Terminates 50,000 admissions "Diversity Visa Program," a fraud plagued program that encourages legal immigration from countries sending relatively few immigrants.
- Does not endorse any temporary guest worker plan or amnesty.

The *Border Protection Act* however, rejected or deferred action on several other important deterrent measures pushed by immigration reform leaders in the House. Among promising measures that appeared in other rejected bills, principally the *True Enforcement and Border Security Act—HR 4313),* but not enacted were:

- Denial of automatic citizenship to children born in the U.S. to illegal alien parents.
- Specific criminal sanctions on employers repeatedly hiring illegals.

- Increase in resources, application to all countries, and faster implementation of "US Visit" program, which will document and help track visiting aliens in the U.S. from entry to departure. (The program now excludes Mexican and Canadian entrants.)
- Complete fencing of the Mexican border from the Pacific to the Gulf of Mexico; 6,000 additional border patrol agents, and 11,000 more worksite and fraud investigators.
- Annual registration of all resident aliens and quarterly registration of temporary foreign visitors.
- Denial of in-state college tuition and other state and local benefits to unlawful aliens.
- Restrictions on acceptance of foreign-issued identification and IRS taxpayer ID numbers.
- Expansion of the existing option of "expedited deportation" (now limited to apprehensions of recently-entered illegals in the border area) to cover illegal aliens apprehended anywhere within-five years of arrival.
- Building or leasing of detention space for 200,000 apprehended aliens.

Getting to Zero Illegal Entries: Raising the Penalties

NPG finds all these measures a hopeful sign of a changing outlook in Washington, though some don't go far enough and other needed measures are absent. Mindful of the growing evidence of strong citizen and legislative support, this position paper outlines some specific recommendations to advance the goals of zero tolerance for illegal immigration. These goals are realistic and attainable, but strict and sustained enforcement over time is vital. Even without new legislation, the regular and consistent application of existing penalties and sanctions could make a major difference. The intent of tough penalties is not to harass or persecute illegal aliens, but to deter them.

Federal law (8USC1325) already makes "entry without inspection" a misdemeanor allowing for up to six months imprisonment and a fine, and an optional administratively imposed fine of $250. Few federal laws have been less frequently enforced. Between 2000 and 2003 only about 13 thousand persons were convicted each year for illegal entry, out of more than a million apprehended each year. Current federal law makes it a felony for an illegal alien to return after deportation, punishable by up to two years imprisonment and a fine. But overloaded U.S. Attorneys have produced only about 4,500 convictions a year in the same period.[1]

First Time Offenders

For all persons who are here illegally and are apprehended for the first time (regardless of whether they are visa overstayers or illegal border crossers, and regardless of the length of time they have been here illegally), there should be a stiff fine and deportation.

While many illegal border crossers may carry few funds, those who have been settled here often have substantial assets. Fines should be levied in any event on those claiming indigence, since the unpaid obligation can become the basis for additional charges, property liens, or garnishment in case of a subsequent apprehension. First time violators should lose the privilege of ever returning here, and be warned that a second illegal entry will subject them to a mandatory one year prison term and larger fines. Visa overstayers should be deemed to be here illegally if they are apprehended over 30 days after their visa has expired.

Section Two

Requiring Verification of Legal Status for Other Transactions

We need a comprehensive Federal program that would make it virtually impossible for an illegal immigrant to remain here undetected. The heart of the program would be to require government authorities or private sector officials to confirm legal status whenever anyone:

- Attempts to open a bank account, purchase bank instruments or securities, or transfer money abroad.
- Applies for a driver's or pilot's license, or any other commercial or occupational license.
- Seeks to enroll in school or college for oneself or one's children.
- Seeks medical care at a hospital.

  (Emergency care would be provided)
- Applies for a marriage license, birth certificate or other vital document.
- Applies for a social security number. (now required)
- Applies for a job. (already required, though verification is inadequate)
- Attempts to buy, sell or rent real estate.
- Applies for a credit card or any other form of credit.
- Seeks to purchase, rent or register a vehicle, aircraft, firearm, explosives, or controlled hazardous materials.

There are precedents for such screening, and databases exist to make it work. A prototype is USCIS's Systematic Alien Verification for Entitlements (SAVE) in use since 1987 to verify the legal status of persons seeking certain federally controlled state and local benefits. A variety of state and local agencies that need to confirm legal status have voluntarily signed on to SAVE, such as the California DMV, City of New York Human Resources Administration, the Palm Beach County Property Appraiser, and the Michigan Tribal Gaming Commission.[2]

Verification of legal status would, for the time being, continue to be by a telephone or online check to a central database maintained by the U.S. government. Until biometric ID documents are adopted, screening should not depend exclusively on any document presented by the applicant. (U.S. passports and some biometric state drivers licenses, for example, would be an exception.) Local law enforcement authorities should be alerted immediately if an illegal alien applicant is detected.

The Role of State and Local Governments

It would be impossible to effectively enforce tougher penalties and more frequent screening without committed cooperation from local and state law enforcement. While there are only approximately 2,000 Interior Enforcement immigration agents to police the entire country, there are approximately 600,000 local and state law enforcement agents. Federal law now provides for training and assistance to state and local law enforcement agencies that volunteer. State and local agencies need full authority to enforce immigration law and their participation should be mandatory.

Public opinion would be behind it. The increasingly apparent link between illegal immigration, crime and drugs has made state and local governments more receptive to a role in immigration. NPG's Roper ASW poll found that 88% of respondents favored Congress requiring state and local governments to apprehend and turn over to ICE illegal immigrants they encounter. A number of states have accepted the option provided in 1996 legislation for federal training and assistance to state and local police on immigration enforcement. HR 4733, passed in December 2005, fully empowers state and local police to enforce immigration laws.

With such laws and procedures consistently and strictly applied, the country would no longer need to debate whether, for example, illegal aliens should be issued a driver's license, or receive favorable tuition rates at colleges. The obvious answer to both questions is that illegal aliens should not remain here at all.

Would the Numbers be Too Great to Control?

Proponents of mass immigration and even some high government officials argue that we must simply accept the fact that nothing can be done to eliminate, or even seriously reduce the number of resident illegal aliens. They claim it to be impossible for the government to round up and deport 10 to 15 million people. Often they put this in terms of the most unappealing and impractical option, a "mass roundup." Another common objection to proposed prison terms, fines and forfeitures is the argument that it would swamp our Federal courts and prisons.

This need not be so. If the penalties and detection processes are sustained and evenly applied, there would be major changes in the illegal aliens' perceptions, leading to their extensive self-deportation over time. The near certainty of detection, apprehension, jail terms and fines would attach a prohibitively high price to violations. Federal court overload in the interim could be avoided by much broader use of "expedited deportation" (i.e., without hearings), and by continuing to treat first-time illegal entry as a misdemeanor with a penalty of a fine and not more than one-year jail time. Misdemeanors can usually be disposed of in one day by federal courts.[3]

There are precedents for believing that large-scale self-deportation is feasible and realistic.

The best example of tough enforcement—changing behavior, of course, is the mass removals of 1954. Then, the apprehensions by INS of some one million illegal aliens over a few months in a determined sweep produced tens of thousands of self-deportations and suppressed illegal immigration for a decade thereafter.

In the summer of 1988, there was a great deal of unrest in Central America, and over 1,000 illegal aliens crossed the Texas border near Brownsville and Harlingen daily. At the outset, for foreign policy reasons, they were released on their own recognizance to apply for asylum. But in a policy switch, then Attorney General Meese ordered that the intercepted aliens denied immediate asylum be held in detention or otherwise prevented from leaving south Texas.[4] Soon the stream of illegals dropped from over 1,000 a day to almost none.

More recently, in December 2005 the flow of Brazilian and some other non-Mexican illegal aliens through Mexico dropped sharply once ICE began detaining and removing them under its "expedited deportation" authority. Full success of this policy will require adequate detention space for sizeable numbers of illegal aliens.[5]

In a November 2003 paper the Center for Immigration Studies, a Washington research organization, took note of the government's 9/11 "Special Registration" program for visitors from Islamic countries. The Muslim nation with the most illegal aliens present was Pakistan with an estimated 26,000. Once it became clear that Homeland Security was serious about enforcing the law on Middle Easterners, Pakistani illegal aliens "self-deported" in droves to Pakistan, Canada, and Europe. The Pakistani embassy estimated that more than 15,000 of its nationals had left the country.

The mass exodus by Pakistani illegals occurred because of the likelihood of detection and without an explicit threat of jail time. With credible high prospects of detection followed by heavy fine and/or prison for illegal presence, we are convinced that a substantial portion of the millions of illegal aliens now living here would, within months, leave the country on their own.

Section Three

Improving Existing Deterrents and Disincentives

Employer Sanctions

The 1986 Immigration Reform and Control Act (IRCA) enacted civil sanctions against employers who knowingly hired illegal aliens. The legislation was, however, fatally flawed. Contrary to common sense, it made employers responsible for verifying the authenticity of the applicants' documentary proof of legal residence. Employers were given an impossible task: to judge the validity of any one of a possible 19 different documents. At the same time IRCA perversely threatened the law-abiding and conscientious employer with sanctions for examining applicants too zealously.

The result was to be expected. Sanctions have not worked, and are now rarely imposed. Many employers preferred hiring low wage illegal aliens and simply accepted whatever documents were offered. Others shifted the responsibility for hiring to scofflaw labor contractors. Still others feared being sued if they turned down an applicant. One study showed that as many as one third of applicants hired in California in recent years were illegal aliens. In part as a result of the failure of sanctions, there are now more than seven million illegal aliens in the U.S. work force.

If properly organized and administered, employer sanctions can prevent illegal aliens from working at all in the formal economy. Government leaders, law enforcement and technical experts have long known that two essential features for effective verification have been missing.

The first is that determination of document validity can not be left to employers. Before hiring, employers should be required to verify applicants' status by a call-in or electronic check against a federally managed database. If the applicant is found to be here illegally, the federal verification site should be required to notify the local ICE or local law enforcement to examine and, if necessary, apprehend him.

The second essential feature would be a system of heavy fines for any employer who failed to carry out a telephone verification check with the national database before hiring a job applicant, or who hired an ineligible applicant. Fines are now authorized but rarely imposed and even more rarely collected. Criminal penalties would be mandatory for those employers who repeatedly failed to comply.

Some states are considering legislation to further penalize errant employers through such laws as 1) denying the deductibility of wages paid to illegals as a business cost for tax purposes; and 2) making offending employers ineligible for government contracts, tax breaks and other state benefits. Similar measures deserve consideration by Washington.

According to NPG's 2003 Roper poll, cracking down on employers would have the support of a solid majority of Americans. That poll found that 79 percent or more of respondents favored these measures: requiring employers to check all job applicants' status with a central federal database; full enforcement of existing fines for knowingly hiring illegal aliens; and criminal sanctions against persistent violators. A January 2006 poll by Polling Point about penalties for hiring illegal aliens found that 55.8 percent of respondents favored both large fines and jail sentences. Another 25.7 percent favored large fines only.[6]

Some opponents of employer sanctions have argued instead for stricter federal and state enforcement of workplace, wage and hour, social security, and safety laws. This supposedly will deprive employers of the inherent advantage of hiring illegals. Sadly, labor laws suffer from the same chronic under-enforcement and interest group manipulation, as do immigration laws. In addition, Labor Department investigators fear reduced workplace cooperation if they report illegal workers. NPG welcomes an increase in the resources and intensity of worksite labor enforcement, though this alone cannot rid us of illegal immigration.

One of the serious threats to eliminating illegal aliens from jobs is the massive spread of the informal economy in major immigrant gateway cities, particularly New York, Los Angeles and Miami. A recent study of the Los Angeles County workforce found over 650,000 people, two thirds of them illegal, working in the informal economy, and costing all levels of government $2 billion in lost taxes.

Uprooting underground jobs will require a sustained, coordinated crackdown by Federal, state and local labor, safety, tax, health and immigration authorities. The system of additional non-worksite immigration status checks discussed earlier in Section Two could be a winning weapon against the underground economy. Another asset is the willingness of millions of American workers and their unions to report illegal immigrants and their workplaces to the authorities. ICE and its predecessor have tended to brush off or shelve such tips. Any reformed system must allow for tips from the public, which resents violations that undermine their wages and labor standards.

An End to Amnesties

Limited and general amnesties going back to 1962 have rewarded millions of illegal aliens for breaking our laws, and have encouraged millions more to come here illegally in the hope of a future amnesty. They have generally been corrupted by massive fraud.

As part of IRCA in 1986 some three million illegal aliens were amnestied. The proponents of that amnesty argued that it would curb the flow of influx of illegal aliens. That did not happen. Instead Congress in 1994 enacted the 245 (i) program that grants legal residence to illegals petitioned for by family or employers in the U.S. on payment of $1000. Nearly 1.2 million more illegals have been amnestied under 245 (i).[7] In spite of the relabeling of immigrants through amnesties, the number of illegal aliens has tripled since 1990. Any amnesty only invites fraud and creates the expectation of future amnesties.

Worst of all, any given amnesty is just the first step that results in a great increase in the size of our resident U.S. population, and for that reason alone should never even be considered. Once an amnestied immigrant achieves permanent resident status, or subsequently becomes an American citizen, he or she is able to bring here legally a seemingly endless chain of relatives and relatives of relatives. This endless process, family" chain migration" has enormous population implications and must be phased out.

A 2002 NPG study showed that, incredibly, 30 to 50 million more foreigners could become candidates for immigration (in the next 15 years alone!) through family ties (i.e. chain migration) if five to six million aliens are amnestied. The complete study, *Amnesty: Overpopulation by Fiat,* is at www.npg.org. We will address the problem of chain migration in a forthcoming NPG Position Paper on Legal and Quasi-Legal Immigration.

Document Fraud's Many Victims

Massive and chronic document fraud enables many violations of immigration and nationality law, as well as identity theft and a wide range of other serious offenses. While Congress has increased the penalties for document fraud to cope with rising foreign crime and terrorism, prosecutions in the immigration field still lag. Annual convictions for immigration-related fraud, forgery and misuse of ID documents have fallen by two-thirds since 1997. There must be more prosecutions and tougher penalties. Admissions of immigrants and provision of benefits should be revoked if a court finds that they were parties to fraud in obtaining them.

A fraud-resistant secure national identification system is essential if we are to minimize fraud while successfully regulating immigration and combating terrorism. See the NPG Forum paper on *Secure Identification: The Weak Link in Immigration Control* at **www.npg.org**.

Automatic Citizenship

Because of a questionable interpretation of the 14th Amendment to the Constitution, the U.S. currently grants automatic citizenship to children born on its territory, even if the mother is a temporary visitor, or an illegal alien. According to the Center for Immigration Studies, 383,000 children were born in the U.S. in 2002 to illegal alien mothers, an astonishing 10% of all births in the U.S. in that year. The parents of such children are rarely deported.

We believe that the law should be applied so that any child born here, to qualify for U.S. citizenship, must have at least one parent who is a U.S. citizen or legal permanent resident. A number of legal scholars believe that automatic citizenship could be restricted by clarifying legislation. We share that view and support legislation introduced so far to that effect. But if the courts find a constitutional amendment is essential, we would support such an amendment.

Our goal should be to reduce births in this country to illegal alien mothers to near zero, by discouraging their presence here. Illegal aliens who give birth here should be subject to the same penalties as all other illegal aliens—a heavy fine for first time offenders followed by deportation and forfeiture of the right to ever return here, and, for repeat offenders, a mandatory one year term in a federal prison or detention center. Maternal responsibilities to minor children should not be a bar to prison sentences any more than it is in the case of citizens and legal residents who are sentenced to prison.

Given the urgency of ending the population growth that is endangering our environment and resources, we simply cannot continue to allow our population to be increased by some half a million a year, due to births to illegal aliens or "demographic tourists." Because of these births, the actual number added to our population each year may even be considerably more since the U.S. citizen child shields the illegal parents from deportation and enables their ultimate legal settlement here, eventually forming a new starting link in a family immigration chain.

Sanctuary Cities: A Shelter for Criminals and Terrorists

Creating a sanctuary for illegal aliens, as many cities have done, is incompatible with the intent of federal immigration law. In her excellent book, *Invasion*, Michelle Malkin writes, "... sanctuary cities across the country continue to declare themselves safe refuges where local government officials must strive to protect the anonymity of illegal aliens, thwarting ICE and local police measures against foreign threats and crime."

Sanctuary cities such as Los Angeles, New York and San Francisco arguably violate federal laws against harboring illegal aliens. Those city councils and/or mayors responsible for maintaining sanctuaries should be held responsible. Tougher and more explicit anti-harboring laws are essential along with greater access in the courts for law suits against sanctuary cities by crime victims.

Asylum: A Magnet for Opportunists

In recent years, U.S. courts and Congress have greatly expanded aliens' rights to political asylum because of alleged persecution abroad. The hope of winning asylum or its legal equivalent, cancellation of removal, is a magnet to prospective illegal immigrants, who see it as a win-win situation. Their claim to asylum might be approved. About one in five are. Of if not, they can abscond. The system of frequent checks of immigration status for day to day transactions outlined in Section Two would ferret out failed asylum seekers. But access to the asylum system for frivolous claimants should also be more tightly restricted to end its magnet effect. (See *Humanitarian Immigration: Third World "Persecution" Swamps the West at* www.npg.org.*)*

Section Four

Why Halting Illegal Immigration is Crucial

Our primary concern with immigration, both legal and illegal, is that it adds weightily to population growth in our crowded country. Our present population of 298 million is already far beyond the long term carrying capacity of our resources and environment. We need to halt, and eventually reverse our population growth so that, after an interim period of population decline, we can stabilize our population at a lower, sustainable level.

Besides its impact on our population size, there are a number of other compelling reasons for halting illegal immigration. First, the violation of our laws by millions of illegal aliens breeds contempt for all laws and nourishes a culture of fraud and deceit. Illegal aliens depress wages of American citizens and legal immigrants, and add to their unemployment. Their access to social services combined with their low tax payments burden our taxpayers. The claim is often made that they do jobs that Americans will not do, but there are no jobs that Americans will not do with proper work conditions and wages. Their presence here invites abuse by unscrupulous employers, and results in the creation of thousands of sweatshops and a pernicious underground economy.

Homeland Security

The annual flow of illegal aliens across our borders and the presence of many millions who live here clandestinely is an open invitation to terrorists to establish themselves in our country and attack us. If there were no other reasons to end illegal immigration, homeland security alone would be sufficient. It is outrageous that over four years after 9/11, our Federal government has done so little to halt illegal immigration and secure our borders.

The "Push Factors," A Nearly Irresistible Force

Principally because of the disparity between our standard of living and that of most third world countries, hundreds of millions of people are determined to come here, whether legally or illegally. Most third world people live in abject poverty, and we sympathize with their plight. World population is growing by some 77 million a year, and almost all of that growth occurs in the developing countries, the countries that send us almost all illegal immigrants. We cannot possibly allow more than a tiny fraction of those millions to come here each year without degrading our quality of life and environment.

Clearly, to believe that the problems of underdeveloped countries can be solved by emigration is delusional. Nothing can permanently and significantly improve living conditions in those countries unless they halt and eventually reverse their population growth, the root cause of their economic and environmental poverty. We should do everything in our power to help those impoverished nations that are determined to halt, and eventually to reverse, their population growth.

If that is ever to happen, it will take decades and perhaps centuries. Because of the tremendous momentum of past population growth in the third world, and the resulting disproportionate numbers of young people, just slowing growth is a gargantuan task. Despite official optimism, an eventual halt to population growth in third world countries may well occur because of increased mortality rather than reduced fertility.

In the meantime, we need not feel apologetic for giving top priority to our own national interest, by halting illegal immigration completely and drastically reducing legal immigration. The U.S. has a long history of generous immigration policies. Our first and primary responsibility now must be to provide for the welfare of present and future generations of Americans, many of them descendants of earlier immigrants, and alleviate environmental pressures in the U.S., such as global warming, that are threatening the whole world.

As world population continues to grow and, and as that growth continues to degrade economic and environmental conditions in many third world countries, the push factors abroad will inevitably increase in force and intensity.

U.S.-bound migration verges on becoming a tidal wave of irresistible force. An irresistible force can only be stopped by an immovable object—and that can only be our own nation's unshakable resolve to stop illegal immigration and reduce to near zero the illegal population now here.

Statement of Purpose

Human population growth in the past century was three times the total growth from the origin of the species until 1900.

Coupled with sharply rising levels of resource consumption and economic activity in the more prosperous nations, that growth has imposed unprecedented strains on the ecological systems that support us and other living things. It has led in many parts of the world to rising unemployment, intensifying water shortages, increasing competition for resources, and the specter of hunger. It is affecting the world's climate, and the consequences—rising sea levels, more powerful hurricanes, heat waves, and more intense floods and droughts—are becoming apparent. Population growth has depended on fossil fuels, which are running down. Future generations must depend increasingly on renewable energy, which is unlikely to be recoverable in amounts sufficient to support more than a fraction of current world populations.

U.S. population has also quadrupled since 1900. The U.S. and the world are in a condition of overshoot.

NPG (Negative Population Growth) is the ideal of a turnaround in U.S. and world population growth until we approach less destructive and more tolerable levels, perhaps at numbers that were passed two or more generations ago.

Our objectives are to

- document the harm humans are inflicting on ourselves and our support systems and arrive at some rough idea of "optimum population"—the human numbers that can live at a decent standard of living within the constraints of environmental sustainability,
- suggest the policies on migration and human fertility that would make it possible to come down to such numbers,
- persuade our government at all levels, and other governments afflicted by population growth, to pursue such policies, and
- dissuade them from the pursuit of policies and behavior that, intentionally or not, lead to population growth.

To those ends, we promote concepts such as "the two-child family", lowered rates of migration to the United States, and the development of conceptual systems such as the steady state economy. And we comment on the demographic implications of present and proposed policies and legislation.

NPG, Inc. is unique among national organizations in calling for a turnaround in population growth and describing the means to achieve it.

About NPG

Negative Population Growth (NPG) is a national nonprofit membership organization with over 30,000 members nationwide. It was founded in 1972 to educate the American public and our political leaders about the devastating effects of overpopulation on our environment, resources, and standard of living. We believe that our nation is already vastly overpopulated in terms of the long-range carrying capacity of its resources and environment.

NPG advocates gradually halting and then reversing our U.S. population growth so that, after an interim period of population reduction, our population can be stabilized at a level that would be sustainable indefinitely, and afford an adequate standard of living for all, in a healthy environment. We believe that in order to be sustainable indefinitely our population should not exceed 150 million, its size two generations ago. We are convinced that goal could be reached within several generations by non-coercive tax incentives to encourage parents to have not more than two children, coupled with a substantial reduction in immigration.

Notes

1. U.S. Customs and Immigration Service. Immigration Statistics. Convictions for Immigration Violations, 1993–2004, table 50
2. Save Program at http://uscis.gov/graphic/services/SAVE.htm
3. Border Security Bill Could Overwhelm Valley Courts. Brownsville, TX, *Herald. January 15, 2006.*
4. Vernon Briggs, Immigration and the National Interest (3rd edition). M.E. Sharpe: Armonk, NY, 2003. p. 160
5. U.S. Jail Program Slows Illegal Immigration. Reuters, January 14, 2006
6. See *www.pollingpoint.com/r esults_121405.html*
7. Briggs: Mass Immigration and the National Interest (3rd edition). p. 265

CHAPTER 9

Challenges of Multiculturalism VS. Pluralism

READING 29

Introduction

Assimilation

By Kebba Darboe

Assimilation is defined as the process of inclusion through which newcomers become full members of another group or society (Gordon, 1964). This is epitomized in the American motto E Pluribus Unum: "Out of many, one" (Putnam, 2007). However, throughout most of American history, mainstream society attempted to blend or assimilate its many ethnic groups, expecting the "melting pot" to provide strength, vitality, and unity, and yet it separated and disenfranchised those it deemed unworthy. Not until the 1970s was this ideology first challenged (Glazer and Moynihan, 1970). Americans then began to realize that the many ethnic and racial groups had not all blended, either culturally or racially. The strength and vitality of America now appears to lie in its diversity of cultures because more and more people recognize that acknowledging their ethnic and cultural roots is a strength and pride, not weakness.

The appeal of pluralism as the preferred route to Americanization has been enhanced by the immigration that is increasing the racial and ethnic diversity of the population. But there is fear on the part of whites that pluralism may slide into separatism, resulting in more racism and nativism. In this historical context the debate between the two competing ideologies of assimilation to Anglo-conformity and cultural pluralism has shaped the multiculturalism and pluralism dynamics (Gordon, 1964). Anglo-conformity ideology is predicated on the complete assimilation of the minority group into Anglo patterns of culture and language. By contrast, cultural pluralists like Kallen (1956) contend that members of every American ethnic group should be free to participate in all of the society's major institutions while simultaneously retaining their own ethnic heritage.

The "melting pot" metaphor was first articulated by the eighteenth-century French immigrant to America, Hector St. John De Crèvecoeur, but popularized in Israel Zangwill's 1908 play *The Melting Pot*. Zangwill called America "God's crucible, the great melting pot where all the faces of Europe are melting and reforming." Horace Kallen (1914), a Jewish philosopher, articulated the cultural pluralism "salad bowl" as the new American reality. This new metaphor of the "salad bowl" was popularized in the 1970s, replacing the melting pot.

Cultural Pluralism VS. Multiculturalism Dynamics

Americanization

- Americanization constituted a nativist movement dedicated to erasing the original cultures, and especially the languages, of the 27 million new immigrants (that is, the Italians and Eastern Europeans) who entered the United States from 1880 to 1920.
- Theodore Roosevelt declared, "We have room for but one language here... . We intend to see that the crucible turns our people out as Americans and not as dwellers in a polyglot boardinghouse" (Portes & Rumbaut, 1996, p. 196).

Melting Pot

- "Melting pot" is a metaphor for a heterogeneous society becoming more homogeneous—a common culture.
- The "melting pot" metaphor was first articulated by the 18th century French immigrant to America, Hector St. John De Crèvecoeur, but popularized in Israel Zangwill's 1908 play *The Melting Pot.*
- Zangwill called America "God's crucible, the great melting pot where all the faces of Europe are melting and reforming"

Cultural Pluralism

Horace Kallen (1915), a Jewish philosopher, argued that members of every American ethnic group should be free to participate in all of the society's major institutions while simultaneously retaining or elaborating their own ethnic heritage. Cultural pluralism emerged in response to a nativist reaction to the massive influx of immigrants from Eastern and Southern Europe. Restrictive immigration laws, the Great Depression, and World War II reduced immigration from those regions.

What is cultural pluralism?

- Cultural pluralism is a term used when smaller groups within a larger society are accepted by the wider culture provided they are consistent with the laws and values of the wider society.
- Often the acceptance of a culture may require that the new or minority culture remove some aspects of their culture which is incompatible with the laws or values of the dominant culture.
- The idea of cultural pluralism has its roots in the transcendentalism supported by the transcendentalist movement.
- Transcendentalism is an American literary, political, and philosophical movement of the early 19th century.

- The transcendentalists operated with the sense that a new era was at hand. They were critics of their contemporary society for its unthinking conformity.
- Cultural pluralism was developed and improved by cultural pluralists, namely William James, Horace Kallen, Randolph Bourne, Louis Adamic, and Leonardo Covello
- Horace Kallen: He advocated that the United States become a "democracy of nationalities, cooperating voluntarily and autonomously in the enterprise of self-realization [utilizing] a common language: English."
- Louis Adamic (1932): The thrust of Adamic's approach to cultural pluralism is captured by his insistence that "in the past there has been entirely too much giving up, too much melting away and shattering of the various cultural values of the new groups. Americanized foreigners became a cultural zero paying lip service to the U.S., which satisfied the Americanizers."
- Leonardo Covello (1958): "A true assimilation means absorption of the foreign groups without destruction of their fundamental characteristics and without the obliteration of an understandable pride in the fine things that come to them from the past history of their races and nations ... ."

Multiculturalism

Multiculturalism (Glazer, 1997) refers to sharing of many cultures:

- Multiculturalism is a social and political movement and position that holds differences between individuals and groups to be a potential source of strength and renewal rather than of strife.
- It values the diverse perspectives people develop and maintain through varieties of experiences and background stemming from racial, ethnic, gender, sexual orientation, and class differences in society.
- The doctrine underlying this position is cultural relativism—the denial that any culture can be said to be better or worse than any other.
- Educators need a definition of multiculturalism that offers the possibility for schools to become places where students and teachers can become border crossers engaged in critical and ethical reflection about what it means to bring a wider variety of cultures into dealing with each other.
- The idea of a mosaic of cultures forming a nation was adopted by Canadian sociologist John Porter (1965) in his study of social class entitled *Vertical Mosaic: An Analysis of Social Class and Power in Canada*. The mosaic theme became a part of Canadian multiculturalism policy in the 1970s.

Cultural Relativism

Cultural relativism (Schnapper, 2009) is a philosophy that contends that when it comes to assessing and evaluating differing peoples' cultural practices, there are no absolutes or any fixed truths but rather that all is relative:

- Cultural relativists view themselves as tolerant; they see other cultures not as wrong but as different.

Table 29.1 Cultural Pluralism vs. Multiculturalism Dynamics

Goals/Objectives	Cultural Pluralism	Multiculturalism
DOMINANCE	with dominant culture	without dominant culture
CONCEPT	TRANS-NATIONALISM Concept refers to multiple links and interactions connecting people and institutions across the borders of nation-states. Concept popularized in the early 20th century by writer Randolph Bourne (1916). Bourne rejects the melting-pot theory because he argues that immigrants are not assimilating easily to another culture.	SALAD BOWL Concept refers to the integration of the many different cultures of the United States like a salad, as opposed to the traditional idea of a cultural melting pot. A new metaphor, the "salad bowl," was popularized in the 1970s replacing the melting pot. In Canada the concept is known as the cultural mosaic
PUBLIC SPHERE	Individuals are treated in a common public sphere.	Multiculturalism is not culturally neutral. Multiculturalism is an arena for cultural negotiation. No group should dominate in a way that excludes other cultural forms.
CULTURAL DIVERSITY	Different cultures are allowed in a separate cultural sphere, but society has no obligation to acknowledge or support alternative cultural forms.	Different cultures are encouraged. Individuals are considered part of collectivities that provide meaning to their lives. Multiculturalism seeks ways to support these collectivities.
EDUCATIONAL GOALS	Mitigate social inequality by ensuring that merit is rewarded.	Cultural pride is encouraged. One goal is to overcome the disjuncture between a child's culture and school culture that excludes a child from participating in the larger society.

Goals/Objectives	Cultural Pluralism	Multiculturalism
EDUCATIONAL GOALS	To support the dominant culture/ hegemony. Individuals are given alternatives. Children have the right to develop their talents and interests, and schools should challenge students by providing different experiences.	To correct hegemony of culture. Cultural respect should be fostered. Different cultural information and historical experiences are provided to the children.
ADVANTAGES	It leads the minority culture into adding a significant aspect of their culture to the dominant culture. There is national unity. There is more stable national identity.	It leads to cultural exchanges. Adds variety in the life of all citizens. It bridges the chasm of ignorance and arrogance.
DISADVANTAGES	The dominant culture is more prominent than the other cultures. It usually leads to dissolution of other cultures. The only aspect accepted in the minority culture is the culture that is compatible to the dominant culture.	It brings anxiety to stability of national identity. It creates national disunity. It leads to questionable loyalties.

Source: Cultural Pluralism by Dr. Diane Mitschke at http://www.slideshare.net/dianemitschke/cultural-pluralism-24876573

References

Adamic, Louis. 1932. *Laughing in the Jungle: The Autobiography of an Immigrant in America.* New York and London: Harper & Brothers. Reprinted by Arno Press and The New York Times, 1969; pp. 10–35.

Bourne, Randolph S. 1916. "The Jew and Tran-national America."

Brooks, Stephen, ed. 2002. *The Challenge of Cultural Pluralism.* Westport, Conn.: Praeger.

Booth, William (1998). "One Nation, Indivisible: Is It History?" Myth of the Melting Pot: America's Racial and Ethnic Divide. *Washington Post.* pp. A1. Retrieved July 15, 2008 from https://www.washingtonpost.com/wp-srv/national/longterm/meltingpot/melt0222.htm

Covello, Leonardo. 1958. *The Heart Is the Teacher* (1st ed.). New York: McGraw-Hill.

Glazer, Nathan. 1997. *We Are All Multiculturalists Now.* Cambridge, Mass.: Harvard University Press.

Glazer, Nathan, and D. P. Moynihan. 1970. *Beyond the Melting Pot.* Cambridge: MIT Press.

Gibbon, John Murray. 1938. *Canadian Mosaic: The Making of a Northern Nation.* Toronto: McClelland & Stewart.

Gordon, Milton M. 1964. *Assimilation in American Life: The Role of Race, Religion, and National Origins.* New York: Oxford University Press.

Hollinger, David A. 1995. *Post ethnic America: Beyond Multiculturalism.* New York: Basic Books.

Kallen, Horace M. 1956. *Cultural Pluralism and the American Idea: An Essay in Social Philosophy.* Philadelphia: University of Pennsylvania Press.

Kallen, Horace M. 1924. *Culture and Democracy in the United States.* New Brunswick, N.J.: Transaction Books.

Kallen, Horace M. 1915. "Democracy versus the Melting Pot: A Study of American Nationality." *The Nation.* 190–194, 217–220.

Porter, John. 1965. *The Vertical Mosaic: An Analysis of Social Class and Power in Canada.* Toronto: University of Toronto Press .

Portes, A., and Rumbaut, R. G. 1996. *Immigrant America: A Portrait* (2nd ed.). Berkeley: University of California Press.

Putnam, Robert D. 2007. "E Pluribus Unum: Diversity and Community in the Twenty-first Century." *Scandinavian Political Studies. 30*(2): 137–74. doi:10.1111/j.1467-9477.2007.00176.x.

Schnapper, Dominique. 2009. "Relativism." *Society, 46*(2), 175–179. https://doi.org/10.1007/s12115-008-9181-6.

READING 30

The Whiteness of America

By William Raspberry

WASHINGTON—My family, someone said at a recent reunion, likes to think of itself as a river stretching back as far as the mind can remember and as far forward as it can imagine.

But the salient feature of this river—the thing we like to boast about—is its ability to take in (through marriage, through adoption, even by "acclamation") a huge variety of streams and rivulets while keeping its own lovely essence.

We are generous about this process, the reunion speaker said. We believe that every new drop of water that enters the river is transformed by it, and that's good. But we believe the process also changes the river, leaving it deeper and stronger and livelier. That's good, too.

We can (and usually do at our reunions) talk for some time about the peculiar culture of that river we call family: its core beliefs and attitudes, reinforced by family fables; its values with the power to improve those who come under its influence; the gentle but firm limits it sets on what is acceptable behavior, and perhaps most of all its willingness to share the benefits of this culture with all who would join.

I was talking about this to a class on race the other day when this unsettling thought occurred: In what way is my family's pride of kinship different from white America's pride of race?

Doesn't each proceed from a quiet confidence that it has found the right path to success, happiness and worthwhileness? Don't both believe that only good things can come from adopting our culture? Aren't both saddened by those who reject the values whose validity we take for granted?

There are, of course, white racists who think no nonwhite could ever measure up to white standards, but those are at least as rare as the family members who would try to bar certain newcomers as unworthy to be kin.

Mostly, though, white Americans share the view so deeply held by my family: that its key values—its beliefs if not always its practices—"work." And white America seems about as willing as my family to take in those who embrace its values. I know we nonwhites tell ourselves that's not so, but what

William Raspberry

else can it mean when white folk tell us with such earnestness what peace and neighborliness we could enjoy "if they were all like you"?

How arrogant that sounds. It seems, as Jeff Hitchcock and Charley Flint have written, to make whiteness the measure of all things good. In a paper they wrote for the Center for the Study of White American Culture (in Roselle, N.J.), they argue that the American culture is regrettably, the white American male culture. Whiteness is so much at the center of things that white people don't even recognize it. What nonwhites see as whiteness, whites see as merely normal—neutral.

Hitchcock (a white man) and Flint (a black woman) argue for deliberate efforts to create a truly multiracial, multicultural society in America by "decentering whiteness." Their argument of the need to do so comes off stronger than their proposals for getting it done.

Nor is theirs the only interesting view of the matter. I've just been reading Eric Liu's book, "The Accidental Asian," in which he wrestles with his own "whiteness."

"I never asked to be white," he writes. "I am not literally white. That is, 1 do not have white skin or white ancestors, I have yellow skin and yellow ancestors, hundreds of generations of them. But like so many other Asian Americans of the second generation I find myself the bearer of a strange new status: white by acclamation."

Liu, a 30ish former speechwriter for President Clinton, has, in short, been "assimilated," a concept many nonwhites find repugnant, because it seems to entail the necessity of giving up one's own culture and accepting the superiority of the dominant American (white) culture.

Probably most African and Asian Americans would be saddened (if not angered) by Liu's self-revealed transformation to "white." And yet, isn't there something to be said about his apparent acceptance into, and success in, the American mainstream?

And to repeat: How different is what he has done from what my own family has taken as a matter of common sense leavened with generosity?

READING 31

American Multiculturalism VS. French Ethno-pluralism

The Debate over Arab and Muslim Assimilation

By Lanouar Ben Hafsa

Abstract

Although they have become more visible across the Western world, Arabs and Muslims remain inadequately described and poorly misunderstood. In the United States, inasmuch as in France, despite their expanding numbers and their growing involvement into the decision making process, both groups still suffer from widespread prejudice, especially the negative image conveyed about them in the media and within some political circles.

Until the 1970s, Arab and Muslim immigrants had been a neglected dimension in either American or French ethnic and religious history. But the rise in the number of such foreign-born residents in both countries added to the growing fear over the upsurge of Islamic fundamentalism, and generated considerable interest and public debate on how well these groups would assimilate into the mainstream culture of their host societies and fit within a pre-established order.

This paper not only aims to cast a fresh and objective look into how American and French citizens of Arab and Muslim descent adjust to their new environment, but also attempts to provide some insights into how the United States and France accommodate Islam, as both nations, because of their different immigration histories and their relatively diverging ideologies, do not have a communality of views on how society should be structured and organized.

Two elements have been decisive for such a study: first, my experience in France as a postgraduate student at Sorbonne University, second, the research I conducted in 2004 on Arab Americans as Senior Fulbright at the Center for Arab American Studies, at the University of Michigan Dearborn. Both encounters not only helped me draw a number of conclusions regarding the respective experiences of two communities, united by common historical and cultural ties, but so different as to the way they adapt to their host societies. They especially enhanced my understanding of what it really means to be Arab or Muslim in France and in the United States.

To support the research's central point, a number of questions will be addressed: Are Arab-Americans in general and American Muslims in particular unwilling to assimilate? Is Islam inherently incompatible with Western and Judeo-Christian values? Should policymakers see Islam as the enemy of the West? Should the prevalent anti-Americanism in the Arab and Muslim world be understood within the broader context of "clash of civilizations" or "war of religions", as stressed by some scholars, or should it be considered as a "natural response" to a temporary conjuncture necessitating reconsideration and change? Finally, what role should Arab and Muslim leaders in both countries play to provide community stability and maintain their identity in an ever-changing world?

Keywords: Arab Americans, American Muslims, French Arabs and Muslims, American Muticulturalism, French Ethno-pluralism, Assimilation.

Background

The epithets "Arab" and "Muslim" are usually muddled up and in most French people's minds—in as much as American people's perceptions—both terms are interchangeable. In practice, they do not even overlap as Arabs can be Muslim, Christian or Jewish, etc. Worldwide, people of Arab descent constitute only a minority. Although Islam is often associated with the Arab world, fewer than fifteen percent of Muslims are Arab.[1] If, however, most Arab residents in France are Muslim, making roughly ten percent of the overall population,[2] in the United States, contrary to popular assumptions, the majority of Arabs are Christian, with Muslims making one-third of the Arab population.[3]

It is onerous to accurately estimate the total number of Arabs or Muslims who live in France[4] and the United States simply because both countries made it illegal to compile data based on religious or ethnic affiliation. The figures provided, therefore, are based rather on contrasted gauging published by non-governmental institutions. As of 2010, according to the French Ministry of Interior (in charge of religious affairs and which does not have the right to enquire straightforwardly about religion and applies criterion of people's geographic origin as a basis for calculation),[5] there are between five to six million Muslims in metropolitan France, the largest Muslim minority in Europe. Those of Maghreb origin represent eighty-two percent of the Muslim population (42.2% from Algeria, 27.5% from Morocco, and 11.4% from Tunisia).[6]

Across the Atlantic, 1,967,219 are of Arab descent, according to the 2010 Census.[7] On the other hand, research by the Arab American Institute and Zogby International suggest that—without taking into consideration ancestry's issue—the Census Bureau's estimation is substantially lower than the actual number which they adjust at 3,665,789. To put it bluntly, that is roughly one percent of the American population. Most of Arab Americans are Christian (sixty-three percent), with Muslims counting merely twenty-four percent.[8]

Contrary to their French counterparts, most Arabs in America are highly educated and have better economic prospects. Whereas Muslims or Arabs in France either suffer from unemployment or typically hold low-paid manual jobs with little chance of upward socio-economic mobility. Arab Americans fare quite well compared even to the average American. With at least a high school, they number eighty-nine percent. More than forty-five percent have a Bachelor's degree and eighteen percent a Post-graduate diploma, respectively twice the American average.[9]

The higher rates of education translate into a pattern of prestigious and remunerative employment. Indeed, seventy-three percent of working Arab Americans are employed in managerial, professional, technical, sales or administrative fields. Most work in the private sector (eighty-eight percent), whereas a mere twelve percent hold governmental positions.[10]

In contrast, French Arabs are doing less well and tend to be poorer, on average, than the nation as a whole. As in much of Europe and contrary to Arab Americans who have been settling since the 1880s, the French Arab community was established largely by waves of immigrant laborers in the 1960s through the mid-1970s, and had continued under family reunification provisions ever since. These populations have grown, but remained, by and large, below average in income and social status, as many of them are at best either semi-skilled or unskilled workers. Recent studies which focus on "immigrants" but refer to Muslim-related issues—describe the more than two million residents of increasingly "ghettoized" suburbs where unemployment and crime rates are disproportionately high—as forming a "*culturally distinct, socially and economically 'excluded' population.*"[11] In an article about the 2005 civil unrest in France, Ralph Peters, a retired U.S. army lieutenant colonel and author, wrote that France's "apartheid" has a distinctly racial aspect. In his view, "France's 5 million brown and black residents (have) failed to appreciate discrimination, jobless rates of up to 50 percent, public humiliation, crime, bigotry and, of course, the glorious French culture that excluded them through an informal apartheid system."[12]

When it comes to political participation, the gap between the two communities widens further, even though both agree on the pressuring need for more political clout and more involvement into the decision making process. Here, Arab Americans who, starting from the early 1980s, decided to take their own affairs in hand, seem more visible and better represented across the political spectrum. While in France, citizens of Arab heritage feel further marginalized by their exclusion from politics—despite their growing numbers—their American counterparts hold public office almost at all levels. To cite but a few examples, five Arab Americans served in the U.S. Senate and nine in the U.S. House of Representatives, three have been governors, and more than thirty have been mayors of U.S. cities.[13] In contrast, there have been only one full minister of Arab descent in France (Rachida Dati, Minister of Justice in Nicolas Sarkozi's first administration), and a handful of Cabinet members, but none among France's 577 members of the National Assembly, and none among France's 36,000 mayors.[14]

Higher official positions are equally rarely occupied by French nationals of Arab or Muslim background. A case in point, when in January 2004, President Jacques Chirac declared Aïssa Dermouche the new prefect (senior state representative) of the Jura region, a bomb destroyed his car just three weeks after his nomination. A few days later, another explosion damaged the front door and glass façade of Audencia, a leading French business school of which he was head, and on January 29, a third detonation caused minor damage to a letterbox at the school of one of Dermouche's sons.[15]

On the whole, by many standards, Arab Americans seem to be offered worthier opportunities for assimilation, thanks notably to the American multicultural context as a whole, but also to the political activism of a socio-culturally integrated Christian Arab community. However, despite their economic and political achievements, and although the U.S. Census Bureau classifies Arabs as white alongside the European majority, a sizable number among them still believe they are not treated as whites, but more like such other minorities as Asian Americans or Hispanic Americans.[16]

The Debate over Assimilation: Are Arabs Unwilling to Assimilate?

Although they have become more visible over the last few decades, Arabs in France and the United States remain inadequately described and poorly misunderstood. Until the 1970s, Arab immigrants had been a neglected dimension in either French or American ethnic and religious history. But the rise in the number of such foreign-born residents, in both countries, added to the growing fear over the upsurge of Islamic fundamentalism, has generated considerable interest and public debate on how well these groups would assimilate into the mainstream of their host societies.

This is not a paper about Islam. Our endeavor is to scrutinize a modus operandi of thinking and of expression through the respective experiences of two communities, united by a common historical and cultural heritage, but remarkably disparate as to the fashion they adjust to their new environments and to the way they respond to the challenges in order to maintain their identity in an ever-changing world.

Perhaps the best way to tackle this controversial and polarizing issue would be first to raise the following questions: What place do Arab Americans and Arabs based in France hold in the social fabric of their host countries? In other words, do they fully make part of the social landscape, or are they simply considered as aliens pursuing a dream that is beyond their reach? What should they do to challenge and overcome the stereotype many of their fellow-citizens make of them as being eternally the members of a foreign creed that is fundamentally alien to the Western experience and history? Now that we unknowingly associate them with Islam, does their Islamic identity constitute an insurmountable hindrance on the path of assimilation? Is Islam incompatible with the Western and Judeo-Christian values? Should the prevalent anti-Americanism in the Arab and Muslim worlds be understood within the broader context of "clash of civilizations" or "war of religions", as stressed by some scholars,[17] or should it be considered as a "natural" response to a temporary conjuncture necessitating reconsideration and change?

In effect, if the first wave of Arab immigrants to the United States who arrived in the 1880s from the province of Mount Lebanon, in Greater Syria, sought to assimilate and blend in what it was perceived as American mainstream culture, that was not the case for North African immigrants, namely Algerians who started to arrive in the early Twentieth Century. Up to 1959, this group constituted the largest non-European immigrant presence anywhere in Europe, and the great public controversy they aroused, generated perceptions of colonial "barbarians" invading the very heart of the empire.[18]

Besides the depiction, some newspapers made of them as being "*animals*", "*primitive savages*", "*rapists*" and "*transmitters of venereal diseases and tuberculosis*", and thus a threat to metropolitan society, it became a real challenge for the French officials to break down their resistance to integration into the French society. Because, contrary to most immigrant groups like Italians, Poles, and Spanish who gradually assimilated by participating into different working class organizations and associations (trade unions, sports clubs, the Communist Party), Algerians reconstituted in France small and "micro-ghettos", impermeable to any outside influence. Their rationale down to the Algerian independence in 1962 was founded on a project to return to the homeland and a definite refusal to strike roots in France.[19]

Up until the early 1980s, and even though they stood for the largest Muslim community in Europe, there was no or limited media focus on such a group named French Arabs or French Muslims.[20] Furthermore, not only the government of Giscard d'Estaing (1974-1981) deepened its anti-immigrant stance by adopting a wide array of measures meant to severely reduce the flux of immigrants from North and sub-Saharan Africa, but Arabs, despite their increasing numbers, were still an invisible community and their prayer rooms were unrecognizable as they were improvised in basements, garages, and council flats (they had none of the external architectural symbolism of the traditional mosque with a minaret and a dome).

The Iranian Revolution of 1979 led to a conspicuous turning point. Both at governmental and public levels, there were no clear signs of a growing anxiety about Islamic fundamentalism beginning to penetrate mainland France. Immediately after a bomb exploded at St. Charles station in Marseilles, in December 1983, The French officials began to apprehend the threat from within, a menace better articulated by Gaston Deferre, Interior Minister and mayor of Marseille who, in 1984, told the press that religious practice until then had been apolitical, "an excellent thing ... But, step by step, the fundamentalists got a foothold in the mosques, became the managers or the leaders, and began to make propaganda and to proselytize. This is dangerous because they can act as intermediaries when bombings are perpetrated."[21]

Interestingly, casting a penetrating glance into Deferre's political discourse reveals a second but equally important anti-Muslim theme, the Arab or Muslim unwillingness to integrate or to assimilate. For across the media and within political and academic circles, the pivotal question was no longer one of controlling the immigration flow from Arab and Muslim countries, but has shifted to a profound disquiet toward those considered as the "inassimilable stock" and the "racially different other". According to Deferre, contrary to other immigrants (namely Italians and Spanish) who had assimilated, become naturalized and now "occupy important position, almost everywhere", "Arabs"[22] and Algerians, more specifically, reconstituted large extended family networks, "groupings after the several dozen people who, in addition, wear traditional clothing and live according to the customs of their country. They roast in the yard, etc."[23] Articulating a shift toward widespread and overt forms of racism, he added that the laws of Islam in the sphere of marriage, divorce, gender roles, and family life "are in contradiction with the rules of the French Law."[24]

The new visibility of Muslims, fostered by the construction of purposely built mosques of which the most controversial was inaugurated at Montes-la-Jolie in 1981, was perceived by almost all major political parties and the general public as an "invasion" and an "aggressive" assertion of the Muslim faith, even though there was no significant change in the number of Muslim immigrants. The worst case scenario of a takeover by radical Islamists and which presented all Muslims as potential terrorists, would not only tighten control around the Arab community, but would further legitimize racist and xenophobic sentiments, a new mobilizing issue of which the still uninspiring National Front would emerge as the uncontested champion. As a consequence, because of the growing homogeneity in the political discourse around the use of anti-immigrant rhetoric as a key electoral card, the National Front, which astutely knew how to substitute a traditional biological racism with one based on cultural differences, moved, within a few years only, from an insignificant party into a central player on the national scene.

Today, the situation of Arabs and Muslims on the other side of the Atlantic is not substantially different. Even though it is the fastest-growing faith in the United States, Islam remains either widely misunderstood or simply viewed as foreign, mysterious, and even threatening to the nation's "Judeo-Christian heritage." In fact, attempts to target Islam as an alien creed and portray Muslims as the members of a cult based on hatred of the American society and associated with terrorist activity abroad and inside the United States, did not emerge after the 9/11 attacks on the World Trade Centre and the Pentagon. Years before the shock, scholars such as Samuel Huntington of Harvard and Bernard Lewis of Princeton, and publicists like Daniel Pipes and Steven Emerson were envisaging the likelihood of clashes between Islam and the West.

Said Karina Rollins, editor of *The American Enterprise*, a neoconservative public policy magazine:

> "The Cold War is over, but the battle of good vs. evil rages stronger than ever. At some point in the future, the human thirst for liberty and self-determination may sweep even the Islamic world. But today, a fresh enemy is at civilization's gate, and it's time we recognized him."[25]

Since 1994 and the airing by Public Broadcasting Service (PBS) of Steven Emerson's documentary, *Jihad in America*, Arab and Muslim Americans have been looked at as suspects. In his article "America's Muslims Against America Jews," Daniel Pipes, director of the neoconservative think tank, Middle East Forum, and Bush's nominee, in 2003, to the U.S. Institute of Peace, went so far as to suggest that Muslims constituted a monolithic bloc, intrinsically anti-Semitic and driven by hatred.[26]

Criticizing American Muslim groups for not distancing themselves from terrorism and anti-American sentiments in their countries of origin, Pipes pointed out Islam's universalizing and missionary impulse and the threat this might represent to religious pluralism in America. "The ambition to take over the United states is not new," he argued, "(t)he first missionaries for militant Islam, or Islamism, who arrived here from abroad in the 1920s, unblushingly declared, 'Our plan is we are going to conquer America."[27] To him converting Americans has always been the central purpose of Muslim existence in the United States, the only possible justification for Muslims to live in an "infidel land."

Assaults on Islam and attempts to reinvent a "religious" Cold War dubbed as the "Green Scare"; and Muslims targeted as the enemies of the West were not the declared targets of neoconservative ideologues alone. They made also part of a huge campaign launched by Islamophobic leaders of the New Christian Right who never miss an opportunity to question the compatibility of the Islamic faith with the American values. Even though implicitly denounced on several occasions by President Bush to whom "Islam, as practiced by the vast majority of people, is a peaceful religion, a religion that respects others,"[28] and later by President Obama in his outreach address to the Muslim World, when he declared: "I consider it part of my responsibility as President of the United States to fight against negative stereotypes of Islam whenever they appear,"[29] their much-publicized remarks not only revived tensions in the Arab and Muslim worlds, but also fuelled an already growing anti-American sentiment. Remarks such as the one made by Franklin Graham, son of televangelist Rev. Billy Graham, who called Islam "an evil religion" inherently at odds with American values, or that made by Rev. Jerry Vines who called the prophet "a demon-possessed paedophile,"[30] to cite but a few, are illustrative of the radical Religious Right view of Islam, fundamentally based on the rejection of the "other."

To Daniel Pipes, finally, the real danger to the American democracy and to the American religious pluralism did not emanate from the pro-Israel Christian Right. More specifically, American Jewish organizations should not devote considerable resources and energy targeting the New Religious Right while virtually ignoring the rise of "*Islamist fascism*". He warned:

> "The real and present danger is by no means the pro-Israel Christian Coalition but the rapidly anti-Semitic Muslim Arab Youth Association; not Jerry Falwell but Sheikh Omar Abdel Rahman;[31] not those who wish, at the very worst, to convert Jews but those who, with every means at their disposal, intend to do them harm, who have already acted on those violent intentions, and who if unchecked will surely do so again."[32]

American Multiculturalism VS. French Ethno-pluralism

"Unlike any other country, America is defined by its spirit and human values, not by its ethnic background. We are the only truly secular country in the world,"[33] wrote once Anne Wortham, one of the most perceptive American sociologists. Such claim may be legitimate in so far that, besides the presence of a socio-culturally integrated and a politically active Christian Arab community, the American multicultural context appears exceptionally convenient for Muslims. To some extent their status is better than their European counterparts as they enjoy the constitutional advantages offered by the "land of the free", especially wider political freedoms, greater economic rewards, and the protection of their worship by the federal and state constitutions.

France-based Muslims, by contrast, are still laying claim to legitimacy alongside the Catholic, Protestant, and Jewish communities. In effect, the debate over how France and the United States accommodate Islam or how Muslims adapt to life in a secular society seems to have deeper implications as perceptions on both sides are grounded at the core of a long history of confrontational but also peaceful existence. Because of their different immigration histories, and, to a certain extent, diverging ideologies, France and the United States do not have a communality of views on how society should be structured and organized.

This is mirrored in the way both countries deal with their Arab and Muslim communities and the place they have reserved for them within the fabric of their respective societies. On April 2003, the French government created the French Council for the Muslim Religion (*Conseil Français du Culte Musulman*)—a body that represents all Muslims in negotiating on practical problems of their religion with the French State.[34] By and large, the council is part of the government's project to mainstream Muslims in the French culture and to give them "a place at the table." Likewise, it has been quite recently (September, 2003) that the first Muslim high school, the *Lycée Averroes*, opened in the city of Lille. The school, which would uphold the strict French rule on "secular" teaching and follow the national curriculum, is intended to provide Muslim youth with the same core education that celebrates the republic's values as public schools.[35]

Undoubtedly, with more than six million people making roughly ten per cent of the French population, the community's religious needs could not be under-estimated. Yet, the simple idea of building a mosque, somewhere, inflames passions among the public and drives local and national political leaders into a collective hysteria. This is despite the fact that there are more than 1,500 mosques and Muslim prayer rooms in France, compared to 40,000 Catholic buildings, 957 temples and 82 synagogues, with only a handful which have domes and minarets.[36] The case of the Cergy mosque which, while still in construction, had already galvanized passions and led one local opposition politician to warn that its minarets might rise higher than the town's church steeples.[37]

On the whole, the feeling that the French integration model does not work quickly or as well for Arabs and Muslims as it did once for other waves of immigrants represents a profound challenge for France's long inherited ideology of Republican citizenship. Deeply hostile, as it might seem, to the kind of multiculturalism and recognition of ethnic minority rights found in the United States or in Great Britain, French republicanism is based on the Jacobin tradition of France "one and indivisible" (*La République une et indivisible*) which had been constructed mainly under the First Republic (1792–1804). According to this universal ideology which emphasized the equality of all citizens within the state, there could be no intermediate bodies or poles of allegiance that might detract from the uniform relationship between each individual citizen and the state. So any articulation of group interests should be discouraged.

In such scheme of things, and in the name of the so-called French ethno-pluralism, some French thinkers like Alain de Benoist, reject the view that Europe can come closer to the United States in order to strengthen Western civilization. Rather, they call for France to defend its civilization from multicultural meltdown and the homogenizing forces of global American media, or what they call the "Coca-Colonizing" and "McDonaldizing" effects of the United States popular culture.[38]

Interestingly enough, France and the United States do not share the same views on the dynamics of civil society only. They also seem to diverge as to the type of relationship that should exist between Church and State. For, unlike the United States where in terms of Alexis de Tocqueville, "... from the beginning politics and religion were in accord, and they have not ceased to be so since,"[39] France, no doubt as a result long history of religious violence (including the Religious Wars, 1562-1598), favours strict separation between the two as a way to guarantee that religious competition and religious proselytizing do not spawn ataxia in the public sphere.

Notwithstanding, if the purpose of separating Church and State in the United States was principally meant to avoid interference of the government in church matters and to protect, ultimately religion from the state, in France, it was exactly the reverse. The purpose of separating Church and State was to protect the new French democracy from the Catholic Church, at the time socially and politically dominant, and staunchly opposed to the establishment of a secular democracy. To Gilles Kepel, no doubt the most prominent specialist in France of the question and who regards Islamic revivalism as an extremely grave threat to Republican assimilation, strict separation of Church and State has been part of the French Constitution since 1905. In his well-known book, *Allah in the West: Islamic Movements in America and Europe* (Cambridge: Polity, 1997), he asserted: "French political tradition actively combated any form of regional, ethnic or religious identity which could weaken the link between the individual and the state."[40]

But nothing better than the so-called "headscarf affair"[41] could further showcase the debate over Muslims' integration and the way they cope with their new secular environment. The event started in 1989, after three schoolgirls of North African descent were expelled from their high school, Gabriel-Havez in Creil (north of Paris), on the grounds that the veil or *hijab* was a provocative religious symbol in breach of the 1905 "*laïcité*" law protecting the secular, nonreligious nature of state education. So what started as a local row snowballed into a nationwide debate as the "affair" gave way to a whole complex of issues confirming French Muslims as perpetual outsiders in French society. For many commentators in the media and across the political spectrum, the young girls were steadfastly being manipulated by invisible forces or forces acting behind-the-scenes to challenge and subvert the foundations of the Republic, namely the principle of separation of church and state.[42]

On March 15, 2004, after a protracted and gruelling debate and to settle down the question once and forever, President Jacques Chirac, based upon the recommendations of the "Stasi Commission,"[43] signed what came to be called as the "French law on secularity and conspicuous religious symbols in schools."[44] It forbids pupils from wearing "conspicuous" signs of belonging to a religion, wearing any visible symbol meant to be seen. Prohibited items would include headscarves for Muslim girls, yarmulkes for Jewish boys, turbans for Sikh boys and large Christian crosses. It allows, however, the wearing of discreet symbols of faith such as small crosses, Stars of David or Fatima's hands. The law concerns only public primary and secondary schools. It does not concern other public spaces, nor does it concern public universities or other establishments of higher education.

According to those who approved the ban,[45] besides the fact that the headscarf stood for female subjugation, wearing such a symbol outrageously violated the secular principle outlined by the 1905 law on "*laïcité*", and ran counter the goal of schools to function as places of neutrality and critical awareness. They also saw the law as, first and foremost, a protection against oppressive patriarchal authority of radical fathers and brothers. Suffice to read Samira Bellil's book, *Dans l'Enfer des Tourmentes (Paris: Gallimard, 2003)*, (*In Gang Rape Hell*), proponents of the ban said, to discover the harsh reality of those Muslim girls who, because they refused to wear the headscarf and adopt a dress code in the poor suburbs, were regarded as "prostitutes" and subjected to gang rape.[46]

The "headscarf affair" was a critical juncture in the unfolding of France's relationship with its Muslim minority. Not only it shook the very bedrock of the French society, but it also served—according to some French Muslims who refuted any allegation accusing them of plotting to thwart the nation's secular heritage—to promote the image of France that restricts personal freedom. A tendency broadly shared across the American public opinion which could not understand how the wearing of such personal symbols in public schools could violate the principles of religious freedom. This is echoed in the diverging perceptions—in both countries—of the kind of relationship likely to exist between Church and State. For the Bush administration which publicly criticized France for practicing a too rigorous separation of church and state, the law was simply inappropriate as

> "all persons should be able to practice their religion and their beliefs peacefully, without government interference, as long as they are doing so without provocation and intimidation on others in society."[47]

But according to French officials and many supporters of the ban, public schools were plainly the bulkiest remaining but most robust institutions for the systematic moulding of all children, regardless of their ethnic origin, into the universal values of the Republic. French public schools, they argued, have long been areas where a new civic identity could be nurtured, free from any anti-democratic influence of any religion, in other words, veritable "mills of citizenship" and "Frenchness".

In *toto*, while it is intricate to predict what kind of relationship that might exist between Islam and the West in the near and farther future, both French and American Arab and Muslim communities seem today decided to react to the clouds of suspicion hanging over them, as they realized that they had little influence on the policies of their host countries. But they need, first, to voice their concerns through the mainstream political organizations, if they want to gain national visibility and recognition.

This seems fairly achievable for Arab Americans and American Muslims as they now have become aware that they could exert greater political pressure if they invest in building grass-roots political structures and, most of all, overcome their ethnic, religious, and cultural differences which, so far, have complicated their ability to reach political cohesiveness. Notwithstanding their small numbers (representing less than three per cent of the American population) Arab and Muslim activists are convinced that if they vote as a bloc, they could make the difference in key electoral swing states where they are concentrated, such as Michigan, Pennsylvania, Ohio, New Mexico, Florida and Wisconsin.[48]

Another reason for persuasive political participation and adequate contribution to organized fund-raising groups, known as Political Action Committees (PACs), is their perception that the Patriot Act, passed in 2001, hinders their civil liberties and allows their communities to be unfairly targeted by law enforcement. Their disappointment with Bush's handling of the national security affairs after the shock of 9/11, not only buttressed the *desideratum* for a power transmission from elite to grass-roots organizations, but also produced a major shift in strategy. Now convinced that no candidate will be likely to change the American Middle East policy and Washington's full and uncontested support for Israel, fighting against rejection and negative stereotyping has become a rallying cry for the disparate Arab and Muslim communities, and the single most important issue for every single Arab and every single Muslim who directly or indirectly experienced discrimination.

On their part, despite the existence of a web of strong historical bonds that links France and North Africa, French Arabs and Muslims still find it difficult to break the vicious circle around them and get acceptance in the country they now call home. Less organized as they obviously lack the political experience and maturity of their American counterparts, they have no choice but to struggle to legalize and protect their status alongside similar lines to the country's Jewish and Protestant minorities.

Paradoxical, as it might seem, the lack of recognition and the widespread anti-Arab and anti-Muslim prejudice are further nurtured by a steadfast refusal, on the part of policymakers, to recognize and seriously tackle the real needs of such "ghettoized" communities and especially the disaffected youth among them, commonly referred to as *Beurs* (Arabs). For, the real problems are not religious or simply related to security matters, as many might allegedly suppose, they are rather social and economic and the row over the "headscarf affair" was but an outright distraction from the integration process. Added to that, the adverse role endorsed by the French media in the dissemination of anti-Muslim stereotypes[49] served only to fuel an already heated context and exacerbated tensions by creating an atmosphere of exaggerated feeling of insecurity. The contention over the wearing of the *niqab* (full head covering) in public places, and its banning in 2011, is another case in point.[50]

Conclusion

To conclude, it seems fair to ascertain that while they utterly consider the founding of Arab and Muslim advocacy organizations as a giant step on the path of interfaith dialogue and a major vestige in the course of integration, France's and America's Arabs and Muslims yearn for more than acceptance. They aspire for respect, respect for their culture, respect for their faith, and respect for them as human beings. In such a case only, could they develop sincere relationships based on mutual respect, act as bridge communities, help boost understanding between the different cultures, and why not serve as the moving force behind the wind of change in their home and host societies.

Over it all, as the nomenclature "global village" has become more supportive of democratic changes in government, time has become ripe for Muslims finally to attain what centuries of internal oppression and subsequent colonialism have prevented them from accomplishing. So far, Muslim policymakers in the Arab World have hidden behind religion to justify oppressive cultural choices. But Islam does not belong to any one country or region. It is committed to diversity.

Notes

1. Nearly one-fourth of the world population today is Muslim and, contrary to widespread attitudes, most Muslims are concentrated in Southeast Asia. As to recent surveys, there are 203 million Muslims in Indonesia, 174 million in Pakistan, 161 million in India, 145 million in Bangladesh, 22 million in China, etc. (See: http://www.islam.about.com/od/muslimcountries/a/population).

2. Pew Research Center's Forum on Religion and Public Life. "The Future of the Global Muslim Population Projections for 2010–2030." (See: http://www.pewforum.org/-The-Future-of-the-Global-Muslim-Population.-aspx).

3. The Arab American Institute. (See: http://www..aaiusa.org/pages/demographics/).

4. Due to a law dating back to 1872, the French Republic prohibits performing census by making distinction between its citizens regarding their race or their religion.

5. See: *Le Figaro.* «5 à 6 millions de Musulmans en France.» June 28, 2010.

6. Michèle Tribalat. Institut National d'Etudes Démographiques (INED, 2010). (See: http://www.fdesouche.com/tag/ined/page/3).

7. U.S. Census Bureau (2010). (See: http://www.census.gov/2010census/).

8. The Arab American Institute. (See: http://www.aaiusa.org/pages/demographics/).

9. U.S. Census Bureau (2010). Op.cit.

10. See: http://www.b.3cdn.net/aai/fcc68db3efdd45f613_vim6ii3a7.pdf.

11. Economic data, such as employment and income, are central for studying both communities, yet they are poorly addressed as there are no official government statistics on religious affiliation in France and the United States.

12. Ralph Peters. "France's Intifada." *New York Post.* Nov. 8, 2005.

13. The Roster of Arab Americans in Public Service and Political Life (see: http://www.aaiusa.org/index_ee.php/pages/arab-american-roster).

14. See: http://www.pbs.org/wnet/wideangle/shows/france/info4.html.

15. See: Valerie Gas. "Attentat conte la voiture d'Aissa Dermouche." RFI. January 2004. (See: http://www.1.rfi.fr/actufr/articles/049/article_26245-asp).

16. For more information, see N. MacMaster. "Islamophobia in France and the Algerian Problem." In: E. Qureshi and M.A. Sells, eds., *The New Crusades: Constructing the Muslim Enemy.* New York: Columbia University Press, 2003.

17. Even though identified with Samuel Huntington in his book, *The Clash of Civilizations and the Making of the World Order.* New York: Simon & Schuster, 1996, the current popularity of the expression "clash of civilizations" stems from an article, "The Roots of Muslim Rage." *Atlantic Monthly.* Sept. 1990, published by Bernard Lewis, then Professor of History at Princeton University.

18. See: G. Meynier. *L'Algérie Révélée.* Genève : Droz, 1981.

19. See: N. MacMaster. "The Rue Fondery Murders of 1923 and the Origins of Anti-Arab Racism." In: J. Winderbank and R. Gunther, eds. *Violence and Conflict in the Politics and Society of Modern France.* Lampter: Mellen, 1995, pp. 149-160.

20. See: F. Gaspard. *Une Petite Ville en France.* Paris : Gallimard, 1990, p. 168.

21. *Les Temps Modernes.* March-May, 1984, pp. 1567–1574.

22. Muslim immigrants were called « Arabs », a stereotype that bore Orientalist assumptions, when in reality many originated in non-Arab societies such as Turks, Kabyles or Berbers, Pakistanis, etc.

23. *Les Temps Modernes*, op.cit.

24. Ibid.

25. "Why They Hate Us?" Editorial, *The American Enterprise.* December 1, 2001.

26. D. Pipes. "America's Muslims against America's Jews." *Commentary*, May 1, 1999.

27. Ibid.

28. Statement to reporters during a meeting with U.N. Secretary General Kofi Annan. The Oval Office, Washington D.C., Nov. 13, 2002.

29. Obama's Speech in Cairo, delivered on June 4, 2009. (See: http://www.whitehouse.gov/the-press-office-university-6-remarks-president-cairo-university-6-04-09).

30. S.J. Freedberg. "The War within Islam." *The National Journal.* May 10, 2003.

31. In 1993, Sheikh Abderrahman masterminded the bombing of the World Trade Center in New York which resulted in the killing of six persons and the injuring of more than a thousand.

32. D. Pipes, "American Muslims against American Jews," op. cit. Noting that the Christian Right have been staunch supporters of Israel. This commitment stems not from guilt over past Christian sins against Jews but from a theological doctrine widely shared in fundamentalist and Pentecostal circles known as "Dispensationalist Premillennialism." In this view, a complete restoration of the nation of Israel, including the rebuilding of the Temple in Jerusalem, is a prerequisite to the Second Coming of Christ and the establishment of his millennial reign.

33. "The Melting Pot, Part 2: America's Cultural-Institutional Core." *Modern Thought.* November, 2001.

34. The CFCM was set up by Nicolas Sarkozy, minister of interior at the time, which the state now officially recognizes as a discussion partner for religious issues. The council, however, is merely a private non-profit association and has no special legal standing, nor is it universally accepted as being representative of the opinions of Muslims residing in France.

35. Consisting of three classrooms and a science laboratory on the third floor of a mosque, the goal of the school is to provide Muslims with an alternative to public education, like those that French Catholics, Protestants and Jews have long enjoyed. Courses are taught in Arabic, Islamic culture and history are offered as electives and Quranic studies are assured for only one hour a week. There is no requirement that the students be Muslim, though all of them are, or that the girls go to school veiled. Like other private schools, if it meets all these requirements, it is eligible for state aid after five years.

36. Best estimates of an interior ministry source in "L'Islam dans la République." *Haut Conseil à l'Intégration.* November 2000, p.36.

37. G.S. Smith. "Minarets and Steeples: Can France Balance Them?" October 1, 2003. (See: http://www.nytimes.com/2003/10/01/international/europe/01M056.html).

38. See: Alain de Benoit. "L'Amerique qu'on aime." *Element,* no. 116. Spring 2005.

39. H. Mansfield and D. Winthrop, eds. *Democracy in America.* Chicago: University of Chicago Press, 2000.

40. Ibid., p. 236.

41. On the "affair" see A. Perotti and F. Thépaut. "L'Affaire du Foulard Islamique." *Migrations Sociétés* 2.7. January 1990, pp. 61–68; A.G. Hargreaves. *Immigration, "Race," and Ethnicity in Contemporary France.* London: Routeledge, 1995, pp. 125–131; F. Gaspard and F. Khosrokhawar. *Le Foulard et la République.* Paris: Découverte, 1995.

42. See: D. Decherf. "French Views of Religious Freedom." U.S. –France Analysis Series. July 2001. See: http://www.brookings.edu/fp/cusf/analysis/relfreedom.htm.

43. An investigation commission which Chirac set up in July 2003 to examine how the principle of *laïcité* should apply in practice and which, on December 11, 2003, published its report ruling that ostentatious displays of religion violated the secular rules of the French school system.

44. "Loi encadrant, en application du principe de laïcité, le port de signes ou de tenues manifestant une appartenance religieuse dans les écoles, collèges et lycées publics." (Translated: "By virtue of the law applying the principle of secularism, the wearing of signs or uniforms showing any religious affiliation at public primary and secondary school".

45. According to a February 2004 survey by CSA for the daily, *Le Parisien*, 69% of the population favored the ban, against 29% who were opposed to it. For Muslims living in France, the same survey showed 42% for and 53% against, and among Muslim women, 49% approved the proposed law, and 43% approved it. (See: http//www.economist.com/world/europe/displayStory.cfm?story-id=2404691). More significantly, a January 2004 survey for *Agence France Presse* showed overwhelming support among the teachers with 78% in favour of the ban. (See: http://www.laic.info/Members/webmstre/Revue_de_presse.2004-0204.2241/view).

46. This is, among others, the daily combat of a recently founded feminist organization, "Ni Putes, Ni Soumises" (*Neither Whores, Nor Submissives*) which was supportive of the law and which rallied in Paris, on March 8, 2003, more than 30,000 people for "The March of Women from the Projects Against Ghettos and for Equality" (*La marche des femmes des quartiers contre les ghettos et pour l'égalité*).

47. See: J.O. Goldsborough. "Separating Church and State." *San Diego Union -Tribune.* January 5, 2004.

48. This is at least what they think they did in Florida, in 2000, claiming that their support for George W. Bush made the difference in favor of the Republican candidate who, thanks in part to the 40,000 Arab and Muslim voters, ended up winning the state by slightly more than 500 votes in the final recount.

49. Noting that France's Islamophobia is just a more subtle form of racism. Overt anti-Arab prejudice is no longer acceptable and is even punished by the law, so now it is masked as an analysis of Islam, with the conclusion that Muslims are a menace to France.

50. See: Steven Erlanger. "Parliament Moves France Closer to a Ban on Facial Veils." *The New York Times.* July 13, 2010.

References

De Benoit, Alain. "L'Amérique qu'on aime." *Element*, no. 116, Spring 2005.

Decherf, Dominique. "French Views of Religious Freedom." *U.S. –France Analysis Series*. July 2001. <http://www.brookings.edu/fp/cusf/analysis/relfreedom.htm>.

Erlanger, Steven. "Parliament Moves France Closer to a Ban on Facial Veils." *The New York Times*. July 13, 2010.

Freedberg, Joseph S. "The War within Islam." *The National Journal*. May 10, 2003.

Gas, Valerie. "Attentat conte la voiture d'Aissa Dermouche." *Radio France Internationale* (RFI). January 2004. <http://www.1.rfi.fr/actufr/articles/049/article_26245-asp>.

Gaspard, F. and Khosrokhawar, F. *Le Foulard et la République*. Paris: Découverte, 1995.

Gaspard, Françoise. *Une Petite Ville en France*. Paris: Gallimard, 1990.

Goldsborough, James O. "Separating Church and State." *San Diego Union –Tribune*. January 5, 2004.

Hargreaves, Alec G. *Immigration, "Race," and Ethnicity in Contemporary France*. London: Routeledge, 1995.

Huntington, Samuel. *The Clash of Civilizations and the Making of the World Order*. New York: Simon & Schuster, 1996.

Lewis, Bernard. "The Roots of Muslim Rage." *Atlantic Monthly*. Sept. 1990.

MacMaster, Neil. "Islamophobia in France and the Algerian Problem." In: Qureshi. E. and Sells, M.A., eds., *The New Crusades: Constructing the Muslim Enemy*. New York: Columbia University Press, 2003.

MacMaster, Neil. "The Rue Fondery Murders of 1923 and the Origins of Anti-Arab Racism." In: Winderbank, J. and Gunther, R., eds., *Violence and Conflict in the Politics and Society of Modern France*. Lampter: Mellen, 1995.

Mansfield, H.C. and Winthrop, D., eds. *Democracy in America*. Chicago: University of Chicago Press, 2000.

Meynier, Gilbert. *L'Algérie Révélée*. Genève: Droz, 1981.

Perotti, A. and Thépaut, F. "L'Affaire du Foulard Islamique." *Migrations Sociétés* 2.7. January 1990.

Peters, Ralph. "France's Intifada." *New York Post*. Nov. 8, 2005.

Pew Research Center's Forum on Religion and Public Life. "The Future of the Global Muslim Population Projections for 2010-2030." <http://www.pewforum.org/-The-Future-of-the--Global-Muslim-Population.-aspx>.

Pipes, Daniel. "America's Muslims against America's Jews." *Commentary*. May 1, 1999.

Smith, Graig S. "Minarets and Steeples: Can France Balance Them?" October 1, 2003. <http://www.nytimes.com/2003/10/01/international/europe/01M056.html>.

The Arab American Institute. <http://www.aaiusa.org/pages/demographics/>.

The Roster of Arab Americans in Public Service and Political Life. <http://www.aaiusa.org/index_ee.php/pages/arab-american-roster>.

Tribalat, Michèle. Institut National d'Etudes Démographiques (INED, 2010). <http://wwwfdesouche.com/tag/ined/page/3>.

United States Census Bureau. 2010 Census Data. <http://www.census.gov./2010census/data/>.

"Why They Hate Us?" Editorial. *The American Enterprise*. December 1, 2001.

Author and Contributor Biographies

Kebba Darboe, (2004-present) is professor and chair, Department of Ethnic Studies at Minnesota State University, Mankato. He earned his Ph.D. in sociology from South Dakota State University, Brookings in 2000. From 2000 to 2004, he taught sociology courses in the Department of Sociology and Anthropology at St. Cloud State University, Minnesota. Dr. Daboe's many scholarly articles are published in peer-reviewed journals, including the *Great Plains Sociologist.* He has also been published by Sage Publications and by Routledge, Francis & Taylor Group, and he is author/coauthor of the following books: *A Reader on Race/Ethnic Relations: Harmonizing Indigenous and Immigrant Voices* (Kendall Hunt Publishing Company), *Introduction to Ethnic Studies: A New Approach* (Kendall Hunt Publishing Company), and *An Empirical Study of the Social Correlates of Job Satisfaction Among Plant Science Graduates of a Midwestern University: A Test of Victor H. Vroom's (1964) Expectancy Theory* (University Press of America, Inc.).

His teaching and research interests include the history of American racial minorities, sociological theories, modern demographics theory and immigration, urban minority problems, and qualitative, quantitative, and evaluation research methods. Dr. Darboe was born in Georgetown, the Gambia. He earned his undergraduate degrees in sociology and French language from the University of Paris, France; a Bachelor of Arts degree in economics from the University of Minnesota Duluth, and a Master of Arts in economics from Mankato State University, Minnesota; and a Master of Arts in educational administration and Multicultural studies from California State University, Bakersfield. He has lived in and attended schools on three different continents: Africa, Western Europe, and North America. His own life experiences help him better relate to many students who struggle with the challenges of what it means to be an "American."

Wayne E. Allen earned his B.A. in anthropology and religious studies summa cum laude in 1989 from Mankato State University and his M.A. in cultural anthropology in 1991 and his Ph.D. in cultural anthropology in 1998, both from the University of California at Santa Barbara. In 1993–94 he was a Fulbright Scholar to Canada and a UCSB IHC Humanities Fellow. He was the recipient of

Minnesota State University, Mankato's Clarence E. Harris Humanitarian Award in 2005-2006 for his support of cultural diversity on campus and in the surrounding community and region, and the Global Citizen Award in 2007, and numerous other awards and certificates for his work on diversity-related issues. Dr. Allen is the coauthor of three books, *Introduction to Ethnic Studies: A New Approach* (2010, with Kebba Darboe, 2016 2nd edition eBook), *An Integrative Approach to Human Geography* (2011, 2012 revised 1st edition, with Javier-Jose Lopez-Jimenez), and *A Reader on Race and Ethnicity* (2012, with Michael T. Fagin and Kebba Darboe), as well as book chapters and articles. His research focuses on Native North Americans, experimental archaeology, resource colonialism, common dilemmas and resource sustainability, community resource management and participatory action research, traditional indigenous cultural and natural resource conservation practices, environmental racism, and environmental justice. Dr. Allen has worked with diverse Native American and Native Canadian populations for over 40 years, Nepali peoples for 15 years, and immigrant Somali, Hmong, Ethiopian, Sudanese, West African, Central American, and South Asian peoples for 18 years. He was also executive director of a museum for three and a half years.

Karamo B. S. Barrow is a full-time instructor in the Business and Social Sciences Department at Clarkston Campus of Georgia State University/Perimeter College. He currently teaches history and political science courses. He began his academic career in 1997 at Georgia Perimeter College as a part-time history instructor. At the same time, he served as a full-time assistant history professor at Clark Atlanta University from 1997–2009, where he also served as Director of the Doctor of Arts in Humanities (DAH) program from 2002–2009. The DAH program is an interdisciplinary degree program with offerings in the disciplines of African and African-American studies, Africana-women's studies, English, history and romance languages. Additionally, Dr. Barrow held an adjunct instructor position with Southern Polytechnic State University in the Department of Social and International Studies from 2004–2009 and taught courses, including history, political science and law (Constitutional and International Law, Environmental and Regulatory Agencies, and Intellectual Property Issues) courses.

With an uncompromising commitment to education, Dr. Barrow armed himself with nine degrees, including two undergraduate degrees in English and history from the University of Wisconsin; an M.A. in English and an M.A. in history from the University of Minnesota; an M.A. (political science) and an M.S. (educational administration) from Minnesota State University, Mankato; a Ph.D. in higher education from Southern Illinois University, Carbondale; a Juris Doctor and an LL.M. (Litigation) from The Atlanta Law School. The nine degrees represent each letter in his country's name: THE GAMBIA.

As an educator, Dr. Barrow considers teaching as a calling: it is both a vocation and an avocation. He is comfortable in the company of a diverse variety of students from traditional and nontraditional undergraduates, as well as international students. He encourages students to be the very best they can be. His philosophy of teaching calls for meeting students where they are at and guiding them to a higher level of learning. He believes that a successful professor creates a comfortable, interactive, and entertaining learning environment by mixing substance with humor. His philosophy of teaching states, "The teacher should go beyond the call of duty as an instructor and mentor: I give valuable tools for students' growth as future world leaders in addition to advising them on issues ranging from professional school to graduate school and to personal life. In short, I support, encourage and inspire my students, so they can do more than they knew they could. I challenge them to learn and instill intellectual curiosity, while never compromising academic rigor. The greatest gift a teacher can give to the students is hope."

Dr. Barrow's current research interests focus on Chief Justice Earl Warren's contributions to the U.S. from 1953–1969, and he is working on a book of poems on African kings from antiquity to the present. He lives in Stone Mountain, Georgia.

Mary Dowd is a dean of students who has devoted her career to helping students seize opportunities, overcome obstacles, and soar to unimagined heights. Other higher education jobs held by Dr. Dowd include serving as director of student conduct, interim affirmative action director/Title IX coordinator, adjunct educational leadership instructor, and acting director of the women's center.

As dean of students, Dr. Dowd works closely with staff in Institutional Diversity to foster student success and enhance campus climate. Dr. Dowd's office is co-located with Institutional Diversity, which fosters communication, collegiality, and joint ventures. Similar partnerships with other offices have been built to better serve international students. Dr. Dowd's collaborative projects, crisis intervention work, and homegrown initiatives have earned state and national awards.

Dr. Dowd's skills and research interests include public policy, systems change, intersectionality, educational equity, and women in leadership. She is a past recipient of the Pathfinder Award conferred by the Dr. Martin Luther King, Jr. Commemorative Board for Noteworthy Contributions to Social Justice. Further examples of her community involvement include participating on the Skyline (MN) city council, previously presiding as president of a local Kiwanis chapter, leading labor union organizations, and volunteering at the Mahkato Wacipi.

Earlier in her career, Dr. Dowd was on call 24/7 as a Licensed Independent Social Worker directing a county rape crisis program. She also started the Catalyst Training and Consulting business that provided violence prevention education in the schools and nonprofit grant writing assistance. In the early 1990s, she recognized higher education as her true calling and embraced her niche. Today, Dr. Dowd is eligible to join her university's Quarter Century Club that recognizes employees with 25 years of service.

Hamdi Elnuzahi is originally from Sudan. In 2008, he immigrated to the United States and continued his higher education at Minnesota State University, Mankato graduating in 2011 with a degree in aviation management and earning a master's in public administration in 2013. In 2011, he was hired as a graduate assistant in the Department of Aviation, advising and recruiting Saudi students. In 2015, he earned a second M.A. in multicultural and ethnic studies from Minnesota State University, Mankato. Traveling and living in different countries has given him the ability to understand different cultures and to communicate with people from these cultures. He is working on a Ph.D. in strategy planning and crisis management at Alnileen University in Khartoum City.

Megan Heutmaker works as director for American Indian affairs in the Multicultural Center at Minnesota State University, Mankato. This position focuses on recruitment and retention efforts for American Indian/Native American students in Minnesota and the surrounding Midwest states. She has earned bachelor's degrees in both anthropology and American Indian studies and a master's degree in counseling and student personnel, specializing college student affairs from MSU, Mankato.

Kelly Meier is a writer and multiculturalist with over 30 years of experience in higher education. She serves as the senior director of institutional diversity at Minnesota State University, Mankato and as an adjunct faculty member in the College of Education. Meier holds a doctoral degree in educational leadership and is the author and co-author of 12 books and several related publications and training resources. Dr. Meier is a regular contributor to The Equity Network and has numerous publications with Talico, Inc. and DynaTEAM Consulting, Inc. She has also served as an administrator in student affairs and university advancement. She is the co-owner of Kinect Education Group and provides equity and inclusion training for K-12 and higher education professionals across the country.

Lu Yan earned her B.A. in English in 2006 from Hebei University of Technology, Tianjin, China, and her M.A. in applied linguistics (TESOL focus) in 2008 from Winona State University and her Ph.D. in education in 2018 from Iowa State University. Her research interests include diversity and inclusion, critical thinking, and student success in higher education. She has published studies on the topics of critical thinking and student success and marginalized college students' experiences.

Dr. Yan has been teaching since 2008 and had taught ESL, women's studies, critical thinking, and diversity-focused classes. In her spare time, she enjoys yoga, cultural events, theater/concerts, movies, dining out, and traveling.

CPSIA information can be obtained
at www.ICGtesting.com
Printed in the USA
LVHW101804150121
676596LV00003B/30